# Analysing Suicide

## Reality Myth Fallacy

## Philip O'Keeffe

Analysing Suicide – Reality Myth Fallacy

Author: Philip O'Keeffe

Copyright © 2024 Philip O'Keeffe

The right of Philip O'Keeffe to be identified as author of this work has been asserted by the author in accordance with section 77 and 78 of the Copyright, Designs and Patents Act 1988.

First Published in 2024

ISBN 978-1-83538-405-3 (Paperback)
      978-1-83538-406-0 (Hardback)
      978-1-83538-407-7 (E-Book)

Book cover design and Book layout by:
    White Magic Studios
    www.whitemagicstudios.co.uk

Published by:
    Maple Publishers
    Fairbourne Drive, Atterbury,
    Milton Keynes,
    MK10 9RG, UK
    www.maplepublishers.com

A CIP catalogue record for this title is available from the British Library.

All rights reserved. No part of this book may be reproduced or translated in any form or by any means, electronic or mechanical, including photocopying, recording or by any information storage and retrieval system without written permission from the author.

The views expressed in this work are solely those of the author and do not reflect the opinions of Publisher, and the Publisher hereby disclaims any responsibility for them.

# Acknowledgements

Almost a decade after beginning this project, and close to an ending, I wanted to acknowledge the encouragement and support that I received and benefitted from during those years.

Initially, my late doctoral supervisor at Ulster University, Professor Dr Peter Weinreich suggested a book might enable me to discuss my considered views on suicide candidly, constructively and comprehensively while access to relevant professional journals seemed unavailable to me. I cannot thank him enough for his wisdom, insights and friendship while we worked together.

Latterly, Conall O'Cuinn has expertly edited my draft manuscript and he merits my sincere thanks for his patience and persistence, not least in communicating his constantly positive evaluation of my humble literary efforts. Thank you, Conall.

Along the way, these good people believed in me and in the value of my work:

Joe Barnes, Peadar McKenna, Alice Seabheanna Finnegan, Noel Farnan, Brian Tanney, Eleanor Meenehan, Brian McAllister, Brian Pelan, Fergus Cumiskey, Dave Lyttle, Gordon Galloway, Patrick Donnelly, Jason O'Rourke, Tony Salvatore, Kate Mellotte, Tony Langlois, Mary Torney, Terence McMackin, Bill McGivern and Hugh O'Neill. Thank you, all.

At all times, my son, Joseph, and my surviving siblings Denis, Rosemary and Peter O'Keeffe were always there for me, and alongside me, as we remembered our deceased parents and siblings Noel, Gerry and Adrian.

Unfortunately, I am unable to record that I received much backing or endorsement from GB/NI or Irish fellow-travellers in suicidology. Fortunately, no one actively discouraged me in my endeavours. But, excluding those named above, my authorial perambulations have been personal, self-directed and solitary.

Consequently, no one except myself is responsible for the book's contents, including any and all errors or omissions.

**Philip O'Keeffe**
Belfast
September 2024

# Preface

This book is important because it offers for both professionals and non-professionals alike a lateral, alternative, 'take' on human suicidal behaviour. It tracks the development of my reluctant interest in suicidology that was triggered by the regrettable, and for our family, traumatic, deaths of my younger brother Gerard Henry Aidan O'Keeffe (aged 28 years) on 13 February 1982, and of my youngest brother, Adrian Francis O'Keeffe (aged 31 years) on 15 December 1989.

# Introduction

My particular interest is understanding suicide in Northern Ireland, Ireland and, to a somewhat lesser extent, Great Britain. This is because I tend towards the view that local culture may be an important and under-rated, but as yet under-researched factor that exerts a strong and significant influence upon suicidal behaviour. Hence what follows will represent in part an exploration of such cultural factors.

Another driver that motivates me relies upon my opposition, in a philosophical sense [see Quinton (1995) below], to an embedded mindset in psychiatry, psychology, and a range of their related disciplines, including sociology and anthropology, which postulates an inherent link, bridge, or cause-effect relationship between an individual's suicidal behaviour and what is referred to colloquially as their mental ill-health, or mental illness, or mental disease or mental disorder. In this book, I propose to describe the inadequate origins of this – for want of better words – assumption or given, and to use an evidence-based approach or methodology to expose what I consider to be this fundamental fallacy that undermines and renders irrelevant much current thinking about society's response to human behaviours that result in self-destruction.

It may well be – if my arguments hold up – that any positive or negative or neutral effect of society's suicide prevention activities upon 'the suicide rate' – or the statistical estimate of its frequency – in a family, community, neighbourhood, district, region, country or continent – may in reality be more closely related to other complex, multifactorial influences that act emotionally, cognitively and behaviourally, upon each 'at risk' individual. Such influences – if they exist – may be additional to, and perhaps other than, that which psychiatry and psychology traditionally and currently contributes to our understanding. These disciplines employ psychiatric diagnoses, appraisals or assessments, pre- and/or post-mortem, including psychological autopsy, of the mental health, or 'state of mind' up to and including the time of death of the deceased individual.

But evidence regarding what any of those 'other' influences might be, seem not yet to have been subject to rigorous excavation and examination. Hence, psychiatric evidence predominates, when decisions and conclusions emerge at a coroner's inquest, 'beyond a reasonable doubt' or 'on the balance of probabilities', following the UK Supreme Court's decision in Maughan (2020) in favour of the latter. Unfortunately in Northern Ireland (NI), public inquests following suspected suicide are convened only exceptionally and where 'circumstances' and/or a 'public interest' threshold is met. An enquiry that I made to NI's Senior Coroner regarding the criteria that the NI Coroner's Service employ to determine whether to hold 'discretionary' inquests elicited the following intriguing response:

"There are no formal criteria. Normally coroners in NI exercise their discretion not to hold an inquest if there is clear evidence that the death is suicidal and the family do not want an inquest held. However the views of the family are not determinative and an inquest would be held if the circumstances/public interest warrants that course"(Personal email from John Leckey, Senior Coroner, NI Coroner's Service, 2 Dec 2013).

I have no reason to believe that the NI Coroner's Office do not apply the relevant legislation correctly and with compassion, particularly for family members bereaved by apparent suicide.

But what disturbs me is the apparent Chinese Wall that restricts, perhaps even to the extent of preventing, open communication about the serious loss involved in each death by suspected suicide, and full disclosure of the known facts about what actually happened and whether and how the death might have been prevented and a life saved. This closed book on suicidal behaviour in Northern Ireland means that effectively, excluding perhaps NI Coroner's Office staff, citizens have little or no opportunity to learn anything about deaths by suspected suicide other than what is written by journalists and published in local print and broadcast media.

While I refer to society's failure to provide citizens with adequate information, I have to confirm that some individuals, excluding this writer, may have been given considerable if conditional access to otherwise restricted, suicide related information held by the NI Coroner's Office at various times for academic research (O'Neill, S. et al., 2014; O'Connor et al., 1999). Any relevant research findings that emerge from such studies are normally published months or years later in limited circulation peer-reviewed professional journals and academic publications. On occasion a university press release about a research project will survive the media editor's 'spike' and find its way into print, online or broadcast media in abbreviated form. Unfortunately, fuller information about such research findings is invariably available only on a restricted basis: online to university staff and registered students, to journal subscribers, by direct purchase or time-limited rental from publishers, or perhaps by inter-library loans.

As for publicly available information, internet site search can offer some limited access that may be just as restricted since much online material originated as the research project findings mentioned above. In short, you may be able to get what you pay for but only if you already know what you are looking for. However, on a brighter note, a recent invention, referred to optimistically as 'open access', has put in an appearance online: one relevant, important and innovatory example is Suicidology Online – open access journal (www.suicidology-online.com) whose articles became generally available from 2010 onwards.

One final remark about published literature on suicide: pace Alvarez (1971, 1974: 14) "[nearly] everybody has his (sic) own ideas about suicide ..." Just as 'no one has ever seen God' (John 1:18) it can reasonably be supposed that no one has read and understood everything that has been said, heard or written about suicide. Thus in what follows, in citing known source references, I rely upon what I have heard, read or written about human suicidal behaviour. Readers are invited to respect this caveat particularly when tempted to challenge anything herein by citing their own view. Why? I welcome your view in advance of knowing about it; I fully respect your view and will defend your absolute right to hold and express that view. I write to stimulate discussion and debate not least because I am convinced that a new paradigm is essential in order completely to transform the way people in Northern Ireland, Ireland and Great Britain think about or interact with human suicidal behaviour.

Quinton's (1995) broad definition of philosophy:

"Philosophy is rationally critical thinking, of a more or less systematic kind about the general nature of the world (metaphysics or theory of existence), the justification of belief (epistemology or theory of knowledge), and the conduct of life (ethics or theory of value)."

Each of the three elements has a non-philosophical counterpart, that is less explicitly rational, critical and systematic, to be found in everyone's general conception of the nature of the world in which they live and of their place in it.

*Metaphysics* replaces the unargued assumptions embodied in such a conception with a rational and organized body of beliefs about the world as a whole. Everyone has occasion to doubt and question beliefs, their own or those of others, with more or less success and without any theory of what they are doing.

*Epistemology* seeks by argument to make explicit the rules of correct belief formation. Everyone governs their conduct by directing it to desired or valued ends.

*Ethics*, or moral philosophy, in its most inclusive sense, seeks to articulate, in rationally systematic form, the rules or principles involved."

**Note:** Each of the 18 sections listed in the Table of Contents represented an area, that in my opinion, is worthy of exploration in relation to human suicidal behaviour in Ireland and the United Kingdom.

**References**

Alvarez, A. (1971) The savage god: a study of suicide. London: Penguin Books

Leckey, J. (2013) Personal email.

Maughan (2020) R (on the application of Maughan) (Appellant) v Her Majesty's Senior Coroner Oxfordshire (Respondent) [2020] UKSC 46 Press Summary, 13 November 2020. Accessed on 1 February 2022 at Supreme Court of the UK, London, SW1P 3BD https://www.supremecourt.uk

O'Connor, R.C., Sheehy, N.P. and O'Connor, D.B. (1999) The classification of completed suicide into subtypes. Journal of Mental Health. Vol. 8. No. 6. Pages 629-637

O'Neill, S., Corry, C. V., Murphy, S., Brady, S. and Bunting, B. P. (2014) Characteristics of deaths by suicide in Northern Ireland from 2005 to 2011 and use of health services prior to death. Journal of Affective Disorders. Vol 168. Pages 466-471

Quinton, A. (1995). "The ethics of philosophical practice". In T. Honderich, ed. The Oxford Companion to Philosophy. Oxford University Press. p. 666.

# Contents

Chapter 1 – Suicidology: not yet a discrete discipline ............... 10

Chapter 2 – Suicide, Law and Medicine – how psychiatry has suicidology by the throat ............... 22

Chapter 3 – The pervasive influence of sociology – Durkheim's outdated ideas? ............... 39

Chapter 4 – Reporting and counting suicides but disregarding the lessons one by one ............... 57

Chapter 5 – Surviving suicide – grief in the aftermath of suicide ............... 91

Chapter 6 – Integration – society's disintegrated response to suicide? ............... 154

Chapter 7 – Cultural factors – suicide as a local phenomenon ............... 168

Chapter 8 – Psychological autopsy – a flawed concept of limited value? ............... 194

Chapter 9 – Theories about Suicide – 15 and counting ............... 223

Chapter 10 – Camus – the only problem ............... 251

Chapter 11 – Suicide – justice for the deceased ............... 268

Chapter 12 – Suicide, murder and accidental death – allocation of state investigative resources ............... 300

Chapter 13 – Suicide, freedom and individual human rights ............... 319

Chapter 14 – Suicide – assisted suicide and murder ............... 343

Chapter 15 – Suicide or penacide – terminology and importance of language ............... 373

Chapter 16 – Suicide – Education for understanding: an approach to reduction and prevention ............... 409

Chapter 17 – Suicide research: impediments, lateral thinking and critical suicidology ............... 444

Chapter 18 – Suicide – Afterthoughts and recommendations ............... 471

Index ............... 479

# Chapter 1
# Suicidology: not yet a discrete discipline

E.S. Shneidman (1964/2001) is credited with ascribing the word 'suicidology' to his own and others' study of and/or research into the science or branch of knowledge concerned exclusively with human suicidal behaviour. This section seeks to explain why suicidology is not yet recognised by the scientific world as a discrete discipline with specific research objectives and bounded aspirations towards new knowledge that is absent from other scientific disciplines.

I shall not attempt here to describe the overlapping boundaries that separate and distinguish suicidology from philosophy, psychology, psychiatry, sociology, anthropology or other behavioural sciences. Each is replete with attempts to understand human suicidal behaviour through the window of its own disciplinary perspective, and with varying and sometimes conflicting outcomes. Initially I rely upon Edwin Shneidman's own succinct, focused explanation of the word 'suicidology' and its specific meaning:

"Suicidology simply defines the field of knowledge of suicide and the practice of suicide prevention." (Shneidman, 1993: x)

and Maris's definition

"... 'suicidology' can be defined as the scientific study of suicide and suicide prevention." (Maris, 1993: 4).

However, an ongoing debate exists about whether understanding suicide necessarily involves its prevention:

"Strictly speaking suicidology is the scientific study of suicide." (Maris, 1993: 19).

The issue of suicide prevention, as an essential component of suicidology, has not been without challenge from advocates of assisted suicide / euthanasia (Battin, 1996; Humphry, 1996) although Shneidman's reported view was that the study of suicide without including 'the suggested clinical intervention' was 'highly inappropriate'(Maris et al., 2000: 4).

This takes us to the definition of 'suicide' – later we shall briefly examine what 'scientific study' comprises and also what 'suicide prevention' might involve. Shneidman's (1985) considered opinion of what the word 'suicide' meant was exhaustively analysed in his iconic text 'Definition of Suicide'. He said his goal was 'to present ... fresh notes about what suicide is and ... to imply realistic and practical measures for preventing suicide' (Shneidman, 1985: v). Shneidman added that his 'special way of looking at the topic [was] advertently idiosyncratic' thus aligning himself with Alvarez's (1971, 1974) opinion that everyone has their own ideas about suicide.

In addition to the NASH, an acronym for the categories of death as Natural, Accidental, Suicidal and Homicidal, Shneidman acknowledged a three fold classification of all deaths, viz. intentioned suicides, unintentioned (many natural, accidental and homicidal) deaths and subintentioned (many natural and some accidental and homicidal) deaths (Shneidman, 1985: 21). He seems to have distinguished 'unintentioned' from 'subintentioned' deaths, describing the latter as deaths where the decedent 'played a covert, partial, latent, unconscious role in hastening their own death' while the former decedent may have 'played some psychological role' in their own demise. However he was clear that his subject was 'suicide, conscientiously defined' i.e. intentioned suicide, while keeping in mind subintentioned deaths.

Ultimately Shneidman's (1985: 203) proposed definition of suicide was as follows:

"Currently in the Western world, suicide is a conscious act of self-induced annihilation best understood as a multidimensional malaise in a needful individual who defines an issue for which the suicide is perceived as the best solution".

Maris et al. (2000) dedicated their voluminous textbook to 'all who died unnecessarily and prematurely, and those who loved them' (p. v). They did not 'define' suicide per se but referred to 'suicidal behaviour' (p. xi), 'self-destructive behaviours' (p. xiii) and 'irreversible cessation of ... consciousness' (p. 6) before directly engaging with their meaning of the word 'suicide':

'At first blush suicide seems simple and clear. Some pained individual ends their own life – period. However, upon reflection it becomes apparent that suicide is not that simple ... suicide is not one thing but many ... suicide has great variety ... what at first seems simple is in fact more complex' (p. 14).

Clearly these writers regarded a 'suicide' as a discrete, observable event, containing particular features and specific attributes inherent to an individual's death by suicide and that were worthy of scientific interest. It's noteworthy perhaps that 'human death' as distinct from 'human life' was not of any interest to them. They limited their studious reflection to suicide's pathways, methods and, with respect to those who mourn or grieve a death by suicide, to its aftermath.

They also mentioned (p. 71) the NASH 'manner of death' classification in the US 'official certificate of death'. This official record was completed primarily by each decedent's 'attending' medical doctor (in addition to the medical examiner or coroner) and filed with each US state's vital statistics department. NASH was also employed by forensic pathology when examining cause / manner of death (http://www.exploreforensics.co.uk/the-four-manners-of-death.html).

Since the dawn of time individual humans have killed themselves and continue to do so with increasing frequency across the globe. According to Befrienders International (2015):

'The World Health Organisation (WHO) estimates that each year approximately one million people die from suicide, which represents a global mortality rate of 16 people per 100,000 or one death every 40 seconds. It is predicted that by 2020 the rate of death will increase to one every 20 seconds. In the last 45 years suicide rates have increased by 60% worldwide. Suicide is now among the three leading causes of death among those aged 15-44 (male and female).' (http://www.befrienders.org/suicide-statistics)

Surviving humanity invariably responds to suicidal fatalities differently (Jordan, 2001; Jordan, 2008) when compared with fatalities experienced as 'natural, accidental or homicidal'. Such quite different responses constitute the factual basis for a massive and growing bibliography accumulated under the rubric of 'suicide and suicide prevention' that includes scientific, idiographic and statistical research (reported via peer reviewed academic journals and/or textbooks), university and college third level courses of study, published output from state / voluntary / community suicide prevention organizations / agencies / individuals, online and print media reportage, history, biography, novels, short stories, and other print and online literature.

Maris et al. (2000) conceded that, suicidology was 'for a long time ... a relatively new subdiscipline' (p. 6). They argued that 'much of the scientific groundwork' had until recently not been done. They modestly opined that now their 650 page textbook will 'consolidate and integrate' research from diverse disciplines and serve 'to further the scientific study of suicide' (p.6). These authors compared suicidology and psychology, albeit in a relatively simplistic and imprecise way. They said that these disciplines were similar:

"...suicidology is the science of self-destructive behaviours, thoughts, feelings and so on in the same way that psychology is the science dealing with the mind and mental processes, feelings, desires and so on. No doubt 'suicidology' sounds alien to many but no doubt so did 'psychology' and 'psychiatry' at first" (Maris et al., 2000: 4).

Interestingly 'psychology' has colonised many if not by now all available known behavioural outcomes of humanity's 'mind and mental processes', including for example 'the psychology of suicidal behaviour' and even perhaps 'the psychology of psychology'. However, suicidology and psychology are not commutative. I am of the view that the scientific study of suicide, otherwise suicidology, has evident integrity, is self-standing and deserves understanding, acceptance and respect by fraternal knowledge-based disciplines, such as philosophy, thanatology, medical psychiatry, psychology, anthropology, sociology and so on as a discrete, bounded scientific discipline. As to the inclusion or exclusion of suicide prevention in its definition, I am agnostic.

## Scientific Study

Both 'scientific study of suicide' and 'suicide prevention' are mentioned in Shneidman's (1993) and Maris's (1993) respective definitions of suicidology. What is 'scientific study'? And what does 'suicide prevention' mean and entail? These questions are considered next.

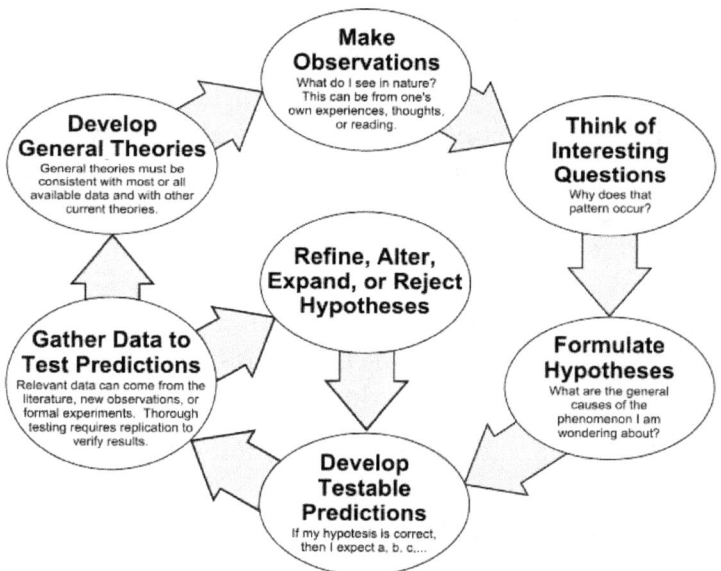

**Fig 1: illustrating steps in scientific method**

Taken with thanks and permission from https://commons.wikimedia.org/wiki/File:The_Scientific_Method_as_an_Ongoing_Process.svg

The diagram above is relatively self-explanatory in describing the research cycle that represents many, if not most, areas of scientific work in discovering new knowledge.

There are obvious difficulties in suicidology research linked to the researcher's inability to access person/s deceased by suicide, as research respondents, other than at the secondary level. Nothing can be done about this intractable obstacle. Consequently the generation of new knowledge in suicidology by research necessarily lacks the relative precision that would otherwise be potentially accessible.

One response to this problem was the generation of the psychological autopsy methodology that contains serious limitations and 'should now be abandoned' (Hjelmeland et al., 2012: 606). Another area of activity that has recently escalated, especially in the USA, involves research respondents who 'made serious but not life-destroying efforts to end their lives' often referred to, confusingly, as 'suicide attempt survivors' (Stack, 2014; O'Brien et al., 2014).

Historically, before and since Durkheim's (1897/2002) seminal sociological study, an enormous volume of published, peer-reviewed, suicidological, research documentation, has been generated involving relevant 'at one remove' respondents, e.g. survivors of bereavement by suicide, family members, friends/colleagues, clinicians, medical and mental health practitioners, psychologists, and a plethora of more remote entities, including various samples and population groups, etc. using quantitative, qualitative and mixed research methodologies. Given real world circumstances, practising suicidologists tend, by way of interest or occupation or both, to choose to specialise in relatively narrow or niche areas of suicidology. This mirrors the status of practitioners across many if not most related professional activities, including, for example, both psychology and sociology.

Ironically Shneidman's (2001b: x) accidental discovery in c1950 at the age of 31 years in the Los Angeles coroner's office vaults of a deceased man's 'suicide note', prefaced his life's work in scientific suicidology, including 160 publications, that extended across most aspects of human suicidal behaviours.

## Prevention of suicide

It may seem self-evident but it is worth asserting in this section the writer's own view that primary responsibility for preventing one's own individual death by suicide rests with the writer, i.e. myself. This is a logical consequence of the fact that by definition suicide is 'self-induced annihilation' (Shneidman, 1985: 203) involving direct agency only and exclusively by the soon-to-be-deceased. Of course hidden so-called pathways to suicide (Maris, 1981) representing discrete stages leading to an individual's death by suicide, and referred to as 'suicidal careers' (Leenaars, 1991: 28, 29), may well be uncovered in retrospective post-mortem by coronial enquiry. Others may not be fully aware of this inner process – including an individual at risk. Suicidal tendencies and traits can indeed be enigmatic, mysterious, subconscious.

Fortunately any vulnerable person who may be at risk of suicidal behaviour can seek support by accessing, or with their informed consent, being referred by a family member, friend or colleague, one or more of a range of helping resources using widely advertised telephone 24/7 helplines. In Ireland/Northern Ireland, the Samaritans Freephone Number is 116 123 while in Northern Ireland, the Lifeline Crisis Hotline Freephone Number is 0808 808 8000.

Community and societal efforts to reduce suicide can involve so-called 'gate-keeper' suicide prevention training packages including Question Persuade and Respond (QPR); Yellow Ribbon International for Suicide Prevention; ASIST; STORM (Skills Training On Risk Management) and safeTALK. Training programmes last anywhere from a few hours to 5 days, with most dedicated to 2 days training (Isaac et al., 2009).

## Suicide Prevention Training

A major study (Ubido and Scott-Daniel, 2014) of suicide prevention training included the somewhat disappointing conclusion:

> "Systematic reviews of gatekeeper training found they were generally successful in imparting knowledge, building skills and moulding the attitudes of trainees. There was generally a dearth of studies showing effectiveness in terms of decreasing suicide ideation, suicide attempts or deaths by suicide (Isaac et al., 2009)" (Ubido and Scott-Daniel, 2014: 15).

A more detailed critique of ASIST is summarised below.

## ASIST (Applied Suicide Intervention Skills Training)

ASIST (Applied Suicide Intervention Skills Training) is a widely employed approach to suicide prevention by way of short-term training for 'Lifeline' crisis hotline telephone counsellors. ASIST is used as a gatekeeper training programme in several countries including Australia, Canada, Ireland / Northern Ireland, Norway, Scotland and the United States. A major recent study by Gould et al. (2013), that evaluated ASIST for effectiveness, monitored 1,507 calls from 1,410 suicidal individuals to 17 US Lifeline centres in 2008–2009. The authors' findings were mixed: they concluded that, although they could see promise in callers' increased disclosure of distress and improved outcomes during interactions with ASIST-trained counsellors, there was reason for concern in ASIST's lack of impact on the thoroughness of counsellors' assessment of suicide risk. Some worrying outcomes are described below.

Mishara et al. (2007a; 2007b) noted that 'while callers appeared to be helped in a significant numbers of calls and some lives may have been saved, counsellors did not consistently evaluate suicide risk, and when risk evaluations were conducted they were usually incomplete.' Two studies (Kalafat et al., 2007; Gould et al., 2007) concluded that in a 'follow-up assessment ... conducted two to four weeks [after calls were conducted] to assess the duration of the [training] effect ... a key finding was that there were significant reductions in callers' self-reported crisis and suicide states from the beginning to the end of the calls; however, without a control group, these effects cannot be definitively attributed to the crisis intervention.'

Notable positive findings were that seriously suicidal individuals were calling telephone crisis services (for example, over half of suicidal callers had made a prior suicide attempt and had a plan when they called), and 11.6% of suicidal callers reported at follow up that the call prevented them from harming or killing themselves. However, a troubling finding was that of the callers who were rated as non-suicidal crisis callers by crisis staff, 12% reported at follow up that they were feeling suicidal either during or since their Lifeline calls. Furthermore, three studies (Coveney et al., 2012; Mishara et al., 2007a; Mishara et al.,

2007b) raised concern about the adequacy of suicide risk assessments conducted by some crisis centre staff.

## Suicide prevention by education for understanding

The writer's view is that alternative and possibly more effective ways of reducing suicidal behaviour may be through programmes of education for understanding at all ages and stages about alternatives to suicide. In straightforward language, this approach acknowledges that each individual human, unless prevented by physical or psychological disability, can decide to make autonomous, freely chosen decisions about their behaviours, for good or ill, for better or worse. Everyone therefore, potentially, can benefit from education in suicidology. What you don't know about suicide can be fatal.

In conclusion, one considered recommendation for suicidology apprentices is the work of the late Dr Israel Orbach (2001) on 'therapeutic empathy with the suicidal wish' that offers a compassionate analysis of his experience-based psychotherapeutic approach that respects each individual's autonomy while supporting her/him to make optimal decisions concerning life and death.

**Myth:** (fictitious popular idea): Approaches to prevention of suicide can be effective, without either, scientific study, or comprehensive understanding of human suicidal behaviour, or both.

**Fallacy:** (misleading argument): Gatekeeper training programmes, including for example, QPR and ASIST, are both necessary and sufficient for reducing the incidence of suicidal behaviour.

## References

Alvarez, A. (1971/1974) The savage god: a study of suicide. London: Penguin Books

Battin, M.P. (1996) The death debate: Ethical issue in suicide. Upper Saddle River, NJ: Prentice Hall

Befrienders International website: http://www.befrienders.org/suicide-statistics . Accessed 3 Nov 2015

Coveney C.M., Pollock, K., Armstrong, S. and Moore, J. (2012) Callers' experiences of contacting a national suicide prevention helpline: Report of an online survey. Crisis, The Journal of Crisis Intervention and Suicide Prevention, 33(6): 313-324

Durkheim, E. (1897/2002) Suicide: a study in sociology. New York: Free Press

Explore Forensics website: http://www.exploreforensics.co.uk/the-four-manners-of-death.html . Accessed on 2 Nov 2015

Gould, M.S., Kalafat, J., Munfakh, J.L.H. and Kleinman, M. (2007) An evaluation of crisis hotline outcomes, Part II: Suicidal Callers. Suicide and Life-threatening Behaviour, 37(3): 338–352.

Gould, M.S., Cross, W., Pisani, A.R., Munfakh, J.L., and Kleinman, M.(2013) Impact of Applied Suicide Intervention Skills Training (ASIST) on National Suicide Prevention Lifeline Counsellor Interventions and Suicidal Caller Outcomes. Suicide and Life-threatening Behaviour, 43(6): 676-691

Humphry, D. (1996) Final exit: The practicalities of self-deliverance and assisted suicide for the dying. New York: Bantam/Doubleday / Dell

Hjelmeland, H., Dieserud, G., Dyregrov, K., Knizek, B.L. and Leenaars, A.A. (2012) Psychological studies as diagnostic tools: are they methodologically flawed? Death Studies. 36, 605-626

Isaac, M., Elias, B., Katz, L. Y., Belik, S., Deane, F. P., Enns, M. W. and Sareen, J. (2009). Gatekeeper training as a preventative intervention for suicide: A systematic review. Canadian Journal of Psychiatry, 54(4), 260-268.

Jordan, J.R. (2001) Is suicide bereavement different? A reassessment of the literature. Suicide and Life-threatening Behaviour, 31(1) 91-102

Jordan, J.R. (2008) Bereavement after suicide. Psychiatric annals, 38:10, October 2008

Kalafat, J., Gould, M.S., Munfakh, J.L.H. and Kleinman, M. (2007) An evaluation of crisis hotline outcomes, Part I: Non-Suicidal Crisis Callers. Suicide and Life-threatening Behaviour, 37(3): 322–337

Leenaars, A.A. (Ed.) (1991) Lifespan perspectives of suicide. Timelines in suicide process. New York: Plenum

Leenaars, A.A., Berman, A.L., Cantor, P., Litman, R.L., and Maris, R.W. (Eds.) (1993) Suicidology: Essays in Honour of Edwin S Shneidman. Northvale, NJ: Aronson

Maris, R.W. (1981) Pathways to Suicide. A survey of self-destructive behaviours. Baltimore: John Hopkins Univ Press

Maris, R.W. (1993) The evolution of suicidology. In A.A. Leenaars, A.L. Berman, P. Cantor, R.L. Litman and R.W. Maris (Eds.) Suicidology: Essays in Honor of Edwin Shneidman. Northvale, NJ: Jason Aronson

Maris, R.W., Berman, A.L. and Silverman, M.M. (2000) Comprehensive textbook of suicidology. New York: The Guilford Press

Mishara, B.L., Chagnon, F., Daigle, M., Balan, M., Raymond, S., Marcoux, I., Bardon, C., Campbell, J.K. and Berman, A. (2007a) Which Helper Behaviours and Intervention Styles are Related to Better Short Term Outcomes in Telephone Crisis Intervention? Results from a Silent Monitoring Study of Calls to the U.S. 1-800- SUICIDE Network. Suicide and Life-threatening Behaviour, 37(3): 291–307

Mishara, B.L., Chagnon, F., Daigle, M., Balan, M., Raymond, S., Marcoux, I., Bardon, C., Campbell, J.K. and Berman, A. (2007b) Comparing Models of Helper Behaviour to Actual Practice in Telephone Crisis Intervention: a Silent Monitoring Study of Calls to the U.S. 1-800-SUICIDE Network. Suicide and Life-threatening Behaviour, 37(3): 308–321

O'Brien, K.H.M., Becker, S.J., Spirito, A., Simon, V. and Prinstein, M.J. (2014) Differentiating Adolescent Suicide Attempters from Ideators: Examining the Interaction between Depression Severity and Alcohol Use. Suicide and Life-threatening Behaviour, 44(1), 23-33

Orbach, I. (2001) Therapeutic empathy with the suicidal wish: principles of therapy with suicidal individuals. American Journal of Psychotherapy, 55(2), 166-184

Scientific Method. Diagram. Diagram illustrating steps in scientific method (accessed via wikipedia on 15 Nov 2015 at: http://idea.ucr.edu/documents/flash/scientific_method/story.htm

Shneidman, E.S. (1964) Grand old man in suicidology. A review of Louis Dublin's Suicide: a sociological study. Contemporary Psychology, 9, 370-371

Shneidman, E.S. (1985) Definition of suicide. New York: John Wiley and Sons Ltd

Shneidman, E.S. (1993) Suicide as psychache. A clinical approach to self-destructive behaviour. Northvale, NJ: Jason Aronson

Shneidman, E.S. (2001a) Suicide: a sociological and statistical study, Louis Dublin. Originally published in New York, 1968. In Comprehending suicide, Chapter 4, page 51. Washington, DC: American Psychological Association

Shneidman, E.S. (2001b) Comprehending suicide. Landmarks in 20th Century Suicidology. Washington, DC: American Psychological Association

Stack, S. (2014) Differentiating Suicide Ideators from Attempters: Violence—A Research Note. Suicide and Life-threatening Behaviour, 44(1), 46-57

Ubido, J. and Scott-Samuel, A. (2014) Suicide Prevention Training. LPHO Report Series, number 99. Rapid Evidence Review Series, number 3. Liverpool: Liverpool Public Health Observatory, Liverpool University

Wikipedia Website (2015) Accessed on 15 November 2015 at: https://en.wikipedia.org/wikipedia.org/wiki/Scientific_method#/media/File:The Scientific Method as an Ongoing Process.svg

\* \* \*

## Chapter 2
# Suicide, Law and Medicine – how psychiatry has suicidology by the throat

The layperson's response to suicide does not appear to match the word association outcome that 'conventional wisdom' might predict, i.e. suicide/depression. Rather, as I discovered by informally surveying students attending my university evening class in basic studies in suicidology (Queen's University Belfast, 2009) that even in an unrepresentative sample, suicide seems more closely associated in public consciousness with 'death' than with 'depression'.

Depression is a condition of the mind – later we may consider just what 'the mind' might be – a condition recognised by way of 'symptoms' by medical psychiatry as a 'depressive disorder' (DSM-IV-TR, 2000: 173 et seq.) that could 'constitute mental disease, mental disorder or mental disability' (DSM-IV-TR, 2000: xi, xii). Medical ethics included the dictum 'primum non nocere' (trans. 'first do no harm') representing 'a guiding principle for physicians that, whatever the intervention or procedure, the patient's well-being is the primary consideration' (http://medical-dictionary. the freedictionary.com/). Death, on the other hand is of limited interest to medicine, other than in a psychiatric context post-mortem, for example regarding 'bereavement' following 'the death of a loved one' (DSM-IV-TR, 2000: 311) where symptoms of 'a major depressive disorder' persist beyond two months after the loss (DSM-IV-TR, 2000: 312). Non-psychiatric medical interest post-mortem seems to cease beyond necessary legal compliance by an attending medical practitioner in completion of a 'death certificate' confirming, if known, deceased's cause of death.

Which takes us back full circle to suicide: when police conclude 'no suspicious circumstances' regarding any death, this is coded language for 'this person's death did not involve any criminal act'. However, since 1961 in GB [excluding Scotland where suicide was never an offence under Scottish Law (https://en.wikipedia.org/wiki/Suicide_Act_1961)], 1966 in N Ireland and 1993 in Ireland, suicide is not a crime: accordingly in police-speak 'no suspicious circumstances' may seem ambiguous, if not premature, regarding suicide as a possible cause of death in a specific circumstance.

## Public Inquests

If suicide is suspected – the deceased person appears intentionally to have killed themselves with no third party involvement – a N Ireland coroner's inquest may, or may not be considered necessary, wise, or legally required by circumstances (for example, the suspicious death occurred in prison or police custody), or public interest (Leckey op. cit. 2013). Relevant conclusions are reached at the coroner's discretion - see separate section below. For example, surviving families' wishes are now taken into consideration: this did not appear to be the case in relation to public inquests on my deceased brothers (Gerard Henry Aidan O'Keeffe, died 1982 and Adrian Francis O'Keeffe, died 1989).

Both inquests were excruciating experiences for the writer and other family members and, for us, served no positive purpose. Sickeningly, a local trash tabloid masquerading as a newspaper disgraced the already tainted reputation of Irish hack-journalism by 'splashing' a prurient report of the latter inquest, apparently for purely sales-related commercial gain. Our family was neither consulted before publication nor able afterwards to take any remedial action. One reason, on reflection 25 years on, for our apparent inaction was perhaps due to the enduring intensity of our ongoing individual and family grief responses.

## Coroner's Discretion

Although O'Neill, S. et al. (2016) analysed a sample from N Ireland coroner's files (2005-2011) totalling 1,671 suicides and undetermined deaths (i.e. insufficient evidence to confirm suicide 'beyond a reasonable doubt' but enough to conjecture suicide 'on the balance of probabilities') only an unknown fraction were subject to a public inquest, with or without a jury. Hence the evidence used in O'Neill, S. et al. (2016) relied upon contents of closed coroner's files. But it was not possible to ascertain what, for whatever reason, was included or left out of any individual file.

See Chapter 5 below for research-based survey of survivor grief in the aftermath of suicide-related bereavement. [Note - The law concerning coroner's inquests differs in each British/Irish jurisdiction: in England/Wales, Scotland, Northern Ireland and Ireland. This text's focus is on suicide in Northern Ireland.]

**Political Violence / Terrorism**

Key to understanding the context for our family's experience, and that of the wider Northern Irish population, of the aftermath of suicidal loss, is the persistent and entrenched nature of the poisonous, unresolved legacy of political violence here. Terrorism – defined as 'unofficial or unauthorized use of violence and intimidation in the pursuit of political aims' (http://www.oxforddictionaries.com/definition/english/terrorism) – was deployed in Northern Ireland / Ireland / Great Britain (1966-1998) during an Irish irredentist 'conflict' ostensibly aimed at reunification of Ireland through 'armed struggle' and recently referred to as 'a just war' by elderly Irish republicans. A similar form of 'terrorism', by British forces and locally-based 'loyalists' (https://en.wikipedia.org/wiki/Gusty_Spence) resisted this 'armed struggle' in a brutally violent 'mirror-image' fashion.

Recently Bryan et al. (2010) argued that from an academic perspective 'terrorism' is indefinable:

> 'Terrorism ... represents a subspecies of warfare [and] can form part of a wider campaign of violent and non-violent attempts at political leverage (English, 2009:24) ... [and] designed to create power where there is none or to consolidate power where there is very little (Hoffman, 2006: 40, 41).'

However the above-mentioned Northern Irish political violence is defined, its outcomes for 1.8 million Irish/British citizens resident here included multiple murders, thousands of physical and psychological injuries and enormous destruction of property, both public and private. No cost/benefit analysis existed: it can safely be concluded that although detailed costs calculations, human and material, are available (Morrissey et al., 1999), no one to this writer's knowledge has to date attempted to address the benefits, human and/or material, if any.

Over 3,620 related fatalities (McKeown, 2001/2009) and multiple tens of thousands of life-changing casualties resulted. During a 32 year 'conflict' period, thousands of inquests appear to have been formally opened, adjourned and left 'on file'. An official report (Doherty and Mageean, 2006) stated that, in Northern Ireland:

The inquest system remains clogged with old cases (at the end of 2001 there were 1,897 deaths still awaiting an inquest) some dating from as far back as the early 1990s (http://www.patfinucanecentre.org/hrights/NIHRC_Feb06.pdf).

## Murder disguised as suicide

In May 1992, a notorious double murder in Northern Ireland committed a year before, was inadvertently concealed by a coroner's inquest conclusion of double suicide until seventeen years later when the serial killer confessed to police (2009), was convicted in December 2010 and imprisoned for life, with a minimum term of 21 years (Henderson, 2011: 203). An accomplice was also convicted in March 2011 of double murder and imprisoned for life, with a minimum term of 18 years (Henderson, 2011: 236). We could perhaps be kind and categorise this unfortunate episode as a sequence of exceptional, although culpable and potentially avoidable, 'human errors' by the authorities, both police and coroner. More importantly, the question arises as to whether these examples of murders, masquerading as suicides, may demonstrate that society's response to death by apparent suicide, when compared with death by murder, appears to attract minimal, state investigative resources.

My students (Queen's University Belfast, 2009) advised me that the difference may lie in fuelling society's urge to find law breaker(s) in the latter cases while responsibility, i.e. 'blame', for suicide was seen by them to rest totally and exclusively with the deceased, QED.

Sociology, however, appears to offer another perspective on society's responsibility for death by suicide pace Durkheim's (1897/2002) iconic book. See Chapter 3 which follows.

## Medicine and Suicide – NICE guidelines

What of psychiatric medicine's relationship with any patient's suicidal behaviour – both apparent and/or concealed – that may or may not result in death by suicide? Just to be clear, the writer is referring to psychiatric medicine, rather than any of its multiple specialities:

Psychiatry is the branch of medicine concerned with the bio-psycho-social study of the etiology, diagnosis, treatment and prevention of cognitive, perceptual, emotional and behavioural disorders. Related non-medical fields include psychotherapy and clinical psychology (https://en.wikipedia.org/wiki/Medicine#Specialties).

In UK, a national institute for health clinical excellence (NICE), published guidelines for practitioners and the public 'to improve outcomes for people using the NHS and other public health and social care services, by:

- Producing evidence-based guidance and advice for health, public health and social care practitioners.
- Developing quality standards and performance metrics for those providing and commissioning health, public health and social care services.
- Providing a range of information services for commissioners, practitioners and managers across health and social care (NICE, 2022).

This body's recommendations represented 'best practice' across the entire field, including psychiatry. NICE offered guidance for 'management' of people, aged 16 and over, at risk of self-harm and/or suicide presenting in primary care, viz. in Ireland/UK, a general practitioner (GP) or doctor in community practice. In effect, such clinician/patient contact should result in an expert assessment of their risk, and their psychosocial needs, together with appropriate support and treatment. Ultimately, NICE stated that 'healthcare professionals have a duty to act in the person's best interests [including] taking the person to hospital for further assessment and treatment against their wishes' (NICE, 2020). Only Szasz (2009) recognised such hospitalisation for 'treatment against their wishes' as involuntary incarceration of patients by medical psychiatrists, facilitated by state law:

> 'The bread and butter of the modern psychiatrist is 1) writing prescriptions for psychoactive drugs and pretending they are therapeutically effective against mental illnesses, 2) prescribing these drugs to persons willing to take them and forcibly compelling persons deemed "seriously mentally ill" to take them against their will, and 3) converting voluntary mental patients who appear to be "dangerous to themselves or others" into involuntary mental patients. Indeed, the modern psychiatrist no longer has the option to reject the use of force vis-à-vis patients: such conduct is considered a dereliction of professional responsibility' (Szasz, 2009: viii).

At this stage, a person at risk might be compulsorily detained in a hospital's psychiatric unit, under the care of a consultant psychiatrist, psychiatric nurses and related staff. Their release from detention would depend upon the professional opinion and consent of these medical personnel. The NICE guidelines recommended management of 'any identified mental health or other problems as appropriate'. A lengthy list of such mental health topics followed including:

> 'Generalised anxiety disorder, depression, depression in children, depression – antenatal and postnatal, psychosis and schizophrenia, Bipolar disorder, post traumatic stress disorder, dementia, alcohol – problem drinking, and opioid dependence' (NICE, 2020).

NICE guidelines were comprehensive and directive, implying that when primary care encountered an at-risk person, an established, approved set of protocols, procedures and practices would click into gear, aimed at caring for and treating, sensitively and compassionately, the person's distress.

## Medicine and suicide: theory and practice

Unfortunately, a gulf existed between the above-mentioned NICE guidelines and the actualité of life as lived and experienced by general practitioners and at-risk citizens in Northern Ireland.

Leavey et al. (2016) offered an insight into that gulf's dimensions, its consequences and what might be done to begin to harmonise practice with theory. Their study's aim was to examine contact by a person deceased by suicide, with health and social care services in the 12-month period prior to suicide and to assess GP recognition of suicidality. NI coroners' office records and general practitioner records for 399 eligible cases of suicide recorded by the Coroner's Office during a two year period 2007/2009 were accessed. Excluding GP records that were unobtainable for 38 individuals (9.5 % of all cases), the analysis of service access, therefore was carried out with a base population of 361 suicides.

It was found that eighty-seven per cent of suicides were in contact with General Practice services in the 12 months before suicide. GP records showed that only 2% of the deceased had access to counselling services. The frequency of contact with services was considerable, particularly among patients with a common mental disorder, for example, depression, anxiety, phobias, stress, psychological disorders and post-traumatic stress disorder (PTSD) or substance misuse problems, for example, those with alcohol and/or drug dependency problems. A diagnosis of psychiatric problems was absent in 40 % of suicides.

Leavey et al. (2016) concluded that 'contact with primary care and psychiatric services prior to suicide may be considerable, presenting opportunities for intervention. However, there is scant knowledge regarding the frequency, nature and determinants of contact'. Such opportunities appeared to be unrecognised and/or missed, particularly if referrals by GPs of at-risk patients to expert, focused counselling and psychotherapy support appeared to be largely absent.

A more recent report by Black (2021) for the NI government, considered 'the complex issue of suicide in the context of mental health

[and] support services'. It made for depressing reading as it highlighted the dearth of state resources allocated to its resolution:

> 'The strong association between suicide and mental illness is well established. Yet around 70% of people who die by suicide in Northern Ireland are not known to mental health services. This is particularly challenging in regard to efforts to prevent suicide. People in Northern Ireland are estimated to experience 20-25% higher levels of mental health illness compared to the rest of the UK. In addition, Northern Ireland has the lowest levels of mental health spend in the UK and Ireland' (Black, 2021: 3).

The physical and psychological legacy for citizens of Northern Ireland's political and community conflicts (1969-1998) cannot but have contributed in a major way to ongoing adverse levels of mental health illness. Over two decades after terrorism ended, the NI devolved government has not yet recognised the importance of adequately resourcing mental health services. This abysmal dereliction of their primary duty to protect citizens was evident in government's neglect in caring for the casualties of 30 years of purposeless violence and mayhem, translated by government spin-doctors into the softer more anodyne, tabloid-appropriate term 'conflict':

> 'Mental ill health is one of the leading causes of disability in Northern Ireland. Moreover, research suggests that Northern Ireland, being a post conflict society, experiences 20-25% higher levels of mental health illness compared to the rest of the UK, and around 1 in 5 adults have a diagnosable mental health condition at any given time. There are also significantly higher levels of depression in Northern Ireland than in the rest of the UK, higher antidepressant prescription rates, higher incidences and presentations for self-harm (albeit that in many cases, people who self-harm do not present for medical attention and are not visible to healthcare professionals) and high rates of post-traumatic stress disorder. Although mental health is said to be as important as physical health, the "parity of esteem" between the two is yet to be realised. Expenditure on mental health care in Northern Ireland remains the lowest in the UK, estimated to be around 7% of the total healthcare budget. According to the

Department of Health (NI), this is 27% less than the mental health budget in England and 20% less than in Ireland' (Black. 2021: 5).

Although the umbrella term 'mental health' features in Black (2021) as a way to interpret Northern Irish suicide statistics, the complexity of human self-destruction cannot begin to be understood unless suicide as a human behaviour is perceived and comprehended as a purposively motivated activity by an individual and/or individuals. In the context of Covid-19's attrition in N Ireland – over 4,000+ related deaths at end 2021 – the Northern Ireland Mental Health Champion, Prof Siobhan O'Neill emphasised the need for government to plan and resource appropriate services for citizens traumatised by their pandemic encounters:

> "Crisis intervention services need to be improved urgently so that people who are suicidal have compassionate support and interventions for safety planning and problem-solving, and there should not be waiting times. It is about providing continuous support within 48 hours of someone feeling suicidal." (Black, 2021: 9)

In later chapters, the weakness of the 'suicide is a mental health issue' mantra will be examined, exposed and rejected. But this aberration was addressed almost three decades ago by Shneidman (1993) a psychologist and suicidologist who held that psychiatry had little to contribute to understanding and ameliorating suicide's catastrophic harvesting of too many of our sisters and brothers.

## Medicalisation of suicide

Shneidman (2001) was strongly opposed to the medicalisation of suicide that he saw as a human condition, not a disease, but as 'a series of acts with a common end point'. He added that although suicide may overlap with mental illnesses, there was a '100% overlap between the commission of suicide and perturbation, upset, unease, anguish, discontent along with the idea of ending it all' (Shneidman, 2001).

Leenaars (1996) rejected as limited and inadequate, a psychiatric approach to understanding suicide:

> 'Suicide is a multidimensional malaise (Shneidman, 1985). There are biological, psychological, intrapsychic, logical, conscious and unconscious, interpersonal, sociological, cultural,

and philosophical/existential elements in the suicidal event. It thus seems reasonable that we would be perplexed and bewildered about answering the question. It is not simply a psychopathological entity in the DSM-IV (Diagnostic and Statistical Manual of Mental Disorders - American Psychiatric Association, 1994). I do not agree ... with those who point to an external stress as the cause of suicide. I also do not agree that it is only pain. I tend to place the emphasis on the multideterminant nature of suicide. Suicide is intrapsychic. It is not simply the stress or even the pain, but the person's inability to cope with the event or pain' (Leenaars, 1996: 221, 224).

Shneidman (1993: 45, 46) acknowledged up to 13 contemporary fields of knowledge with a legitimate interest in suicidology, including psychological, sociological, demographic / epidemiological, and philosophical / theological domains, alongside the predominant psychiatric approach to understanding and addressing suicide and suicidal behaviour. He cited five general notions about suicide that helped to inform his own perspective:

i) Suicide was not so much a movement towards death as a movement away from something that was always the same: intolerable emotion, unendurable pain, or unacceptable anguish. Reduce the level of suffering, and the individual will choose to live.

ii) Suicide was best understood – not in terms of depression, or any of the symptom-related labels of the DSM – but rather in terms of perturbation (i.e. their level of psychic disturbance) and lethality (i.e. how deathfully suicidal they are). The effective way to reduce the suicidality level is to do so indirectly by reducing the elevated perturbation. Reduce the individual's anguish, tension and pain and the level of lethality will come down, since it was elevated perturbation that drives or fuels elevated lethality.

iii) Suicide was best understood not as a psychosis or a neurosis or a character disorder but rather as a more or less transient psychological constriction of affect and intellect. The presence of constriction in an at-risk person of high perturbation and high lethality was one of the most dangerous aspects of the suicidal state. Pathological constriction must be dealt with before any attempt at rescue or remediation.

iv) Suicide was best understood not so much as an unreasonable act (or defect in cognition) but as a reaction to frustrated psychological needs. Shneidman (1980a) held that there are no suicides in the absence of thwarted needs. Address the frustrated needs and suicide will not have to occur.

v) Suicide is best understood not so much in terms of death, per se, but in terms of the idea of cessation – the complete stopping of one's consciousness of unendurable pain – when seen by the suffering individual as a solution, indeed the perfect solution, to life's painful and pressing problems. The moment that the idea of the possibility of stopping consciousness occurs in the mind as the answer or the way out, in the presence of unusual constriction, elevated perturbation and high lethality, then the active suicidal scenario has begun (Shneidman, 1993: 23-25).

The pathway to suicidal behaviour was unique to each at-risk individual, since the architecture of their psychache and consequent lethality was dependent upon a multitude of distinct, circumstantial motivating factors. However, despite the 'suicide prevention' mantra promulgated by mental health advocates, most of us lack the necessary skills, either personal or knowledge based, to act appropriately if and when we encounter suicidal behaviour – otherwise than 'call a doctor' or 'ring the police'. Almost invariably this would lead, in Northern Ireland, to the casualty being routed to a hospital emergency room, en route to a psychiatric ward. What happens next would depend upon the availability and quality of medical/nursing staff on duty. Our expectations of local health services are now contrasted with the actuality of the drivers of suicidal behaviour.

## The limits to medicine: Illich's insights and legacy

Black (2021: 4) listed 20 factors that 'drive' or may have an impact upon suicide risk:

1. A single adverse event
2. A series of adverse events over time
3. Mental illness (treated or untreated)
4. Self Harm
5. Drug and alcohol misuse
6. Imprisonment
7. Family history of suicide
8. Violence
9. Chronic disease, disability, or pain
10. Legacy of conflict and transgenerational trauma
11. Unemployment/financial loss
12. Family breakdown
13. Social isolation
14. A previous suicide attempt
15. Poverty
16. Abuse
17. Poor social conditions
18. Homelessness
19. Damage to reputation
20. Trauma.

Most of these drivers are not amenable to medicine-based health related remedies. Excluding obvious medicine-related factors – mental illness (treated or untreated), self-harm as in cutting, non-fatal bodily injury, chronic disease, disability or pain, and trauma – the vast majority (80%) were not medical issues, and appropriate only for non-medical intervention. Space and time restrictions prevented further examination of Northern Ireland's societal response to alleviating the psychache /perturbation generated in our neighbours that contributed to multiple deaths of despair, in suicide.

O'Mahony (2016) reflected upon Illich (1976) whose attack on modern medicine opened with the statement, 'The medical establishment has become a major threat to health'. It should not take more than a glance at Black's (2021) list – above – to isolate the handful of 'health-related' issues that contributed to suicide risk. Illich (1976) did not include suicidal behaviour as a 'health' issue in his diatribe. But he did not miss the 'suicide' target by much arguing that:

'modern medicine had hubristically taken on a mission to eradicate pain, sickness, even death. These were, he argued, eternal human realities, which we must learn to cope with: in fact, coping with these verities is what it means to be "healthy"; [he was concerned by] the three types of harm done by doctors – iatrogenesis – clinical, or the direct harm done by various medical treatments; social, or the medicalisation of ordinary life; and cultural, meaning the loss of traditional ways of dealing with suffering' (O'Mahony, 2016: 135).

Illich (1976) held that, rather than scientific medicine, sanitation, nutrition and housing were more important determinants of health. He coined the term 'Sisyphus syndrome', meaning the more healthcare given to a population, the greater its demand for care. He attacked the 'the medicalisation of death':

'The patient's unwillingness to die on his own makes him pathetically dependent. He has now lost faith in his ability to die, the terminal shape that health can take and has made the right to be professionally killed into a major issue' (O'Mahony, 2016: 136).

Illich's (1976) remedies lacked practical application, and were less astute than his diagnosis of medicine's woes, including 'vague proposals' like handing back to lay people responsibility for their health, and limiting the power of doctors, insurance companies, and the pharmaceutical industry. The sub-title of Illich's (1976) book was 'the expropriation of health': this phenomenon, he argued, was resistant to medical remedies, being a spiritual, rather than an organisational or societal, malaise:

'It can be reversed only through a recovery of the will to self-care among the laity, and through the legal, political and institutional recognition of the right to care, which imposes limits upon the professional monopoly of physicians' (O'Mahony, 2016: 136).

O'Mahony (2016) suggested that as medicalisation continued apace 'Illich would have been wryly amused by the invention of new diseases, such as social anxiety disorder (shyness), male pattern alopecia (baldness), testosterone-deficiency syndrome (old age) and erectile dysfunction (impotence)' (p138).

What Illich might have made of the ongoing discussion in psychiatric literature about possible inclusion of 'suicidality disorder' or 'suicidal syndrome' as a new addition to the burgeoning list of treatable (appropriate fees payable?) symptoms in the next DSM revision by the American Psychiatric Association (APA) remains unknown. Oquendo (2014), Obegi (2019), Silverman and Berman, A.L. (2020) and Fehling and Selby (2021) represented a small sample of interested parties, both for and against, active in this exclusive debate.

## Conclusions

At the outset of writing and reviewing this section, I wondered if I had gone too far in adding my sub-title: 'how psychiatry has suicidality by the throat' and whether a question mark would be appropriate in recognition of an ongoing debate in psychiatry. Being a professional, self-governing body, the APA was a 'law unto itself'. The real question remained regarding the DSM and its voluminous, expanding contents: cui bono?

**Myth:** (fictitious popular idea) Suicide is self-murder and our society is as concerned about suicide as it is about murder.

**Fallacy:** (misleading argument) Monitoring changes in annual suicide rates is a reliable way to measure success levels in a state's suicide prevention policy.

## References

American Psychiatric Association (1994) Diagnostic and Statistical Manual. DSM-IV Washington, DC: American Psychiatric Association

American Psychiatric Association (2000) Diagnostic and Statistical Manual. DSM-IV-TR Washington, DC: American Psychiatric Association

Black, L-A. (2021) Suicide: Northern Ireland. 14 April 2021. Research and Information Service Research Paper. Northern Ireland Assembly, Stormont, Belfast

Bryan, D., Kelly, L. and Templar, S. (2010) The failed paradigm of 'terrorism'. Behavioural Sciences of Terrorism and Political Aggression. First published on: 17 September 2010 (iFirst Article)

Doherty, F. and Mageean, P. (2006) Investigating lethal force deaths in Northern Ireland. The Application of Article 2 of the European Convention on Human Rights. February 2006 ISBN 1 903681 53 7© Belfast: Northern Ireland Human Rights Commission

DSM-IV-TR – Diagnostic and Statistical Manual (2000) Quick reference to the diagnostic criteria. Washington, DC: American Psychiatric Association

Durkheim, E. (1897/2002) Suicide: a study in sociology. New York: Free Press

English, R. (2009) Terrorism: How to respond. Oxford: Oxford University Press

Fehling, K. B. and Selby, E. A. (2021) Suicide in DSM-5: current evidence for the proposed suicide behaviour disorder and other possible improvements. Frontiers in Psychiatry, February, 2021, volume 11, article 499980

Henderson, D. (2011) Let this be our secret. Dublin: Gill & Macmillan

Hoffman, B. (2006) Inside terrorism (revised and expanded edition). New York: Columbia University Press

Illich, I. (1976) Limits to Medicine – Medical Nemesis: the expropriation of health. London: Pelican Books

Leavey, G., Rosato, M., Galway, K., Hughes, L., Mallon, S. and Rondon, J. (2016) Patterns and predictors of help-seeking contacts with health services and general practitioner detection of suicidality prior to suicide: a cohort analysis of suicides occurring over a two-year period. BMC Psychiatry (2016) 16:120

Leckey, J. (2013) Personal email.

Leenaars, A. A. (1996) A multidimensional malaise.1996 Presidential address to the American Association of Suicidology. Suicide and Life-Threatening Behaviour, 26(3) Fall 1996

McKeown, M. (2001/2009) Post-Mortem: an examination of the patterns of politically associated violence in Northern Ireland during the years 1969-2001 as reflected in the fatality figures for those years. http://cain.ulst.ac.uk/victims/mckeown/mckeown01.pdf

Morrissey, M., Smyth, M. & Fay, M.T. (1999) The Cost of the Troubles Study. Derry / L'derry: INCORE (University of Ulster & The United Nations University)

NICE (2020/2022) Acute management of a person at risk of self-harm. Last revised August 2020. Accessed on 28 January 2022 at https://www.nice.org.uk/about/what-we-do

Obegi, J. H. (2019): Is suicidality a mental disorder? Applying DSM-5 guidelines for new diagnoses, Death Studies, DOI: 10.1080/07481187.2019.1671546

O'Connor, R.C., Sheehy, N.P. and O'Connor, D.B. (1999b) A classification of suicides into sub-types. Journal of Mental Health. 8(6): 629-637

O'Mahony, S. (2016) Medical Nemesis 40 years on: the enduring legacy of Ivan Illich. J R Coll Physicians Edinb 2016; 46: 134-9. Accessed on 22 April 2022 at https://www.rcpe.ac.uk/college/journal/medical-nemesis-40-years-enduring-legacy-ivan-illich

O'Neill, S., Corry, C., McFeeters, D., Murphy, S., and Bunting, B. (2016) Suicide in Northern Ireland: an analysis of gender differences in demographic, psychological, and contextual factors. Crisis 37(1): 13-20

Oquendo, M. A. and Baca-Garcia, E. (2014) Suicidal behaviour disorder as a diagnostic entity in the DSM-5 classification system: advantages outweigh limitations' World Psychiatry, 13, 2

Queen's University Belfast (2009) Notes of students' informal survey responses.

Shneidman, E. S. (1980a) A possible classification of suicidal acts based on Murray's need system. Suicide and Life-Threatening Behaviour, 10, pp175-181.

Shneidman, E. S. (1993) Suicide as psychache : a clinical approach to self-destructive behaviour. Northvale, NJ: Jason Aronson Inc

Shneidman, E. S. (2001) Psychologic factors in suicide: risk factors for suicide. Summary of a workshop. Washington (DC) National Academies Press (US) 2001. Institute of Medicine (US) Board on Neuroscience and

Behavioural Health. Accessed on 29 January 2022 at NCBI Bookshelf ID: NBK223745

Silverman, M. M. and Berman, A. L. (2020) Editorial: Feeling Ill at Ease With a New Disease Labeling Suicide-Related Behaviours as a DSM-5 Diagnosis. Crisis, 41(4), 241-247

Szasz, T. S. (2009) Antipsychiatry: quackery squared. Syracuse, New York, NY: Syracuse University Press.

\* \* \*

## Chapter 3

# The pervasive influence of sociology – Durkheim's outdated ideas?

Emile Durkheim's 1897 study of suicide is regarded as 'a seminal study, significant in the history and development of sociology as a science' (The Guardian, 2015). From 2015 however, the largest UK exam board for sociology A-levels, the Assessment and Qualifications Alliance (AQA), removed suicide from its syllabus and as a central part of A-level sociology, apparently because 'some students may be distressed by the topic'. This 'out of sight – out of mind' dichotomy applies only to A-level sociology since 'suicide' may be mentioned in some current examiners' feedback re AQA A-level studies in English Language and Literature, Health and Social Care, History, Religious Studies, Law, German, Music, Spanish, French, Drama & Theatre, and Psychology (Assessment and Qualifications Alliance, 2015).

For students of suicide and suicidology, sociology's contribution continues to be strongly represented by the ideas of that discipline's co-founder (alongside Auguste Comte) Emile Durkheim (2002, first published in 1897), augmented by over a century of comments, opinions and analyses of the Great Man's celebrated study. Durkheim's work regarding suicide was focused as sociology is, upon relevant phenomena 'attributed to society at large, rather than being limited to the specific actions of individuals' (Wikipedia, 2010).

Durkheim's continuing influence upon national and international approaches to understanding and controlling the phenomenon of suicide in society, is evident in the universal and unquestioning use of so-called 'suicide rates' to denote success or failure in such endeavours. Durkheim's 100+ year-old analysis and his difficulty with some of it, influenced Dr Mike Tomlinson's important published work on suicide in Northern Ireland in relation to the so-called Troubles (1968-1998) and their aftermath (Tomlinson, 2007, 2012).

I recall an informal comment by Dr Tomlinson, Queen's University Belfast (QUB) Emeritus Sociology Professor, at a suicide prevention a while ago, along the lines that the one aspect of suicide that our society is good at is 'our ability to count them'.

Ian Rockett (2010) among others disputes this. He characterises the issue of misclassification of suicides as a consequence, inter alia, of

i) under-resourced investigations when compared with homicide counterparts

ii) deliberate policy driven decisions, linked to budgetary constraints and media criticism, to wilfully misclassifying suicides under 'accidents'

iii) absence of 'compelling corroborative evidence ... in drug-related and other poisoning suicides'.

Rockett (2010) goes so far in his admitted speculations about the extent of undercounting of global suicide quanta to suggest that 'the true annual toll could easily double or triple the World Health Organisation's (WHO) conservatively estimated 1 million deaths (WHO, 2010)' (Rockett, 2010: 229).

**Durkheim's Major Conclusions**

Durkheim's sociological thesis postulated four main suicide categories, that he related to an individual's lesser or greater 'social integration' and an individual's lesser or greater 'social regulation'. These were:

- Egoistic suicide that corresponds to a low level of social integration. When one is not well integrated into a social group it can lead to a feeling that they have not made a difference in anyone's lives.
- Altruistic suicide that corresponds to too much social integration. This occurs when a group dominates the life of an individual to a degree where they feel meaningless to society.

- Anomic suicide that occurs when one has an insufficient amount of social regulation. This stems from the sociological term anomie, meaning a sense of aimlessness or despair that arises from the inability to reasonably expect life to be predictable.
- Fatalistic suicide that results from too much social regulation. An example of this would be when one follows the same routine day after day. This leads to a belief that there is nothing good to look forward to. Durkheim suggested this was the most popular (sic) form of suicide for prisoners (Wikipedia, 2010).

An American sociologist Corrigall-Brown (2020: 14) states that social inequality, social institutions and social change are the 'core foci' of sociology. She believes that social institutions are the norms, values and rules of conduct that structure human interaction (p 16). She then lists five core institutions - the family, education, religion, the economy, and the government. When supplemented by mass media, medicine and science (including the ongoing 'war' on Covid-19 global plague), these can perpetuate social inequality or create social change (p 17). In the context of Northern Ireland, local 'institutions' that we can add are the justice system, including police, courts, prisons and military, and post-1998 GFA legacy organizations, lawful and outlawed, that constitute our unique social / political culture.

Corrigall-Brown (2020) highlighted the negative influence of secularization on religious practice while contending that context is all-important in understanding religion's changing role as a social institution. For example, so-called 'Peace' walls or barriers, 116 in all, separating perceived Roman Catholic populations from their Protestant fellow-citizens in Northern Ireland remain 'as visible symbols of community segregation and division' (The World, 2020).

The 'brilliance' of Durkheim's study, according to Corrigall-Brown (2020: 27), is the way it shows how a phenomenon that is generally thought to be purely psychological, the decision to die by suicide, is shaped by the structure of the society in which the person lives (and dies). She acknowledges the criticism of later researchers that there is a logical error in his research in his attempt to explain micro-level individual behaviour (the act of suicide) with macro-level country statistics (suicide rates). Wray et al. (2011: 518) suggest that an opportunity exists now for sociology to acknowledge a multidisciplinary approach to understanding suicide:

'... recent suicide research... reveals a trend toward studies that examine suicide as something that happens not just within groups or societies, but also to individuals who inhabit those groups and societies. By this we do not mean to suggest that sociologists either adopt an overly individualistic approach to the study of suicide or abandon the study of aggregate measures; rather, this suggestion calls both for incorporating our own insights on the individual level and for pushing past the current insularity of the sociology of suicide to consider research from other disciplines [since] over the past three decades, scientific research and conceptual thinking have converged to suggest that suicide comes from a combination of genetic, developmental, environmental, physiological, social, and cultural factors operating through diverse, complex pathways (Goldsmith et al., 2002)'.

## Complex social and psychological factors beyond Durkheim's sociological thesis

Tomlinson (2012: 464) critically evaluated the applicability to Northern Ireland of Durkheim's conclusions by way of 'a case study of suicide trends by age, gender and cause of death over a forty-year period.' His key finding was that the cohort of children and young people who grew up in the worst years of violence during the 1970s, have the highest and most rapidly increasing suicide rates, and account for the steep upward trend in suicide following the 1998 Belfast/Good Friday Agreement (GFA, 1998). In a parallel study of the community response to perceived 'youth suicide clusters', Forbes et al. (2012) suggested 'that social deprivation, the trauma legacy of the conflict and the transition out of conflict were highly significant in creating a sense of hopelessness in the community in which these young people were growing up.' Torney (2014) reported that 'In the last 10 years [from 2002 to 2012] the suicide rate per 100,000 of the population [across all age ranges] in Northern Ireland has increased from 10.8 in 2002 to 15.2 in 2012'. This was equivalent to a percentage increase of 40.7%.

Although Tomlinson (2012) cites several studies (Lester, 2002; McGowan et al., 2005; McKitterick et al., 1999; and O'Connor and Sheehy, 1997) addressing suicide and the Northern Ireland conflict, his case study's sources and findings are largely based upon complex statistical analysis of data from the Government's Registrar General Northern Ireland Annual Reports over a 45 year period (1965-2010).

Although conceding that Durkheim's 'work has had an enduring influence on the understanding of suicide for more than a century (Van Poppel and Day, 1996)', Tomlinson (2012) does not dwell upon Durkheim's fundamental notions of social integration and social regulation with regard to explaining changes in the incidence of suicide during and following the end of Northern Ireland conflict via the Belfast / Good Friday Agreement (GFA, 1998). Contrary to Durkheim, he argues that the post-GFA rise in suicide involves a complex of social and psychological factors including:

i) Direct effects of war on the mental health and behaviour of individual witnesses, survivors and perpetrators of violence

ii) Expressions of aggression and violence are no longer 'socially approved' and instead become internalised in suicidal behaviour

iii) The growth in social isolation, poor mental health arising from the experience of conflict, and ensuing greater political stability

iv) Imprisonment and increased social isolation in families and households

v) Transition to peace has involved mass medication with anti-depressants, alcohol and non-prescription drugs

vi) Drug use and the illicit drugs trade have flourished during the peace process.

(Tomlinson, 2012).

## Sociology underpins a 'big data' approach to suicide

Moving beyond Durkheim's thesis that attributed the phenomenon of suicide to 'society and culture', rather than to an individual decedent's behaviour, this section surveys Durkheim's, and thus sociology's somewhat grandiose ambition 'to demonstrate how social factors determine individual consciousness and behaviour' (Tomlinson, 2012: 464-482), with particular reference to the unique, idiosyncratic phenomenon that is an individual human being's death by self-destruction.

An important source is a 35 page section, headed 'Society and Culture', of a comprehensive 500+ page report, 'Reducing Suicide' (2002), published by the US Institute of Medicine, whose aims included:

i) To assess the science base for suicide etiology (= cause or origin, per Merriam-Webster)
ii) To evaluate the current status of primary and secondary prevention, including risk and protective factors
iii) To develop strategies for studying suicide and comment on gaps in knowledge, research opportunities and strategies for prevention.

(Reducing Suicide, 2002: xi)

At its date of publication, US deaths by suicide numbered 'about 30,000' (Reducing Suicide, 2002: x). A later estimate, cited by the US Centers for Disease Control and Prevention (CDC, 2015), stated that 'in 2001 there were 30,622 deaths from suicide' (Hogan and Grumet, 2016: 1085). Seventeen years on, latest published statistics for deaths by suicide for 2018 were 48,344, i.e. 58% higher (Chapterland.org).

Tomlinson's (2012) analysis provided important insights into some drivers and causes of N Ireland's 'Troubles legacy' 40% hike in suicide numbers (2002-2012). Durkheimian explanations of drivers/causes of the 58% spike in US suicide numbers (2001-2018) are suggested by Dr Ben Miller of a Health Policy Center in Aurora, Colorado: 'One is in health care, and one is in society.' Dr. Miller attributed the increasing disparities in health care and inequalities in income as crucial factors in the feelings of despair, loneliness and a lack of belonging that contributed to suicides among many Americans (New York Times, 2019):

'Suicides can be the result of trauma that goes unrecognized or unaddressed — the loss of a job, home or death of a loved one', said Mr. John Auerbach, president of a major non-profit US health trust, adding that 'without the social cohesiveness and social support built within family ... people are experiencing trauma without what gave them resilience historically' (New York Times, 2019).

One available but seemingly immoveable aspect of US suicide is the use of 'plentiful and accessible' firearms: the New York Times (2019) reported that almost 50% of 2017's 47,173 suicides were by gunshot. Suicide by poisoning, including deaths by overdose of prescription drugs, including opioids, have escalated by 50% between 2016 and 2017. American life expectancy continues to decline with high mortality rates largely fuelled by suicide and drug overdoses. Numerous factors can be attributed to this worrying trend, with failures in democratic institutions and regulations, economic stagnation and increasing medical costs cited. Besides social and economic strife, the opioid crisis has been further exacerbated by misconduct in the pharmaceutical industry and dangerous prescribing practices for an extremely addictive class of drug. Suicide and drug overdoses — both growing public health crises – reflect deficiencies across many social determinants of health, from housing to employment to family connections. Deaths from suicide and opioid overdose fall into the category of deaths of despair:

'"There's a reason why these conditions have been called conditions of despair, because I think they represent a disconnect between a kind of world that generates health and the kind of world (in which) most people live," [said] APHA member Sandro Galea, MD, DrPH, MPH, dean and professor at the Boston University School of Public Health' (The Nation's Health, 2019)

However suicide and opioid addiction are not the same having different causes and [potential] solutions. But as conditions of despair, marked by secrecy, shame and stigma, preventing people from accessing care, both opioid addiction and suicidality are rooted in social and socio-economic adversities, many of which are widespread in the U.S. and contribute to mortality (The Nation's Health, 2019):

'"There are many communities in America where it is hard to find the road to economic opportunity, and we have observed escalating rates of economic inequality in our country that drive fundamental barriers to individual well-being that affect health," said Professor Colleen Barry,

PhD, MPH, from Johns Hopkins Bloomberg School of Public Health. "Health and secure employment and secure housing are all inextricably linked. And to the extent that it is harder to make ends meet than it has been in many communities in America, which inevitably affects our health."' (The Nation's Health, 2019).

On the face of it, the above US suicide numbers suggested that the Institute of Medicine's 'Reducing Suicide' (2002) report and recommendations were less than effective in their application. A better question, perhaps, was whether its 'Society and Culture' section's findings help us to understand, or even to come to terms with this almost 58% surge in suicide deaths over 17 years. For example, if there was value in a Durkheimian approach, what further societal and/or cultural factors might explain, or even illuminate in some way, this escalation in self-destructive behaviour by individuals?

## Societal factors that correlate with suicide

Under the report's 'Society and Culture' rubric, relevant factors that 'correlate' with suicide were considered at four different levels: individual, geographic, societal and historical influences:

i) <u>individual</u>: specific events in a person's life and participation in social groups. Critical life events and circumstances are responsible for suicides. Examples include divorce, economic strain or political repression;

ii) <u>geographic</u>: focus is on distribution of suicide events within countries (or neighbourhoods). 'Socio-cultural profiles' are assessed to see if they contribute to suicide rates. Examples include individuals living in areas or locales of 'low social integration', e.g. high divorce and/or unemployment rates;

iii) <u>societal</u>: differences in suicide rates are examined cross-nationally. Different countries have different 'institutional arrangements'; political factors may influence suicide rates related to 'a general worsening of health conditions in a time of societal turmoil and crisis with vast economic, political and social changes'; discrepancies between male and female suicides are much smaller in Asian, especially East Asian countries; and

iv) <u>historical</u>: suicide rates can be compared over time periods to examine short period effects or longer term trends. Trends can be examined and correlated with changes over time in social and cultural indicators for various societies. The point here is to acknowledge the importance of understanding context and historical period.

(Reducing Suicide, 2002: 196)

## Actual factors considered to influence suicide

The report cites actual factors that can be considered to influence suicide, under all or any of the above four headings, including the following:

i) <u>Family and other social support</u>: Family attachments influence suicidal probability. Family and other social support are protective factors. Living alone increases the risk of suicide

ii) <u>Marital status</u>: Its influence on suicide rates varies by gender, culture and across the life course. In general marriage is associated with lower overall suicide rates while divorce and marital separation are associated with increased suicide risk

iii) <u>Parenthood</u>: this appeared to reduce the risk of suicide

iv) <u>Family discord and connectedness</u>: 'Discord within a family ... has an impact on suicide' (Reducing Suicide, 2002: 189). More positively, some researchers reported that 'perceived parental and family connectedness significantly protected against suicidality for youth' (Reducing Suicide, 2002: 189)

v) <u>Social support</u>: Close relationships with others enabled better coping with life stresses such as bereavement, rape, job loss, and physical illness. Multiple studies across 'sundry countries and ethnic groups' revealed increased suicides among those who were socially isolated, and/or lacked supportive family and friendships. Other evidence showed that social support can represent 'part of a protective process that increases self efficacy and thereby reduces suicidal behaviour' (Reducing Suicide, 2002: 200)

vi) <u>Religion, religiosity, religious affiliation, religious beliefs</u>: Participation in religious activities was reported to be a protective factor for suicide. Studies showed that higher suicide rates were reported in areas with a higher percentage of individuals without religious affiliation. Durkheim famously found that Catholics had lower suicide rates than Protestants that he linked with 'increased social contact and affiliation in practiced Catholicism' (Durkheim, 1897/2002). Overall, 123 years on, it is clear that religion per se is a neutral factor in suicide risk. What does seem to be relevant are the protective effects upon the behaviour of individual believers of the programming and conditioning that are implicit in religious belief and practice (Reducing Suicide, 2002: 201-204)

vii) <u>Occupation</u>: Some professions have higher risk of suicide than others. Examples are physicians, dentists, police officers and manual labourers. However specific influences of occupation-related factors on suicide remain unclear

viii) <u>Unemployment</u>: Unemployment is clearly associated with increased rates of suicide. Three explanations are possible: a) unemployment may confer vulnerability by increasing the impact of stressful life events; b) it may indirectly cause suicide by increasing the risk of factors that precipitate suicide (for example, mental illness, financial difficulties); or c) it may be a non-causal association because of confounding or selection by factors that predict both unemployment status and suicide risk (Blakely et al., 2003)

ix) <u>Socioeconomic status</u>: A strong predictor, across levels, time and countries is socioeconomic disadvantage. Overall suicide rates appear to be associated with indicators of economic distress (Stack, 2000)

x) <u>The political system</u>: According to David Easton (1971), "A political system can be designated as the interactions through which values are authoritatively allocated for a society". Essentially, this factor is of sociological interest regarding suicide because politics is all about the exercise of power, who holds it within the relationship of government and people and how this power is used. The report acknowledges the complex relationship between power and suicide, citing examples including how to disentangle the power a certain group has at a macro-social level from individuals' perceived personal and interpersonal control, economic power and self-perception of the ability to foster change (Reducing Suicide, 2002: 210). In Northern Ireland, from 1969 to date, 'certain groups', mentioned above, may have included armed paramilitary organizations and criminal gangs spawned, nourished and tolerated by political organizations, some of whom currently exercise political power there via democratically elected office.

(Reducing Suicide, 2002: 193-210)

## Durkheim's contribution to suicidology today

As stated above, since Durkheim's (1897/1952) seminal sociological study 'On Suicide', a voluminous, suicidological literature has been published. However it is useful to reflect upon and to critique Durkheim's technical study of some key social factors over a century ago, that he believed contributed directly to the incidence of suicide at that time in human societies. He was convinced that the personal, individual circumstances pertaining to any and every suicide event were 'almost infinite in number' (Durkheim, 1897/1952: 262). However Durkheim did not totally dismiss the potential value of a psychological examination of what caused each such event (Kivisto, 2011: 108). Rather he preferred to seek an understanding of the causes of suicide in what he termed a 'suicidal aptitude in each society' that was located within the nature of societies themselves. Hence his invention of a 'social suicide rate' as his way to illustrate the 'moral situation of society' that gave rise 'for each people a collective force of a definite amount of energy impelling men towards self-destruction' (Durkheim, 1897/2002: 263).

It is clear from the above that the trouble with understanding and perhaps reducing the incidence of suicide using sociological analysis is suicide's complexity. Yur'yev et al. (2011) cited Durkheim's classic theory that elevated suicide rates are associated with times of significant socio-economic change (Durkheim, 1897/2002). They said that, in accordance with Durkheim's theory, abrupt changes temporarily reduce the social regulation of individuals, because their social equilibrium is disturbed (Durkheim, 1897/2002). Durkheim had identified 'four categories' – see above – that located human self-destruction within the influence upon an individual of social factors – integration and regulation – and their capacity to determine that individual's consciousness and behaviour (Tomlinson, 2012: 464-482).

Yur'yev et al. (2011) investigated the role of social welfare provision in suicide prevention in several European countries. They relied upon Durkheim's theory to conjecture that levels of state-provided welfare support would moderate 'abrupt changes' related to socioeconomic adversity. They concluded that:

1. Higher social expenditure was inversely associated with suicide mortality in the majority of the European countries studied; and
2. Confidence in welfare provision appeared to have a suicide-preventive effect.

Wray et al. (2011) asserted the 'truly impressive durability' of Durkheimian theory. However they argued that two separate goals appear to underlie sociological research on suicide: first, development and testing of sociological theory, and second, 'a more latent concern for the amelioration of social problems' (Wray et al., 2011: 522). They suggested that sociologists might pursue 'new directions ... [including] ... treating suicide as a significant social problem in and of itself (not merely a symptom of larger pathologies) ... [that] aim[s] strategically at intervening in public discourse and policy debates around suicide' (Wray et al. 2011: 523). Otherwise they fear that future sociologists will become less interested in pursuing answers to the riddle of suicide, such that the role for sociology in the multidisciplinary study of suicide will eventually die, as it were, a self-inflicted death (Wray et al., 2011: 523).

## Suicide: Six Psychological Theories & One Sociological Theory

Some existing theories of suicide were reviewed by Stanley et al. (2015) in relation to understanding elder suicide. Locating suicide as

a critical public health priority, they summarized seven theoretical approaches – one sociological and six psychological - that 'move beyond psychiatric risk factors alone in considering why older adults die by suicide' (Stanley et al., 2015). These were:
  i) Classical sociological theory – Durkheim (1897/2002)
  ii) Hopelessness theory: Beck et al. (1985)
  iii) Escape theory: Baumeister (1990)
  iv) Emotion dyregulation theory, 50: Linehan (1993)
  v) Psychache theory: Shneidman (1993)
  vi) Interpersonal-psychological theory of suicide: Joiner (2005) and Van Orden et al. (2010)
  vii) integrated motivational-volitional model (IMVM) of suicidal behaviour: O'Connor (2011)

Stanley et al. (2015: 118) concede that these theories have not yet been subject to 'direct empirical tests', are limited to studies published in English language and conducted in the United States, and that they disregard 'qualitative reports', viz. the findings and conclusions of qualitative, ideographic, case study based, peer-reviewed research studies. Stanley et al. (2015) add that these seven theories await testing among older adults at particularly elevated risk of suicide, inter alia veterans, sexual minorities, and those living in long-term care. In a somewhat over-optimistic concluding paragraph, these authors state their opinion that 'to advance the science of the understanding and prevention of suicide among older adults, researchers and clinicians should draw from and apply [these seven untested] theories of suicide' (page 119).

One major, unavoidable consequence of the quantitative, 'big-data' approach inherent in each of these seven theoretical approaches to the human suicide phenomenon is relegation to non-scientific speculation concerning the actuality of the unique, idiosyncratic death by suicide of any human individual. Perhaps what is meant by 'the riddle of suicide' is summed up in Durkheim's view that individual circumstances pertaining to any and every suicide event were 'almost infinite in number' (Durkheim, 1897/2002: 262).

## World Suicide Prevention Day 2020

At the time of writing, the Covid-19 global pandemic has for almost two years dominated the lives, well-being and future prospects of millions of our fellow humans. Coincidentally, World Suicide Prevention Day (WSPD, 10 September) drew attention to the pandemic's lethal potential with regard to suicide. Initiated by the International Association for Suicide Prevention (IASP) in 2003, the annual event aims 'to encourage us to engage with each other and to join together to spread awareness of suicide prevention' (IASP, 2020). A local (Northern Ireland) media report, headlined 'Tackle Suicide Risk Caused by Pandemic Says Royal College of Psychiatrists' (The Irish News, 2020), published on 10 September 2020, included references to Covid-19 pandemic-related factors, that 'could lead to an increase in suicides'. They included:

i)   Pressures of lockdown
ii)  Job losses
iii) The economic downturn
iv)  Financial stressors
v)   Bereavement
vi)  Isolation
vii) A rise in domestic violence
viii) A rise in addictions

(The Irish News, 2020)

Many of these negative consequences match those factors described above as 'correlates' and 'influencers' for suicide. It will be interesting to observe sociology's contribution, if any, to the public discourses and policy debates around the incidence of suicide, at home and around the world, as this 'once in a lifetime' catastrophe enveloped our world.

**Myth:** (fictitious popular idea) Sociology and psychology are complementary ways of understanding the suicide phenomenon

**Fallacy:** (misleading argument) Removing the study of suicide from the A-level sociology syllabus will prevent suicides in schools

# References

AQA (2015) Teaching guide: An overview of the new AS and A-level Sociology specifications. Accessed on 25 September 2024 at https://www.aqa.org.uk/subjects/sociology/as-and-a-level/sociology-7191-7192/specification-at-a-glance

Baumeister, R.F. (1990). Suicide as escape from self. Psychological Review, 99, 90-113

Beck, A. T., Steer, R. A., Kovacs, M. & Garrison, B. (1985) Hopelessness and eventual suicide: a 10-year prospective study of patients hospitalized with suicidal ideation. American Journal of Psychiatry, 142(5), 559-563

Blakely, T. A., Collings, S.C.D. and Atkinson, J. (2003) Unemployment and suicide. Evidence for a causal association. J Epidemiol Community Health, 2003 (57), 594–600

CDC (2015) Centers for Disease Control and Prevention. Fatal injury reports [Internet]. Atlanta (GA): CDC

Chapterland.org (2020) Suicide Facts and Figures: United States 2020. Source: CDC, 2018 Fatal Injury Reports, on 3 January 2020. Accessed at https://chapterland.org/wp-content/uploads/sites/13/2017/11/US_FactsFigures_Flyer.pdf on 12 September 2020

Corrigall-Brown, C. J. (2020) Imagining Society: an introduction to sociology. London: Sage Publications Inc

Durkheim, E. (1897/2002) Suicide: a study in sociology. London: Routledge (first English edition published 1952)

Easton, D. (1971) The political system: an enquiry into the state of political science. New York, NY: Knopf

Forbes, T., Sibbett, C., Miller, S., and Emerson, L. (2012). Exploring the Community Response to Multiple Deaths of Young People by Suicide, Belfast: Centre for Effective Education, Queen's University Belfast

GFA (1998) The Belfast / Good Friday Agreement. NI Government. Belfast.

Goldsmith, S., Pellmar, T., Kleinman, A. and Bunney, W. (2002) Reducing Suicide: A National Imperative. Washington, DC: Natl. Acad. Press [See 'Reducing Suicide' 2002, below]

Hogan, M. F. and Grumet, J. G. (2016) Suicide prevention: an emerging priority for public health. Health Affairs, 35(6) (2016), pages 1084-1090

IASP (2020) International Association for Suicide Prevention. Accessed on 14 September 2020 at https://www.iasp.info/wspd2019/

Joiner, T. E. (2005) Why people die by suicide. Cambridge, MA: Harvard University Press

Kivisto, P. (2011) Key ideas in sociology. London: Sage Publications Ltd

Lester, D. (2002) 'The "troubles" in Northern Ireland and suicide'. Psychological Reports 90 (3, Part 1): 722.

Linehan, M. M. (1993) Cognitive-behavioural treatment of borderline personality disorder. New York, NY: Guilford Press

McGowan, I., Hamilton, S., Miller, P. and Kernohan, G. (2005) 'Contrasting terrorist-related deaths with suicide trends over 34 years', Journal of Mental Health 14 (4): 399-405.

McKittrick, D., Kelters, S., Feeney, B., McVea, D. and Thornton, C. (1999) Lost Lives: The Stories of the Men, Women and Children Who Died as a Result of the Northern Ireland Troubles. Edinburgh: Mainstream Publishing

New York Times (2019) Deaths from drugs and suicide reach a record in the US. Adeel Hassan. New York Times, 7 March 2019 accessed on 25 September 2020 at https://www.nytimes.com/2019/03/07/us/deaths-drugs-suicide-record.html?auth=login-google

O'Connor, R.C. (2011). Towards an Integrated Motivational–Volitional Model of Suicidal Behaviour. In R.C. O'Connor, S. Platt, J. Gordon (Eds.) International Handbook of Suicide Prevention: Research, Policy & Practice. Chichester: Wiley Blackwell

O'Connor, R.C., and Sheehy, N. P. (1997) 'Suicide and Gender', Mortality 2(3): 239-254.

Reducing Suicide (2002) Reducing suicide, a national imperative. Institute of Medicine. Washington, DC: National Academies Press [See Goldsmith et al. (2002) above]

Registrar General Northern Ireland (1965-2010) Registrar General Northern Ireland Annual Reports (Forty-Fourth to Eighty-Eighth). Belfast: Stationery Office.

Rockett, I. (2010) Counting suicides and making suicide count as a public health problem. In Crisis, Journal of Crisis Intervention and Suicide Prevention. September 2010. Vol 31(5): 227-230

Shneidman, E. S. (1993) Suicide as psychache: a clinical approach to self-destructive behaviour. Lanham, MD: Jason Aronson

Stack, S. (2000) Suicide: A 15 year review of the sociological literature. Part 1: Cultural and economic factors. Suicide and Life-Threatening Behaviour, 30(2):145-162

Stanley, I.H., Hom, M.A., Rogers, M.L., Hagan, C.R. and Joiner, T.E. (2016) Understanding suicide among older adults: a review of psychological and sociological theories of suicide. Aging & Mental Health, 2016, 20(2), 113-122

The Guardian (2015) 'Suicide dropped from sociology lessons – are some topics too sensitive for school?' Sharmini-Selvarajah. 15 June 2015. Accessed 23 Sept 2020 at https://www.theguardian.com/profile/sharmini-selvarajah

The Irish News (2020). 'Tackle suicide risk caused by the pandemic say Royal College of Psychiatrists' Suzanne McGonagle, The Irish News, 10 September 2020, page 10. Belfast: The Irish News. Accessed on 14 September 2020 at http://www.irishnews.com /epaper/aviator/aviator.php?newspaper=IN&issue=20200910&edition=IRISHNEWS&startpage=1&displaypages=2

The Nation's Health (2019) Suicide, opioids tied to ongoing fall in US life expectancy: Third year of drop.' Julia Haskins. A publication of the American Public Health Association. Accessed on 25 September 2020 at https://thenationshealth.aphapublications.org/content/49/1/1.2.full

The World (2020) Public radio programme. Accessed on 24 September 2020 at https://www.pri.org/stories/2020-01-14/northern-ireland-still-divided-peace-walls-20-years-after-conflict

Tomlinson, M. W. (2007) The Trouble with Suicide. Belfast, N Ireland: DHSSPS Available from http://www.investingforhealthni.gov.uk/

Tomlinson, M. W. (2012). War, peace and suicide: The case of Northern Ireland. International Sociology, 27(4), 464-482.

Torney, K. (2014) Suicide kills as many as the Troubles. The Detail - Investigations and Analysis. The Detail, Fifth Floor, The Warehouse, 7 James Street South, Belfast, Northern Ireland, BT2 8DN Telephone + 44 28 9031 5930. Accessed on 16 April 2014 at www.thedetail.tv

Van Orden, K. A., Witte, T. K., Cukrowicz, K.C., Braithwaite, S. R., Selby, E. A. and Joiner, T. E. (2010) The interpersonal theory of suicide. Psychological Review, 117(2), 575-600

Van Poppel, F. and Day, L. H. (1996) A test of Durkheim's theory of suicide – without committing the "ecological fallacy". American Sociological Review. 61-3, 500-507

WHO (2010) World Health Organisation. Suicide prevention (SUPRE). Available at hppt://www.who.int/mental_health/prevention/suicide/suicideprevcent/en/

Wikipedia (2010) https://en.wikipedia.org/wiki/%C3%89mile_Durkheim. Accessed on 6 September 2020

Wray, M., Colen, C. and Pescosolido, B. (2011) The sociology of suicide. Annual Review of Sociology, 2011(37), 505-528

WSPD (2023) World Suicide Prevention Day. https://www.who.int>campaigns

Yur'yev, A., Varnik, P., Varnik, A., Sisask, M. and Leppik, L. (2011) Role of social welfare in European suicide prevention. International Journal of Social Welfare, January, 2011

\* \* \*

## Chapter 4
# Reporting and counting suicides but disregarding the lessons one by one

As mentioned in Chapter 3 above, Prof Tomlinson remarked a while back that we – he meant society, since he's sociologist – were quite good at counting suicides. Understanding the phenomenon and doing something to alleviate its catastrophic legacy – well, perhaps that was something else.

We also examine here the related issue of the role of media in the reporting of suicide in UK/Ireland. All that most people know about suicide (a 2% issue) is the media's reporting and characterising of it. The predicament of survivors, i.e. those people bereaved by a suicide death, added to speculation about 'the reasons why', comprise the media's main response. Coroner's inquests in N Ireland are held at the Coroner's discretion. This power however is limited. Not being a lawyer, but using common sense, I can only surmise that precedent applies here as in much judge-made law. Even when an inquest is reported, its limited remit - who, when, where and how – facilitates further journalistic rumination around 'why'. I provide same summary evidence of this below, at paragraph headed 'newsworthiness'.

### New Zealand is an outlier

I can find only one jurisdiction – (NZ) – where media reporting of suicide, including via online and social media, was until recently (2016) limited by statute. Almost three decades earlier, reporting suicide was restricted by the Coroners Act 1988. This meant that:

'where a death was believed to be self-inflicted and an inquest was not completed, no one could make public any details of the manner of death. Following a determination that the death was self-inflicted, only the name, address and occupation of the dead person could be published unless the coroner authorised further publication – a rare occurrence.

'Following Law Commission recommendations in 2014, the Coroners Amendment Act 2016 was passed. This allowed the news media (including social media) to report a death as 'suspected suicide' before a coroner's inquiry if the facts supported such a description. The chief coroner was able to allow the reporting of a suicide if the risk of copycat behaviour was small and outweighed by public interest. Restrictions on reporting the details of methods of suicide used by individuals remained' (Teara: the Encyclopedia of New Zealand, 2019).

At present, the NZ Coroner must inquire where a person appears to have died from unexplained, violent or suspicious circumstances. There also has to be an inquiry if the person who died was:

- In police custody
- In prison
- In an Oranga Tamariki - Ministry for Children home
- In foster care or if they were a ward of state
- Under a mental health compulsory treatment order
- In an institute for alcoholism or drug use
- Intellectually disabled and in compulsory care or rehabilitation

The coroner's finding is a report written by the coroner about the facts of the death. The finding can also include comments or recommendations to help prevent similar deaths in the future.

The immediate family of a person who died, or other interested parties, may apply to the coroner for a non-publication order that prohibits specific details or evidence given during a coronial inquiry being made public.

This means publishing it in a newspaper, a book, a journal or similar document, broadcasting it, putting it online or releasing an audio or visual recording (Coronial Services of New Zealand, 2021).

## Definition

There's a whole branch of suicidology devoted to the definition of suicide – Shneidman (1985: 47,48) wrote a book about this conundrum – when is/was a death an act of suicide – much of it devoted to investigating the deceased's behaviour, their motivation and intention. [Chapter 8 below engages with 'psychological autopsy' in this regard.] Coroners and statisticians invented a term 'undetermined cause of death' (otherwise coroner's 'open conclusion/finding') to be assigned to cases of unnatural death when a clear preponderance of evidence supporting a specific category (homicide, accident, or suicide) was not available. This ensured a statistical slot where evidence did not prove that death was 'suicide beyond a reasonable doubt'.

[As mentioned earlier, in a related and highly significant appeal case, the UK Supreme Court considered whether, in inquest proceedings in the case of a prison suicide in 2016, the criminal standard – 'beyond a reasonable doubt' – or the civil standard – 'the balance of probabilities' was the applicable standard of proof. By a majority, the Court ruled in favour of the civil standard, i.e. 'the balance of probabilities' (Supreme Court – Maughan, 2020; Inquest, 2020)].

## The Aftermath

Yet for relatives, friends, colleagues, associates and neighbours of the deceased – estimated from 6 upwards – the aftermath of a death by suicide, however categorised by a coroner, extends well beyond family:

'It has long been stated that six people are left behind following every suicide. Despite a lack of empirical evidence, this has been extensively cited for over 30 years. Using data from a random-digit dial survey, a more accurate number of people exposed to each suicide is calculated. A sample of 1,736 adults included 812 lifetime suicide-exposed respondents who reported age and number of exposures. Each suicide resulted in 135 people exposed (knew the person). Each suicide affects a large circle of people, who may be in need of clinician services or support following exposure' (Cerel et al., 2019).

Of course in this age of media-generated celebrity, when a 'well-known' person dies by (suspected) suicide, tabloid journalism allied with its sturdy, adolescent cousin, viz. social media, ensures that those 135 people, researched by Cerel et al. (2019), balloons into hundreds of thousands of readers near and far. Recent tragic examples of excessive publicity following a 'celebrity suicide' involved Robin Williams (hanging, 2014), David Foster Wallace (hanging, 2008), Alexander McQueen (hanging, 2010), Nicholas Plath (hanging, 2009: son of Sylvia Plath, suicide, 1963) (see 'List of celebrity suicides', 2020) and Caroline Flack (hanging, 2020).

One disturbing example of such 'excessive publicity' was evident in media reports following actor Robin Williams' (2014) suicide:

'... researchers in America looking into the rates of suicide following the death of Robin Williams noted a rapid increase in suicides, specifically suffocation suicides, in the five months following his death that paralleled the time and method of Williams' death. They also noted a dramatic increase in news media reports on suicides and Robin Williams during the same period. The researchers make clear that it is uncertain whether his death led to the increased number of suicides ...' (Independent Press Standards Organisation, IPSO: Guidance on Reporting Suicide, 2020).

Celebrity inquest conclusions found that both actor Philip Seymour Hoffman (drug overdose, 2014) and singer Dolores O'Riordan (drowning/intoxicated, 2018) died accidentally. The death of singer Keith Flint (found hanged, 2019), was ruled by the coroner not as suicide, but as death by undetermined cause, as follows:

'The Prodigy singer Keith Flint died by hanging [on 4 March 2019] and had unspecified amounts of cocaine, alcohol and codeine in his system at the time, an inquest has heard ... The senior coroner for Essex, Caroline Beasley-Murray, recorded an open conclusion, adding: "We will never quite know what was going on in his mind on that date ... Explaining how she reached her conclusion, she said: "I've considered suicide. To record that, I would have to have found that, on the balance of probabilities, Mr Flint formed the idea and took a deliberate action knowing it would result in his death. Having regard to all the circumstances I don't find that there's enough evidence for that." She also found insufficient evidence to conclude Flint's death was an accident, where he may have been 'larking around and it all went horribly wrong'. "I'm going to conclude an open conclusion," she said. "We will never quite know what was going on in his mind on that date and so that's why I'm going to record an open conclusion.'" (The Guardian, 2019)

## Werther Effect

I have not yet found research evidence whether media reporting of celebrity deaths by suicide adversely affected those bereaved to a lesser or greater extent than equivalent reporting of celebrity deaths by accidental / undetermined cause. However an authoritative research study published in the British Medical Journal (BMJ, 2020) concluded that a 'media related imitation' effect – dubbed the Werther effect – appeared to be associated with media reports of celebrity suicide:

'Reporting of deaths of celebrities by suicide appears to have made a meaningful impact on total suicides in the general population. The effect was larger for increases by the same method as used by the celebrity. General reporting of suicide did not appear to be associated with suicide although associations for certain types of reporting cannot be excluded. The best available intervention at the population level to deal with the harmful effects of media reports is guidelines for responsible reporting. These guidelines should be more widely implemented and promoted, especially when reporting on deaths of celebrities by suicide' (Niederkrotenthaler T. et al., 2019; BMJ, 18 March 2020).

The Werther effect related to a reported spike in suicides by young men in Germany and across Europe 246 years ago following publication of a novel by Goethe entitled 'The sorrows of young Werther' in 1774. This depicted the circumstances leading to the suicide of the fictional male protagonist Werther, who shoots himself with a pistol after he is rejected by the woman he loves.

Perhaps it may help to define three terms related to the Werther effect that have emerged in the literature:

'Imitation is the process by which one suicide exerts a modelling effect on subsequent suicides. Clusters are a number of suicides that occur in close temporal and/or geographical proximity, with or without any direct link. Contagion is the process by which a given suicide facilitates the occurrence of a further suicide, regardless of the direct or indirect knowledge of the prior suicide' (Gould, M. S., 1990).

Bridge et al. (2006) enter an important caveat regarding a cause/effect relationship between media coverage of suicide and subsequent suicidal behaviour:

'Even if it is accepted that media can have an effect on suicidal ideation, it is not a <u>sufficient condition</u> to drive people to commit suicide. The effects that media can have on suicidal behaviour are certainly less important than individual psychological and social risk factors (Bridge et al., 2006).

Journalism at all levels, from trash tabloid [including social media] all the way up to so-called 'newspaper of record', publish articles or what some journalists call 'stories', resorting as necessary to 'the public interest' or even 'the national interest' to explain or justify editorial decisions. The only effective legal constraint in UK/Ireland on published journalistic content, commonly referred to as 'freedom of the press', is the law of defamation. Suicide stories are few and far between since 'newsworthiness' determines editorial content. Recent research on suicide-related 'journalistic challenges' in Ireland included the comment:

'... one radio reporter noted, "A typical ordinary suicide we wouldn't cover ... For instance, if a body is found in a river, we would try to find out if it's a suicide and if it is then we wouldn't report on it," (Radio Reporter 3).' (Headline, 2018).

## Newsworthiness

Local N Irish print media appear to use a 'newsworthiness test' in their reporting of 'ordinary' viz. non-celebrity suicide. Earlier the World Health Organisation's (WHO, 2000) 'preventing suicide' resource booklet for media professionals commented on an auxiliary factor that appeared to trigger media interest:

'However, the suicides most likely to attract the attention of the media are those that depart from usual patterns. In fact, it is striking that cases presented in the media are almost invariably atypical and uncommon, and to represent them as typical further perpetuates misinformation about suicide' (WHO, 2000).

Recent examples may reveal some relevant criteria:
i) Prison suicides
ii) Suicide and Irish paramilitary criminality
iii) Murder-suicide
iv) Consecutive family suicides
v) Child suicide
vi) Suicide immediately prior to facing serious criminal charges
vii) Suicide linked to social media
viii) Irish ex-paramilitaries and suicide, and
ix) Suicide by domestic violence

## Prison Suicides

A Belfast inquest on 14 February 2020 concluded that JR, a 20 year old prisoner in a Young Offender's Centre, died in Belfast City Hospital on 19 April 2013, 10 days after he was found hanging by bed sheets in his cell on the evening of his first day in prison custody.

He was arrested at 745pm on 7 April 2013, and was held by police for two nights – 7th & 8th April - until he was remanded to prison by a court at 09.19am on 9 April 2013 and transferred to the Offender's Centre arriving at 13.20hrs on that day. No information was available about why police arrested JR but he apparently had been 'in prison on four occasions for theft and criminal damage [and] was on prescription medication for depression' (The Irish News, 2020d). JR's suicide was facilitated by multiple errors of judgment, of which one of the most critical is summed up here:

'JR was placed in an ordinary cell [at 18.14 hrs], rather than an observation cell (which provides anti-ligature furniture and bedding, and CCTV observation) as the senior officer did not assess him as having a serious and immediate intent to self-harm' (Ombudsman, 2015: 22).

JR was found unresponsive by prison staff on 9 April 2013 at 22.16 hrs, after four hours locked in his cell and less than nine hours after his incarceration.

The inquest jury said 'errors made by the prison authorities and [a local] Health Trust contributed to JR's death' (The Irish News, 2020d). On 15 December 2015, several years before that delayed inquest, the N Ireland Prisoner Ombudsman published an investigation report, with consent of his next-of-kin, into the circumstances surrounding [his] death in hospital while in prison custody. The Ombudsman's methodology resembled some aspects of a psychological autopsy:

'including interviews with staff, prisoners, family and friends, analysis of all prison records in relation to the deceased's life while in custody; and examination of evidence such as CCTV footage and phone calls. Where necessary, independent clinical reviews of the medical care provided to the prisoner are commissioned. In this case, Dr Seena Fazel, Consultant Forensic Psychiatrist, undertook a clinical review of the healthcare provided to Mr Rainey whilst he was in [custody]' (Ombudsman, 2015: 5).

The Ombudsman's findings were limited to consideration of the deceased's period in custody. They recorded multiple errors in carrying out policy guidelines by prison service staff including 'senior officers' throughout JR's nine hours in prison custody. In response to the coroner's findings that the prison service failed 'to train staff in suicide and self-harm prevention [and failed] to adequately assess JR' (The Irish News, 2020d) the Northern Ireland Prison Service director-general issued a lengthy statement. He said 'when someone is placed in our care, the family has every right to expect that everyone whether prison or healthcare staff, will do all we can to keep their loved ones safe'. He also offered 'my deepest apologies to [JR's] family, [adding] we have introduced a range of measures with the focus on a person-centred approach over recent years' (The Irish News, 2020d).

Neither the Ombudsman's report (Ombudsman, 2015) nor the local newspaper's report (The Irish News, 2020d) included any message, regarding access to help and support by anyone in distress.

Afterthought - Prison policy regarding 'someone placed in [the Northern Ireland Prison Service's] care' might benefit if the philosophy and practice of the 'Zero Suicide' initiative was considered for implementation across their estate. Northern Ireland Association for the Care and Resettlement of Offenders (NIACRO) published a short paper by Professor Dr Siobhan O'Neill (2018) confirming that 'Zero suicide appears to be gaining momentum and elements are being adopted in healthcare settings across the UK and internationally'. She cautioned however that 'a focus on the eradication of suicide deaths without leadership and culture change would risk placing individual clinicians at risk of being blamed for suicide deaths.' Prison governors, senior officers and wardens are not, and do not consider themselves to be, 'clinicians'. An unanswered issue remains, therefore, whether prisons, where individuals are compulsorily incarcerated by state forces and closely supervised by uniformed wardens, can be considered to be 'healthcare settings' as normally defined.

### Suicide and Irish Paramilitary Criminality

In February 2020, a West Belfast parish priest, Fr Martin Magill commented in a news report (The Irish News, 2020c) that he had 'no doubt whatever' about a link between young people living under fear of attack and suicide rates in areas where paramilitaries still hold sway. He added: 'We know of the links between drugs and suicide and we often hear of people, either under threat or who have been attacked in the past, self-medicating as a result of the trauma.'

Fr Magill cited research (Hamill, 2011) that informed his stated view:

'One of the few studies carried out into the link between those under threat for alleged anti-social criminality and suicide, found that just over one third of participants had experienced long periods of depression and had suicidal thoughts in response to being threatened, while 22 per cent admitted having attempted suicide' (The Irish News, 2020c).

This same general view was shared by a university researcher, Dr Sharon Mallon, who believed:

'... communities within Northern Ireland continue to be blighted by an insidious form of violence in the form of intimidation often in the form of paramilitary punishment attacks (PPA).' (Mallon, 2017: 2)

Her recent research paper, Mallon (2017) investigated the proposition that 'acts of intimidation' can and do lead to death by suicide. She reviewed 403 Northern Ireland coroners' files relating to individuals who died by suicide between 2007 and 2009. She also accessed 360 GP's medical records and interviewed 78 bereaved family members, regarding their deceased family members' experience of intimidation, if any, in the 12 months before death.

She identified 19 men as experiencing intimidation during the last year of their lives. These unfortunate men were mostly unemployed (n=15) and single (n=13). However, Mallon (2020: 7) viewed with caution any causal link between intimidation and suicide adding that 'it is impossible ... to fully assess the issue of intimidation and its contribution to the suicides of these [19] men'. She concluded that 'suicide is likely to take place when a person experiences 'entrapment' (Williams, 1997; 2001; O'Connor, 2011) in the form of a mental or physical state in which they cannot get away from something they wish to flee' (Mallon, 2017: 8).

**Murder-Suicide**

On 7 February 2020, a local newspaper published a detailed, full-page article, with by-line, including two colour photographs, reporting inquests into the deaths in early March 2019, of two women, 37 year old GMH and her daughter AMH, aged 15 years and a man, RS, age unknown, who were found dead on 7 March 2019 in an apartment in Newry, Co Down. The coroner found that RS murdered the older woman before raping and murdering her daughter. The report described how GMH died by 'asphyxiation and suffocation' while AMH died by 'manual strangulation and suffocation'. The coroner found that neither of the women 'would have been likely to have been able to fend off RS'. He said:

'The killing of GMH and her daughter AMH by RS was barbaric. GMH was a woman of small stature. [She and her] 15 year old daughter would have been unable to offer any resistance against an attack by RS. I am satisfied that he acted alone for a reason that is unknown. The killings were an impulsive act carried out by an individual with a history of aggression and violence' (The Irish News, 2020a).

The coroner also found that RS 'died by hanging and had intended to die.' The newspaper report, headlined 'Man murdered partner before raping and killing her daughter' ended somewhat abruptly without any message, regarding access to help and support by anyone in distress, that is, per suicide reporting guidelines, routinely added to reports about suicide (The Irish News, 2020a).

Several murder-suicide tragedies were extensively reported in recent years by Irish media. A particularly brutal and 'out of the blue' family slaughter was written up in some detail by tabloid and 'serious' media, after the event (29 August 2016) and later following a two-day inquest (18 & 19 December 2017). This savage and inhuman atrocity involved Alan Hawe's murder of his wife, Clodagh (39), and their three sons, Liam (13), Niall (11), and Ryan (6) and his (Alan Hawe's) subsequent suicide. The coroner said:

'this particularly emotive inquest ... was intended to establish four limited but factual questions – who the deceased were, when and where they died, and how they died [and] was precluded from questioning civil or criminal liability' (The Irish News, 20 December 2017c).

A consultant psychiatrist reviewed Hawe's GP's medical records, his psychotherapist's notes on his counselling sessions with Hawe from 15 March to 21 June 2016, and Hawe's suicide note. He concluded that he believed that Hawe:

'was troubled [and] that at the time [he] carried out the murder-suicide he had progressed from long-term depression to a severe depressive episode with psychotic symptoms. When people act in the course of severe mental illness, such as very severe psychotic mental illness, their judgment is severely impaired. [Referring to his review] he added hindsight is always a very unfair advantage' (The Irish News, 20 December 2017c).

The jury of six women and one man concluded that Clodagh, Liam, Niall and Ryan were unlawfully killed and that Hawe died by suicide. An axe and a small knife were used in the murders but Hawe's suicide method was not disclosed. As usual, the 'why' question remained unasked and unanswered, although a solicitor, acting for Clodagh's sister and mother, speculated that Hawe:

'a school vice-principal ... was concerned at his imminent fall from his position as a pillar of the community and the breakdown of his marriage' (The Irish News, 20 December 2017c).

When asked by a journalist if Alan Hawe's mental illness would explain his actions, the solicitor Mr K said:

'"Not really. An inquest examines the how, where and when of the death but not the why. It's not the role of the inquest to stray into that territory," he said. "In truth, I don't think anything can explain how a father can do that to his wife and children," he added' (The Irish Times, 20 December 2017a).

Days after the Hawe inquest, the killer's written messages, including a lengthy suicide note, were the subject of journalistic scrutiny and comments from a clinical psychologist and a psychiatry professor were reported (The Irish Times, 2017b). The former expert described the killer's distorted belief system, referring to Joiner's (2005) theory of 'burdensomeness' – a deepening belief that you are a burden on those around you - as a 'potent driver of the desire for death'. The psychiatry professor opined that Hawe was 'delusional' and that killing his family and himself were his way of avoiding the suffering he believed was about to happen to him because of his 'mess and the anger that Clodagh and the boys would have to live with forever' (The Irish Times, 2017b).

Most of the several articles referenced above included lengthy advice and information about accessing support for anyone in distress. These articles were headlined:

'Husband murdered wife and eldest son so they wouldn't fight back'. Ed Carty. The Irish News, 19 December 2017(b), front page

'Mother had sense of foreboding when she saw note'. Ed Carty. The Irish News, 19 December 2017(b), p. 6

'Everything appeared normal evening before murder-suicide'. Ed Carty. The Irish News, 19 December 2017(b), p. 7

'Evidence so far beyond harrowing'. Morris, A. The Irish News, 19 December 2017(b), p. 7

'Family killed because husband thought marriage breaking up'. Ed Carty. The Irish News, 20 December 2017(c)

'Family says Clodagh Hawe and her three sons "savagely and brutally killed"'. Conor Lally. The Irish Times. 20 December 2017(a)

'Hawe killings fit characteristics of other murder-suicides'. Simon Carswell. The Irish Times. 23 December 2017(b).

There have been more than 30 murder-suicide cases in Ireland since 2000, but according to the Republic's National Suicide Research Foundation they remain relatively rare.

It has called for in-depth investigations of each case to identify risk factors and patterns and help prevent more occurring, stressing the need for sensitive and factual reporting to minimise harm and increase awareness.

In Northern Ireland, nine murder-suicide tragedies involving the murders of 14 innocents and 9 suicides by their killers were reported from 2005 to 2017 (The Irish News, 8 March 2019). (This article concluded: Anyone in distress can contact Samaritans on 116 123).

## Consecutive Family Suicides

On 18 February 2015 a local newspaper published three suicide-related articles, including two large colour photographs (front page and inside page 6) of the deceased, and an editorial two days after a 19 year-old woman died by suicide on her late father's birthday – he had died by suicide in December 2012 (Belfast Telegraph a b c d, 2015). The editorial commented, in the context of 303 suicides being registered in Northern Ireland in 2013:

'The Department of Health has introduced a strategy to combat suicide but there remain some pertinent concerns. Are the right groups being targeted and in a consistent and cohesive manner across Northern Ireland? Do we need to put more resources into counselling to offer quicker assistance to those facing a crisis in their lives? ... Perhaps it would be best if ... collective abilities [of] very active anti-suicide charities ... were harnessed more closely to statutory bodies to create a holistic approach to reach those at risk' (Belfast Telegraph, 2015c).

This extensive coverage did not include any detailed contact information for people in distress about how to access help and support.

In September 2020, a local newspaper published a lengthy, full-page article, with by-line, including three colour photographs, one week after the apparent suicide of a 32 year-old woman [C] whose sister [K], then also aged 32 died by apparent suicide 10 years earlier. Their father [J] had died by apparent suicide 8 years earlier. The surviving family members were reported to have 'organised a suicide and drug-awareness walk'. They were said to be highly critical of politicians for the lack of public services for vulnerable people:

'... the family had tried to find [C] help but were told that "nothing" could be done. "There's no residential place where people can come in and detox under supervision ... Unless you have thousands and thousands of pounds to go private, there is nowhere in Northern Ireland that [you] can bring someone troubled in and help them"' (The Irish News, 2020b).

The newspaper report, headlined 'Don't let my family be another statistic pleads Derry man', concluded with a routine message: "Anyone in distress can contact Lifeline on 0808 808 8000 or Samaritans on 116 123."(The Irish News, 2020b)

## Child Suicide

Fortunately this ghastly phenomenon is very rare. It does happen however and it attracts media interest. An Irish newspaper reported the inquest on an eleven year old girl (M) who had posted online ("Instagram") on 8 November 2015 that she was unhappy about her appearance and wanted to die. Her parents eventually discovered this 'out of the blue'. They followed their GP's advice to arrange for M to see a psychologist at a private clinic. This was not possible due to the psychologist's non-availability. Instead, on 24 November 2015, M was assigned to an art therapist for weekly appointments and 'encouraged to explore her feelings through verbal and visual means'. After M's first appointment, the therapist recommended that M should attend the Irish Child and Adolescent Mental Health Service (CAMHS) and an appointment for 30 January 2016, two months later, was made. On 8 December 2015 M's mother found 'a suicide diary along with medication' in M's bedroom. On 17 December 2015, her appointment was brought forward to 5 January 2016. M died in hospital on 4 January 2016, after she was found at home on 1 January 2016 'in a critical condition' (The Irish Times, 2017c). The coroner concluded at the inquest that M had died by suicide.

Extensive, detailed consideration of M's inquest by Rosita Boland (The Irish Times, 2017 d & e) disclosed that M completed a Youth Self-Report Questionnaire that an Irish CAMHS consultant child and adolescent psychiatrist (Dr McD) sent to her parents, on 14 December 2015, along with a child behaviour checklist, following their GP's contact on 8 December 2015 with the CAMHS. These forms were completed and hand-delivered on 22 December 2015. Dr McD stated that these forms were 'scored' on 30 December 2015.

The director of research for the Irish National Suicide Research Foundation, Professor Dr Ella Arensman, called as an expert witness, commented on M's responses in the questionnaire:

'The combination of the escalation of self-harm methods over a short time period and high scores on the ... screening questionnaires, which M had completed, reflected high risk of self-harm and suicide, and therefore would have warranted an immediate full biopsychosocial assessment, followed by the required treatment and support' (The Irish Times, 2017e).

Since her tragic death, M's parents have been campaigning for the establishment of a Suicide Prevention Authority. They have argued that three times as many die by suicide in Ireland than on the roads yet ten times more is spent on road safety, than on suicide prevention. M's mother said:

'In the absence of such an authority, there is absolutely no chance of the entire structure of suicide prevention being ring-fenced to prevent something like this happening. At the moment, it is a series of islands that you have to navigate between' (The Irish Times, 2017d).

Postscript – Over seven years after M's tragic and lamentable death, in April 2024, a 'wrongful death' action that was taken by M's family against 'several defendants' was settled, in the Dublin High Court following mediation. Terms agreed included an award of E65,000 plus costs and letters of regret to the family. The family's legal representative 'outlined a story of missed opportunities and systemic failures after the family sought help for M in the eight weeks before her dying by suicide, and expert opinion concluding "individual breaches of duty of care led to a systemic failure in addressing [M's needs] which very likely prevented her life from being saved"' (The Irish Times, 2024). M's mother, FT, is the founder and chief executive of Hugg (Healing Untold Grief Groups), suicide bereavement charity. [The lengthy article, by Deirdre Falvey, upon which the above is based concluded: 'If you are affected by any of the issues in this story, you can contact The Samaritans on freephone 116123. Hugg can be reached at www.hugg.ie and 3ts at www.3ts.ie .]

The author has located recent media reports on deaths by suicide of children, as follows:

i) February, 2018, death of N O'C, aged 14, reported on 4 April 2018
ii) April, 2018, death of K C, aged 18, reported on 9 April 2018
iii) November, 2018, death of K A-S, aged 16, reported on 20 November 2018
iv) April, 2005, death of D McC, aged aged 18, reported in June, 2007, following an independent inquiry into his death. Further extensive reporting in a two day 'special feature on mental health' on 17 February 2020.

An article in a local paper on 13 February 2020, headlined 'Schools received emergency help after 25 sudden deaths since 2018', stated that 'over the last three years [2017-2020] the Northern Ireland Education Authority Critical Incident Response Team responded to 141 "critical incidents"'. It was unclear how many of the above 25 deaths were found to be by suicide. The article continued:

'The startling figures were revealed ... to the Stormont [devolved Northern Ireland government] education committee ... Mr McC (an elected member) said ... "Last summer [2019] I attended the funerals of three young people who were very close friends who took their own lives very close together'... Ms M (an elected member) said "... availability of counselling services in schools is insufficient ... It's shocking to hear that in a school which has 1,000 pupils there are only five sessions a week'. The Education Authority representative Ms T said "We are largely constrained by the funding ... we are given ... in relation to [providing] the new Independent Counselling Service for Schools [established in September 2019]'" (The Irish News, 13 February 2020e).

The article did not include contact information for anyone in distress.

**Suicide Immediately Prior to Facing Serious Criminal Charges**

The most notorious recent example of a suspected suicide appeared to be related to the impending prosecution of serious criminal charges against US billionaire Jeffrey Epstein. This was exhaustively reported in US and European media in part due to Epstein's death in prison awaiting trial but also to the subsequent arrest and scheduled prosecution (at time of writing) of his alleged accomplice, UK national Ghislaine Maxwell.

The tragedy in Ireland of Paul Kelly's suicide on 9 September 2019 was compounded by his role, until his resignation in July 2016, as founder in 2002 and chief executive of a suicide prevention and bereavement charity, Console. At the inquest on 29 September 2020 into his death at Kildare Coroner's Court, sitting at Naas, the Kildare Coroner, Prof Cusack, concluded that Mr Kelly's death 'was caused by asphyxiation due to hanging' (Kildarepost.com). He did not refer to Mr Kelly's death as 'suicide'. A Garda witness, who attended the death, said in their statement 'there was no evidence of foul play or suspicious circumstances at the scene' (Kildarepost.com). In extending his sincere condolences to the deceased's family, friends and work colleagues, Prof Cusack said:

'The advice I give to all bereaved families in the Coroner's Court is to remember not just the last few weeks or months of life, but all the good and happy times as a husband, father, family member, friend and colleague'(Kildarepost.com).

Over six months before Mr Kelly's inquest, his wife Patricia, who was a former director of Console, was charged with fraudulent trading (2006-2016) and money laundering (2010-2016). Her husband, Paul Kelly, according to Patricia's solicitor, 'died by suicide the night before he was [due] to be charged [with financial irregularities at Console]' (The Irish Times, 2020).

The Kildare Post report, headlined 'Console charity boss left "loving note" to his family, inquest hears', featured a colour photograph, but did not include a message regarding access to support and help by anyone in distress. The Irish Times report, with by line, headlined 'Wife of suicide charity founder is charged with fraudulent trading' also did not include information regarding access to help and support by anyone in distress.

**Suicide Linked to Social Media**

'Catfishing' involves using a fake online identity to target other online users, and facilitates sexual abuse, exploitation and blackmail. In Belfast on 11 March 2024, following a six-year police investigation, a 26 year old former Northern Irish university computer science student [AMcC] pleaded guilty to manslaughter of a 12 year old girl [name and nationality withheld] whom he admitted blackmailing online six years ago [2018]. This unfortunate, innocent child 'took her own life in May 2018 after being blackmailed online over a four day period' (The Irish Times, 2024a). The convicted defendant 'admitted' to 185 offences from 2013 to 2018, mainly connected to the sexual abuse of more than 60 child victims from as far away as New Zealand and the United States. He was remanded into custody until a sentencing hearing in May 2024. [The extensive 'The Irish Times' report included a significant 'Support and Helplines' section.]

On Friday 30 September 2022, a senior coroner concluded, following an inquest into the death of a 14 year old girl (MR) that it would not be 'safe' to rule the cause of M's death as suicide. He opined that the teenager 'died from an act of self-harm while suffering depression'. She had lost her life 'while suffering from the negative effects of online content ... that was not safe as [it] allowed [her] access to adult content [images, video clips and text] that should not have been available for a 14 year old child to see'. Her bereaved family argued that she accessed material from 'the ghetto of the online world' before her death in November 2017. The coroner reported his intent to issue a Prevention of Future Deaths (PFD) notice which would recommend action on how to stop a repeat of the tragic MR case. Her bereaved family's lawyer [OS-KC] asked the coroner to send the PFD to Instagram, Pinterest, UK media regulator OfCom and the UK Department for Digital, Culture, Media and Sport (The Independent, 2022). [A UK Online Safety Act 2023, that sets out to minimize online abuse, grooming and exposure to content that is illegal or harmful, came into force in October 2023.]

A County Tyrone 17 year old schoolboy, RH, died by suicide on Friday 5 June 2015 after being blackmailed on social media. A lengthy, detailed report (The Irish News, 2015) published on 16 June 2015 described how several days earlier the boy 'was tricked into posting images on a social networking site after receiving photographs from a girl.' RH confided to his parents 'three days before his death about a fake Facebook account threatening to send the images to his online friends - unless he paid £3,300 within 48 hours'.

Local police were informed by RH's father and they 'traced the site to Nigeria and closed it down within two days. For [RH's family], this was "too late" and [they] feel that police should have acted beforehand'.

On the car journey home after meeting police, RH said to his father 'I think I've just committed social suicide, dad'.

'The couple said they anxiously waited for the police to get in touch over the next two days but didn't hear anything.

"We were very disappointed but we sat Ronan down and told him that if the images were published it would blow over in a couple of weeks and we'd deal with it. We told him it wasn't the end of the world," added RH's father.

"I had a chat with him on the Thursday night. I asked him if he was okay about the fact the images might appear the next morning and he replied, 'whatever'. He had changed. He had accepted that it wasn't going to be sorted and he was going to have live with it. That's what I thought. I never thought he would go down the route he went down."

On the day of her son's death [Friday], RH's mother received a telephone call from RH who said that his friend contacted him to alert him that she had received a link containing private images - but she had not opened them (The Irish News, 2015).

RH's mother tried to reassure her son and told him "not to worry" and immediately rang her husband who was working in Keady [County Armagh].

An emotional Mr. H said he had a "bad feeling" and asked his boss if he could leave work early:

"I knew coming down the road…something was telling me in my heart I was going to find him. My biggest fear was how I was going to find him and how I was going to tell T [RH's mother]. I had a feeling in the pit of my stomach.

"He was always sitting in an armchair in the living room with his headphones on. I didn't see him. I came in through the front door and shouted for him. I went into the kitchen and the lap-top was sitting open and a pile of notes sitting. I grabbed the notes…I wrecked the house looking for him.

"There on one of the notes for me he'd written 'back field'. I knew instantly where he was. That was the worst experience of my life, going round that corner. I can't get it out of my head at all."

In November 2016, it was reported that 256 blackmail cases were recorded in Northern Ireland of which over 100 involved online sex scams (The Irish News, 2016).

In 2017, a Romanian criminal (IE) was jailed for 4 years for crimes including extortion by blackmail of young RH, and also of several of his friends. This despicable wretch was eligible for release in 2019 (The Irish News, 2017).

It is clear that in this case, any Papageno effect (see below) in reporting this tragedy was almost totally absent not least because 'alternatives to dying by suicide' were not persuasive enough to moderate deceased's lethal behaviour. Education to raise awareness of internet crime was mentioned but without reference to specific resources or guidance for young people.

A note in bold typeface: 'Any child affected by these issues can contact Childline on 0800 1111 or Lifeline on 0808 808 8000' concluded The Irish News (2015) article.

## Irish Ex-Paramilitaries and Suicide

Considering the significant numbers of activists imprisoned (and subsequently released under the Belfast/Good Friday Agreement) for paramilitary-related offences during the 'Troubles', only a very small number of relevant suicides have been reported. These include UVF's Billy Giles (1998) who died by hanging at home on 25 September 1998, LVF's Mark Fulton (2002), and INLA's John Kennaway (2007). The last two named were convicted paramilitaries, both of whom were found dead by hanging in their cells in Maghaberry Prison.

Billy Giles: This man, an active member of the UVF, was convicted of a sectarian murder at the age of 25 in 1982 of a former workmate, Michael Fay. He served 14 years of a life sentence, and was released in July 1997. He died in 1998 aged 41 – Taylor (1999) believed Giles took his own life because of remorse he felt about his involvement in UVF violence (Wikipedia, 2020).

Mark Fulton: The life and death of this 'cold, sectarian and callous' man who died 'by apparent suicide' on 10 June 2002, merits several pages on Wikipedia (2020), that contain the caveat 'This article needs additional citations for verification'. He was in prison on remand on a conspiracy to murder charge, having been jailed for 4½ years in December 1998 on firearms charges. Reputed to have been involved in at least a dozen sectarian murders, including the killing of a prominent solicitor, Rosemary Nelson, 'prison staff found [Fulton] dead in his cell [having] hanged himself with his belt, it is understood' (The Irish Times, 11 June 2002).

John Kennaway: This convicted killer was one of three INLA paramilitary prisoners jailed for murdering LVF paramilitary Billy Wright, in the Maze Prison (formerly Long Kesh) in 1997. Released under the Belfast / Good Friday Agreement in 2000, he was returned to prison in February 2007 when his parole was revoked. He was found dead in his cell on 8 June 2007. The Prisoner Ombudsman's investigation report extended to 169 pages. It appeared that Kennaway was isolated from most other prisoners, meeting few other than prison staff, and was assessed as vulnerable by medical staff. Just prior to his death he was found by medical staff to be experiencing PTSD symptoms. Extract from the Ombudsman's report:

'From prison records and CCTV, it is evident that John was last seen alive at 16.00 [on 8 June 2007] when he was observed through the door by an officer carrying out a headcount check. At 17.15, an officer checked John's cell and saw him hanging (Page 24) John committed suicide by hanging himself using a shoe lace attached to the grille at the opening of the cell window. He was discovered by an officer at 17.15 (Page 27) and was pronounced dead by a doctor at 18.55 (Page 28)' (Ombudsman, 2009: 24, 27, 28)

Two months after John Kennaway's death, the NI Prison Service changed the regime (Special Supervision Unit - SSU) under which Kennaway, and others, were living in jail:

'In August 2007, the Prison Service issued a set of revised procedures to be followed in relation to the accommodation, care, discipline and control of prisoners in the SSU. The procedures recognise that prisoners held in the SSU may be especially vulnerable and include a requirement that every prisoner is treated with humanity and as an individual' (Ombudsman, 2009: 32).

The Prisoner Ombudsman's report is worrying not least because the deceased prisoner appears to have been left without supervision, and with means to self-harm/suicide (viz. boot laces and access to a ligature point), for 75 minutes, alone in a locked cell, having been very recently medically assessed as 'vulnerable with PTSD symptoms'. I have not had access to any inquest's conclusions.

## Suicide by Domestic Violence

According to a press report, hundreds of UK women who kill themselves each year may have suffered abuse: now there are calls for better police enquiries (Roberts, 2022).

A UK campaign by a charity, Advocacy After Fatal Domestic Abuse (AAFDA), highlighting domestic abuse, including intimate partner violence, and its links to victims' deaths by suicide and homicide, is demanding that police treat all sudden, unexpected deaths of those known to be victims of domestic abuse as potential femicide [and/or homicide] at the outset (Roberts, 2022). 'Femicide' is defined as 'gender-based murder of a woman or girl by a man (Merriam-Webster, 2024).

Two deaths by apparent suicide, cited by Roberts (2022), were shown to feature domestic abuse as a prominent factor:

i) Eight months before she took her own life, Abigail Patterson, 29, was brutally assaulted by her partner, Robert Holiday. She had suffered five (5) years of violence and on this occasion received a fractured cheekbone, bruising and a head wound. Holiday was convicted of assault causing actual bodily harm and damage to property. He received a sentence of two and a half years, half of which was to be served in jail, the rest on licence. The judges's remarks before sentencing, pointed to the need to address a lacuna in current law:

Judge Bury said: 'She (Abigail) was left in a lot of pain. She couldn't eat properly and needed help with washing and dressing. She was worn down by you. It is clear that the family blame you for her death and her mental health had deteriorated since the last assault and they may well be right, but you have not been charged in a way that allows you to be blamed for her death'.

Roberts (2022) added that 'coercive and controlling behaviour [built] an invisible prison around the isolated woman, stripping her of liberty, choice and the person she was. Abigail Patterson blamed herself for Holiday's behaviour'; and

ii) Justene Reece, 46, was subjected to harassment and abuse by Nicholas Allen, 47, from September 2016 to February 2017. Allen made 3,500 attempts to contact Reece via calls, texts and social messages. He had convictions for violently abusing women going back to 1998. After Reece took her own life, Allen was jailed for 10 years, and a further five (5) years on licence. He was initially charged with coercive behaviour and stalking. Later, the UK Crown Prosecution Service brought a charge of unlawful killing – believed to be a legal first. In the five years since Allen's conviction, a charge of unlawful killing in a domestic abuse related suicide has proved rare to nonexistent.

Roberts (2022) acknowledged that the causes of suicide were complex. But she added that the lacuna in UK/NI law, pointed out by Judge Bury, had been addressed in France. Since 2020, if domestic abuse was a prominent factor, under French criminal law the perpetrator can expect a sentence of up to 10 years and a fine of €150,000. No such law existed in UK/Ireland at the time of writing.

## Homicide/Suicide and Domestic Violence in Northern Ireland

According to a press report, 'more women are murdered in Northern Ireland as a result of domestic violence than in any other part of western Europe per head of capita, frightening statistics have revealed' (Barnes, 2021). The Police Service for Northern Ireland (PSNI, 2022), later corrected this erroneous statement - that was based on a statistical error - to distinguish between data for 'domestic abuse homicide involving an intimate partner' from data for 'domestic abuse homicide, involving all victims, i.e. an intimate partner or other family members'. In short, this meant that, in 2017, fewer women were murdered in Northern Ireland as a result of domestic violence than in some neighbouring countries, as the misleading press report had asserted.

Earlier figures indicated that in NI in 2012/13, five murders were recorded with a domestic abuse motivation. The number of all recorded murders in that year was 17. Therefore, 29% of all murders in NI had a domestic abuse motivation (Belfast Domestic Violence Partnership, 2015).

A recent Belfast Domestic Violence Partnership seminar (2015) presented data on aspects of abuse that represented victims' perception of high risk factors for serious harm, homicide, and/or suicide. These included:

Separation (child contact), Pregnancy/new birth (under 18 months), Escalation, Community issues/isolation, Child abuse, Animal/pets abuse, Stalking, Sexual assault, Credible threats to kill, Strangulation (choking/suffocation/drowning), Alcohol/drugs/mental health, Controlling (aka coercive) and/or excessive jealous behaviour, Suicide/homicide (Slide #72, Belfast Domestic Violence Partnership, 2015).

An Ulster University (2018) research study, supported by Women's Aid Federation (Northern Ireland), revealed that victims of domestic violence benefitted from societal changes that have taken place in Northern Ireland since the Belfast / Good Friday Agreement in 1998. Researchers interviewed approximately 120 women victim/survivors of domestic violence – 56 individuals during in 1992, and 24 years later, interviewed 63 individuals in 2016, two decades after the communal conflict ended. The study's key findings showed that:

- The threat of firearms that previously existed in domestic violence situations has been greatly reduced as a result of the decommissioning of weapons and the demobilisation of paramilitary groups.
- Perpetrators of domestic violence still draw on paramilitary connections to threaten their partner in 2016 but this has less impact than it did in the 1992 study.
- Paramilitary style attacks are much less likely to be used to punish perpetrators of domestic and sexual violence in 2016 compared to 1992.
- Post conflict, police officers have become more responsive to domestic violence. The increase in training, quicker response times and greater accessibility for police to nationalist/republican and loyalist working class areas are significant factors here.
- A strong link continues to exist between domestic violence and poor mental health, with one in four women in the 2016 study reporting that they had attempted to take their own life and one in two reporting suicidal thoughts.
- Sexual abuse in domestic violence relationships is more prevalent than official statistics suggest. Almost half of those interviewed in 2016 reported that they had been raped or sexually assaulted by their husband/partner.
- Religious attitudes still exert a strong influence on decision-making processes and help seeking for victims/survivors of domestic violence (Ulster University, 2018).

At date of writing, I cannot find evidence of inquest findings of suicide by domestic violence in Northern Ireland. Arguably, the above mentioned lacuna in the law may prevent adequate consideration of its occurrence in N Ireland as in the rest of the UK. Walby (2004) had estimated that one in eight of all female suicides and suicide attempts in the UK were due to domestic violence and abuse (Roberts, 2022). Meanwhile, Munro and Aiken (2020) argued that the distress, sense of entrapment and hopelessness arising from domestic abuse (DA) could sometimes cause victims to feel that suicide was "the only way out" (O'Connor & Nock, 2014).

## Suicide Methods

UK/Irish journalism, follows IPSO Guidance on Reporting Suicide (2020), being generally cautious and responsible regarding disclosure of the lethal method used by a suicide deceased. This is closely related to fear of contagion (Headline, 2018) or the risk of 'media related imitation' (BMJ, 2020). Although this conviction appears logical and sensible, it may not fully acknowledge the complexity and idiosyncratic nature of each suicidal event, including self-inflicted death. It also seems somewhat at odds with current, understandable advice to the general public to 'talk about suicide' that to an extent dominates suicide awareness exercises. Coroners, at their discretion, can investigate the circumstances of an unnatural death resulting from murder, suicide, accident, and/or undetermined cause. Necessarily these enquiries will involve when appropriate, consideration of medical evidence confirming, when relevant, the self-destructive method used by the deceased. Their limited purpose seeks to ascertain the 'who/where/when/how' of such deaths and to summarise these facts in a 'conclusion' – formerly a 'verdict' – or a concluding statement, as in the case (see above) of the late Keith Flint's death. Significantly, the coroner has no formal role in ascertaining 'why' the deceased made their lethal choice.

## Papageno Effect

An 'equal and opposite' effect, viz. discouraging suicide, has unfortunately received much less media attention than the Werther Effect. This so-called Papageno effect relies upon:

'(R)eporting of suicide in an appropriate, accurate and potentially helpful manner by enlightened media [that] can prevent tragic loss of lives by suicide.' (WHO, 2000)

It appears to have initially been conceived as a hypothesis related to Mozart's opera 'The Magic Flute'. This proposed that there was:

'an indirect association between media reporting on lived experiences of coping with adverse circumstances and subsequent suicides, the so-called Papageno effect. This protective effect has been termed the Papageno effect in honour of the [eponymous] character in Mozart's opera The Magic Flute. When Papageno fears that he has lost his love, Papagena, he prepares to kill himself. But three boys save him at the last minute by reminding him of alternatives other than dying' (Niederkrotenthaler, 2020).

IPSO Guidance on Reporting Suicide (2020) notes that 'sensitive' reporting of suicide can contribute to suicide prevention efforts:

'... there is a growing body of evidence showing the benefits of sensitive coverage of suicide, including interviews with people who have overcome a crisis. It can actually help vulnerable people by encouraging them to seek help and reducing the stigma around the subject' (IPSO, 2020).

Niederkrotenthaler et al. (2010, abstract) noting its potentially harmful 'contagion' effect – the Werther Effect – investigated 'associations between specific media content and suicide rates... [adding that less] is known about the possible preventive effects of suicide-related media content.' They specifically tested the notion (hypothesis) that such 'other' media may be associated with a decrease in suicide.

It seems to me that a Papageno effect may indeed be a way ahead for suicide prevention but if, and only if, an individual who is perceived to be some way along a suicide pathway, is willing and able to communicate empathically with a competent compassionate human. The desired alternative to 'dying' for a person contemplating suicide is, of course, identification by the affected person of both means and motivation to change direction from death to life. Suicide statistics confirm the intricate complexity therein.

## Miscounting Suicides

For statistical purposes, the official definition of suicide in Northern Ireland, as in the rest of the UK, includes deaths from self-inflicted injury and also those from 'events of undetermined intent' (BBC, 2020). In October 2020, government statisticians in the Northern Ireland

Statistics and Research Agency (NISRA) published revised statistics for deaths registered as suicides in 2019. They said that in conjunction with the Northern Ireland Coroners' Service, they had carried out a review of deaths believed to have been by suicide that included drug overdoses or were drug-related. Using what was referred to as 'additional scrutiny', 86 deaths registered in 2019 that resulted from such 'undetermined intent' events, particularly where drugs played a part, were analysed by the coroner. 57 of these were reclassified as 'accidental' and were thus removed from 2019's suicide deaths quanta. This reduced by 57, to 197, provisional statistics for deaths by suicide in N Ireland in 2019. The Agency said that a similar planned review by the coroner of their suicide statistics for the years 2015 to 2018 'will see a drop in the suicide rate for each of those years of between 20% and 30%' (BBC, 2020).

**Myth:** (fictitious popular idea) 'Ordinary' suicide is seldom worth reporting but 'celebrity' suicide is always newsworthy

**Fallacy:** (misleading argument) Censoring print and/or broadcast media from disclosing suicide methods is an acceptable, effective way to prevent suicide

## References

BBC (2020) NI suicide rate expected to fall following review. Online article by Karen Atkinson. Accessed on 15 October 2020 at https://www.bbc.co.uk/news/uk-northern-ireland-54436324

Barnes, C. (2021) Northern Ireland is most dangerous place for women in Europe. Accessed on 5 April 2022 at https://www.belfasttelegraph.co.uk/sunday-life/northern-ireland-is-most-dangerous-place-in-europe-for-women-41095214.html

Belfast Domestic Violence Partnership (2015) Slides presented at the seminar. Accessed on 5 April 2022 at https://belfastdvp.co.uk/themainevent/wp-content/uploads/Listening-Sharing-Final-sPPT.pptx-2.pdf

Belfast Telegraph (2015a) 'Family's double suicide anguish'. Deborah McAleese. 18 February 2015

Belfast Telegraph (2015b) 'No parent ever thinks their child is suicidal'. Bobby Cosgrove. 18 February 2015

Belfast Telegraph (2015c) 'Strengthen fight against suicide'. Editorial. 18 February 2015

Belfast Telegraph (2015d) '"Now Lauren is gone too" – heartbreak as teen found dead on the birthday of dad who took his own life'. Deborah McAleese. 18 February 2015

BMJ (2020) Association between suicide reporting in the media and suicide: systemic review and meta-analysis. Niederkrotenthaler, T., Braun, M., Pirkis, J., Till, B., Stack, S., Sinyor, M., Tran, U.S., Voracek, M., Cheng, Q., Arendt, F., Scherr, S., Yip, P.S.F. and Spittal, M.J. British Medical Journal. Published 18 March 2020. Downloaded from http://www.bmj.com/ on 10 Oct 2020

Bridge, J. A., Goldstein, T. R., and Brent, D. A. (2006). "Adolescent suicide and suicidal behavior". Journal of Child Psychology and Psychiatry. 47 (3–4): 372–394.

Cerel, J., Brown, M. M., Maple, M., Singleton, M., van de Venne, J., Moore, M. and Flaherty, C. (2019) How many people are exposed to suicide? Not six. Suicide and Life-threatening Behaviour, 49(2), 530-534

Caroline Flack (2020) Suicide by hanging. Accessed on 27 September 2020 at https://extratv.com/2020/08/06/caroline-flacks-cause-of-death-revealed/

Coronial Services of New Zealand (2021) Information accessed on 4 April 2022 at NZ Govt website at https://coronialservices.justice.govt.nz/what-to-expect-during-an-inquiry/#inquiry

Gould, M. S. (1990) Suicide clusters and media exposure. In: Blumenthal, S. J. & Kupfer, D.J., (eds.) Suicide Over the Life Cycle. Washington DC: American Psychiatric Press, 1990. Cited in WHO (2000)

Hamill, H. (2011) The hoods: crime and punishment in Belfast. Princeton: University Press

Headline (2018) Reporting mental health & suicide: challenges facing journalists. Research report by Dr Anne O'Brien, Dept of Media Studies, NUI Maynooth on behalf of Headline

Inquest (2020) Supreme Court lowers standard of proof for unlawful killing and suicide inquest conclusions to balance of probabilities. Accessed on 4 April 2022 at https://www.inquest.org.uk/maughan-supreme-court

IPSO Guidance on Reporting Suicide (2020) Independent Press Standards Organisation: Guidance on reporting suicide. Accessed on 12 October 2020 at https://www.ipso.co.uk/member-publishers/guidance-for-journalists-and-editors/guidance-on-reporting-suicide

Joiner, T. E. (2005) Why people die by suicide. Cambridge, MA: Harvard University Press

Kildarepost.com (2020) 'Console charity boss left "loving note" to his family, inquest hears'. Accessed on 19 October 2020 at https://www.kildarenow.com/news/home/579995/console-charity-boss-left-loving-note-to-his-family-inquest-hears.html#:~:text=Kildare%20Coroner%20Prof%20Denis%20Cusack,Clane%20by%20his%20wife%20Patricia.&text=Mr%20Kelly%20was%20later%20pronounced%20dead%20by%20a%20doctor

List of celebrity suicides (2020) Examples. Accessed on 27 September 2020 at https://en.wikipedia.org/wiki/List_of_suicides_in_the_21st_century

Mallon, S. (2017) The role of paramilitary attacks and intimidation in death by suicide in Northern Ireland. Knowledge Exchange Seminar Series (KESS) presentation on 21 June 2017. Published by the Northern Ireland Assembly. Accessed on 25 October 2020 at http://www.niassembly.gov.uk/globalassets/documents/raise/knowledge_exchange/briefing_papers/series6/mallon210617.pdf

Maughan (2020) R (on the application of Maughan) (Appellant) v Her Majesty's Senior Coroner Oxfordshire (Respondent) [2020] UKSC 46 Press Summary, 13 November 2020

Merriam-Webster (2024) Femicide: gender-based murder of a woman or girl by a man, Accessed on 18 July 2024 at http://www.merriam-webster.com

Munro, V. E. and Aiken, R. (2020) From hoping to help: Identifying and responding to suicidality amongst victims of domestic abuse. International Review of Victimology, 2020. Vol. 26(1) 29–49

Niederkrotenthaler, T., Voracek, M., Herberth, A., Till, B., Strauss, M., Etzersdorfer, E., Eisenwort, B. and Sonneck, G. (2010) Role of media reports in completed and prevented suicide: Werther v. Papageno effects. Br J Psychiatry, 2010, 197(3): 234-43

Niederkrotenthaler, T., and 12 others (2019) Association between suicide reporting in the media and suicide: systemic review and meta-analysis. University of Vienna, Austria. See BMJ (2020) above

Niederkrotenthaler, T. (2020) The Papageno Effect. Wiener Werkstaette for Suicide Research. Accessed on 15 October 2020 at http://www.suizidforschung.at/papageno-effect/#:~:text=Research%20on%20associations%20between%20content,suicides%2C%20the%20so%2Dcalled%20Papageno

Ombudsman (2009) Report by the Prisoner Ombudsman into the circumstances surrounding the death of John Martin Gerard Kennaway [dob 12/05/1962] in Maghaberry Prison on 8 June 2007. 10 December 2009. Accessed on 31 October 2020 at https://niprisonerombudsman.gov.uk/publications/death-in-custody

Ombudsman (2015) Prisoner Ombudsman investigation report into the circumstances surrounding the death of Joseph Rainey aged 20 post release from Hydebank Wood Prison & Young Offender's Centre on 19th April 2013. Publisher: Prisoner Ombudsman for Northern Ireland, Unit 2, Walled Garden, Stormont Estate, Belfast, BT4 3SH. www.niprisonerombudsman.gov.uk

O'Connor, R. C. (2011) Towards an integrated motivational–volitional model of suicidal behaviour. In: O'Connor R.C., Platt S. and Gordon J., eds. International handbook of suicide prevention: research, policy and practice. Chichester: John Wiley & Sons, 2011: 181–98

O'Connor, R. C. and Nock, M. K. (2014) The psychology of suicidal behaviour. The Lancet Psychiatry, 30 April, 2014

O'Neill, S. (2018) Zero suicide, an approach to be considered in criminal justice systems. Accessed on 22 October 2020 at https://niacro.co.uk/news/zero-suicide

PSNI (2022) Clarification and correction of data referring to Northern Ireland's ranking in respect of Domestic Abuse Homicide rates across Europe. 3 February 2022. Accessed on 10 April 2022 at https://www.psni.police

Roberts, Y. (2022) Suicide by domestic violence: call to count the hidden toll on women's lives. Observer Campaign – End Femicide. Yvonne Roberts. The Observer, page 20; 27 Feb 2022

Sisask, M. & Varnik, A. (2012) Media roles in suicide prevention: a systematic review. Int J Res Environ Public Health, 2012, 9, 123-138

Shneidman, E. S. (1985) Definition of Suicide. London: Jason Aronson Inc

SPRC (Suicide Prevention Resource Centre) (2018) Zero Suicide in health and behavioural health care. https://zerosuicide.sprc.org

Supreme Court – Maughan (2020) R (on the application of Maughan) (AP) (Appellant) v Her Majesty's Senior Coroner for Oxfordshire (Respondent) Case ID: UKSC 2019/0137. Hearing 26-27 February 2020. Accessed on 18 August 2020 at file:///C:/Users/woppo/Documents/Suicide%20-%20UK%20-%20Supreme%20Court%2026-27%20Feb%202020%20-%20Maughan%20(Appellant)%20v%20HM%20Senior%20Coroner%20Oxfo%20(Respondent)%20-%2020180820.pdf

Taylor, P. (1999) Loyalists. London: Bloomsbury Publishing PLC

Teara: the Encyclopedia of New Zealand (2019) Jock Phillips, 'Suicide – Preventing suicide', accessed on 6 April 2022 at http://www.TeAra.govt.nz/en/suicide

The Guardian (2019) 'Keith Flint: not enough evidence for a suicide verdict, coroner rules.' Accessed on 25 May 2019 at https://www.theguardian.com/music/2019/may/08/keith-flint-inquest

The Independent (2022) 'Global first' ruling that online content contributed to Molly Russell's death. Josh Payne. Fri 30 September 2022. www.theindependent.co.uk Accessed 27 March 2024.

The Irish News (2015) 'Ronan Hughes' devastated parents warn of dangers of cyber blackmail'. Seanin Graham. The Irish News, 16 June 2015. Accessed on 21 October 2020 at https://www.irishnews.com/news/2015/06/16/news/devastated-parents-warn-of-dangers-of-cyber-blackmail-136926/

The Irish News (2016) 'Record levels of blackmail sweep the north'. Andrew Madden. 28 November 2016. Accessed on 21 October 2020 at https://www.irishnews.com/news/2016/11/28/news/record-high-levels-of-blackmail-offences-sweep-the-north-804963/

The Irish News (2017a) 'Ruthless Romanian criminal tried to blackmail friends of Tyrone teenager Ronan Hughes.' Bimpe Archer. 1 September 2017. Accessed on 21 October 2020 at https://www.irishnews.com/news/2017/09/01/news/ruthless-romanian-criminal-tried-to-blackmail-friends-of-tyrone-teenager-ronan-hughes-1125523/

The Irish News (2017b) 'Mother had a sense of foreboding when she saw note.' Ed Carty. 19 December 2017

The Irish News (2017c) 'Family killed because husband thought marriage was breaking up.' Ed Carty. 20 December 2017

The Irish News (2019) 'More than 30 murder-suicide cases in Ireland since 2000.' Bimpe Archer. 8 March 2019. Accessed on 29 October 2020 at https://www.irishnews.com/news/northernirelandnews/2019/03/08/news/more-than-30-murder-suicide-cases-in-ireland-since-2000-1568016/

The Irish News (2020a) 'Man murdered partner before raping and killing her daughter.' Rebecca Black. 7 February 2020

The Irish News (2020b) 'Don't let my family be another statistic pleads Derry man'. Marie Louise McConville. The Irish News, 29 September 2020

The Irish News (2020c) Links between suicide and paramilitary attacks 'needs addressing'. Alison Morris. The Irish News, 17 February 2020. Accessed on 25 October 2020 at https://www.irishnews.com/news/northernirelandnews/2020/02/17/news/links-between-suicide

The Irish News (2020d) 'Prison service and trust failings contributed to death, jury finds'. No by-line. 15 February 2020

The Irish News (2020e) 'Schools received emergency help after 25 sudden deaths since 2018'. No byline. 13 February 2020

The Irish Times (2002) 'Wright associate takes own life in Maghaberry cell' No by line. The Irish Times 11 June 2002

The Irish Times (2017a) 'Family says Clodagh Hawe and her three sons "savagely and brutally killed"'. Conor Lally. 20 December 2017

The Irish Times (2017b) 'Hawe killings fit characteristics of other murder-suicides' Simon Carswell. 23 December 2017

The Irish Times (2017c) 'Girl (11) posted on Instagram about intentions to die'. Carl O'Brien. 1 December 2017

The Irish Times (2017d) 'Milly was set adrift, as we were'. Rosita Boland. 23 December 2017, page 3

The Irish Times (2017e) 'Child spoke of "killing herself" in HSE form.' Rosita Boland. 23 December 2017, page 4

The Irish Times (2020) 'Wife of suicide charity founder is charged with fraudulent trading'. Tom Tuite. 7 March 2020,

The Irish Times (2024a) Catfishing: online blackmail of girl (12) led to her suicide. Seanin Graham. 16 March 2024

The Irish Times (2024b) 'Milly could have been saved'. Deirdre Falvey. 27 April 2024

Ulster University (2018) Study shows how victims of domestic violence benefitted from the peace process in Northern Ireland. Accessed on 5 April 2022 at https://www.ulster.ac.uk/faculties/arts-humanities-and-social

Walby, S. (2004). The Cost of Domestic Violence. London: Women and Equality Unit.

WHO (2000) Preventing suicide: a resource for professionals. Dr J. M. Bertolote, Coordinator, Mental and Behavioural Disorders, Department of Mental Health. World Health Organization

Wikipedia (2020) Billy Giles. Accessed on 22 October 2020 at https://en.wikipedia.org/wiki/Billy_Giles

Wikipedia (2020) Mark Fulton. Accessed on 31 October 2020 at https://en.wikipedia.org/wiki/Mark_Fulton_(loyalist)#:~:text=Fulton%20was%20alleged%20to%20have,and%20had%20a%20quick%20temper

Williams, J. M. G. (1997; 2001) Cry of pain. London: Penguin Books

\* \* \*

# Chapter 5
# Surviving suicide – grief in the aftermath of suicide

## Suicide is No Accident

Suicide is no accident. Think about it. The implication becomes clear: that a cause/effect relationship within the human mind links unbearable psychological pain (Shneidman, 1993) to irreversibly lethal behaviour that kills the pain but that tragically and coincidentally destroys the decision-taking mind. Hence an aeons long search goes on for a General Theory of Suicide, exemplified perhaps most recently in the innovative work of O'Connor (2011) and Joiner (2005) [Chapter 9 below addresses several theories about suicide.]

I hasten to add that I am not a member of any global search squad. Rather I am interested in understanding the idiosyncratic nature of each lethal event of human self-destruction. For me, and many others, shocked and distressed by family suicide, prevention is no longer possible: we have become survivors of bereavement by suicide. Frank Campbell's (2005: 16) view was that:

'The nature of suicide as a cause of death generates both trauma and confusion for most survivors ... the top concerns expressed by survivors of suicide are a variety of afterlife considerations based on their own recollections of teachings by their respective faiths ... [they] may be reinforced by those who attempt to comfort the family with comments like: "I will pray for your son's redemption for this cowardly act" or "I know s/he will miss being reunited with you for eternity"... [such] stigmatizing and inappropriate comments are often expressed ... at times when survivors are especially vulnerable ... cruel assumptions and suggestions are certainly not comforting and worse yet, often awake or reinforce worst fears of survivors' (Campbell, 2006: 16).

Beyond some unknowable, existential considerations, choices exist that are inevitable, unavoidable and necessary, regarding our behavioural response to what has happened. Either, we can invest scarce energy in analysis of the impossible, i.e. how I, and/or others, might have prevented our family suicides, and/or we might consider, in some systematic and disciplined way, how to deepen our understanding about what happened, not least inter alia to secure some fraction, large or small, of absolution in relation to our catastrophic loss.

## After a Suicide

To the layperson, the notion of 'surviving suicide' is an oxymoron – in other words it sounds like a contradiction in terms. But a moment's thought reveals that its meaning is only too clear – a survivor of suicide, or a suicide survivor, is someone who is bereaved after the death of someone that they knew. Suicide survivors therefore include all those who felt that they were related to, or connected with the suicide deceased, in some meaningful way, i.e. someone with whom they had a significant relationship or emotional bond (American Association of Suicidology, 2007).

As mentioned in Chapter 4 above, research by Cerel et al. (2019) concluded that up to 135 people are exposed to, or left behind following every suicide. This is a remarkable revision of Shneidman's (1969) estimate of six survivors per suicide:

'Regarding the number of survivors, Shneidman (1969: 22) first suggested that on average a "half-dozen" of survivors would be left behind after a suicide, and this estimate of six survivors per suicide has been perpetuated in the literature' (Andreissen, 2014: 339).

A range of writers have successively made estimations, e.g. 10 survivors per suicide (Wrobleski, 2002), that remained hypothetical without research evidence:

'Only recently, Berman (2011) reported the first systematic estimation of the number of suicide survivors among members of US suicide survivor support groups. The survey found that the estimated numbers varied depending on who actually made the estimate, that is, the kinship relationship. In addition, the numbers varied depending on the frequency of contact between the deceased and the bereaved, and the age of the deceased. For example, parents who lost a child by suicide estimated that the death has left 80 suicide survivors behind, the spouses and/or partners of the suicides estimated the number at 60, while siblings and/or friends estimated 45–50. Five survivors after one suicide, the estimate of survivors limited to the members of a typical nuclear family, was almost identical to the original guesstimate of Shneidman (1969)' (Andreissen, 2014: 339).

Irrespective of the actual estimated numbers, this study (Berman, 2011) clearly showed that there is no fixed number of survivors per suicide, but the number varies depending on the kinship relationship and the quality of the relationship (Andreissen, 2014: 339). As a survivor myself, an unplanned opportunity arose for me over two decades ago, to investigate further, i.e. by research, what happened to other survivors, who were not my family members.

**Research – The Lead In**

My research interest began in 1998 while I was a counselling student at Ulster University (N Ireland) on a diploma course. Since 1982, sixteen years earlier, any feeling of wanting to know about or to look closely at suicide was submerged in my personal, and our family grief response to the loss of a loved sibling. When a further sibling loss occurred in 1989, my personal response sent me – at the suggestion of my then employer – to talk to a consultant psychologist. Following this support, about a year or so later, I worked for several sessions with an expert psychotherapist. This work included an 'ending ritual' involving a practical exercise focused upon saying good-bye and moving forward in my life. In the meantime, my 18 year long relationship with my son's mother concluded with an amicable separation, while I did my best to maintain an ongoing, close, loving, paternal relationship with my son. My positive response as a client in counselling triggered an interest in the whole psychotherapy process – hence several years later, my counselling diploma course.

## Research – The Beginning

A course research module set me the task of carrying out a pilot research exercise of my own choice. I was drawn to look further into the experience and response of others who had lost loved ones to suicide. A letter to the editor of a local newspaper led to my meeting in her home with a suicide survivor (J) who had recently lost her son (M) to suicide.

So over two decades ago, I found myself listening and audio-taping with her consent, for over two hours as this suicide survivor – like me – recalled, reflected on and updated their painful feelings of loss and bereavement. I resurrected my typed up report of this interaction recently and re-read it in full for this exercise. I was reminded of where I was, personally and psychologically back then, autumn 1999, less than a decade following my sibling's death. I seemed to have been able to almost fully detach myself from my personal woundedness in order, respectfully, to be fully present to witness as compassionately as possible, the enduring rawness of my research respondent's (J) deep maternal loss by suicide of her son (M).

Re-reading my 30+ page report (O'Keeffe, 1999), I noted Shneidman's (1984) assertion that 'the largest public health problem in dealing with suicide is provision of postvention efforts for survivors of suicide (Stillion and McDowell, 1996).' Over a decade earlier, Shneidman (1972) had noted:

'the importance of what Erich Lindemann ... labeled "preventive intervention" and what I have called postvention – that is "working with survivor-victims of a committed suicide to help them with their anguish, guilt, anger, shame and perplexity"' (Cain, 1972: ix).

## What Happened

Over 20 years ago, the attitude and response of medical and justice (viz. police) services in N Ireland to protecting a reportedly vulnerable young man (M, aged 19) were somewhat inadequate, and that, in my humble opinion is something of an understatement. His mother J had summoned the family doctor (GP Dr Mi) after she became concerned about M's perceived depression and related this to his recent accumulation of medications and alcohol. The doctor visited M's home, spoke to M for a while but left without speaking to his parents, J and L.

Most of our audiotaped interview consisted of J's reflections on her troubled life, including her life-threatening overdose and her interactions with police, neighbours, and medical practitioners, following her son's death. J said that, several months after M's death, her local newspaper reported a case brought against her for alleged assault of a police officer and her strenuous rejection of this charge. She also described how at times she felt stared at in her local street – possibly stigma-related – but not when out and about elsewhere.

The fact that M was found dead at home by shotgun wounds, ostensibly from his father's shotgun, when his parents and sibling were 'away for the weekend' and that police initiated a murder enquiry are only mentioned in passing by J. It's not possible to even begin to understand the complexities and the highways and byways of M's young life, without some further detail about his life circumstances and events in the period leading up to his death. Little is learned from the audiotape about who M really was.

We know he was loved by his parents and his sibling, and that he was in his early 20's at his death. But we find out little if anything about his personality, interests, education or occupation. We learn only that J's marriage to L appeared to be experiencing some undisclosed issues, that M's psychological health was poor, that he had been using cannabis, that he was regarded by his parents and GP as 'depressed' and that he had signalled his suicidal ideation when he said to her 'Mum, my life's over' after she had found his 'stash' of medication and alcohol. It seems that M was being treated by a psychiatrist (S) and his GP but that the opportunity to consider hospitalizing him, to interrupt his potential pathway to suicide appears to have been missed after the 'stash' discovery and M's 'my life is over' comment.

J remarked that one of the clinicians ostensibly charged subsequently with caring for her, showed a disappointing lack of empathy two years after her son's death, and close to his anniversary:

'It was a counsellor (Ms D) I saw initially in 'X' Hospital [who] noticed that coming up to M's anniversary ... about the time of M's death

... she thought I should see one of their [psychiatrists]. It was Dr D and he said I'd been coming for a matter of months ... and he just looked at me and he said "I've one word of advice for you and that is to stop feeling sorry for yourself" ... and I looked at him because I was amazed at his inconsideration and unsympathetic manner and I said maybe if you were sitting in my shoes you would also feel sorry for yourself' (O'Keeffe, 1999).

Although J talks briefly about her attendance at two inquest hearings, her demonstrable need to talk - and be listened to - about what the loss of her son had done to her, produces an episodic, at times disconnected, narrative covering the period immediately before his death, and the several years since.

What inter alia appears to be missing here, as in many if not most deaths in UK/Ireland by suicide, is any attempt at a psychological autopsy (PA) of M. Despite its somewhat flawed nature (Hjelmeland et al., 2012), PA can be much more authentic and informative, than journalistic adventures or limited, coronial discussions and conclusions. Everyone merits an accurate obituary, if not a detailed biography. M does not appear to have received either.

**What I Learned**

Reflecting back on my interaction with J, 21 years ago and reading through my report, I'm struck by the distance that has developed between she (J), my research respondent, and I, such that I cannot actively recall much other than my now renewed feelings of compassionate empathy for her. These emotions are similar to those I feel when, from time to time, I briefly remember – at anniversary time or when otherwise triggered – my own personal loss of my siblings, 31 and 38 years ago, respectively.

**Research Project #2**

My postgraduate diploma-level research report achieved a sufficient grade for me to be permitted to join the taught Master's Degree in Guidance and Counselling Programme, at Ulster University. This included several examined modules and a research dissertation over one academic year, 2000-2001. My master's research project used my diploma-level work as a pilot. The letter to print media editor(s) that located J had produced several additional responses from survivors of suicide loss in my immediate area. Six of these individuals were agreeable to become 'target group' research respondents. I recruited several non-suicide 'mourners' as 'control' respondents.

My research exercise involved securing respondents' written consent, meeting with them, arranging audio-taped interviews and obtaining from each of them a completed identity exploration instrument, based on an innovative research instrument, Identity Structure Analysis (ISA), designed by Dr Peter Weinreich (1992, 1997, 2003). My work was approved by the Ulster University's Research Ethics Committee. In compliance with the university's academic requirements, I formulated appropriate hypotheses upon which to structure my research work and my dissertation. These related to examining three propositions:

i) That suicide survivors are more likely than the general population to take their own lives

ii) That survivors traumatized by their loss who engage in psychotherapeutic counselling achieve loss integration more quickly and more fully than survivors who do not benefit from an effective counselling relationship

iii) That suicide survivors' experiential insights are a potentially effective therapeutic resource for self and others (IAS, 2006).

For my purposes here, I plan to rely upon a presentation that I made at a bereavement seminar during a conference organized by the Irish Association of Suicidology (IAS) in Armagh City, N Ireland in 2005 based upon my master's dissertation (O'Keeffe, 2001). [The presentation was published in full in the proceedings of the conference (IAS, 2006).]

## Armagh Presentation 2005

The term 'postvention' was coined by Shneidman (1974) as 'activities that reduce the after-effects of a traumatic event in the lives of survivors. Its purpose is to help survivors to live longer, more productively and less stressfully than they are to do otherwise' (Shneidman, 1974: 33, 34). An earlier more comprehensive definition by Shneidman et al. (1971) states:

'Postvention is to come after—that is, to do those things after the dire event has occurred that either (a) serve to mollify the after-effects of the event in the chief protagonist, specifically, to work with a person after he has attempted suicide; or (b) deal with the inimical sequels in other persons affected by the event, for example, the family members of a [severely distressed] person or, in the case of a suicide, with the obvious mental health needs of the survivor-victims. I prefer "postvention"'(Shneidman et al., 1971: 452).

My interest was, through a postvention counselling process, to help survivors 'to work through their special type of grief' (Stillion and McDowell, 1996). I noted that suicidologists, many but not all, did not dispute that, in general, survivors were regarded as at higher risk of suicide than the general population but there was no agreement on how much higher that risk might be. Bereaved individuals grieved in their own way regardless of whether the loss was by natural causes, accident, homicide or suicide. But clinical observations, according to Farberow (1996: 1), confirmed that the suicide survivor's experience was different: more difficult, more complicated, more intense and longer lasting.

Counselling and psychotherapy were variously defined but principally their purpose was to help individuals and groups, including families to process issues brought to counselling by these 'clients' for exploration and possible resolution. The chair (Mr E) of the bereavement seminar commented in his review that, in his opinion, 'the key purpose of counselling or listening/support is to give people options, to be able to recognize their individual requirements and to be aware of the pathways to such services'.

My research employed a case study approach involving working with a small number of individuals and carrying out content analysis of interview material. Each individual respondent completed an analytical instrument, Identity Structure Analysis (ISA), that explored their identity development, i.e. how their sense of themselves changed as a result of their suicide survivor experience.

I explained in some detail what 'identity' and 'identity development' meant in the particular context of my study:

'My identity has been said to be "all things a person may legitimately and reliably say about her/himself – status, name, personality and past life"' (Klapp, 1969).

Weinreich (1992) deployed a more nuanced explanation that deepened and enriched our understanding of 'my identity':

'When I speak of ME: "the ME can mean many things; the ME of yesterday, today and tomorrow or the ME of everyday, the ME in this particular action or situation, or the ME in all actions or situations" (Reizler, 1950) ... so one's concept of oneself is situated within the social context of one's family and the broader community within which one experiences the trials and tribulations of everyday life' (Weinreich, 1992).

Shannon (2000) argued that undoubtedly the loss of a loved one by suicide affected the survivor's identity or sense of self: the survivor's self-image or their image of that dead person has been damaged. Identity Structure Analysis (ISA) enabled the researcher to assess each target group member and each control group member. This outcome was an assessment of each respondent's 'individual appraisal of self and others in a way that takes account of the wider social context and self's idiosyncratic ways of relating to that context ... It is custom designed to reflect the uniqueness of the individual' (Weinreich, 1992).

Identity Structure Analysis (ISA) comprised a metatheoretical framework that employed 'concepts in the psychodynamic approach, social comparison theory, reference group theory, symbolic interactionism, personal construct theory and cognitive-affective consistency theory' (Black and Weinreich, 2000). Many of these concepts were integral to recognised counselling therapies while ISA-related concepts facilitated a deeper understanding of the client–counsellor relationship.

## Case Studies – Methodology (1)

Six target group suicide survivor case studies and two control group non-suicide mourner case studies were written up using narrative content analysis of transcriptions of audiotaped interviews and computer-supported analysis of identity instruments.

## Content Analysis – Methodology (2)

Content analysis of interview material used an approach devised by the researcher 'since there was no simple correct way to undertake content analysis'. The researcher had to judge what was most appropriate for the purpose of the research project (Weber, 1994, cited in Hickey and Kipping, 1996: 91). This idiosyncratic analytical method involved the generation of issues, and emergent themes from which linked attributes/concepts emerged. These attributes were tabulated in order of numerical frequency and integrated into an objective narrative summary of each respondent's experiences.

## Identity Structure Analysis (ISA) – Methodology (3)

Identity Structure Analysis (ISA) used personal bipolar constructs and entities – explained below. Measurement of a person's identity was achieved through the filter of that person's identification with or dissociation from significant others in her/his social world, including 'father', 'mother', 'my partner/spouse', and 'my closest friend', with perceptions of self including 'me as I used to be', 'me as I am now' and 'me as I would like to be' and others' perceptions of self including 'me as my family sees me', and so on. These significant others, perceptions of self, and others' perceptions of self were known as 'entities'.

Bipolar constructs were designed to: 'incorporate people's value and belief systems and their "everyday ideologies" [and] include items that allow different people to opt for one or other pole as representing something to which they aspire' (Weinreich, 1992). Since this project was about suicide, six bipolar constructs, out of a total of 23, concerned suicide, e.g. 'feels that a suicide survivor's grief is like any other' / 'feels that a suicide survivor's grief is uniquely painful'; a further seven were personal, e.g. 'is/are pessimistic about the future' / 'is/are optimistic about the future'; five were social, e.g. 'feel/s at ease when acting as a member of a group / 'feel/s uncomfortable when acting as a member of a group'; five concerned family; and five were about health. These constructs related to the target group. (Note: Summation of constructs exceeded 23 due to overlapping membership of categories.) Similarly, appropriate entities and bipolar constructs were created for control group respondents.

Each entity could be linked with each side of the bipolar construct to form two opposing statements. For example, consider the entity 'me as I would like to be' and the bipolar construct ' ... can be trusted' / ' ... cannot be trusted'. The two opposing sentences are:

1 "Me as I would like to be ... can be trusted"

2 "Me as I would like to be ... cannot be trusted

Each respondent could express a preference for only one of these statements. This process of expressing a preference was repeated for all entities and all bipolar constructs. Computer software was then used to analyse these preferences for all respondents, target and control. Outcomes were then interpreted by the researcher particularly in relation to each respondent's value and belief system, their identification processes including their role models, the extent of their identity diffusion, self-evaluation and ego-involvement and their global identity states.

**Observations Emerging From This Research**

Case studies were composed for each respondent that integrated both narrative and identity structure analyses. Survivors were found to be at different stages in their identity process but all were strongly impacted upon by their only common identity forming experience – their loss by suicide.

The 'key' grief variable appeared to be the degree of attachment between survivor and the deceased rather than degree of kinship or mode of killing.

Dysfunctional families could be breeding grounds for suicidal behaviour, both ideation and acting out. A completed suicide may point to the existence of past or current suicide ideation in surviving family members.

The general practitioner (GP) of a patient who died by suicide required the option of availing of the support of a deputised colleague to care for the survivors of her/his patient for up to one year.

The status of suicide survivor was a readily identifiable predisposing factor for depression.

Suicide's black reputation appeared to block proactive behaviour by support mechanisms in family and community that are triggered by 'normal' bereavement. Inability to anticipate suicide conspired with shock, silence, stigma, and taboo to render these mechanisms impotent.

The human cost of suicide was incalculable. But life expectancy data inferred that 'lost time' for suicide deceased was assessable as a key indicator of the economic cost of suicide to society. It seemed there was a massive imbalance between public investment in suicide prevention and postvention and the societal costs of suicidal loss.

Identity differentiation related to bereavement was shown to be significantly connected to the mode of death, i.e. by suicide or otherwise.

Factors such as age, chronology of the bereavement, availability and access to personal, family, medical and counselling support did not affect the impact of mode of death on the identity development of either survivors or non-suicide mourners.

## Conclusions and What I Learned

1. Suicide survivor risk

    It was likely that survivors were at some greater risk than non-suicide mourners although this could not be quantified. Four survivor respondents engaged in one or more activities that pre-disposed towards possible future completed suicide – self harm, suicide ideation, or attempted suicide – while one control group respondent engaged in a self-harming activity related to childhood trauma.

2. Survivor counselling and loss integration

    One survivor respondent obtained effective one-to-one and group counselling. Their ISA outcomes inferred that s/he achieved some loss integration and confirmed that her/his identity process was designed so that s/he would avoid their deceased family member's fate. Although it was not possible to isolate counselling as a significant factor that secured loss integration and a positive prognosis, there may be a causative relationship of some kind between the combination of self-help activities, of their access to tailored counselling, and of their identity development. Again it was not possible to infer a causative relationship between lack of effective counselling in relation to the remaining five survivors and their identity development.

3. Survivors as a therapeutic resource

All of the survivor respondents expressed an interest in the outcome of this study in relation to the wellbeing of other survivors. Active participation by suicide survivors in therapeutic programmes for other survivors was conditioned upon the level of resolution of their own loss trauma and provision of any necessary training and organisation. It seemed that the goodwill of these wounded, recovering individuals was an invaluable basis upon which to consider therapeutic programmes at some future date (IAS, 2006: 20-25).

**Research Project #3**

Successful completion of the Master's Programme in 2001 led me to consider further advanced study and research. I had by then retired from full-time pensionable employment and commenced working as a trainee counsellor, en route to accreditation. I completed a period of voluntary practice with local organisations caring for the bereaved, the homeless, and with individuals enmeshed within the justice system. At this time I began to work, part-time, as an associate lecturer in certificate/diploma level counselling courses in Further Education (FE) colleges and at Queen's University Belfast (QUB) and to present part-time classes in suicidology at QUB. I learned that a colleague with whom I studied on the master's programme had commenced a full-time doctorate level course and decided to consider my further study options. I preferred part-time study, not least on financial grounds, and enrolled on a part-time M Phil course, at Ulster University, that offered an option to doctoral level by research. Having addressed family suicide and its aftermath at master's level, I chose to study client or patient suicide and the clinician's predicament in its aftermath.

In due course I completed this research project and was awarded the degree PhD in December 2010. Besides the PhD dissertation, I subsequently prepared a related draft book chapter (unpublished) and delivered an address to local medical staff, both of which were based on my research findings. What follows is a reflection, using my dissertation and the afore-mentioned book chapter and address to staff, on what I learned from my research about the aftermath of suicide for health professionals, aka clinicians, bereaved in the aftermath of their client's suicide.

## Client Suicide and Clinician Identity

Caveat: Statistical data and its interpretation relied upon acceptance by a lay person of statistical theory, principles and practice and the reputation and integrity of the interpreter of such data. Similarly, understanding the application of Identity Structure Analysis (ISA) data to real-world circumstances and situations, such as suicide, relied upon the lay person's acceptance of ISA core definitions and principles as well as the reputation and integrity of the interpreter. ISA is complex, like suicide. As a research methodology for understanding the predicament of the suicide survivor, ISA is considered by many to be superior to psychology's traditional psychometric approach. [See Weinreich & Saunderson (eds.) (2003) Analysing Identity (Routledge), for comprehensive presentation of theory and principles in addition to several detailed case studies].

## Clinician Survivor

A suicide survivor was an individual who remained alive following the death by suicide of someone with whom they had a significant relationship or emotional bond (American Association of Suicidology, 2007). A 'clinician' was a psychological counsellor, a counselling psychologist, psychotherapist or similar qualified counselling practitioner. A 'client suicide' referred to the death by suicide of an individual who was the clinician's current or former client or patient. Hence a 'clinician survivor' was a clinician who experienced one or more client suicides. The research also considered the plight of the 'clinician survivor by proxy' described as the coincidental status of a colleague clinician who, although not a clinician survivor per se, shared a professional relationship with a clinician survivor. Their 'predicament' was investigated in my research by appraisal of their identity development (Weinreich and Saunderson, 2003) in relation to their experience.

[Note:- Suicidology continues to suffer from non-recognition by the scientific hierarchy as a discrete discipline, having been colonised by psychology, sociology and more recently psychiatry. Fitzpatrick et al. (2014) suggested that this aeons-old study of lethal human self-destructive behaviour, viz. suicidology, could be better re-defined as 'a social practice'.]

**Client Suicide**

Reliable data on the frequency of client suicide was lacking though an early US investigator opined that it 'was not a rare event' (Litman, 1965: 572). Estimates for its occurrence ranged from 22% (Kahne, 1968a) to 82% (Cryan et al., 1995) of psychotherapists who reported the loss by suicide of one or more of their clients. Swiss professionals reported that up to 70.1% had been 'confronted' by client suicide during their career (Gulfi et al., 2010: 203) while 69% of German therapists reported at least one patient suicide (Wurst et al., 2011). 'Relatively sparse' research studies into client suicide (Foley and Kelly, 2007: 134) represented, perhaps, 'a collective avoidance' (Soderland, 1999).

**Aftermath of client suicide**

Numerous studies from Litman (1965) to Foley and Kelly (2007) and Darden (2008) looked into clinicians' responses in the aftermath of client suicide that included components that were both personal and professional. At the personal level these were thought to be equivalent to those experienced by family suicide survivors (Farberow, 2001), for example following parental suicide (Soderland, 1999). Clinician survivors' personal reactions included 'grief, guilt, depression, personal inadequacy and ... anger' (Wurst et al., 2011). The intensity (Litman, 1965) of the clinician's professional relationship with their now-deceased client, and the former's personal attributes, e.g. age (Farberow, 2001), and gender (Grad et al., 1997) affected the characteristics of some clinician survivors' responses. Gaffney et al. (2002) confirmed that the quality of the client/clinician relationship was a key factor affecting a clinician survivor's response. Hendin et al. (2004) found that the clinician survivor's feelings of grief and guilt were linked to their emotional connectedness and closeness of involvement with their client, although a clinician survivor's distress level was inversely related to the length of their professional experience.

## Research into clinician survivors' experience of client suicide

Most research studies relied upon a range of methods including interview and content analysis, psychological autopsy, survey questionnaire, literature review, psychometric scales and multiple methods. What emerged from many of these studies were estimates of the relative frequency of client suicide as reported by clinicians and clinician survivors together with descriptions of some commonalities and dependencies in the experiences of some respondents. These valuable studies invariably recognised the need for healthcare professionals to take account of potentially deleterious outcomes for clinicians in the aftermath of their client's death by suicide. But an evident weakness was a consequential but unrecognised error in failing to acknowledge respondents' individual differences by often inferring, at least indirectly, that such outcomes were unavoidable, perhaps even inevitable.

## Research by way of case studies

A minority of writers on client suicide acknowledged, that while many clinician survivors may experience a range of emotional and professional consequences, it was vital that individual differences were respected given the uniqueness of each client suicide event and consequently the appropriateness of tailored postvention responses (Marshall, 1980; Berman, 1985; Farberow et al., 2001; Gaffney et al., 2002). Furthermore Hendin et al. (2000) referred to evidence of idiosyncratic processing of their experience by clinician survivors while Horn (1994) noted variations in clinician survivors' responses.

A modest number of published research studies investigated idiographically the lived experience of an individual clinician survivor. Several case studies written by clinician survivors (e.g. Gorkin, 1985; Foster, 1987; Phillips, 1995; Grad, 1996; Gitlin, 1999; Meade,

1999; Valente, 2003; Grad and Michel, 2005; Kapoor, 2008) and by clinician survivors by proxy, describing their own responses to a colleague's client suicide experience (Maltsberger, 1995; Misch, 2003), analysed bereaved practitioners' individual experiences. These studies confirmed that although some commonalities existed in their responses, there were significant differences that reflected individual personal characteristics and professional circumstances. For example, unique influences included each clinician's personal and professional attributes, each client's presenting and underlying issues, the nature of the 'therapeutic alliance' (Kahn, 2001: 151), and the influence, conscious or otherwise, of the presence in clinicians' attitudes of unaddressed countertransference hate and its negative mixture of aversion and malice (Maltsberger and Buie, 1974; Watts and Morgan, 1994; Jobes and Maltsberger, 1995).

## Coping in the aftermath of client suicide

If you thought that peer-reviewed researchers would by now have reached a consensus on approaches to postvention for clinician survivors you stand to be somewhat disappointed. That is not to say that the predicament of bereaved clinician survivors has not been subject to serious, wide-ranging, compassionate, and ongoing consideration. [For information updated to May 2016, please refer to the Clinician Survivors Task Force (CSTF) of the American Association of Suicidology (AAS)]. Published research studies offered contrasting perspectives. Some writers advocated organizational/institutional responses (Ruskin et al., 2004; Foley and Kelly, 2007) while others held that clinician survivors' postvention was the responsibility of each affected individual (Grad and Zavasnik, 1998; Meade, 1999; Campbell, 2006) at their own discretion (Soderland, 1999). One writer referred to a minority of clinician survivors who were less resilient and therefore more vulnerable and who risked a long-term adverse prognosis (Ruskin et al., 2004).

## Doctoral research: aims and approach

The specific aims of this research project included:

a) To explore with clinicians the extent to which their interpersonal relationships with significant others were affected by clinicians' exposure to client suicide
b) To investigate the influence on clinicians of personal knowledge of the suicide phenomenon and of their experience of client suicide
c) To examine how clinicians' professional orientation was influenced as regards their belief and value systems by exposure to client suicide.

An approach was adopted as a research strategy in order to obtain primary evidence from clinicians about their concrete, individual, personal, experiential responses to loss by suicide of their client(s). The approach was capable of recognizing the totality of each clinician survivor's experience and is 'well suited to describing and making sense of the processes of change' (McLeod, 1997: 104). It was hypothesized that, when studied in depth and in detail, each clinician survivor's experience of client suicide was likely to be as unique to that person as their individual coping response. It was further postulated that each clinician's assimilation of their client's suicide was similar to those of other clinician survivors only in their particular experience of the stark fact of a sudden, unannounced, potentially calamitous and catastrophic conclusion to the life of their client.

## Ethical research

This research project was approved by the University of Ulster Research Ethics Committee. Conditional confidentiality was offered to each respondent; some caveats applied:
a) Information disclosed by a respondent about, or intent to commit, serious criminal offence/s including offences against or involving children, terrorism or drug-trafficking or
b) Serious intent to self-harm and/or
c) Information required under sub-poena by any properly constituted court of law.

The researcher also undertook not to disclose any personally identifiable material gained from a respondent in any published report or document without that respondent's informed, written consent (British Association for Counselling, 1996: 8).

## Research cohorts

A total of 22 respondents agreed to participate although considerable difficulty was encountered in recruiting eligible individuals. Client suicide has long been regarded as an inevitable 'occupational hazard' for clinicians (Chemtob et al., 1988a: 227; Chemtob et al., 1988b: 420; Alexander et al., 2000: 1573). The American Association of Suicidology (AAS) featured a caution on their 'Clinician Survivor Task Force' website:

'the odds that [a clinician] will lose a client to suicide during their career are slim but they are not zero' [American Association of Suicidology (AAS) 2007].

At the outset it was envisaged that the existence of 'taboo' (Palmer, 2008: 134) and 'stigma' (Cain, 1972: 15) in relation to death by suicide as well as potential legal ramifications including litigation fears, might inter alia restrict clinician participation in the research. Eligible respondents were sought in the population of eligible clinicians in the UK and Ireland. Following publicity in Ireland and the UK via local and national counselling associations and letters to the media, little interest was generated in UK/Irish psychotherapy professions. Four years after commencement, an adequate number of respondents was assembled and the final cohort structure, that met eligibility criteria ascertained during interview, was arranged as follows:

a) Target group: clinician survivors: 11 members (including 'Matthew', 2005)

b) Comparison group: clinician survivors by proxy: 6 members

c) Control group: non-clinicians: 6 members (including 'Matthew', 2002)

Respondent 'Matthew' was interviewed as a 'Control Group' respondent before commencing employment as a psychological counsellor. When he contacted the project in 2005 following the death of his client by suicide he was subsequently interviewed as a 'Target Group' respondent. Target and comparison group members included psychological counsellors employed in agency work and private practice, and clinicians employed in clinical psychology and medicine. Control group members included social workers and teachers.

**Research Instruments**

It is worth noting Weinreich's (1992) caveat about the vagaries of ISA identity instrument construction:

'ISA forces the investigator to be aware that only portions of a person's identity and social world can be assessed at any moment. There is no pretence that by precise honing of a psychometric scale or the refinement or elaboration of a questionnaire, the ultimate "truth" of the matter in question can be ascertained. The construction of an identity instrument makes one aware that much has to be left out – features of self [viz. identity] that cannot be covered, matters of the person's relationships with others that cannot be included, and many possible discourses for which there is insufficient space' (Weinreich, 1992 : 18).

Weinreich (1992: 35) noted that a risk of bias existed as a result of over-inclusion or omission of certain kinds of entities and constructs: caution was therefore exercised by the researcher in their interpretation of computer-generated indices for each respondent on the basis of their completed instruments.

Three ISA research instruments, A, B and C – see Appendices 1, 2, and 3 – were created by reviewing earlier discourse-based ISA instruments – entities and bipolar constructs – that were used in the earlier study (O'Keeffe, 2001). A sample range of influential or significant people in the life of a clinician survivor and some events that may have influenced that survivor in important ways (Weinreich, 1992) were ascertained. This facilitated the generation of appropriate entities and bipolar constructs for use with clinician survivors and clinician survivors by proxy, viz. Instrument A. An adaptation of these lists was used with the control group, viz. Instrument C, while a variation of the latter was used with one control respondent 'Kevin' early in the fieldwork, viz. Instrument B.

## Data Processing and Capture

Each respondent completed a consent form after which a semi-structured interview was audiotaped and ISA instruments completed. Audiotapes were transcribed for use in case study reports for illustrative and contextual purposes only and respondents' entries to ISA instruments were analysed using ISA IDEX software (Weinreich and Ewart, 1999a). Software outputs for each respondent were represented in printed reports by ISA indices, which were estimates of underlying quantitative parameters. The researcher's task then was to interpret the ISA indices so as to highlight certain attributes of the identity structures of individual respondents. Relevant attributes, as defined in Weinreich (2003), were further interpreted by the researcher 'to tell the story' of each research respondent in case study narratives and summaries. [The technology that underpins the analytical process need not be elaborated here as detailed, comprehensive expositions (Black, 2002; Weinreich, 2003b) may be consulted as necessary].

## Case Study Summaries

The ISA approach facilitated comprehensive exploration of clinicians' individual responses, whether personal, professional or otherwise to client suicide in the context of their identifications with their social world. It focused upon client suicide as a unique event in each clinician's personal and professional autobiography. Its objective was to ascertain, in the context of their duty of care and through the windows of their clinician survivors' experiences, the impact of the loss of a client(s) through suicide on clinicians' identity development, and concomitantly to illuminate their coping strategies and mechanisms. The idea of 'identification with' was a key element in ISA's approach to identity analysis:

'Identity formation owes a good deal to ways in which a person tries to be like or not to be like another... ISA is intended to follow the patterns of 'identification with (or not with)' that seem to have been important in someone's life manifested in self-construals' (Harré, 2003: xix-xx).

In particular, respondents' identifications in a range of contexts with two entities: 'a suicide survivor' and 'a client who died by suicide' were key parameters in each case study.

A total of 23 case studies were written: however in view of space limitations herein, three of these – one from each cohort – are summarised below. The studies considered respondents' global identity variants, their conflicted and empathetic identifications and their systems of values and beliefs in order to 'tell the story' for a clinician survivor, a clinician survivor by proxy and a control group respondent. Data relating to each case study, viz. 'Hannah', 'Sheila' and 'Danny', were accessed from relevant ISA IDEX software outputs, and interpreted by the researcher to inform each respondent's identity transitions, summarised below.

Note: For clarification, definitions of ISA's identification parameters and processes, in particular global identity variant, conflicted identification and empathetic identification, idealistic identification and contra identification, self-evaluation, identity diffusion and ego-involvement are now outlined. In addition, ISA's meaning and use of structural pressures as indicators of respondents' aspirational systems of values and beliefs are also summarised below.

## ISA's Identification Processes and Structural Pressures

*Global identity variant:* This characteristic provided an overview, located in time and situation, of a person's identity state in specified social contexts. It is derived from one's self-evaluation and one's identity diffusion, linked to one's acknowledgement of, or defence against one's conflicted identifications. A person's identity may be confident, diffused or foreclosed according to context and circumstance but is unlikely to be achieved for all time. It offers an accessible summary of one's state of identity within a nine-fold 3 X 3 classification (see Table 1 below) of low, moderate or high levels of self-evaluation against low, moderate or high levels of identity diffusion: most adults are classified as 'indeterminate' or 'confident' i.e. they reflect moderate levels of identity diffusion, with moderate or high levels of self-evaluation and are considered to be psychologically well-adjusted. Other identity states are regarded as vulnerable.

| Identity Variants | Low Diffusion | Moderate Diffusion | High Diffusion |
|---|---|---|---|
| High Self-evaluation | Defensive High Self-regard | Confident | Diffuse High Self-regard |
| Moderate Self-evaluation | Defensive | Indeterminate | Diffusion |
| Low Self-evaluation | Defensive Negative | Negative | Crisis |

Table 1: Global Identity Variants. Accessed at Weinreich, 2003b, page 106 in Analysing Identity, Weinreich and Saunderson, 2003. Page 106 London: Routledge. Reproduced with permission.

*Empathetic identification:* The extent of one's empathetic identification with another is defined as the degree of similarity between the qualities one attributes to the other, whether 'good' or 'bad', and those of one's current self-image.

*Idealistic-identification:* The extent of one's idealistic identification with another is defined as the similarity between the qualities one attributes to the other and those one would like to possess as part of one's ideal self-image;

*Contra-identification:* The extent of one's contra identification with another is defined as the similarity between the qualities one attributes to the other and those from which one would like to dissociate;

*Identification conflict:* In terms of one's self-image, the extent of one's identification conflict with another is defined as the multiplicative function of one's current empathetic identification and contra-identification with that other;

*Structural pressure:* Structural pressure is an ISA index that estimates the extent to which an individual consistently attributes favourable and unfavourable characteristics to particular entities. In simplistic terms, structural pressures offer reliable indications concerning an individual's aspirational system of values and beliefs;

*Self-evaluation:* One's self-evaluation is defined as one's overall assessment of self in terms of positive and negative evaluative connotations of the attributes one construes in oneself, in accordance with one's value system;

*Identity diffusion:* The extent of one's identity diffusion acknowledges the optimal presence of residually conflicted identifications – optimal levels – or defends against them – low levels – or exhibits extensive unresolved conflicted identifications – high levels; and

*Ego-involvement:* One's ego-involvement with another is defined as one's overall responsiveness to the other in terms of the extensiveness both in quantity and strength of the attributes one construes the other as possessing (Weinreich & Saunderson (eds.) 2003).

## Case study: a clinician survivor: 'Hannah' (case A11)

'Hannah' was a pseudonym for a practitioner counsellor employed full-time in a counselling agency following work experience in psychiatric nursing and in counselling for substance abuse. Two of her clients had taken their own lives: one was Hannah's former psychiatric patient several years before. More recently, her current client was found hanged after six months in counselling with Hannah and four days after his last appointment. Two of Hannah's immediate family had killed themselves: an uncle many years ago and a cousin only a few years before interview but after her former psychiatric patient's death. Hannah learned of her client's death on returning to work from a brief period of leave to keep her appointment with this now deceased client.

Hannah's seven global identity variants were regarded as well-adjusted being either 'confident' or 'indeterminate'. But her problematic identifications with suicide were very high in two contexts: after client suicide and when overwhelmed by life's cruelties. Hannah's problematic identifications with actively suicidal clients, viz. those with 'ideation' and 'depression', were more intense than with clients in the aftermath of suicidal behaviour, viz. 'a client who recovered after serious suicide attempt', 'a suicide survivor' or 'a client who died by suicide'. When 'working' she construed herself as 'a suicide survivor' while recognising herself more so in the characteristics of 'an admired person', of professional colleagues (e.g. 'my counselling supervisor') and of family members (e.g. 'my partner/spouse').

Hannah's past encounters with family suicide emerged in her highest pre-counselling problematic identification with 'a client who recovered after serious suicide attempt' which intensified in 'life's cruelties' but remained at its pre-counselling level when Hannah worked with vulnerable clients. This pattern was repeated for 'actively suicidal' clients in these transitions. Family suicide during Hannah's adolescence heightened an awareness that was intensified through more recent patient and family suicides. It was evident that Hannah's most problematic current issues would be with 'suicide in counselling', its potential, its actualité and its aftermath while she continued to have substantial issues with her family, e.g. 'mother'.

Hannah's positive role models spanned her professional, personal and family worlds with her strongest models being 'an admired person' and 'my counselling supervisor'. Her negative role models were suicide-related depressed/suicidal clients.

Hannah aspired to contend with distress, pointed up by low structural pressures (SPs), including existential issues, levels of responsibility for certain others and suicide-related concerns: suicide being a brave act, 'out of the blue' suicide and whether suicide can be anticipated. She did this by implementing core evaluative dimensions of identity, by way of high SPs, about suicide including: that grief after suicide was uniquely painful, being highly sensitised to the issue of suicide, that suicide could be prevented and that suicide totally changed survivors. Other strong aspirational beliefs included developing personal values and beliefs, the irreplaceable value of each human being, developing human relationships and continuing to be the person that she is.

The ISA instrument was unable accurately to discriminate between Hannah's evaluation of her deceased relatives (uncle and cousin) and her deceased clients (patient and client). So it was not immediately possible for the researcher to identify 'family' as an evaluative influence in this regard. Yet an apparent paradox existed for Hannah: she appraised four suicide related clients as people that she valued least, her deceased client being least valued. These data contrasted overwhelmingly with Hannah's highest aspirational self-evaluation 'me as I would like to be'. Yet the single most essential component for effective counselling was the quality of the relationship between client and counsellor:

'There is an increasingly wide acceptance of the importance of the relationship between the client and therapist as the agent of therapeutic efficacy...something about the process between therapist and client and the way they relate...is much more important to successful outcome than...content of sessions...or the knowledge, skills and techniques of the practitioner' (Wilkins, 2003: 73)

Hence the possible paradox: negative evaluation of the suicidal, or any, client by a counsellor conditioned some potential for an ineffective outcome. The related notion of 'countertransference hate' (Maltsberger and Buie, 1974; Watts and Morgan, 1994; Jobes and Maltsberger,1995) may also be an influential dynamic. Whether there was any identifiable connection between low client evaluation and client suicide in any individual case required further research.

## Case study – clinician survivor by proxy – 'Sheila' (case A8)

'Sheila' was a pseudonym for an experienced and highly qualified counselling psychologist working in an agency setting. Two years before interview, her client died suddenly: Sheila was advised that her client's family were unsure whether or not her client had died by suicide. A year later a coroner's inquest found that the client's death was accidental: the client had overdosed on prescribed medication but no firm evidence existed of suicidal intent. Sheila worked currently with a client who was a clinician survivor, having lost a client by suicide. Consequently Sheila was considered to be a clinician survivor by proxy. Sheila had also experienced family suicide a few years before interview when a family member was found hanged. Hence Sheila's experience of others' suicidal behaviour was considerable but absent in relation to self.

Sheila was unable or unwilling to appraise either 'a client who died by suicide' or 'mother'. In the former case, she wrote 'N/A' against all ISA instrument 'A' entries. In the latter case she wrote 'deceased' against the initial ISA construct '...takes life for granted'/ '...wonders what life is all about' and left all subsequent entries blank. Sheila did not wish to contemplate the meaning of her mother's death or that of 'a client who died by suicide', the latter being represented by her clinician survivor client's loss of their client by suicide.

Sheila was intensely ego-involved with 'a suicide survivor' but did not recognise herself in that entity's characteristics in any current context. Indeed she highly dissociated from this person and regarded them very unfavourably. Her three encounters as 'a suicide survivor', viz. family, accidental death of client where suicide was ultimately ruled out, and clinician survivor by proxy, focused her attention on the entity in the context of current research but not more pervasively in her life.

Sheila placed a very low evaluation upon depressed and suicidal clients and upon a suicide survivor. Although she was currently working in trauma-related psychotherapy following earlier work experience devoted to suicide assessment of vulnerable clients, Sheila believed her clients valued her very highly and almost as highly as her colleagues. Countertransference dynamics, referred to earlier, may also be influential here.

Sheila's identity processes revealed that she construed herself quite strongly in the characteristics of her counselling supervisor, her partner and, less emphatically, her father. Sheila's past problematic identifications with depressed and suicidal clients were only partially resolved in the current contexts of life's wonders (CS2), working (CS3) and relaxing (CS4) as she distanced herself only slightly from these people. However these parameters of conflicted identification maintained high or very high levels.

All Sheila's identity variants were regarded as vulnerable except when she was relaxing. High levels of identity diffusion reflected her high and widely dispersed conflicted identifications across all but one context (CS4) with all entities except her partner and an admired person.

Sheila's system of beliefs and values as revealed in core evaluative dimensions of identity, via high SPs on constructs, indicated aspirations to continue to develop personal values and beliefs, to seek and develop human relationships, to believe that each human being was of irreplaceable value, to continue to be the person she was into the foreseeable future, to feel that safe expression of emotional feelings was always healthy and never feeling lonely or uncomfortable when alone with self. Sheila's low evaluation of depressed and suicidal clients suggested that her aspirational belief regarding the 'irreplaceable value of each human being' was somewhat unrealistic.

Areas of stress for Sheila, by way of low SPs on constructs, included existential issues around questioning who she is and taking life for granted, whether she could rely on family support at times of crisis and being highly sensitised to the issue of suicide while believing that suicide demanded considerable bravery. Her core aspirations represented her attempt to achieve personal certainty in the face of these unresolved dilemmas.

Sheila did not construe herself strongly as 'a suicide survivor' following her own client's suspected suicidal behaviour. She was reluctant to explore, via the ISA instrument 'A', the meaning of her mother's death or of her own 'clinician survivor by proxy' status via her client's clinician survivor experience. When asked whether she believed herself prepared for the possibility of a client's suicide she replied:

'I don't feel I am anyone's saviour... if someone kills themselves...it's their choice... counselling is not for everyone...counselling does not save everyone...and that's why it doesn't surprise me...clients of reputable therapists have killed themselves and I wouldn't put the blame on them or see them or their work as having failed [adding that she would not] put blame on [a clinician survivor] or see them or their work as having failed' ('Sheila' - clinician survivor by proxy – case A8).

## Case study: control group member 'Danny' (Case C5)

'Danny' was a pseudonym for a highly qualified college lecturer in the social sciences, teaching for over five years having previously worked for seven years as an approved social worker following periods of community work. He also previously volunteered for a period with a suicide prevention organisation.

He disclosed four past incidents involving suicidal behaviour by others including a former social work client who died by suicide some time after Danny changed career, less than five years before interview. He had also worked professionally with the partner of a person who died by suicide following discharge from a psychiatric unit and with a mother, whose son and his best friend were found hanged together.

The fourth incident involved the self-reported attempted suicide by drowning of Danny's social work client. Danny also recalled from memory up to eight social worker colleagues whose clients had taken their own lives. His lecturing work included presentations involving learning resources related to suicide prevention, intervention and postvention.

Dominant influences for Danny were 'me when I'm overwhelmed by life's cruelties', 'a person who died by suicide' and with 'me as I would like to be'. He valued the last-mentioned much more highly than the others, respectively. His positive role models were located in family and friends while negative exemplars included depressed and suicidal people.

He recognised in himself many of the characteristics of depressed and suicidal people in the context of being 'overwhelmed by life's cruelties' and less so when working. In these contexts, Danny construed in self, respectively, many of the qualities of 'a person I admire' and 'my partner' which were highest when Danny was working. In the past, when Danny knew about suicide (PS3), there was much more in him, respectively, of the qualities of 'my partner', 'a person I admire' and 'my parents' than of depressed or suicidal people. These data showed that the influence on Danny's sense of self, of suicidal behaviour in others when working or volunteering, was moderated by his experiences with friends and family.

Danny's conflicted identifications were currently highest with depressed and suicidal people in the context of life's cruelties. When working, Danny's lower levels of empathetic identification effected a reduction in his levels of conflicted identification with depressed and suicidal persons, pointing to an appropriate resolution of his conflicted identifications in the transition from 'cruelties' to 'working'. Danny's dissociation currently, from past 'suicide survivor' characteristics were evident in the partial resolution of related conflicted identifications with 'a suicide survivor'.

This respondent's global identity variants were regarded as vulnerable except when he was 'relaxing' (CS4: 'indeterminate'), a well-adjusted identity state. Danny's very low levels of self-evaluation, in the past and currently, allied with high identity diffusion, resulted in identity variants 'crisis' in these contexts. Danny's remaining vulnerable identity states were 'diffusion', based in moderate self evaluation and high identity diffusion (PS3, CS2, CS3).

His metaperspectives (viz. 'as work colleagues see me' and/or 'as my family sees me') pointed to higher involvement with colleagues than family while feeling less valued by the former than by the latter. This pointed to his commitment to his profession while his family role contributed more significantly towards achievement of his aspirations.

Danny's core evaluative dimensions of identity confirmed aspirational values and beliefs including wondering what life is all about, believing in the irreplaceable value of each human being, continuing to develop personal values and beliefs, feeling a special responsibility and having warm feelings for others and believing safe expression of emotion is healthy. Areas of uncertainty for Danny included feeling momentary bouts of psychological discomfort, being alone without feeling lonely and uncomfortable, using alternative/complementary remedies, being sensitised to the issue of suicide and its prevention, developing human relationships and continuing to be the person he was into the foreseeable future.

Danny's core values and beliefs were capable of addressing problematic areas to a limited extent because of some contradictory areas concerned with human relationships, existential issues and suicide prevention. His identity development was strongly influenced by his past experiences of others' suicidal behaviour during his previous career as an approved social worker. While he exhibited some current characteristics of 'a suicide survivor' in his college lecturer role, there were many more qualities in him that resonated of family, friends and colleagues when working.

**Emergent themes**

A synthesis of empirical literature-based research outcomes, summarised above, produced the following themes:
1. Clinician survivors' response is dependent upon their respective levels of resilience and vulnerability

2. The clinician survivor's response reflects the unique impact of their client's death by suicide
3. Postvention for clinician survivors is the responsibility of each affected individual
4. A collective avoidance concerning how clinicians deal with client suicide is reflected in the scarcity of research into this phenomenon
5. The levels of emotional connectedness and closeness of involvement of clinician and client are the determinants of the clinician survivor's grief and guilt
6. The relationship, or therapeutic alliance, is a key factor in facilitating benevolent outcomes for clinician survivors
7. Unaddressed countertransference hate can adversely affect the therapeutic alliance resulting in sub-optimal outcomes when the client presents with suicide ideation
8. The apparent imbalance in relation to the incidence of client suicide between trainee clinicians and their more experienced colleagues may be an avoidable consequence of an inappropriate case assignment strategy
9. Clinician survivors by proxy will exhibit similar affects in the aftermath of client suicide but at reduced levels of intensity.

    These themes evidenced multidimensional aspects of the client suicide phenomenon in relation to how it affected clinician survivors, both personally and professionally. Shneidman (1985) referred to suicide as 'a multidimensional malaise' (Shneidman, 1985: 203) and the form and content of each clinician survivor's response to client suicide evidenced a similarly intricate configuration. Two further themes, emerging from Rubin's (1990) lists of personal and legal 'do's and don'ts' for clinician survivors when a patient dies by suicide, reflected some of this complexity:

10. Personal responsibilities: reach out to client's family and to colleagues; avoid discussion or appraisal of fault or blame; work with a trusted professional on own feelings

11. Legal responsibilities: know relevant law and engage a private/institutional lawyer; keep accurate records about the prelude to and aftermath of client's death; do not alter any records: they are liable to discovery/subpoena in subsequent legal process; discuss case only in privileged settings; maintain client confidentiality.

Brown (1989: 426) described a related five stage process, based on Resnik (1969) and Cotton et al. (1983), specifically for trainee programmes which could structure institutional responses to patient suicide:

i) Anticipation

ii) Acute impact – within hours up to 8 weeks

iii) Clarification and working through – 2 to 6 months

iv) Reorganisation and addressing ongoing doubts – 6 to 18 months

v) Preparation for reactivation and post-training practice.

To date no theoretical framework existed that attempted to understand and to integrate for the purposes of postvention, the dynamics of clinician survivors' responses to client suicide. In a recent study, Darden (2008) interviewed a small number (N=6) of clinical psychologist survivors and confirmed earlier findings (Kleespies et al.,1993) that these individuals experienced 'anguish' that met the criteria for complicated grief (Darden, 2008: 72). Two later studies, viz. Gulfi et al. (2010) and Wurst et al. (2011) made recommendations for helping clinician survivors. The former study mentioned that 'beyond the emotional and professional impact, patient suicide may have a formative influence, encouraging [clinician survivors] to review and improve their working practices' (Gulfi et al., 2010: 202). The latter study estimated that up to 30% of clinician survivors 'suffer from severe distress after a patient's suicide' (Wurst et al., 2011: 99) including up to 60% of psychiatrists in training. The writers recommended that 'specific and intensified help' should be made available for affected individuals. Although none of the above mentioned themes are at odds with these inclusive findings, a complicated grief response to loss by client suicide, including severe distress for some clinician survivors, represents one of several influences that may impact the clinician's identity.

Identity structure analysis facilitated measurement of individual research respondents' identity development, for example, in their appraisal and reappraisal of a key entity 'me when I am overwhelmed by life's cruelties' in a range of contexts. Much existing research-based work on the clinician survivor's predicament including one of the most recent (Wurst et al., 2011), reached conclusions that included broad generalisations purporting to describe what happened to clinician survivors' sense of self in the aftermath of client suicide. The current research showed that such findings were likely, at best, to be only partially correct and that each clinician survivor's experiential response, as reflected in their identity transitions, was unique to them.

**Theoretical Postulates**

[To understand the following postulates and derived theoretical propositions that follow, it is necessary to be familiar with and to refer as appropriate, to ISA's identification parameters and processes, as outlined above.]

In exploring how clinician survivors' experience of client suicide impacts upon their identity and in the light of this doctoral ISA-based research, several theoretical postulates are now presented that make identity redefinition meaningful and that describe how the clinician survivor makes sense of their loss experience. These postulates investigate the dynamic processes that engage clinician survivors and clinician survivors by proxy, in their efforts to understand modulations in their identifications with significant others, and to learn from related issues that challenge the clinician survivor's beliefs and values system (Black, 2002).

**The clinician's exposure to suicidal behaviour – immediate aftermath**

*Postulate 1*: The clinician's direct appraisal of their client's suicide will differ from a colleague's experience by proxy of the same event.

*Postulate 2*: The clinician's direct appraisal of their client's suicide will be unique to the individual clinician.

## The clinician's experience of client suicide

*Postulate 3*: The clinician's orientation towards their social world, whether defensive or open, influences the extent and nature of their experience of client suicide.

*Postulate 4*: Clinicians, in appraising the psychache and lethality (Shneidman, 1996) that brought about their client's suicide, will contra-identify with that client, wishing to dissociate from those characteristics.

## Consequences for the clinician of experience of client suicide

*Postulate 5*: A clinician's assimilation of their client suicide experience will give rise to a redefinition of identity that will be evidenced in modulation of identification conflicts and self-evaluation, the extent of which will depend upon the clinician's orientation to their social world.

*Postulate 6*: The clinician's experience of client suicidal behaviour will result in modulations of empathetic identification with a suicidal client from their past self, as appraised before the suicidal behaviour, to their current selves.

*Postulate 7*: Conflicted identification with a client at risk of suicide (by suicide ideation, serious suicide attempt or death by suicide) will be indicative of the clinician's level of suicidality.

## The clinician as 'a suicide survivor'

*Postulate 8*: Client suicide in conjunction with past experiences of suicidal behaviour in personal, collegial or societal contexts or as communicated in media, literature or history will influence how clinician survivors appraise self and others, in a suicide-related context when working and when relaxing.

## Self-care in the aftermath of client suicide

*Postulate 9*: Clinicians' experience of client suicide will result in decreasing empathetic identifications with colleagues accompanied by feelings of isolation arising from the absence of shared experience.

*Postulate 10*: Clinician survivors' experience will result in closer empathetic identifications with professional colleagues – who also have experience client suicide – and so provide an appropriate basis for assimilating their client suicide experience.

## Respondents' beliefs and values systems

*Postulate 11*: Clinicians' experience of client suicide will affect their systems of values and beliefs and this will be evidenced in conflicted dimensions of identity.

*Postulate 12*: Clinician survivors' core evaluative dimensions of identity are indicative of their coping resources for integrating a client suicide experience.

## Derived theoretical propositions

Following Black and Weinreich (2003), the results of current research, presented as case studies, were idiosyncratic in nature. They revealed 'the complex of processes...by which respondents construct and reconstruct their identities' (Black and Weinreich, 2003: 345) when exposed to suicidal behaviour in self and others. Although each case study and the ISA indices upon which it was based were unique to the particular respondent, Lange (1989) argued that:

'the nature of [ISA] indices makes it possible to perform comparisons between individuals, however idiosyncratic the material from which the indices are derived may be...ISA anchors the analysis in the value system of the individual, the latter being determined from data almost entirely provided by the individual [respondent]' (Lange, 1989: 170)

Detailed analyses of ISA indices that structured the current researcher's 23 case studies, in the context of the study's hypotheses, aims and objectives, facilitated the derivation of theoretical propositions from theoretical postulates that enabled and informed the study's conclusions and implications. An example of such an analytical process was offered to explain how one theoretical proposition – viz. proposition #6 – was arrived at from a theoretical postulate – viz. postulate #7. Eight further theoretical propositions (viz. Propositions #1 to #5 incl. and #7 to #9 incl.) were arrived at by similar research based data analyses and they are stated below (following Proposition #10).

## Postulate #7 as a basis for Proposition #6

Postulate #7 states that a clinician's conflicted identification with a client at risk of suicide (by suicide ideation, serious suicide attempt or death by suicide) will be indicative of the clinician's level of suicidality.

It could be considered highly likely that, when currently working, clinicians' identification conflicts with depressed or suicidal clients, including a client who died by suicide, may be the most challenging in a psychotherapeutic context (Pope and Tabachnik, 1993; Simon and Hales, 2006). Recall that identification conflict represents the degree of self's dissociation from qualities that one attributes to the other that are also present in one's current self-image.

Analysis of respondents' conflicted identifications with depressed and suicidal clients confirms that similar proportions of target (82%) and comparison (83%) group members experience high or very high levels. Almost all control group (94%) members, i.e. non-clinicians, share similar levels of identification conflicts with depressed or suicidal people, i.e. non-clients. Again similar proportions of target (73%) and comparison (75%) group members experience high or very high conflicted identification levels with 'a client who died by suicide'. Fewer control group members (50%) experienced high or very high conflicted identifications with 'a person who died by suicide'.

These data resonate with survey findings by Rogers et al. (2001) that 20% of counsellors 'have seriously considered suicide' (Rogers et al., 2001: 368). Current research data confirm that some clinician survivors and clinician survivors by proxy could have an, as yet, unquantified propensity towards such behaviour. Postulate #7 therefore represents an evidential basis for a theoretical proposition, as stated below:

*Proposition #6*: A clinician's conflicted identification with a client's propensity to suicide (by way of suicide ideation, serious suicide attempt or death by suicide) will be indicative of that clinician's level of suicidality.

## Clinicians' attitudes to suicidal clients

A further theoretical proposition (Proposition #10) emerged from an analytical synthesis of case study findings about clinician attitudes to clients at risk of suicide. The existence of unaddressed countertransference hate (CTH) (Maltsberger and Buie, 1974; Watts and Morgan, 1994; Jobes and Maltsberger, 1995) was mentioned earlier. In current research, the negative mixture of aversion and malice that CTH contained was evident when some respondents' attitudes were explored.

Observation of respondents across three cohorts in their evaluation of and ego-involvement with depressed, suicidal and 'deceased by suicide' clients and with suicide survivors, offers possible insights regarding the presence of CTH in clinicians' attitudes to clients with suicide-related issues. Weinreich and Saunderson (eds.) (2003: 89) defined one's evaluation of another as 'the extent to which another is favoured or disfavoured [involving] one's overall assessment of [that other] in accordance with one's value system'. The existence of CTH in clinicians towards their vulnerable clients may therefore be indicated by consistently low or very low evaluation levels.

Research findings illustrated the above-mentioned evaluations across all three cohorts. All control group respondents make broadly comparable low or very low evaluations of all ambivalent/depressed and suicidal persons, suicide attempters or 'deceased by suicide' people. Target group members' evaluations are seen to be low or very low for 95% of depressed or suicidal clients, for 91% of clients deceased by suicide and for 55% of clients who recovered after serious suicide attempt. Comparison group members' evaluations for these clients are, respectively, 83%, 50% and 83%. These evaluation data show that the influence of varying levels of client suicidal behaviour, directly (target group) or indirectly (comparison group) upon clinicians is somewhat less than the more uniformly baleful influence that knowledge and awareness of others' suicidal behaviour has for non-clinicians.

In explaining ego-involvement, Weinreich and Saunderson (eds.) (2003: 48) defined this parameter as a measure of one's 'intensity of involvement' with self, others, institutions or emblems, including behaviours or actions, that may 'have [an] unusually powerful impact despite being quite removed from the person's daily encounters' (Weinreich and Saunderson, 2003: 88). As defined, respondents' degree of ego-involvement with an entity will measure how dominant, influential and powerful its impact is. The question now arises regarding the meaning, in relation to identity development, of respondents' high ego-involvement with suicide-related clients when coincident with very low, low or higher evaluation levels of these individuals.

Research findings showed that 82% of target group respondents are very highly ego-involved with 'a client who died by suicide'. Comparison (50%) and control (67%) group members are also ego-involved with that key entity but at reduced levels. Further, 55% of target group members are both highly ego-involved with 'a client who died by suicide' and place a very low value on that entity. Comparison (50%) and control (50%) group members evidence this specific relationship but somewhat less so. Additionally, a parallel relationship was identified with regard to 'a client with suicide ideation' but at reduced levels for the three groups, respectively, 45%, 33% and 33%. Analysis of results for depressed/ambivalent and attempted/recovered entities show much weaker relationships, if any, linking low evaluation and high ego-involvement levels.

Study findings revealed that 64% (N=7) of target group respondents and 67% (N=4) of comparison group respondents are very highly ego-involved with 'a suicide survivor'. However results indicated that 36% (N=4) of target group members are both very highly ego-involved and place a moderate or better evaluation upon this entity. This contrasts with 17% (N=1) and 33% (N=2) respectively for comparison and control groups. This indicates that some target group clinician survivors experience lower CTH levels with regard to suicide survivors.

Considered collectively, these results confirm that clinicians' responses to their vulnerable clients are related to their perceptions of clients' levels of suicide risk. Higher levels of suicide risk are associated with suicide ideation and previous suicide attempts (Simon and Hales, 2006: 586) while suicide survivors are believed to be at increased risk for suicidal behaviour (Cain, 1972: 10; Campbell, 2006: 460). Fawcett (2006: 256) notes that, while suicide is not predictable in any individual (McKinnon and Farberow, 1976; Pokorny, 1983, 1993), assessment for suicidality in a depressed client seeks to assign them to risk groups, in relation to lethality, ranging from a) acute high risk of suicide in the immediate future, to b) chronic high risk of suicide over a period of years but moderate immediate risk and c) low risk of suicide for the foreseeable future.

Clinicians' perceptions will be critically informed by their knowledge, experience and competency in assessment for suicide. It seems evident that, where it exists, CTH and its potentially debilitating effects might best be addressed by enhancing clinicians' ability, insights and expertise in assessing clients for suicide.

This could alleviate clinicians' fears (Pope and Tabachnik, 1993), anger (Dressler et al., 1975) and antipathy (Scheurich, 2001) towards vulnerable clients at risk of suicide (Simon, 1998: 480).

*Proposition #10:* Clinicians' perceptions of suicidal clients will be critically informed by their knowledge, experience and competency in assessment for suicide. Relevant ability, insights and expertise will therefore address, where present, adverse consequences of unaddressed countertransference hate (CTH), including malignant alienation from the client, so as to moderate CTH's potential for undermining and weakening the therapeutic relationship.

## Derived theoretical propositions - #1 to #5 and #7 to #9 inclusive

*Proposition #1* A clinician's direct appraisal of their client's suicide will differ from a colleague's experience by proxy of the same event and will be unique to that clinician.

*Proposition #2* A clinician's orientation towards their social world whether defensive or open will influence the extent and nature of their experience of client suicide.

*Proposition #3* Clinicians, in appraising the psychache and lethality (Shneidman, 1996) that brought about their client's suicide will contra-identify with that client, wishing to dissociate from those characteristics.

*Proposition #4* A clinician's assimilation of a client suicide will give rise to a redefinition of identity, evidenced in modulations of identification conflicts and self-evaluation the extent of which will depend upon the clinician's orientation to their social world.

*Proposition #5* A clinician's experience of client suicidal behaviour will result in modulations of empathetic identification with a suicidal client, from their past life, as appraised before such behaviour, to their current selves.

*Proposition #7* A clinician's direct experience of client suicide, in conjunction with past experiences of suicidal behaviour in personal, collegial or social contexts or as communicated in media, literature or history, will influence how clinician survivors appraise self and others in a suicide-related context, when working or relaxing.

*Proposition #8* A clinician's experience of client suicide will result in decreasing empathetic identifications with colleagues accompanied by feelings of isolation arising from the absence of shared experience.

*Proposition #9* A clinician's experience of client suicide will affect their system of values and beliefs, evidenced in conflicted dimensions of identity. In this context, a clinician survivor's core evaluative dimensions of identity are indicative of their coping resources as they contend with integration of a client suicide experience.

## Significance of research findings

Each clinician survivor's response to a client suicide experience was shown to be idiosyncratic, being unique to that individual clinician, as stated in proposition #1, above. Case study findings demonstrated the individuality within each respondent's identity development in the aftermath. In particular, the extent to which clinician survivors believed themselves to possess the attributes of 'a suicide survivor', while working or relaxing, differed for each individual, ranging from low to very high. This key finding indicated that for effective postvention, each clinician survivor's particular needs, as perceived and expressed by that individual, should be addressed. The remaining empirically derived theoretical propositions, stated above, represent equally significant research outcomes. Each is a discrete statement based in analysis of respondents' identification modulations.

Propositions #2 and #4 emphasise the strong influence upon the clinician survivor of their orientation towards their social world, whether 'defensive' or 'open'.

Propositions #3 and #10 evidence the crucial influence upon the quality of the therapeutic relationship of the clinician's skills in assessment for suicide while maintaining core conditions of empathy, congruence and respect (Wilkins, 2003: 64-84).

Propositions #5 and #7 show that a clinician survivor's engagement with past suicidal behaviour in self and others will affect how they respond currently to a client at risk of suicide.

Proposition #6 resonates with Orbach's (2001: 171) view that the clinician's own level of suicidality is a critical factor in relation to facilitating effective psychotherapy with suicidal clients.

Proposition #8 confirms the empirical evidence that debilitating isolation for the clinician survivor may intensify in the absence of non-judgemental access to colleague clinician survivors' shared experience of client suicide (Gitlin, 2006; Hendin et al., 2000; Hendin et al., 2004).

Finally proposition #9 suggests that the clinician survivor's system of values and beliefs may be so disrupted by their client suicide experience, that their coping ability will be challenged and tested.

The overall significance of this research rests primarily in related consequences for postvention protocols and procedures particularly in organisational settings. Incorporation of these propositions within the design and delivery of postvention support frameworks for clinician survivors, whether directly or by proxy, offers potential to positively transform existing ad hoc practices. This work explains diversity in clinicians' responses when faced with this serious loss experience. This is evidenced in each clinician survivor's identification processes, while paying due regard to acknowledged differences based inter alia in their gender (Grad et al., 1997), therapeutic experience (Hendin et al., 2004) and theoretical orientation (Tillman, 2006).

## Limitations

This doctoral research would have benefitted from comparable quanta of target, comparison and control group members. Thus a total of 33 respondents should ideally have been recruited, 11 for each cohort, instead of 11, 6 and 6 respectively. This limitation was due to a combination of recruitment difficulties and time constraints.

Grad et al. (1997) investigated gender differences in clinicians' responses to patient suicide. Doctoral research respondents were 43.5% (N=10) female and 56.5% (N=13) male. Target group membership was 45.4% (N=5) female and 54.5% (N=6) male; comparison group was 83% (N=5) female and 17% (N=1) male while control group was 100% male. Although respondent gender was not a variable in current research, gender balance for all cohorts might have been preferred.

One respondent (A17; C1; 'Matthew') featured as an eligible member of both target and control groups. This could have adversely influenced research findings although balancing advantages are evident in researcher's ability to access Matthew's identity development from 'control' to 'target' status.

Only one control group member, viz. B1 'Kevin', completed ISA instrument 'B' which did not include the entity 'a suicide survivor' thereby potentially diluting resultant findings.

Late in the doctoral research following completion of respondent interaction, the researcher noted that the inclusion of an entity 'a clinician survivor', in addition to 'a suicide survivor', in ISA instruments might have been helpful. This possible deficiency was acknowledged although, as noted earlier, the ISA model for research investigations is always constrained by the vagaries of instrument construction (Weinreich, 1992).

Doctoral research did not investigate longitudinal aspects. Its findings are therefore restricted to respondents' identity development at the time of interview.

## Directions for future research

Doctoral research did not investigate longer term identity development in clinician survivors. Several respondents had experienced more than one client suicide. A possibility existed for renewing contact with target and comparison group respondents to investigate identity development in the interim.

Postulate #10 referred to empathetic identifications with colleague clinician survivors. This dynamic is a potential research topic although practical difficulties are acknowledged in recruitment of eligible respondents.

The rarity of suicide – 'a very low frequency event' (Gitlin, 2006: 477) – combined with relatively few suicides per clinician means that 'the topic [client suicide] never becomes one that demands an agreed-upon set of coping skills that has been shaped and taught over the generations' (Gitlin, 2006: 478). Further research, in addition to the current study, to address this deficiency is suggested.

## Implications of research findings

Each clinician survivor's identity development in the aftermath of their client's suicide was shown to be idiosyncratic, evidencing unique personal, professional and other elements. Consequently their assimilation process for the experience will reflect elements that are peculiar to each clinician survivor. This means that available individual, family, social and organisational resources should be configured so as to match each clinician survivor's distinct, ascertained, support needs. Proposition #8 (above) in conjunction with postulate #10 (above) points to potential benefits for clinician survivors of a networking facility for mutual, therapeutic interaction. A clinician colleague of a survivor, described in current research as a clinician survivor by proxy will also have an idiosyncratic response to their colleague's loss. Their identified needs should also be similarly addressed.

It is not possible to predict suicide in any individual (Fawcett, 2006). However there is some evidence that a clinician survivor's propensity to suicidal behaviour may match the increased risk for suicidal behaviour in non-clinician survivors (Cain, 1972; Campbell, 2006). The evident implications for effective provision of clinician survivors' support resources should be noted and actioned.

A potentially traumatising aftermath of 'out of the blue' client suicide was experienced in a uniquely personal way by several target research respondents including 'Michael', 'Hannah', 'Ruth', 'Debbie' and 'Matthew'. It is indisputable that for vulnerable clients during each clinician/client interaction, appropriately documented and effective assessment for suicide risk, is essential to protect both clinician and client. Each of these bereaved clinicians benefitted from family, collegial and organisational support. But essential self-support to reinforce that crucial human support in the aftermath also depended upon each clinician's level of competency in effective approaches to assessment for suicide. Education and training in suicide assessment protocols and procedures should therefore be mandatory for trainee clinicians and prioritised in continuous professional development programmes for clinicians.

**Myth:** (fictitious popular idea) Everybody experiences grief in much the same way after someone close to them takes their own life.

**Fallacy:** (misleading argument) Clinicians encounter clients/patients at risk of suicide so rarely that current approaches to education and training in suicide assessment protocols and procedures are considered to be adequate.

### Appendices

A Table 2 PhD Instrument A Entities and Constructs;

B Table 3 PhD Instrument B Entities and Constructs; and

C Table 4 PhD Instrument C Entities and Constructs.

### Table 2:

| | APPENDIX A: IDENTITY STRUCTURE ANALYSIS: INSTRUMENT A: ENTITIES AND CONSTRUCTS | | | |
|---|---|---|---|---|
| | Instrument A: ENTITIES | | Instrument A: CONSTRUCTS | |
| 1 | IDEAL SELF | me as I would like to be | ...takes life for granted | ...wonders what life is all about |
| 2 | CURRENT SELF 1 | me when I'm overwhelmed by life's cruelties | ...carries a terrible responsibility for the fortunes or misfortunes of people with whom s/he had significant relationship or emotional bond | ... believes that people with whom s/he had a significant relationship or emotional bond are entirely responsible for their own circumstances |

| | | | | |
|---|---|---|---|---|
| 3 | CURRENT SELF 2 | me when I feel enhanced by life's wonders | ...believes that suicide demands considerable bravery | ... believes that suicide is the act of a coward |
| 4 | PAST SELF 1 | me before I became a psychotherapist/counsellor | ...feels that safe expression of emotional feelings is always health | ...feels that expression of emotions often indicates lack of control |
| 5 | PAST SELF 2 | me before my client's suicidal behaviour | ...considers that most suicides could be prevented | ...considers that most suicides are unavoidable |
| 6 | PAST SELF 3 | me after my client's suicidal behaviour | ...questions who s/he is | ...remains sure of who s/he is |
| 7 | CURRENT SELF 3 | me when I'm working | ...feels that grief following suicide is like any other | ...feels that grief following suicide is uniquely painful |
| 8 | CURRENT SELF 4 | me when I'm relaxing | ...relies mainly on prescribed medication to relieve psychological pain | ...always uses complementary / alternative remedies where possible |
| 9 | META-PERSPECTIVE 1 | me as colleagues see me | I have warm feelings towards... | I loathe... |
| 10 | META-PERSPECTIVE 2 | me as my clients see me | ...does not think about people committing suicide | ...is highly sensitised to the issue of suicide |

| | | | | |
|---|---|---|---|---|
| 11 | | Mother | ...sticks rigidly to values and beliefs of parents and guardians | ...continues to develop personal values and beliefs |
| 12 | | Father | I feel a special responsibility for the well being of ... | I don't have any particular responsibility for the well-being of... |
| 13 | ADMIRED PERSON | A person I admire (nominate) | ...believes that suicide cannot be predicted by overt behaviour | ...believes that suicide may be anticipated by perceptive observation |
| 14 | DISLIKED PERSON | A person I dislike (nominate) | ...relies on family support at times of threat or crisis | ...does not need family support at difficult times |
| 15 | | A client with suicide ideation | ...believes that depression and suicide are inextricably linked | ...believes suicide can occur 'out of the blue' without depression being evident |
| 16 | | A depressed client | ...does not value some human beings very highly | ...believes each human being is of irreplaceable value |
| 17 | | A client who recovered after serious suicide attempt | I feel distressed by... | I feel encouraged by... |
| 18 | | A client who died by suicide | ...continues to be the person s/he was into the foreseeable future | ...feels that the person s/he was is dead |

| 19 | | My counselling supervisor | ...never feels lonely or uncomfortable when alone with self | ...often feels the need for human contact when alone with self |
|---|---|---|---|---|
| 20 | | A psychiatrist | ...withdraws from human contact | ...seeks and develops human relationships |
| 21 | | My partner/spouse | ...was totally changed by suicide of person with whom s/he had significant relationship or emotional bond | ...was not much affected by suicide of person with whom s/he had significant relationship or emotional bond |
| 22 | | A suicide survivor (person remaining alive after suicide death of individual with whom s/he had significant relationship or emotional bond) | ...feels momentary bouts of psychological discomfort | ...suffers unendurable psychological pain |

## Table 3

| APPENDIX B: IDENTITY STRUCTURE ANALYSIS: INSTRUMENT B: ENTITIES AND CONSTRUCTS | | | | |
|---|---|---|---|---|
| | INSTRUMENT B ENTITIES | | INSTRUMENT B CONSTRUCTS | |
| 1 | IDEAL SELF | me as I would like to be | ...is highly sensitised to the issue of suicide | ...does not think about people committing suicide |
| 2 | CURRENT SELF 1 | me when I'm overwhelmed by life's cruelties | ... was totally changed by suicide of person with whom s/he had significant relationship or emotional bond | ... was not much affected by suicide of person with whom s/he had significant relationship or emotional bond |
| 3 | CURRENT SELF 2 | me when I feel enhanced by life's wonders | ...takes life for granted | ...wonders what life is all about |
| 4 | PAST SELF 1 | me before my professional career experiences | ...remains sure of who s/he is | ...questions who s/he is |
| 5 | PAST SELF 2 | me before my client's suicidal behaviour | ...feels that the person s/he was is dead | ...continues to be the person s/he was into the foreseeable future |
| 6 | PAST SELF 3 | me after my client's suicidal behaviour | ...suffers unendurable psychological pain | ...feels momentary bouts of psychological discomfort |

| # | | | | |
|---|---|---|---|---|
| 7 | CURRENT SELF 3 | me when I'm working | ...carries a terrible responsibility for the fortunes and misfortunes of people with whom s/he had significant relationship or emotional bond | ...believes that people with whom s/he had significant relationship or emotional bond are entirely responsible for their own circumstances |
| 8 | CURRENT SELF 4 | me when I'm relaxing | I feel a special responsibility for the well being of ... | I don't have any particular responsibility for the well-being of ... |
| 9 | METAPERSPECTIVE 1 | me as colleagues see me | ...feels that grief following suicide is uniquely painful | ...feels that grief following suicide is like any other |
| 10 | METAPERSPECTIVE 2 | me as my clients see me | ...relies on family support at times of threat or crisis | ...does not need family support at difficult times |
| 11 | | Mother | ...believes each human being is of irreplaceable value | ...does not value some human beings very highly highly |
| 12 | | Father | ...believes suicide demands considerable bravery | ...believes suicide is the act of a coward |

| 13 | ADMIRED PERSON | a person I admire (nominate) | ...feels that safe expression of emotional feelings is always healthy | ...feels that expression of emotions often indicates lack of control |
|---|---|---|---|---|
| 14 | DISLIKED PERSON | a person I dislike (nominate) | ...withdraws from human contact | ...seeks and develops human relationships |
| 15 | | a client with suicide ideation | I loath... | I have warm feelings towards... |
| 16 | | an ambivalent client | ...considers most suicides could be prevented | ...considers most suicides are unavoidable |
| 17 | | a client who made a serious suicide attempt | ...continues to develop personal values and beliefs | ...sticks rigidly to values and beliefs of parents and guardians |
| 18 | | a client who died by suicide | I feel encouraged by... | I feel distressed by... |
| 19 | | my professional supervisor | ...believes suicide may be anticipated by perceptive observation | ...believes suicide cannot be predicted by overt behaviour |
| 20 | | a psychiatrist | ...never feels lonely or uncomfortable when alone with self | ...often feels the need for human contact when alone with self |

| 21 | | my closest friend | ...relies on prescribed medication to relieve psychological pain | ...uses complementary / alternative remedies where possible |
| 22 | | my partner/ spouse | ...believes depression and suicide are inextricably linked | ...believes suicide can occur 'out of the blue' without depression being evident |

**Table 4**

| APPENDIX C: IDENTITY STRUCTURE ANALYSIS: INSTRUMENT C: ENTITIES AND CONSTRUCTS ||||
| --- | --- | --- | --- |
| | Instrument C ENTITIES | | Instrument C CONSTRUCTS |
| 1 | IDEAL SELF | me as I would like to be | ...does not think about people committing suicide | ...is highly sensitised to the issue of suicide |
| 2 | CURRENT SELF 1 | me when I'm overwhelmed by life's cruelties | ...wonders what life is all about | ...takes life for granted |
| 3 | CURRENT SELF 2 | me when I feel enhanced by life's wonders | ...remains sure of who s/he is | ..questions who s/he is |
| 4 | PAST SELF 1 | me before I started work | ...feels that the person s/he was in the past is dead | ...feels that s/he continues to be essentially the person s/he was into the foreseeable future |

| 5 | PAST SELF 2 | me before I knew about suicide | ...suffers unendurable psychological pain | ...feels momentary bouts of psychological discomfort |
|---|---|---|---|---|
| 6 | PAST SELF 3 | me after I knew about suicide | I feel a special responsibility for the wellbeing of... | I don't have any particular responsibility for the wellbeing of... |
| 7 | CURRENT SELF 3 | me when I'm working | ...feels that grief following suicide is uniquely painful | ...feels that grief following suicide is like any other |
| 8 | CURRENT SELF 4 | me when I'm relaxing | ...does not need family support at difficult times | ...relies on family support at times of threat or crisis |
| 9 | METAPERSPECTIVE 1 | me as my work colleagues see me | ...believes in the irreplaceable value of each human being | ...does not value some human beings very highly |
| 10 | | my parents or guardians | ...believes that suicide is the act of a coward | ...believes that suicide demands considerable bravery |
| 11 | ADMIRED PERSON | a person I admire (nominate) | ...feels that any expression of emotional feelings indicates lack of control | ...feels that safe expression of emotional feelings is healthy and natural |
| 12 | DISLIKED PERSON | a person I dislike (nominate) | ...seeks and develops good relationships | ...withdraws from human contact |

| | | | | |
|---|---|---|---|---|
| 13 | METAPERSPECTIVE 2 | me as my family sees me | I loathe... | I have warm feelings towards... |
| 14 | | a person with suicidal thoughts | ...considers that most suicides could be prevented | ...considers that most suicides cannot be prevented |
| 15 | | a depressed person | ...continues to develop personal values and beliefs | ...sticks rigidly to values and beliefs of parents/guardians |
| 16 | | a person who attempted suicide | I feel distressed by... | I feel encouraged by... |
| 17 | | a person who died by suicide | ...believes that suicide cannot be predicted by overt behaviour | ...believes that suicide may be anticipated by perceptive observation |
| 18 | | a psychiatrist | ...can usually be alone without feeling lonely or uncomfortable | ...cannot be alone for long without feeling the need for human contact |
| 19 | | my friend/partner/spouse (nominate) | ...relies on prescribed medication to relieve psychological pain | ...uses alternative or complementary remedies to relieve psychological pain |

| 20 | | A suicide survivor (or person remaining alive after suicide death of person with whom s/he had a significant relationship or emotional bond) | ...believes suicide can occur 'out of the blue' without evident symptoms of depression | ...believes depression and suicide are inextricably linked |

**References**

Alexander, D. A., Klein, S., Gray, N. M., Dewar, A. G. and Eagles, J. M. (2000) Suicide by patient: questionnaire study of its effects on consultant paychiatrists. British Medical Journal, 320, 1571-1574

American Association of Suicidology (AAS) (2019) Clinician Survivor Task Force. Accessed on 28 November 2020 at https://jmcintos.pages.iu.edu/therapists_mainpg.htm

American Association of Suicidology (AAS) (2007) Available from http://mypage.iusb.edu/~jmcintos/basicinfo.htm Accessed 28 December 2007. Washington, DC: AAS

American Association of Suicidology (AAS) (2007) Available from http://mypage.iusb.edu/~jmcintos/therapists_mainpg.htm Accessed 20 November 2007. Washington, DC: AAS

Andreissen, K. (2014) Suicide Bereavement and Postvention in Major Suicidology Journals: Lessons Learned for the Future of Postvention. Crisis, 2014; Vol. 35(5):338–348

Auge, Andrew J. (2016) "Surviving Death in Heaney's Human Chain." "The Soul Exceeds Its Circumstances": The Later Poetry of Seamus Heaney, edited by Eugene O'Brien, University of Notre Dame Press, NOTRE DAME, INDIANA, 2016, pp. 29–48. JSTOR, www.jstor.org/stable/j.ctvpj77d1.6 Accessed 14 Nov. 2020.

Berman, A. L. (1985) "To engrave herself on all our memories": the impact of suicide on psychotherapists. In B. L. Mishara (ed) The Impact of Suicide. 85-99. New York, NY: Springer

Berman, A. L. (2011). Estimating the population of survivors of suicide: Seeking an evidence base. Suicide and Life-Threatening Behaviour, 41(1), 110–116.

Black, S. and Weinreich, P. (2000) An exploration of counselling identity in counsellors who deal with trauma. MSc dissertation, Unpublished. Jordanstown: University of Ulster

Black, W.E.S. (2002) An exploration of the long-term experience of trauma upon counsellors' identity. PhD dissertation, Unpublished. Jordanstown: University of Ulster

Black, S. and Weinreich, P. (2003) An exploration of counselling identity in counsellors who deal with trauma. In P. Weinreich and W. Saunderson (eds.) Analysing Identity: cross-cultural, societal and clinical contexts. London: Routledge

British Association for Counselling (1996) Code of ethics and practice for counsellors. Rugby, Warks: BAC

Brown, H. N. (1989) Patient suicide and therapists in training. In D. Jacobs and H. N. Brown (eds.) Suicide: understanding and responding. 415-434. Madison, CT: International Universities Press

Cain, A. C. (ed.) (1972) Survivors of suicide. Illinois: Charles C. Thomas

Campbell, F. R. (2006) Spiritual and ethical issues survivors face following suicide. Pages 16-19. In IAS (2006) Proceedings of the Tenth Annual Conference – Spiritual & Ethical Issues of Suicide. October 2005. Armagh City Hotel, Armagh: The Irish Association of Suicidology

Cerel, J., Brown, M.M., Maple, M., Singleton, M., van de Venne, J., Moore, M. and Flaherty, C. (2019) How many people are exposed to suicide? Not six. Suicide and Life-Threatening Behaviour, 49(2), 530-534

Chemtob, C. M., Hamada, R. S., Bauer, G. and Kinney, B. (1988a) Patients' suicides: frequency and impact on psychiatrists. American Journal of Psychiatry, 145(2), 224-228

Chemtob, C. M., Hamada, R. S., Bauer, G. and Torigoe, R. Y. (1988b) Patients suicide: frequency and impact on psychologists. Professional Psychology: Research and Practice, 19(4), 416-420

Cotton, R.G., Drake, R.E., Whitaker, A. and Potter, J. (1983) Guidelines for dealing with suicide on a psychiatric inpatient unit. Hospital and Community Psychiatry, 34, 55-59

Cryan, E.M.J., Kelly, P. and McCaffrey (1995) The experience of patient suicide among Irish psychiatrists. Psychiatric Bulletin, 19, 4-7

Darden, A. (2008) Complicated grief as it relates to client suicide: a qualitative study of clinical psychologists. Psy.D. dissertation. Unpublished. Colorado: University of the Rockies

Dressler, D.M., Prusoff, B., Mark, H. and Shapiro, D. (1975) Clinician attitudes to the suicide attempter. Journal of Nervous and Mental Disease, 160(2), 146-155

Farberow, N. L. (1996) Grief and mourning after suicide. Accessed on 19 December 1999 at http://www.afsp.org/research/Fawcett - American Foundation for Suicide Prevention Southeast: American Foundation for Suicide Prevention:

Farberow, N. L. (2001) The therapist-clinician as survivor. In O. T. Grad (ed.) Suicide risk and protective factors in the new millennium. 11-20. Ljubljana: Cankarjevdom

Farberow, N.L. and McKinnon, D. (1975) Prediction of suicide: a replication study. Journal of Personality Assessment, 39, 497-501

Fawcett, J. (2006) Depression disorders. In R.I. Simon and R.E. Hales (eds.) Textbook of suicide assessment and management. 255-275. Washington, DC: American Psychiatric Publishing

Fitzpatrick, S. J., Hooker, C. and Kerridge, I. (2014) Suicidology as a social practice. Social Epistemology. Online first on 12 March 2014. Accessed 27 May 2021 at http://imhlk.com/wp-content/uploads/2019/09/suicidology-as-social

Foley, S. R. and Kelly, B.D. (2007) When a patient dies by suicide: incidence, implications and coping strategies. Advances in Psychiatric Treatment, 13, 134-138

Foster, B. (1987) Suicide and the impact on the therapist. In J. L. Sacksteder, D. P. Schwartz and Y Akabane, Attachment and the therapeutic process: essays in honour of Otto Allen Will, Jr. 197-204. Madison, CT: International Universities Press

Gaffney, P., Russell, K., Collins, K., Bergen, A., Halligan, P., Cahill, T. and Maguire, J. (2002) The impact of client suicide on front-line staff in the North Eastern Health Board. In Proceedings of the 7th Annual Conference (Sept 2002) of the Irish Association of Suicidology (IAS), Belfast. 80 -101. Castlebar, Co Mayo, Ireland: IAS

Gitlin, M. J. (1999) A psychiatrist's reaction to a patient's suicide. American Journal of Psychiatry, 156(10), 1630-1634

Gitlin, M.J. (2006) Psychiatrist reactions to patient suicide. In R.I. Simon and R.E. Hales (eds.) Textbook of suicide assessment and management. 477-492. Washington, DC: American Psychiatric Publishing

Gorkin, M. (1985) On the suicide of one's patient. Bulletin of the Menninger Clinic, 49, 1-9

Grad, O. T. (1996) Suicide: how to survive as a survivor? Crisis, 17(3), 136-142

Grad, O.T., Zavasnik, A. and Groleger, U. (1997) Suicide of a patient: gender differences in bereavement reactions of therapists. Suicide and Life-Threatening Behaviour, 27(4), 379-386

Grad, O. T., and Zavasnik, A. (1998) The caregiver's reaction after suicide of a patient. In R. J. Kosky, H. S. Eshkevari, R. D. Goldney and R. Hassan (eds.) Suicide prevention: the global context. 287-291. New York, NY: Kluwer Academic

Grad, O. T. and Michel, K. (2005) Therapists as client suicide survivors. In K. M. Weiner (ed.) Therapeutic and legal issues for therapists who have survived a client suicide. 71-81. New York, NY: Haworth Press

Gulfi, A., Castelli Dransart, D. A., Heeb, J-L and Gutjahr, E. (2010) The impact of patient suicide on the professional reactions and practices of mental health caregivers and social workers. Crisis, 31(4), 202-210

Harré, Rom (2003) Foreword. In P. Weinreich and W Saunderson (eds.) Analysing Identity: Cross-cultural, societal and clinical contexts. xix-xx. London: Routledge

Hendin, H., Lipschitz, A., Maltsberger, J. T., Haas, A. P. and Wynecoop, S. (2000) Therapists' reactions to patients' suicides. American Journal of Psychiatry, 157(12), 2022-2027

Hendin, H., Haas, A. P., Maltsberger, J. T., Szanto, M. D. and Rabinowicz, H. (2004) Factors contributing to therapists' distress after the suicide of a patient. American Journal of Psychiatry, 161(8), 1442-1446

Hickey, G. and Kipping, C. (1996) A multi-stage approach to the coding of data from open-ended questions. Nurse Researcher, 4(1), 81-91

Hjelmeland, H., Dieserud, G., Dyregrov, K., Knizek, B. l. and Leenaars, A. A. (2012) Psychological autopsy studies: are they methodologically flawed? Death Studies, 36, 605-626

Horn, P. J. (1994) Therapists' psychological adaptation to client suicide. Psychotherapy, 31(1), 190-195

IAS (2006) Proceedings of the Tenth Annual Conference – Spiritual & Ethical Issues of Suicide. October 2005. 1-190. Armagh City Hotel, Armagh: The Irish Association of Suicidology

Jobes, D. A. and Maltsberger, J. T. (1995) The hazards of treating suicidal patients. In M. B. Sussman (ed.) A perilous calling: the hazards of psychotherapy practice. 200-214. New York, NY: John Wiley

Joiner, T. (2005) Why people die by suicide. Cambridge, MA: Harvard Univ Press

Kahn, M. (2001) Between therapist and client: the new relationship. New York, NY: Henry Holt

Kahne, M. J. (1968a) Suicide among patients in mental hospitals: a study of the psychiatrists who conducted their psychotherapy. Psychiatry, 31(1), 32-43

Kahne, M. J. (1968b) Suicide in mental hospitals: a study of the effects of personnel and patient turnover. Journal of Health and Social Behaviour, 9(3), 255-266

Kapoor, A. (2008) Client suicide and its effect on the therapist. In S. Palmer (ed) Suicide: strategies and interventions for reduction and prevention. 124-136. London: Routledge

Klapp, O. E. (1969) Collective search for identity. New York, NY: Holt

Kleespies, P.M., Penk, W. E. and Forsyth, J. P. (1993) The stress of patient suicidal behaviour during clinical training: incidence, impact and recovery. Professional Psychology: Research and Practice, 24(3), 293-303

Lange, A. (1989) Identifications, perceived cultural distance and stereotypes in Yugoslav and Turkish youths in Stockholm. In K. Liebkind (ed.) New identities in Europe: immigrant ancestry and the ethnic identity of youth. 169-218. Aldershot: Gower.

Litman, R. E. (1965) When patients commit suicide. American Journal of Psychotherapy, 19(4), 570-576

MacKinnon, D. R. and Farberow, N. L. (1976) An assessment of the utility of suicide prediction. Suicide and Life-threatening Behaviour. 1976. Summer. 6(2), 86-91

Maltsberger, J. T. (1995) A career plundered. In M. B. Sussman (ed.) A perilous calling: the hazards of psychotherapy practice. 226-234. New York, NY: John Wiley

Maltsberger, J. T. and Buie, D. H. (1974) Countertransference hate in the treatment of suicidal patients. Archives of General Psychiatry, 30, 625-633

Marshall, K. A. (1980) When a patient commits suicide. Suicide and Life-threatening Behaviour, 10, 29-40

McLeod, J. (1997) Doing counselling research. London: Sage

Meade, J. F. (1999) A counsellor's journey of loss and healing after losing a client to suicide. Journal of the California Alliance for the Mentally Ill, 10(2), 31-32

Misch, D. A. (2003) When a psychiatry resident's patient commits suicide: transference trials and tribulations. Journal of the American Academy of Psychoanalysis and Dynamic Psychiatry, 31(3), 459-475

O'Connor, R.C. (2011) The Integrated Motivational-Volitional Model of Suicidal Behaviour (IMV). Accessed on 18 July 2017 at http://www.suicideresearch.info/the-imv

O'Keeffe, P. (1999) Research methods: Coursework assignment: Conduct an in-depth interview, transcribe it and write a report. (Unpublished report). Postgraduate Diploma in Guidance and Counselling, University of Ulster, Jordanstown, N Ireland

O'Keeffe, P., MSc (2001) "Suicidology, Counselling and Identity Exploration: an investigation of postvention strategies for suicide survivors." A dissertation submitted for MSc in Guidance and Counselling. Unpublished. Jordanstown, N Ireland: Ulster University. [Accessible at www.philipokeeffe.com; or http://www.identityexploration.com/Completed_ISA]

O'Keeffe, P. (2006) Effective counselling for suicide survivors. Pages 20-24. In IAS (2006) Proceedings of the Tenth Annual Conference – Spiritual & Ethical Issues of Suicide. October 2005. Armagh City Hotel, Armagh: The Irish Association of Suicidology.

O'Keeffe, P., PhD (2010) "Client suicide and clinician identity: an investigation of identity development in clinician survivors of client suicide". A dissertation submitted for degree doctor of philosophy (PhD). Unpublished. Jordanstown, N Ireland: Ulster University. [Accessible at www.philipokeeffe.com; or http://www.identityexploration.com/Completed_ISA]

O'Keeffe, P. (2011) Outline for book chapter based upon PhD dissertation "Client suicide and clinician identity: an investigation of identity development in clinician survivors of client suicide". 11 June 2011. Unpublished

O'Keeffe, P (2012) Notes for an address entitled – "Application of research findings to families and healthcare professionals bereaved in the aftermath of suicide" – to medical staff at Downe Hospital, South Eastern Social Care Trust, N Ireland. March 2012. Unpublished

Orbach, I. (2001) Therapeutic empathy with the suicidal wish: principles of therapy with suicidal individuals. American Journal of Psychotherapy, 55(2), 166-184

Palmer, S. (ed.) (2008) Suicide: strategies and interventions for reduction and prevention. London: Routledge

Phillips, M. (1995) Patient suicide. British Medical Journal, 310, 1542-1543

Pokorny, A.D. (1983) Prediction of suicide in psychiatric patients: report of a prospective study. Arch Gen Psychiatry, 40, 249-257

Pokorny, A.D. (1993) Suicide prediction revisited. Suicide and Life-threatening Behaviour, 23, 1-10

Pope, K.S. and Tabachnik, B.G. (1993) Therapists' anger, hate, fear and sexual feelings: national survey of therapist responses, client characteristics, critical events, formal complaints and training. Professional Psychology: Research and Practice, 24(2), 142-152

Reizler, K. (1950) Man: mutable and immutable. Chicago, Ill: Regnery

Resnik, H.L.P. (1969) Psychological re-synthesis: a clinical approach to the survivors of a death by suicide. International Psychiatric Clinics, 6, 213-224

Rogers, J.R., Gueulette, C.M., Abbey-Hines, J., Carney, J.V. and Werth, Jr., J.L. (2001) Rational suicide: an empirical investigation of counsellor attitudes. Journal of Counselling and Development, 79(3), 365-372

Rubin, H. L. (1990) Surviving a suicide in your practice. In S. J. Blumenthal and D. J. Kupfer (eds.) Suicide over the life cycle: risk factors, assessment and treatment of suicidal patients. 619-636 Washington, DC: American Psychiatric Press

Ruskin, R., Sakinofsky, L., Bagby, R. M., Dickens, S. and Sousa, G. (2004) Impact of patient suicide on psychiatrists and psychiatric trainees. Academic Psychiatry, 28(2), 104-110

Scheurich, N. (2001) Medicine and the arts. Academic Medicine, 76(10), 1036

Shannon, P. (2000) Bereaved by suicide. Surrey: Cruse Bereavement Care,

Shneidman, E. S. (1969) Prologue: Fifty-eight years. In E. Shneidman (ed.) On the nature of suicide (pp. 1–30). San Francisco, CA: Jossey-Bass

Shneidman, E. S. and others (1971) "The Management of the Presuicidal, Suicidal, and Postsuicidal Patient." Annals of Internal Medicine 75, no. 3 (1971): 441–58

Shneidman, E. S. (1972) Foreword. In A. C. Cain (Ed.) Survivors of suicide. Oxford, UK: Charles C Thomas

Shneidman, E. S. (1974) Deaths of Man. New York, NY: Quadrangle/The New York Times Book Co

Shneidman, E. S. (1985) Definition of suicide. Northvale, NJ: Aronson

Shneidman, E.S. (1993) Suicide as psychache. Journal of Nervous and Mental Disease. v181:145–147

Shneidman, E.S. (1996) The suicidal mind. Oxford: Oxford University Press

Simon, R.I. (1998) Psychiatrists awake! Suicide risk assessments are all about a good night's sleep. Psychiatric Annals, 28, 479-485

Simon, R.I. and Hales, R.E. (2006) Textbook of suicide assessment and management. Appendix: APA Practice Guideline, 577-597. Washington, DC: American Psychiatric Publishing

Soderland, J. (1999) When clients kill themselves. New Therapist, 2. Accessed on 22 July 2008 at http://www.newtherapist.com/suicide.htm

Stillion, J.M. and McDowell, E. E. (1996) Suicide across the lifespan. New York, NY: Taylor and Francis

Tillman, J. (2006) When a patient commits suicide: an empirical study of psychoanalytic clinicians. International Journal of Psychoanalysis, 87, 159-177

Valente, S. M. (2003) Aftermath of a patient's suicide: a case study. Perspectives in Psychiatric Care, 39(1), 17-22

Watts, D. and Morgan, G. (1994) Malignant alienation. British Journal of Psychiatry, 164, 11-15

Weinreich, P. (1992) Identity Exploration Workshop Notes. Jordanstown: Ulster University

Weinreich, P. and Ewart, S. (1997) Identity exploration using Identity Structure Analysis: IDEXwin computer software operation with MS Windows. Belfast: Ulster University

Weinreich, P and Ewart, S. (1999a) IDEX-Basic for Windows Version. Identity exploration computer software for basic case studies. Belfast: University of Ulster

Weinreich, P. and Saunderson, W. (eds.) (2003) Analysing Identity – Cross cultural, societal and clinical contexts. London: Routledge

Weinreich, P. (2003b) Identity exploration: theory into practice. In P. Weinreich and W. Saunderson (eds.) Analysing Identity: Cross-cultural, societal and clinical contexts. 77-110. London: Routledge

Wikipedia (2020) Postvention. Accessed on 17 November 2020 at https://en.wikipedia.org/wiki/Postvention

Wilkins, P. (2003) Person-centred therapy in focus. London: Sage

Wrobleski, A. (2002) Suicide Survivors: A Guide for Those Left Behind. Minneapolis, MN: SAVE.

Wurst, F.M., Kunz, I., Skipper, G., Wolfersdorf, M., Beine, K.H. and Thon, N. (2011) The therapist's reaction to a patient's suicide: results of a survey and implications for healthcare professionals' wellbeing. Crisis, 32(2), 99-105

***

## Chapter 6
# Integration – society's disintegrated response to suicide?

### Integration – What it Means

What does 'integration' mean in relation to suicide? I've pondered that since I sketched an outline for this book, while reflecting upon my life experience in observing the aftermath of suicide in Belfast and further afield. The closest I can get to what 'integration' herein might mean is in considering how ecological studies, in relation to conservation:

'address the how and why of integrating human well-being into conservation practice focusing predominantly on local perspectives. Authors focus on how engagement with local populations is driven, implicitly or explicitly, by the pursuit of a more just conservation and recognition of local voices in deciding their fate' (Biedenweig and Gross-Camp, 2018).

Hence, paraphrasing the above in relation to suicide, I hope to attempt to examine 'the how and why of integrating human well-being into society's response in the aftermath of suicide, focusing predominantly on local perspectives . . . how engagement with local populations is driven, implicitly or explicitly, by the pursuit of a more just response and recognition of local voices in deciding that response.'

### Aftermath of Death by Suicide

Our personal family history during the 1980's demonstrated clearly that each suicide event, whether fatal or non-fatal was, and is, essentially unknowable except, and then only partially, to the actor: indeed the aftermath to each suicide remains for ever unknown by the actor, now deceased. Here, I am less concerned with non-fatal attempts at self-destruction, since 'where there's life, there's hope', perhaps, for the 'attempt' actor. What interests me therefore, as mentioned above, is the aftermath of death by suicide for suicide survivors: "A suicide survivor is someone who experiences a high level of self-perceived psychological, physical, and/or social distress for a considerable length of time after exposure to the suicide of another person" (Jordan, J.R. and McIntosh, J.L, 2011: 7).

**Society's Response**

The issue of euthanasia, or so-called lawful assisted dying, a somewhat oxymoronic term, is also considered to be out with this discussion. In Western societies, where suicide, excluding the crime of aiding and abetting another's suicide, was decriminalized decades ago, criminal justice systems become inactive as soon as a death is believed, either beyond reasonable doubt, or on the balance of probabilities, to be by suicide, without any third party involvement. Thus, any response in the aftermath remains with survivors and civil authorities. This section, therefore, will examine that response, focusing upon the degree of integration, if any, therein between the civil authorities and survivors, as well as community and voluntary organisations, and concerned individuals including professionals, academics and researchers. The apparent disconnect between society's response to increased incidence of suicide and any realistic hopes of reducing deaths by suicide, seems to be evidence of its (i.e. society's) disintegrated approach, both strategically and tactically. It's almost as if genuine, praiseworthy activities ostensibly aimed at preventing suicide, may not have objectives that always include saving vulnerable lives.

Why this may be so is not easy to understand. One way to investigate is to check out the identities of those who work in the field: suicide prevention personnel – volunteers, survivors, clinicians, counsellors/psychotherapists, social workers, researchers, academics, and teachers: then to consider the contrast with the rest of humanity, many or most of whom model themselves, albeit subconsciously perhaps, on all but one of the characters featured in the Good Samaritan parable (World English Bible, 2000), and in relation to suicide, pass by on the other side.

## Passing by Suicide on the Other Side

Recall that the Samaritan tribe was detested by Jews in Jesus's Palestine. Why? We don't need to know the detail of this historical enmity. Let's just call it racism. One interpretation of the thousand years of their mutual loathing, Jews of Samaritans and Samaritans of Jews, is offered by U.S. Catholic Magazine's website:

'By the first century C.E., the worst thing you can call a Jew is a Samaritan—which is what Jesus' detractors call him in John's gospel.

'How daring, then, for Jesus to tell a story about a good Samaritan! To share an extended conversation with a Samaritan woman he meets at a well, then to welcome her whole community as they seek an encounter with him. Citizens of Judea had spent centuries walling Samaritans out of their society with laws and mistreatment. Jesus raises the possibility that it's time to admit these outsiders. A thousand years of bickering and division, perhaps, is enough. When the first-generation church sends Philip to evangelize in Samaria, it's a bold and shattering proposition. And it results in "great joy in that city" (Acts 8:8).

'We hate our enemies for a lot of reasons: politics, history, religion, blood, strangeness, a sense of grievance, an inherited disapproval.

'We hate people because they're not like us, and that makes us uncomfortable. We resent what they've taken from us or what they might take if we give them a chance. Hate begins somewhere. So does acceptance.'

https://uscatholic.org/articles/202005/why-didnt-the-jews-and-samaritans-get-along/

A possible connection, in the opinion of this author, between a person at risk of suicide, commonly but imprecisely referred to as a suicidal person, and a first century CE Samaritan rests in their shared status, being feared, hated and rejected by most of humanity, who prefer to 'pass by on the other side'.

## A Rare Exception

Rarely, as in the following example, does an 'ordinary person', as media too frequently refer to a so-called non-celebrity who has strayed across media's 'story-seeking' obsessive gaze, achieve column inches as a 21st century, modern day Samaritan, being celebrated as a hero. In November 2018, a 66 year old father (P1McC) of two daughters, was jailed for three years after pleading guilty to sexually assaulting them and their neighbour (OL), when all three children were still at primary school. The abuse lasted from 1987 to 2000. Each waived their right to anonymity to have the perpetrator named. One daughter (P2McC) saved her father's life when she found him hanging in a shed, after he learned that gardai had received a complaint against him. She then placed herself under her father to take his weight and held him up until gardai arrived and cut him down. The other daughter (JMcC) said she had only decided to make a complaint after learning that the sisters' school-friend (OL) had done so. I can find no evidence that this courageous woman received any award in recognition of her remarkable life-saving endeavour (The Irish Times, 2018). (Afternote: Had her father (P1McC) chosen to drown himself and she (P2McC) had 'dived in' to rescue him, she would have been eligible – presumably.)

**Unaddressed Countertransference Hate**

Earlier, in chapter 5 above, I referred to issues around the possible existence in clinicians' attitudes to suicidal clients of 'unaddressed countertransference hate' (UCH) (Maltsberger and Bui, 1974) containing a mixture of aversion and malice. Peter Weinreich linked this to what he described as one's evaluation of another: 'the extent to which another is favoured or disfavoured' in relation to one's value system (Weinreich and Saunderson (eds.) 2003: 89). Simply put, such an adverse mindset in a clinician conflicted with a core condition for effective psychotherapy: acceptance or unconditional positive regard (Rogers, 1980/95).

Incidentally, in chapter 5, in the paragraph headed 'What Happened', the research respondent 'J' reported a UCH-related response, by her psychiatrist (Dr D), to her, his vulnerable patient, a survivor of a life-threatening overdose. Described by this author as 'his disappointing lack of empathy', it's clear that his remarks: "I've one word of advice for you and that is to stop feeling sorry for yourself" also evidenced the disappointing presence of underlying UCH, in an experienced medical professional.

## Unacknowledged Unaddressed Countertransference Hate (UUCT)

Clinicians engage professionally with vulnerable people, a number of whom may be at risk of suicide. However, most of humanity are not 'clinicians'. A handful of compassionate people from various backgrounds, engage in helping others through print and, increasingly, social media. I recall one so-called 'agony aunt' (MF) – an attractive, middle-aged and widely respected minor, female celebrity – who was tasked in a lengthy weekly column with addressing dilemmas in family life, in a non-tabloid weekend newspaper column. Knowingly or otherwise, she displayed a negative attitude, resonant of unacknowledged unaddressed countertransference hate (UUCH), in advising a widow whose husband had taken his own life, leaving her 'struggling to see how life can be enjoyable again now that my husband and best friend is gone'. MF wrote in reply to this grieving, childless 40 year old, in an article headed 'My husband took his own life. I can't face being on my own . . .':

'I'm so sorry. What a terrible loss for you to endure [but] there are plenty of people who offer counselling (The Samaritans is on 116 123). Your husband was suffering from depression, an illness that impacts heavily on the people around. You describe him as your best friend, but I sincerely hope you have others. Although your husband has permanently concluded his own suffering, the residue has unfortunately been passed to you. *Taking your own life is an irrational, desperate, tragic act, but it's also an extremely selfish choice. It's rarely embarked on with mental clarity so it's important to acknowledge the terrible legacy those left behind are lumbered with.* I urge you to seek . . . professional help [to] negotiate the aftermath of this trauma. The guilt you are feeling is as entirely natural as it is absolutely unfounded and a good therapist will help you realise that and make better sense of *his unthinkable act'* (The Observer Magazine, 2018).

Following an internet search, I found an online version of MF's article, that included (some) of the response cited above. This was edited and extended, as follows:

i) The reference to counselling and the Samaritans (116 123) was removed. The Samaritans are a listening organisation that offer neither counselling nor advice;

ii) The two inappropriate, judgmental, evidence-free, generalised sentences (in italics above) that resonated with UCH, were deleted;

iii) The evidence-free description of a human's self-destruction as 'his unthinkable act' (in italics above) was retained; and

iv) Support information, as follows, was added:

*In the UK, Samaritans can be contacted on 116 123 or email jo@samaritans.org. In the US, the National Suicide Prevention Line is 1-800-273-8255.In Australia, the crisis support service Lifeline is 13 11 14. Other international suicide helplines can be found at www.befrienders.org

It is clearly unfair and unreasonable to assess MF's value system, based upon her stated attitude to death by suicide in a one-off article. The online version generated 513 'comments' from readers and so it could not be said to have been uninfluential. Each of us, in a psychological sense, is a complex, largely unfathomable maelstrom of current feelings, thoughts, attitudes, aspirations, behaviours and experiences. Also, we are emotionally affected by recollections of the same in our unreliable memory of half-remembered past feelings, et seq. So we cannot know anything about MF's current value system due to the influence upon that system of her life experiences since May 2018. So far I have not found any views on suicide expressed by MF before or since then.

## Community and Voluntary Suicide Prevention Efforts

During Northern Ireland's civil and religious conflict from 1966 to 1998, the absence of governmental support services gave rise to a network of community and voluntary organisations, mainly staffed by volunteers including survivors of bereavement by suicide, some formally qualified but mostly unqualified. These good people attempted to bridge, during the mayhem that then dominated Northern Ireland society, an unaddressed societal need for therapeutic counselling resources. Ironically, levels of reported deaths by suicide diminished somewhat at times during this period (Registrar General Northern Ireland - Annual Reports). When hostilities ended and an uneasy peace settled post-Belfast/Good Friday Agreement (1998), an upward trend in suicide death statistics was noted by researchers in the following decade and a half (Tomlinson, 2012). Indeed this research finding, based upon comprehensive case study evidence, demonstrated that while legacy issues continue to divide the political discourse in Northern Ireland, it's difficult to envisage much change regarding the incidence of suicide here until this 'damned' generation's needs are recognized and acted upon:

'The main finding of the case study is that the cohort of children and young adults growing up in the worst years of violence now have the highest suicide rates and the most rapidly increasing rates. These generations were the most acculturated to division and conflict, and to externalised expressions of aggression. The consequence of peace is that such expressions of aggression and violence are no longer socially approved. They become internalised instead' (Tomlinson, 2012).

**Unreliable Statistics**

It might have been hoped two decades into the 21st century, that 'counting suicides' was a more straightforward element of conventional suicide prevention endeavours. That this is not so was recently reported. Counting suicides in Northern Ireland has for some time been a governmental task performed by the Northern Ireland Statistics and Research Agency (NISRA). However in October 2020, an unintentional byproduct of a joint review, by NISRA statisticians and coroners of the NI Courts Service of deaths registered as suicide in 2019, was a welcome, albeit technical, reduction in the extent of suicide's perceived attrition in Northern Ireland for that year. As mentioned above in chapter 4: Miscounting Suicides, 86 deaths registered as 'undetermined event' fatalities, viz. where insufficient evidence was available to rule out suicide intent by the deceased, and that included drug overdoses or were drugs related, were reviewed and re-analysed, using 'additional scrutiny' by coroners. They decided that 57 out of the 86 should be reclassified as 'accidental deaths', meriting exclusion from 2019's suicide statistics for that calendar year. Thus NI's suicide 2019 statistic was reduced by 57, from 254 to 197 (BBC, 2020). Further 'additional scrutiny' was promised for both earlier and later reported NISRA suicide statistics.

There is an added significance in this revelation of systemic bungling in relation to certifying suicide deaths in Northern Ireland: this relates to the efficacy of suicide prevention efforts by volunteers and professionals. No one so far has been able to demonstrate conclusively 'what works' effectively, efficiently and economically, in relation to eliminating suicide in human societies. This aspiration would require additional evidence of progress in 'integrating human well-being into society's response in the aftermath of suicide, as mentioned above at paragraph 1, 'Integration – what it means'.

This author considers that much, if not most charitable, well-intentioned engagement with vulnerable individuals by volunteers located in agencies and organisations in Northern Ireland devoted to helping, is both laudable and worth encouraging and supporting in relation to increasing human welfare and well-being here. Much publicity is given to 'sloganised' encouragement to vulnerable individuals, perhaps on the edge of despair. Examples include 'It's good to talk'; 'Look after your mental health'; and 'There's help out there – just ask for it' and such like. This kind of largely government funded publicity campaigning no doubt channels some vulnerable people towards helping organisations and agencies. However, I can find no evidence of a provable relationship between such activities and interactions, and any measurable reduction in the incidence of suicide here.

This disappointing but realistic insight is accepted in the N Ireland government's latest iteration of its suicide prevention strategy policy document:

"Protect Life 2 - Suicide Prevention Strategy: Protect Life 2 [2019-24] is a long-term strategy for reducing suicides and the incidence of self-harm with action delivered across a range of Government departments, agencies, and sectors. It recognises that no single organisation or service is able to influence all the complex interacting factors that lead someone to harming themselves or, ultimately, to taking their own life" (Protect Life 2, 2019).

Unfortunately, at first sight what is missing in this 'how to prevent suicide here' strategy statement is any recognition that ultimate responsibility for our own and our neighbour's life, livelihood and well-being rests with each one of Northern Ireland's citizens (Population: 1.8 million). This contrasts starkly in the time of Covid-19 with our UK/Ireland 'all in it together' mantra regarding avoidance of lethal infection via 'the Covid-19 plague' that has been repeated ad nauseam since its outbreak in early 2020 by government, political parties, community leaders, media actors, 'Uncle Tom Cobley' and all. The question therefore remains yawningly open as to how all N Ireland citizens might yet be enrolled, encouraged and motivated to develop raised levels of awareness about how to save a life at risk of suicide.

It is proposed now, with 'integration' in mind, to assess the outcomes of efforts by professionals in suicide prevention by way of their direct engagement with patients and clients regarded as 'at risk of suicide'.

**Suicide Prevention Efforts, and Outcomes, by 'Clinicians', Including Counsellors/Psychotherapists, Social Workers, Researchers, Academics, and Teachers**

Every neophyte Samaritans' volunteer is advised during their practical training regarding the importance, when appropriate, of asking 'the suicide question' viz. 'Are you thinking of suicide?' or 'Have you had thoughts about suicide?' - when engaging with callers or visitors to the organisation's branches. Asking someone directly if they have thought about suicide can bring relief, because someone else finally acknowledges how badly they are feeling (JED Foundation, 2019). Note that the Samaritans (2024) in UK/Ireland is a listening organisation: volunteers do not purport to engage in counselling or psychotherapy: perhaps they do, when it is helpful, use some basic 'counselling skills' including reflection, clarification, and accurate empathy. But their typical interactions with callers or visitors are time-limited, unplanned and one-off in nature. The contrast with a clinician's relationship with a vulnerable patient/client could not be more complete: longer-term, scheduled, sequential and potentially long-lasting.

## Roush et al. (2018)

Roush et al (2018) investigated almost 300 mental health professionals, most of whom identified as social workers, psychologists and/or counsellors, in relation to their 'fear [of] suicide-related outcomes' and/or their 'comfort in working with suicidal individuals' (p56). Worryingly, up to one third (31.1%) of these professionals, most (87.6%) of whom were educated to master's or doctoral degree level, with an average of more than 14 years experience, admitted in a self-reported, anonymous online survey that they did not 'routinely ask every patient about suicide ideation at a first appointment' (p59). Finally, over a fifth (22.1%) of respondents reported ensuring 'that they had a "no-suicide contract" in the medical record for individuals ... with suicide ideation' (p60). The latter practice has no empirical support regarding suicide risk management (p62) (Hendin el al., 2006).

## Hendin et al. (2006)

Hendin et al. (2006) acknowledged the complexity of psychotherapeutic treatment for suicidal patients (p67). They examined respondents' therapeutic practices in the cases of 36 patients who died by suicide while in psychotherapy and on medication. Of the 36 respondent clinician therapists, 29 were psychiatrists, of whom 4 were trainees, 5 were psychologists of whom 4 were trainees, and 2 were social workers. These respondents completed 'clinical, medication and psychological questionnaires and wrote detailed case narratives' (p67). Six critical problems were identified in these cases:

i) Poor communication with another therapist involved in the case
ii) Permitting patients or relatives to control the therapy
iii) Avoidance of issues related to sexuality
iv) Ineffective or coercive actions resulting from the therapists' anxieties about a patient's potential suicide
v) Not recognising the meaning of the patient's communications
vi) Untreated or undertreated symptoms.

The researchers concluded that these cases 'illuminate common problems therapists face in working with suicidal patients' (p67). They stated that their detailed recommendations 'will help address a clearly apparent gap ... an unmet need for education (p67) ... in therapists' clinical training in psychotherapy with suicidal patients' (p71).

## John Terry Maltsberger et al. (2015)

John Terry Maltsberger (1933-2016) was a colleague researcher for the above referenced paper by Hendin et al. (2006). He was regarded by his fellow researchers as a suicidologist of the highest repute. Goldblatt et al. (2019) cited two memorable extracts from a peer-reviewed paper (Maltsberger et al., 2015) published not long before Maltsberger's death, that exemplify the need, in my opinion, to consider abandoning the current, simplistic 'mental disorder' mantra as the principal, but relatively useless, explicator for human suicidal behaviour:

'The emphasis on counting and statistical analysis of larger bodies of data continues to increase. While 50 years ago [1965] there was a fuller emphasis given to individual idiosyncrasies of patients, this is no longer true. Detail, not overall gestalt, rules the day. The era of checklists, questionnaires and tables is full upon us' (Maltsberger et al., 2015: 388).

'... "not everything that counts can be counted, and not everything that can be counted counts ..." (Cameron, 1963). Counting is of course indispensable, but sometimes it can get in the way of deeper more productive thinking. The human condition cannot be reduced to a series of risk factors and correlations; the drive to empiricism, as helpful as it is on the one hand, risks drowning out other ways of understanding people, on the other ... we need to free ourselves from the constriction of general, homogenising diagnosis. We need more reports that reflect the deeper experiences of our patients, including more qualitative research' (Maltsberger et al., 2015: 389)

## Conclusions

In this chapter, I have tried to survey some of the 'suicide prevention' landscape in Northern Ireland. Suicidology remains without mainstream educational courses here at senior school, college and university level. Yet, no one denies that society here urgently desires to tackle the catastrophic legacy that each suicide generates. Surely suicide is far too important, vital, complex and idiosyncratic for weekend, etc. short courses, ditto occupation-related modules, a two hour lecture on counselling diploma courses, etc. that do no more than, perhaps, enable a handful of people to begin to think about considering one's own level of suicidality (what that might mean . . .) and thus beginning to develop accurate empathy for those (viz. clients, patients, family members, neighbours, fellow citizens, etc., etc.) at potential risk for suicide.

Sadly current disintegration in policy and practice regarding saving lives at risk of self-destruction seems ever more distant from society-wide integration of policy and practice through popular involvement and activity. The question remains: are we all in it together – suicide prevention – or not?

**Myth:** (fictitious popular idea) The internet is a reliable source of information about how to prevent suicide.

**Fallacy:** (misleading argument) Diagnosable mental disorder underlies all human suicidal behaviour.

# REFERENCES

Acts 8.8 (2020) Extracted from New Testament and Psalms. Page 312. The Gideon International. Leics., England.

BBC (2020) NI suicide rate expected to fall following review. Online article by Karen Atkinson. Accessed 15 October 2020 at http://www.bbc.co.uk/news/uk-northern-ireland-54436324

Belfast/Good Friday Agreement (1998) A negotiated outcome of a peace process aimed at ending political violence. Stormont, Belfast, N Ireland

Biedenweig, K. and Gross-Camp, N.D. (2018) A brave new world: integrating well-being and conservation. Ecology and Society, 23(2), 32 https://doi.org/10.5751/ES-09977-230232

Cameron, W.B. (1963) Informal sociology, a casual introduction to sociological thinking. New York, NY: Random House

Clinician Survivor Task Force (2020) Accessed on 21 December 2020 at https://jmcintos.pages.iu.edu/therapists_mainpg.htm

Goldblatt, M.J., Ronningstam, E., Herbatman, B, and Schechter, M. (2019) John Terry Maltsberger – Suicidologist extraordinaire. News, Announcements and IASP. Crisis, 2019, 40(1), 67-71

Hendin, H., Haas, A.P., Maltsberger, J.T., Koestner, B. and Szanto, K. (2006) Problems in psychotherapy with suicidal patients. Am J Psychiatry, January, 2006, 163:1, 67-72

JED Foundation (2024) The JED Foundation: preventing suicide in teens and young adults. https://jedfoundation.org Accessed 5 March 2024

Jordan, J.R. & McIntosh, J. L. (eds.) (2011) Grief After Suicide: Understanding the Consequences and Caring for the Survivors. New York, NJ: Routledge, Taylor & Francis Group

Maltsberger, J.T. and Buie, D.H. (1974) Countertransference hate in the treatment of suicidal patients. Archives of General Psychiatry, 1974, 30, 625-633

Maltsberger, J.T., Schechter, M., Herbstman, B., Ronningstam, E. and Goldblatt, M.J. (2015) Suicide studies today: Where do we come from? What are we? Where are we going? Crisis, 2015, 36, 387-389

Northern Ireland Government (2019) Protect Life 2 – Suicide Prevention Strategy (2019-2024). Available from and accessed on 10 January 2020 at https://www.health-ni.gov.uk/protectlife2

Northern Ireland Statistics and Research Agency (NISRA) (2020) Suicide statistics. Statement re 'Review'. 9 Oct 2020. Accessed at https://www.nisra.gov.uk/publications/suicide-statistics

Protect Life 2 (2019) A strategy for preventing suicide and self-harm in Northern Ireland 2019-2024. Policy statement. 10 September 2019. Department of Health. NI Government, Stormont, Belfast, N Ireland

Registrar General Northern Ireland (2012) Source for data presented / analysed by Tomlinson (2012) – Figures 1 to 4 (incl) and Tables 1 to 4 incl.

Registrar General Northern Ireland (1965-2010) Registrar General Northern Ireland Annual Reports (Forty-Fourth to Eighty-Eighth). Belfast: Stationery Office

Rogers, C.R. (1980/95) A way of being. Pages 113-136. New York, NY: Houghton Mifflin

Roush, J.F., Brown, S.L., Jahn, D.R., Mitchell, S.M., Taylor, N.J., Quinnett, P. and Ries, R. (2018) Mental health professionals' suicide risk assessment and management practices. Crisis, 2018, 39(1), 55-64

Samaritans (2024) A registered charity (UK/Ireland) providing emotional support to those in distress or at risk of suicide via free telephone helpline (116123) and confidential email support. Online accessed on 5 March 2024 at http://Samaritans.org

The Irish Times (2018) Woman halted abuser's suicide. Barry Roche. 24 November 2018

The Observer Magazine (2018) Dear Mariella – My husband took his own life. I can't face being on my own... The Observer Magazine, 20 May 2018, page 62

The Observer Magazine (2018) Guardian Media Group Limited. Online version of 'Dear Mariella etc' accessed on 3 January 2021 at http://guardian.com/lifeandstyle/2018/may20/my-husband-recently-killed-himself-and-i-cant-face-being-on-my-own

Tomlinson, M. (2012) War, peace and suicide: the case of Northern Ireland. International Sociology, 27(4), 464-482 https://doi.org/10.1177/0268580912443579

US Catholic (2020) Why didn't the Jews and Samaritans get along? Published May 2020. Accessed on 16 December 2020 at https://uscatholic.org/articles/202005/why-didnt-the-jews-and-samaritans-get-along/

Weinreich, P. and Saunderson, W. (eds.) (2003) Analysing Identity: Cross-cultural, societal and clinical contexts. London: Routledge

World English Bible (2000) Gospel of Luke, 10: 25-37. Published by Rainbow Missions. Accessed on 6 Jan 2021 at https://en.wikipedia.org/wiki/Parable_of_the_Good_Samaritan

\* \* \*

## Chapter 7
# Cultural factors – suicide as a local phenomenon

It's one of those words – culture – that means what you want it to mean. A bit like umbrella terms such as mental health, mental illness / disorder, love, evil, etc. For the London 'Guardian' culture means 'the Arts'. As part of their Orange heritage, some Ulster Unionists, known as Orangemen, turned out on July 12th to march in annual 'Twelfth Day' parades in many towns and cities in Northern Ireland, regardless of the wishes of a small number of communities who did not wish for the marches to pass through their neighbourhoods. Part of the reason to march was a celebration of the unionists' unique culture, but there was another reason: to flaunt the symbols of Orange domination (Dana, 1998). Some parade routes – euphemistically referred to as 'traditional routes' - took marchers directly through nationalist neighbourhoods, where the residents had openly complained that the marchers were not welcome. In April, 1998, Northern Ireland legislation – the Public Processions (NI) Act - establishing an independent Parades Commission to regulate disputed parades, effectively reduced the number of contentious marches to a mere handful (Parades Commission, Bryan, 2000).

My own sense is that culture is shorthand for 'how we do things round here', hence 'cultural dominance':

'The dominant culture in society refers to the established language, religion, behaviour, values, rituals, and social customs. These traits are often the norm for the society as a whole. The dominant culture is usually but not always in the majority and achieves its dominance by controlling social institutions such as communication, educational institutions, artistic expression, law, political process, and business.

The concept is generally used in academic discourse in fields such as sociology, anthropology and cultural studies. In a multicultural society, various cultures are celebrated and respected equally. Dominant culture can be promoted with deliberation and by the suppression of other cultures/subcultures' https://www.definitions.net/definition/dominant+culture).

**Suicide and Culture – Understanding the Context**

Hjelmeland, 2011 (Norway), Colucci and Lester, 2013 (US), and others have recognised the importance of the interaction of culture upon suicidal behaviour. Questions that arise include: Does culture determine suicide? Can the meaning of 'culture' as influencer of suicide be explained in readily understandable ways that might input helpfully and effectively in suicide prevention protocols in N Ireland?

Durkheim's (1897/2002) insight into why people die by suicide, briefly stated, was that 'lacking meaningful social relationships that support us during difficult times and celebrate us when times are good, is extremely harmful to individual well-being' (Mueller et al., 2021). These writers offered useful insights into the effect of culture – however defined – on individuals' behaviour that they said were largely neglected in suicidology:

'Groups of all sizes have cultures, and these cultures are shared – within reason – providing individual members with a sense of who they are, what they are supposed to feel, think, and do under various conditions, and what it means to belong to that group (Fine, G.A., 2010). Culture is activated every time members interact in real life or when one member anticipates or imagines interacting with another member; culture is also activated whenever we come into contact with externalized representations of it (Patterson, 2014), such as a Catholic individual seeing a crucifix. Members watch each other and sanction each other ... to regulate each other's behaviour. However, culture also is internalized in our conceptions of the generalised other: people do not just act because they do not want to be sanctioned by others, but rather are motivated to act by the cultural schema, scripts, and frames they are exposed to and internalize and come to take for granted as normative

(D'Andrade, 1984; Vaisey, 2009; Lizardo et al., 2016)' (Mueller et al., 2021: 6).

Mueller et al. (2021: 6) asserted that recent theories by psychologists Joiner (2005) and O'Connor and Kirtley (2018):

'largely neglect the simple fact that suicide is a social act and therefore is replete with cultural meanings (Boldt, 1988; Kral, 1994) that attempters symbolically externalize to their intended and unintended audiences, who make sense of the suicide via meanings they too have internalised ... that suicide is not just about acquiring the proper cognitive and practical capacities to attempt, but also the normative capacity, or the belief that suicide is a viable and socially acceptable option for expressing outwardly something felt internally (Canetto, 1993; Kral, 1994; Abrutyn et al., 2019)'.

Chu et al. (2019) suggested that 'cultural pathways' to suicidal behaviour were evidenced in half to two thirds of 'youth and ethnic minority samples'. They mentioned associations between cultural risk factors, such as family conflict, minority stress, cultural idioms of distress, and cultural suicide sanctions as identified by the cultural theory and model of suicide (Chu et al., 2010), as well as general distress risk factors (depression and hopelessness) as predictors of suicidal ideation and behaviours. They also analysed the 'existence of pathways to suicide that primarily involve cultural life event risk factors, independent from psychopathology-related constructs such as depression and hopelessness' (Chu et al., 2019).

Colucci and Lester (2013) eloquently demolished the unsubstantiated claim asserted by psychiatry regarding its attempt at an exclusive explanation of suicidal behaviour. Although neither author referred to a cultural theory of suicide, Chu et al. (2010) had earlier identified four cultural factors that they integrated into a Cultural Model of Suicide, namely cultural sanctions, idioms of distress, minority stress, and social discord, with regard to three major ethnic groups (African Americans, Asian Americans, and Latinos) and LGBTQ sexual minority groups:

'Three theoretical principles emerge: (1) culture affects the types of stressors that lead to suicide; (2) cultural meanings associated with stressors and suicide affect the development of suicidal tendencies, one's threshold of tolerance for psychological pain, and subsequent suicidal acts; and (3) culture affects how suicidal thoughts, intent, plans, and attempts are expressed. The Cultural Model of Suicide provides an empirically guided cohesive approach that can inform culturally competent suicide assessment and prevention efforts in future research and clinical practice' (Chu et al., 2010: abstract).

Colucci and Lester (2013) argued persuasively that culture played a major albeit relatively unexplored role in suicidal behaviour, in understanding the meaning of suicide and thus – potentially – in its reduction and prevention.

Hjelmeland (2013: 3) held that suicide was widely recognised as a multifactorial, multidimensional phenomenon. She cited Shneidman's (1985) listing of multiple perspectives of suicide including theological, philosophical, demographic, sociological, psychodynamic, psychological, cognitive, biological, evolutionary, constitutional, biochemical, legal, prevention, global, political and supranational. She added:

'The importance of the sociocultural context in the development, treatment, and prevention of suicidal behaviour should be self-evident from this and this is widely acknowledged' (Hjelmeland, 2013: 3).

She noted that Shneidman (1985) 'did not mention psychiatry explicitly' (p3) as a perspective that interested him. Nonetheless, she acknowledged that psychiatry currently occupied a powerful base in suicidology. This had led indirectly to the 'biologification of suicidology' in parallel with psychiatry's development in a very biological direction (p4). A consequence of this was manifested in an increase in the deployment of prescribed pharmaceuticals to address what albeit erroneously was perceived as a 'chemical imbalance' in the brain of the suicidal client (p4).

Hjelmeland (2013) strongly contested the notion that suicide could 'be reduced to a simple biological condition that can be treated with medicines, for by doing so we would go back to a very mechanistic view of human beings' (p5). She went on to argue that:

'to increase our understanding of how culture contributes to suicidal behaviour, we need a paradigm focusing on meaning and interpretation where the [research] methodology employed is qualitative [such that] the meanings of suicidal behaviour in different cultural contexts [and] the understanding of suicide at the individual level in different sociocultural contexts contribute to our suicide prevention objective' (p17-18).

Although we share Shneidman's disinterest in psychiatry's suicide paradigm, we would be equally unwise were we to replace 'mental illness/disorder' with 'culture' as a comprehensive explicator of suicidal behaviour. The latter does have the advantage of primary 'in your face' contextual evidence 'before-the-event', while the former, being at best an 'after the event', opinion-based guesstimate, has indeterminate predictive value.

Downtown New York (or other more modest metropolises, like Belfast and Dublin) suffered the hollowing out of the coffee shop/restaurant – viz. non-work 'relax' venues – aka 'culture' through post-March 2020 Covid-19 restrictions, prescribing that people 'worked' from home or just obeyed government diktat to 'stay at home'. So it's true – culture in this shade of its multifarious meanings is 'what we do, how we behave, willingly or not, round here'.

In this chapter, we're focusing on – culture and suicide: their relationship, connection, cause/effect, utility and outcomes. Culture or 'cultural context' herein is also perhaps a convenient but lazy, diversion from the more resource heavy task, nay societal duty, of investigating [fact-checking?] each secret, individual self-destructive act. Conversely perhaps, our homeland's culture may provide an open window into a complex set of herd / group influences upon a susceptible, vulnerable individual, our neighbour and fellow citizen, that carve out and lubricate, psychologically and behaviourally, the lethal pathway to their suicide.

## Culture and Northern Ireland

## Prologue

Northern Ireland, a separate, GB governed jurisdiction, emerged a century ago from Ireland's bloody revolution 1916-1921. It currently comprises six (viz. Antrim, Down, Armagh, Tyrone, L'Derry, & Fermanagh) of the nine ancient counties of the northern province of Ireland, Ulster, whilst excluding the remaining three Ulster counties

(Donegal, Monaghan, Cavan). The North, as it (Northern Ireland) has recently (i.e. post 1998) become known by a rump of reformed, Irish republicans and fellow-travellers, was forcibly hived off from the embryo Irish Free State (1921), later known as the Irish Republic (1949), that comprised 26 counties including the three excluded Ulster counties, 12 counties of Leinster (Carlow, Kildare, Kilkenny, Longford, Louth, Dublin, Meath, Westmeath, Laois, Offaly, Wexford, Wicklow), six counties of Munster (Cork, Kerry, Clare, Limerick, Tipperary, Waterford) and five counties of Connaught (Galway, Leitrim, Sligo, Mayo, Roscommon). This violent rupture in Irish polity generated, conditioned, and shaped most aspects of Irish life and continues to overhang and influence what in Ireland might now be known as Northern Irish culture.

Half a century later, the 'Troubles' (1966-1998) in the North exploded coincidentally with a pacific, civil rights movement seeking social, political and economic equality for all Northern Ireland's citizens. Many of the alleged architects of 'The Troubles' were the progeny of 'old' IRA / UVF veterans from 1920's. Hence, to some degree, the 'Troubles' were a more brutal, destructive and vicious re-run of the Irish revolution (1916-1921). They were aimed this time at over-throwing – or maintaining – the democratically elected Northern Irish – albeit unrepresentative, and in practice discriminatory - jurisdiction and replacing both the North's and the Irish Republic's jurisdictions with an as-yet to be defined all-Ireland jurisdiction. This attempted putsch failed totally in respect of the Irish Republic but its political outworking via the Northern Ireland 'Peace Process' (1994-1998), resulted eventually in a cessation of overt Irish republican, terrorist violence and British/loyalist counter-terrorist violence, as documented in the Belfast/Good Friday Agreement (1998). Post 1998, a linguistic swivel partially elided 'The Troubles' from political and academic discourse, as a descriptor of the North's 30 years of green, orange and red campaigns of sectarian murder, political assassination and concomitant, chaotic economic disruption, and substituted a slightly more meaningful, albeit grossly understated, lower-case term 'the conflict'.

Any examination of suicide and culture in the North of Ireland must of necessity be located within the historical and political context outlined above, but in particular with due regard to the catastrophic, traumatising impact - physical, psychological and economic - and continuing influence of a 30 year brutal, internecine, armed conflict that included alleged war crimes by all sides. This unjustified, illegal, lethal, futile, terrorist conflagration killed 3,700 people from N. Ireland and elsewhere, physically injured tens of thousands, and psychologically damaged most, if not all, of the Northern Irish people who lived through and survived all or part of three decades of terror. Also seriously wounded psychologically, rather than physically, were many of the uncounted thousands who left the North, voluntarily or otherwise, to escape possible death and destruction by choosing to live somewhere else - anywhere else - including in the Irish Republic, in Scotland, in Britain, in Europe, in the US & Canada, in Australia and New Zealand and elsewhere.

[Note: See M Tomlinson's 'War, Peace and Suicide – The case of Northern Ireland (2012 :472)': "The main finding ... is that the cohort of children and young adults growing up in the worst years of violence now have the highest suicide rates and the most rapidly increasing rates. These generations were the most acculturated to division and conflict, and to externalised expressions of aggression. The consequence of peace is that such expressions of aggression and violence are no longer socially approved".]

## Social and Economic Impact of Post Traumatic Stress Disorder (PTSD [DSM, 4$^{th}$ Ed. (1994)]) in Northern Ireland

A major N Irish investigation into direct medical service costs, and indirect costs (e.g. related to 'lost work productivity') associated with NI's post-conflict-related PTSD, assessed the prevalence of PTSD related to psychologically traumatic experiences, and their consequent economic costs (Ferry et al., 2012). These costs in one year, 2008, were estimated at sterling £173 million (p16). It was suggested that '39% of N Ireland's adult population have had one or more traumatic experiences linked to the conflict' (p4). Overall, it was 'estimated that 61% of the NI adult population have experienced a traumatic event in their lifetime' (Ferry et al., 2012: 7). Further, they asserted that N Ireland had 'the highest level of ... PTSD among comparable studies across the world, including in other areas of conflict' (p4). Two years later, O'Neill, S. et al. (2014) relied on data from the World Health Survey's NI Study of Health and Stress - NISHS (Bunting et al., 2013) to suggest that:

'traumatic events associated with the NI conflict may be associated with suicidal ideation and plans, and this effect appears to be in addition to that explained (sic) by the presence of mental disorders. The reduced rates of suicide attempts among people who have had a conflict-related traumatic event may reflect a higher rate of single, fatal suicide attempts in this population' (O'Neill, S. et al., 2014: abstract).

However, a direct link – causal or correlational – between conflict-related traumatic events, PTSD and suicidal behaviour has yet to be proven: the best that can be said is that, in Northern Ireland, a significant, but unknown number of citizens deceased by suicide may have experienced PTSD symptoms along the pathway to their self-inflicted death.

A possible influence recently has been the promulgation locally of Joiner's (2010) assertion that, in the USA, 'virtually everyone, approaching if not 100%, who dies by suicide had a mental disorder or a subclinical variant at the time of death' (Joiner, 2010: 188). It is perhaps ironic that Joiner's book (2010) is entitled 'Myths about Suicide', since his argument has located suicidology, i.e. the scientific study of suicidal behaviour, including the causes of suicidalness [or suicidal tendency] and approaches to suicide prevention (Maris et al., 2000: 3), within a psychiatric epidemiology, psychiatry being a branch of medicine that deals with mental, emotional, or behavioural disorders (Merriam-Webster, 2020). This position statement was robustly challenged, modified or qualified by some of Joiner's peers in suicidology who argue that:

'One of the most well-established truths in suicidology is that mental disorders play a significant role in at least 90% of suicides, and a causal relationship between the two is often implied. [But they argue] the evidence base for this truth is weak and there is much research questioning the 90% statistic [adding that] ideology, politics, power and vested interests among influential professionals obstruct argument-based discussion of this issue [and] that constant iteration of the 90% statistic has unfortunate consequences' (Hjelmeland and Knizek, 2017).

These included the notion that unless there were signs of mental disorder there was no suicide risk (Dyregrov, 2008). Also, as Rasmussen (2013) noted, although the suicide bereaved might not have seen signs of serious mental disorder, it was only realised in hindsight that there had been a number of signs of imminent risk of suicide that had not been interpreted as warning signs by them (Rasmussen et al., 2014). In a telling insight, Shahtahmasebi (2015) noted that 'linking suicide to mental illness automatically attaches the label "mentally ill" to the suicide ideation. It is highly plausible that someone with suicidal tendencies may not seek help in order to avoid being labelled as mentally ill'.

Crucially, constant repetition of the 90% statistic can lead to the perception that one needs to be a psychiatrist or a psychologist to be able to prevent suicide. This hinders the World Suicide Prevention Day's important message – 'Suicide prevention is everybody's business' – that seeks to get across to the public that everyone can contribute to reducing the scourge of suicide.

## Culture in N Ireland – its constituents

A single key, unavoidable, cultural identifier and marker in the North, signifies a UK/Irish region that is divided inter alia across demography, geographic location, financial and economic resource distribution, availability and access, and local, national and international politics. That characteristic or criterion is the perceived religious denomination, as universally ascribed therein to individuals, families, organisations, neighbourhoods /communities, districts, et al. The extensive definition of this immutable label includes cultural attributions:

Religion/s of birth parent/s, evidence of one's own religious persuasion, e.g. for Catholics: Pioneer Pins, Rosary Beads, Crucifixes, displays of religious illustrations such as the Sacred Heart, the Virgin Mary, various Saints, the Pope, et al., at home and/or in the workplace; for Protestants aka non-Catholics: Union Flags, illustrations of the Queen/King and UK Royal Family, et al., Orange Sashes and related ephemera on display at home and/or in the workplace, etc; attendance at churches / places of worship; residence in a housing area, aka ghetto, predominantly inhabited by those of one perceived religious denomination; some albeit fewer professions than prior to NI Fair Employment laws (1976 et seq.); state / government employment, particularly police, law & justice; various 'reserved occupations' including teaching in nursery, primary and second-level schools / colleges that may, consciously or otherwise, use religious denomination to include / exclude candidates from consideration; service in the military, Irish, British, other; and so on and on (Encyclopaedia Brittania, 2022).

In the US, skin colour is a visible cultural identifier. For centuries following European colonisation and the subsequent, strategic destruction, nay genocide, of its indigenous, aboriginal 'Indian' nations, succeeded by its associated African slave economy, each citizen's or resident's degree of skin 'blackness' or 'brownness' has been and remains the predominant cultural denominator in that catastrophically racist nation. In the North, matters are more diverse, although cultural identifiers sometimes include first name (viz. Siobhan, Declan, etc. not Daphne, Sammy, etc.) and surname (O'Hara, O'Sullivan, etc. not Galloway, Kirk, etc.); blue eyes; length of fore lip; width of eyes; breadth of nose, etc. These and others have been potential signals of a person's likely Irish Catholic religious denomination or otherwise. One particularly insidious marker is – allegedly – one's pronunciation in English of the H-sound, either as 'aitch' or 'haitch', that - presumably – may echo back to centuries old use of vernacular Irish / Gaeilge, by the ancestral, pre-colonised, Catholic Irish:

'Given that Irish immigrants in Australia were predominantly working class, to say 'haitch' rather than 'aitch' (runs the folk etymology) marks you as some mixture of proletarian, Irish and Catholic-educated. This – though only anecdotal evidence [exists] for the Catholicism claim - is to be avoided, lest you appear rude or—worse—poor' (Web T., The Web Wars: aitch or haitch, 2016).

Only when we move past religious denomination as a Northern Irish cultural marker, can we begin to investigate what, if any, other cultural influences are directly or otherwise linked to suicide. This cultural labelling is unavoidable although some optimistic commentators appear to have identified, albeit at a political level, 'a middle ground', betwixt and between two apparently immutable religious markers, represented in an increasing vote share by the non-sectarian, neither 'unionist nor nationalist', cross-community NI Alliance Party:

'Northern Ireland has always been a polity noted for its strong links between national identity, religion, and voting, and acute British unionist versus Irish nationalist divisions. The constitutional question of whether Northern Ireland should be part of the UK or a united Ireland dominates. Yet, recent surveys have suggested that a sizeable and growing section of its electorate declares itself neither unionist nor nationalist. This development may have assisted the growth of the centrist Alliance Party, which rejects unionist and nationalist identities and claims to be neutral on Northern Ireland's constitutional status. Alliance doubled its vote across three elections in 2019 and is now the third largest party in the region. This article examines the importance of ideological de-alignment relative to other factors, such as Alliance's opposition to Brexit, in explaining the rise of a non-binary party in a divided society' (Tonge, 2020).

## Religious denominations of Northern Ireland's suicide deceased

The Northern Ireland Statistics and Research Agency (NISRA) does not normally publicly disclose a breakdown of the religious denomination of our suicide deceased. However, these data, as stated in death certificates, were recently made available to academic researchers into the North's suicide. A preliminary internet search identified a single peer-reviewed paper by O'Reilly and Rosato (2015).

They reported the findings of a government funded joint study by Northern Ireland Public Health Agency (PHA) and NISRA, using census data for 2001, that linked 53,617 registered deaths, of which 1,119 were by suicide or undetermined cause over 8.7 years until end of 2009 (p467). Census 2001 included two questions: i) 'Do you regard yourself as belonging to any particular religion?' and ii) 'If "Yes" then specify the religion'. Using this primary data source, the study investigated statistically, in a longitudinal follow-up analysis, the question: Does religion still protect against risk of suicide – as promulgated by Durkheim (1897/2002)? It concluded, as follows:

'The relationship between religious affiliation and suicide established by Durkheim (1897/2002) may not pertain in societies where suicide rates are highest at younger ages. Risks are similar for those with or without a religious affiliation, and Catholics (who traditionally are characterised by higher levels of church attendance) do not demonstrate lower risk of suicide. However religious affiliation is a poor measure of religiosity [belief & practice], except for a small group of conservative Christians, although their lower risk of suicide may be attributable to factors such as lower risk behaviour and alcohol consumption' (O'Reilly and Rosato, 2015: 466).

Rees (2015) commenting on O'Reilly and Rosato (2015), noted their conclusions, that 'the non-religious, Protestants and Catholics all have about the same risk of suicide'. He added that:

'the tribal divide between Protestants and Catholics is extremely strong. So if social identity and affiliation aspects of religion affect suicide rates, you would expect to see it here. This study suggests that regular religious affiliation has no effect on suicide rates, and that religion itself does not protect against suicide' (Rees, 2015).

## Multiple deprivation & Northern Ireland's suicide deceased

A later study (Bunting et al., 2017) confirmed that the key NI cultural marker – religious denomination – was not useful in understanding NI's suicide incidence. They analysed coroners' office data for suicide deaths in N Ireland's 462 electoral wards, within 80 local government districts and 11 councils from 2005-11. Their statistical analysis concluded that 'area deprivation', especially in urban locations, was a stronger factor than either age structure or religious composition when considering incidence of deaths by suicide. Bunting et al. (2017) stated that 'a strong association' existed between 'deprivation' and suicide. Logic therefore suggested that easing / reducing / alleviating levels of 'deprivation' may, probably would, positively affect suicide rates. So what does 'deprivation' mean regarding suicide risk and what could be done to alleviate it?

IJpelaar et al. (2019) described seven factors contributing to measurement of Northern Irish 'multiple deprivation' domains :

• Income Deprivation – 25 per cent • Employment Deprivation – 25 per cent • Health Deprivation and Disability – 15 per cent • Education, Skills and Training Deprivation – 15 per cent • Access to Services – 10 per cent • Living Environment – 5 per cent • Crime and Disorder – 5 per cent

The 'health deprivation and disability' domain, representing but a 15% (or one seventh) contribution to 'multiple deprivation', was summarised by IJpelaar et al. (2019: 169):

'The Health & Disability domain ... included a number of indicators, covering different aspects of health. Commonly used indicators are those representing (a) mortality or life expectancy, (b) receipt of health-related benefits, (c) emergency admissions and (d) mental health. Regarding the latter, data on prescriptions for anxiety, depression or psychosis have been commonly used, alongside suicide rates and mental health emergency admissions'.

It is striking to this writer, that our conventional focus upon mental health, as a necessary and sufficient lens into effective suicide prevention, appears to largely ignore many of the above-mentioned, modifiable factors / domains that contribute to multiple deprivation.

Many of these influences exist to an alarming degree in a Belfast electoral ward, Ardoyne (2013), as described below, that offers a brief 'real life' window into what 'multiple deprivation' within an area in Belfast actually means for citizens resident there:

'Ardoyne is a residential area in North Belfast. North Belfast is sometimes described as "a patchwork of small communities, often separated by walls and peace lines, in which people have an intense sense of belonging". The majority of people living in this "patchwork" landscape of communities are from different national, religious, economic and social backgrounds. Historically, Ardoyne has been faced with numerous challenges due to years of conflict. This has impacted on the ... wider community within our area. Following the Northern Ireland Multiple Deprivation Measure, Ardoyne is currently ranked nine of 582 wards in regards to multi-deprivation (NIMDM 2010) with one (viz. Water Works) being the most deprived. Such deprivation is manifested in the high proportion of residents with little or no educational qualifications, low economic activity, high generational unemployment, high levels of low self-esteem and confidence, along with health problems'. (https://www.poverty.ac.uk/community/northern-ireland/ardoyne)

Black and McKay (2019) updating an earlier analysis (2008), offered a partial, albeit hazy insight into how N Irish divisions, the conflict and its legacy – for many – of unresolved post-traumatic stress disorder (PTSD) symptoms, multiple deprivation and suicidal behaviour may be inter-related. Their map (2) illustrated earlier statistics for self-destruction at ward level, in three parliamentary constituencies with the highest average annual suicide rates- 2013 to 2018:

Belfast North (31 per 100,000); Belfast West (26 per 100,000) and Fermanagh and South Tyrone (19 per 100,000).

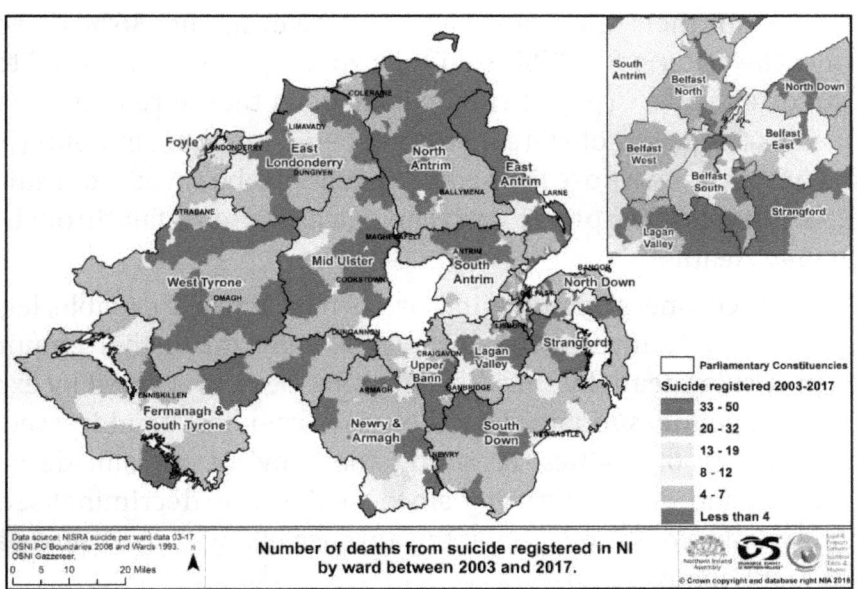

Map [2]: shows the number of deaths from suicide in Northern Ireland at ward level shown within parliamentary constituency boundaries between 2003 and 2017(Black & McKay, 2019). Licensed under the Open Government Licence v3.0.

'Both Belfast North and Belfast West are small urban geographical areas with dense populations, whereas Fermanagh and South Tyrone is a much larger geographical area, with a slightly larger and more rural population. The data also shows that the number of registered suicides has increased in North Belfast from 26 in 2017, to 40 in 2018. It must also be noted that North Belfast had the highest number of registered suicides in 2016, with 43; this is also the highest number for any constituency between 1997-2018' (Black and McKay, 2019).

It remains of continuing concern, given the robust equality legislation in place in N Ireland, and is totally beyond dispute, that all citizens regardless of the location of their home address, or religious denomination / affiliation or absence of same, were and are legally entitled to the highest level of expert psychotherapeutic and psychological care and consideration, on request and 'free at the point of service' from the UK's National Health Service (NHS). But Ferry et al. (2012) found that only 61% of those who met the criteria for PTSD ever sought help for their relevant symptoms. However, "just 36% of people who met the criteria for PTSD said they got help they considered to be 'helpful or effective'" (p7). It can be concluded therefore that, in spite of considerable levels of state investment – £27 million, in 2008 (p13) – too many citizens whose lives could potentially be saved from suicide by expert psychotherapeutic / psychological support, fall through the net to their deaths.

Whether coroners' inquests in Northern Ireland are capable, legally or competently, to investigate – or even to refer for further enquiry – how a particular death by suicide might have been prevented by expert psychotherapeutic support, or otherwise, remains unaddressed by UK/Irish policy or politics. Presently, the 'why' of any suicide event remains beyond official scrutiny since suicide was decriminalised, in UK and Ireland, conditional upon the absence of any illegal, third party involvement, many decades ago.

## Case study evidence regarding cultural influence upon deaths by suicide

Research investigations using an idiographic, case study methodology into a family's response to a deceased relative's suicide (O'Keeffe, 2001) and a clinician's response to their deceased client's suicide (O'Keeffe, 2010) offered a window into evidence of acknowledged, cultural influences, and their presence, strength and/or intensity and influence, if any, upon the deceased's demise in 17 cases, comprising 6 families and 11 clinicians. Sample family suicide cases are summarised below:

Case Study 'A': A 19 year-old college student was found hanged in her study bedroom by a staff member in late 1977. Almost 22 years later, her 46 year old sister, 'A', was interviewed. She said she was living abroad when her sister died and was unable to attend her funeral. She said that her family – parents and two brothers – received no medical or therapeutic support and that she did not seek any help. 'A's family were traumatised by this catastrophic loss and its circumstances and were unable to support each other. It was clear that 'A' had not been facilitated to talk deeply about her serious loss other than to her husband:

'All life events affected and altered identity but traumatic life events changed identity significantly. A [suicide] survivor's identity was inevitably changed as a result of a suicidal loss experience. Recovery was aided by recognition and acknowledgement of such change and its accommodation and integration within the psyche.' (O'Keeffe, 2001: 84).

The ongoing Northern Irish conflict overshadowed and dominated all aspects of living before, during and following 'A's family tragedy. Over 400 conflict-related deaths occurred in two years 1977 & 1978 (Cain, 2021). 'A's approach to the researcher in 1999, following the Belfast/Good Friday peace agreement (O'Keeffe, 2001), exemplified a potential, cultural shift, generated by that seismic, political event.

Case Study 'B': In 1996, a 23 year old man was found dead, by suicide, in bed at home by his younger brother. Three and a half years later, his bereaved mother, 'B', agreed to be interviewed for research into suicide's aftermath for survivors. Counselling did not 'work' for 'B' and she embarked on a study, and completed a dissertation, into how people cope with suicide bereavement, several months after her own drastic loss. She found that 'she herself was unable to talk deeply about her own loss to a compassionate listener' (p95). She felt 'this terrible sense of isolation, loneliness, fear of death, fear of what it can do, how final it is ... it was a long struggle and ... I had to do it on my own ... my family were all there for about the first two weeks ... after that I just don't feel I got much support ... I think they left me quite ... alone far too much' (p95). The death of her father at 9 years of age meant a less-than-ideal upbringing for this eldest child of a 'very demanding, strict mother [who] had to work hard' (p100). Identity structure analysis (ISA) confirmed that:

'five entities occupying pivotal positions in 'B's social world, including an admired person, her closest friend, those in the caring professions, her spiritual adviser and workplace colleagues, indicated her reliance upon an active support framework outwith her family, that balanced alienation from the latter ... evidence of unresolved post-suicide trauma appeared to be focused in her conflicted identifications with her mother' (p103).

Case Study 'C': A man, now aged 42 years, learned that his father, aged 29 years, died presumably by suicide, in a gas-filled room at home in 1965: 'C' was then aged 7 years, born in 1958. 'C' and his five siblings were staying with relatives because both parents were in hospital. His mother was still in hospital at the time his father took his own life. Eleven years later aged 18, and married, 'C' began searching for 'the truth about his father's life and death' (p107) but 'it was during a recent period of disruption of his [own] family life that he deepened his search' (p107). 'C' said: 'I believe he should have got more help and support. He shouldn't have been on his own ... to do it ... only out of a mental hospital and left to go back to the house on your own? It doesn't sound right to me ... it definitely doesn't ... I've said to them [his late father's brothers] ... why didn't you support him ... definitely if it was my brother I would have been with him' (p116/117).

'C' recalled how he and two of his siblings learned of their father's death from an aunt who 'just came straight out ... just turned round and dead cold [said] "I have to tell you now your daddy's dead ... and he was buried yesterday" ... because we were so young there was no big response' (p108). Background evidence from 'C' confirmed that neither in-law family members offered or provided support to 'C's parents, seeming to have disapproved of their marriage – even to the extent of mutilating 'the other' in respective wedding photographs – and withholding friendship or support even after 'C's father's death. 'C' does not refer to supportive input at any time from police, 'social services', GP., local representatives or minister of religion although his former neighbours were helpful in recalling what actually happened to 'C's father in 1965. 'C's ISA analysis indicated a present-day support framework including his closest friend, his partner/spouse, an admired person and his work colleagues. 'C's continuing search for the truth about his father, 24 years on from age 18, represented the outworking of a post-suicide trauma, that focused to an extent upon his complex relationship with his mother (p117).

Case Study 'D': In 1994, 'D's sister, a 39 year old female patient (MN) in a psychiatric unit, was found hanged, in the hospital bathroom. Then aged 45, 'D' volunteered in 1999 to join the research study. At interview, she spoke uninterrupted for over 30 minutes, describing with some emotion what happened to her deceased sister. 'D' confirmed that other than a single phone call to Cruse [Cruse Bereavement Support], on the advice of her GP 'when I felt dreadful ... a year or so after MN ['D's sister] died ... I don't suppose I've had any help really apart from myself ... och FG ['D's husband] has been very good too but FG doesn't talk much'(p123). 'D' said Cruse undertook to get back to her but she said they never did and so 'D' did not contact them again.

The awful calamity that was MN's suicide was intensified by the fact that 'this suicidal person, benefitting from a medical diagnosis for clinical depression and hospitalised for her own safety, became isolated from medical, nursing and religious/spiritual personnel ... [and] in the absence of patient support, she took her own life' (p125). 'D's chronic grief 'six month's after her sister's death was compounded ... following a second serious loss through miscarriage, twelve weeks into 'D's first pregnancy after eighteen years of marriage' (p122).

Non-specific, organisational cultural influences may have contributed in an appalling way to MN's death following just 10 days in a hospital ward that was deemed 'a place of safety'. Based upon 'D's albeit anecdotal evidence, these included local personnel mismanagement of medical, nursing and religious/spiritual resources, tasked with protecting the life of a highly vulnerable patient, believed to be at risk of suicide. It is not known whether a coroner's inquest and/or a major incident investigation were convened in relation to what and/or who may have been accountable and/or responsible in relation to the catalogue of missed opportunities to intervene that may have cost MN's life.

Case Study 'E': This respondent's 37 year old younger brother was found hanged in London in June 1998. 'E' learned of this tragedy over a week later, at home in Belfast. Interviewed in late 1999, 'E' said that his brother had issues around alcohol and sexuality. He was also involved in some non-specific way in a so-called 'cult'. 'E' said he experienced 'initial shock that transformed into ... a terrible anger directed at his deceased brother and at anyone and everyone involved with his brother's death, including his friends in England, his family, his sister-in-law, his parents and alcoholism' (p139). His family in Belfast were 'totally shattered so we weren't really in a position to support each other ... I didn't get any help from my doctor... [he] doesn't really know me ...and he wouldn't have known about this' (p139). 'E' said he had 'a belief about talking about what's going on ... and feeling my feelings ... and trying to go through it ... in a healthy way without looking for medication or other things' (p140). He 'went to Cruse for support ... I persisted until I got face-to-face counselling ... and went to a group for relatives of victims of suicide ... also talked to a lot of friends ... I believe in talking to people ... twelve-step friendship support' (p140).

A significant factor for 'E' was being given permission to grieve and freedom to express his pain in whatever appropriate way he wished (p140). 'E's description of his response to serious loss is almost that of an exemplar for what to do after a suicide and how to survive it. He said 'I can talk to people easily about it because I've been there ... I know what the story is ... one benefit of the whole experience ... if you can call it a benefit ... it is hard for people ... afraid to upset you or say the wrong thing ... so they say nothing ... assume you don't want to talk about it ... now I do know what it's like so I'm able to talk to people ... about my experience ... they're not going to turn round and say "What do you know about it?" I do know about it' (p144).

Summing up 'E's reported aftermath of his brother's suicide 18 months before, it's clear that local cultural supports included his freedom to choose his response, the existence of accessible charities like Cruse, that deliver expert psychotherapeutic services for the bereaved and other 12 step programmes that provided him with ongoing support. The absence of accessible, statutory resources providing equivalent, expert support as necessary for anyone in need who might benefit from them, remains to be addressed by a more socially progressive polity in UK/Ireland. The current Covid-19 emergency shows what can be done to protect and care for all citizens in need, if and when the state decides.

Case study 'F': In October 1992, a 49 year old single lady was found dead (Tuesday) at her home in Belfast. She had died about two days earlier (Sunday). Her only sibling, 'F', a professional actor, was informed by a police telephone message to his home in England of his younger sister's death. Interviewed seven years later, he said his late sister had written a six page letter to him 'as to why and what it was all about' (p156). Only later did police confirm 'no suspicious circumstances', i.e. suspected suicide, compounding 'F's grief. He got back to Belfast on Friday, 5 days after his sister's death. 'F' was next-of-kin, other survivors were his elderly aunt and some cousins. 'F's week-long response was 'a lot of drinking and smoking ... not much eating ... people in the [theatre] company ... were absolutely marvellous ... extremely supportive ... emotionally ... just the holding ... just to feel something to hold on to is a great, great help' (p157). 'F' recalled that he had been home two months before. They had 'enjoyed each other's company for the first time in a long time ... again I didn't know she was being treated for depression ... someone told me that afterwards ... her doctor told me' (p158). 'F' said he did not avail of counselling 'but I had ears to bend in all these friends who were prepared to have their ears bent' (p159). 'F' widened the discussion to include 'a human right to suicide, defined as being an individual's right to dispose of their own life as they see fit' (p159). In relation to suicide survivors' responses 'F' said ' ... it's selfish of us to feel ... terribly chewed up and upset and distressed about it. Of course we do and of course we should but an awful lot of it is the people who are left behind floundering. We've got to latch on to the fact that ... that the person who left didn't see it that way.'(p160).

'F' also raised the subject of his sister's religious beliefs that would have considered suicide to be morally wrong: '... but she had seemingly worked it out – that if she confessed to Jesus long time since that she was a sinner, Jesus is there to save confessed sinners ... that's how she sorted it out ... how she could end her own life ... as opposed to waiting for the great call' (p160).

'F' contrasted attitudes to suicide in GB with those in N Ireland, possibly due to influential religious mores such that people in Belfast found it difficult to talk about an act that was still considered by many to be a sin and a crime: 'They don't like to talk about it. There's still a great deal of shame attached ... I'm talking today ... having lived outside Northern Ireland virtually all my adult life ... and in the [theatrical world] we're a lot more upfront. I'll always be at the head of the queue to air the subject' (p160). 'F' added that 'the word "suicide" is something I try not to use now. I prefer to try to use "ended their own life" because I think "suicide" is a very dramatic word ... we who are left behind ... make it dramatic ... because we can't understand it' (p163).

'F's identity state, as assessed by Identity Structure Analysis when interviewed, appeared to lean towards reasonable adjustment, evidencing considerable accommodation to his suicidal loss: 'I try to see it from the other person's point of view ... the person who actually ends their life ... because we can't touch the thing beforehand ... we then ... feel more awful afterwards than we do even if you're watching someone dying a malingering, painful disease ... to see it from the other person's point of view can help or get things into a slightly different perspective' (p169).

## Conclusions

Although statistical evidence on the incidence of suicide across the globe is tentative at best, there's no dispute that where you live, and the way your life is lived within the context and constraints of your material and political environment, affects and influences in a fundamental way, your thinking, behaviour, decisions and actions and those of fellow citizens, regarding suicide. In this section, I have tried to describe some cultural aspects within our attitudes and responses to human suicide in our midst. Understanding these more deeply and broadly is one way to engage compassionately with neighbours and citizens at risk of ending their life, and with survivors of bereavement by suicide.

**Myth:** (fictitous popular idea) Causes of suicide are the same all over the globe – mental disorders.

**Fallacy:** (misleading argument) To ensure zero suicide in Belfast / Northern Ireland, what's needed is more expert psychiatry

## References

Abrutyn, S., Mueller, A. S., and Osborne, M. (2019). Rekeying cultural scripts for youth suicide: how social networks facilitate suicide diffusion and suicide clusters following exposure to suicide. Soc. Ment. Health 10, 112–135. doi: 10.1177/2156869319834063

Ardoyne (2013) Information from https://www.poverty.ac.uk/community/northern-ireland/ardoyne Accessed in February 2021

Belfast/Good Friday Agreement (1998) Underpins Northern Ireland's peace process, its constitutional settlement and its institutions. Published 10 April 1998. Northern Ireland Office, Stormont, Belfast, N Ireland

Bell, J. (2018) Revealed: Northern Ireland's most deprived areas. Belfast Telegraph. Accessed on 8 February 2021 at https://www.belfasttelegraph.co.uk/news/northern-ireland/revealed-northern-irelands-10-most-deprived-areas-37157128.html

Black, L-A. and McKay, K. (2019) Suicide statistics and strategy in Northern Ireland: Update. Accessed on 9 February 2021 at https://www.assemblyresearchmatters.org/2019/11/28/suicide-statistics-and-strategy-in-northern-ireland-update/

Boldt, M. (1988) The meaning of suicide: implications for research. Crisis 9, 93–108

Bryan, D. (2000) Orange Parades. London: Pluto Press

Bunting, B. P., Ferry, F., Murphy, S., O'Neill, S. and Bolton, D. (2013) Trauma associated with civil conflict and post-traumatic stress disorder: evidence from the NI study of health and stress. J Traumatic Stress, V26(1), 134-141

Bunting, B., Corry, C., O'Neill, S. and Moore, A. (2017) Death by suicide at the ward level in Northern Ireland. Psychological Medicine. Volume 48, Issue 8, June 2018, pp. 1375 – 1380

Cain (2021) Deaths (number) due to the security situation in Northern Ireland (only), 1969-2015. Accessed on 10 February 2021 at https://cain.ulster.ac.uk/ni/security.htm#death

Chu, J. P., Goldblum, P., Floyd, R. and Bongar, B. (2010) The cultural theory and model of suicide. Applied and Preventive Psychology Volume 14, Issues 1–4, June 2010, Pages 25-40

Chu, J., Maruyama, B., Batchelder, H., Goldblum, P., Bongar, B., and Wickham, R. E. (2019, November 7). Cultural Pathways for Suicidal Ideation and Behaviours. Cultural Diversity and Ethnic Minority Psychology. Advance online publication. http://dx.doi.org/10.1037/cdp0000307

Canetto, S. S. (1993). She died for love and he for glory: gender myths of suicidal behavior. J Death Dying. 26, 1–17. doi: 10.2190/74YQ-YNB8-R43R-7X4A

Colucci, E. and Lester, D. (2013) Suicide and Culture: understanding the context. Cambridge, MA: Hogrefe Publishing

Dana, J. (1998) A Brief History of Orangeism in Ireland. Accessed on 15 June 2024 https://www.his2rie.dk/kildetekster/irland-engelsksprogede-kildetekster-om-nordirland/kilde-5/

D'Andrade, R. G. (1984). "Cultural meaning systems," in Culture Theory: Essays on Mind, Self and Emotion, eds. R. A. Shweder and R. A. LeVine (Cambridge: Cambridge University Press), 88–119

DSM, 4th edition (1994) Diagnostic and Statistical Manual. DSM IV. Washington, DC: American Psychiatric Association

Durkheim, (1897/2002) Suicide. A study in sociology. London: Routledge

Dyregrov, K. (2008) En farlig diskurs ved forstaelse av selvmordi [A dangerous discourse in understanding suicide]. Tidesskrift for norskpsykologforening, 45, 2-3

Encyclopaedia Britannica (2022) Cultural life - Northern Ireland. Accessed on 25 September 2022 at http://www.britannica.com

Ferry, F., Bolton, D., Bunting, B., O'Neill, S., Murphy, S. and Devine, B. (2012) Economic impact of Post Traumatic Stress Disorder (PTSD) in Northern Ireland. The Lupina Foundation, NI Centre for Trauma & Transformation and Ulster University

Fine, G. A. (2010). The sociology of the local: action and its publics. Sociol. Theory 28, 355–376. doi: 10.1111/j.1467-9558.2010.01380.x

Hjelmeland, H. (2011) Cultural context is crucial in suicide research and prevention. Crisis, 2011, 32(2), 61-64

Hjelmeland, H. (2013) Suicide research and prevention: the importance of culture in 'biological times'. Pages 3-23. In E. Colucci and D. Lester (eds.) with Heidi Hjelmeland and B. C. Ben Park, Suicide and culture: understanding the context (2013). Cambridge, MA: Hogrefe Publishing

Hjelmeland, H., Dieserud, G., Dyregrov, K., Knizek, B. L. and Rasmussen, M. L. (2014) Suicide and mental disorders. Tidsskrift for den norskelegeforening, 134(14), 1369-1370

Hjelmeland, H. and Knizek, B. L. (2017) Suicide and mental disorders: a discourse of politics, power and vested interests. Death Studies, Vol 41, 2017, 481-492

IJpelaar, J., Power, T. and Green, B. (2019) Northern Ireland Multiple Deprivation Levels 2017. Journal of Statistical and Social Inquiry Society of Ireland, Vol 48, p163-174

Joiner, T. E. (2005) Why people die by suicide. Cambridge, MA: Harvard University Press

Joiner, T. E. (2010) Myths about suicide. Cambridge, MA: Harvard University Press

Kral, M. (1994) Suicide as social logic. Suicide Life Threaten. Behav. 24, 245–255. doi: 10.1111/j.1943-278X.1994.tb00749.x

Lizardo, O., Mowry, R., Sepulvado, B., Stoltz, D. S., Taylor, M. A., Van Ness, J., et al. (2016). What are dual process models? Implications for cultural analysis in sociology. Soc. Theory 34, 287–310. doi: 10.1177/0735275116675900

Maris,R. W., Berman, A. L. and Silverman, M. M. (2000). Comprehensive Textbook of Suicidology. 72 Spring Street, New York, NY 10012: The Guilford Press. p. 3

Macdonald, C. J-H. (2007) Uncultural behaviour: an anthropological investigation of suicide in the Southern Philippines. Hololulu, Hawai'i: University of Hawai'i Press

Merriam-Webster (2020) Online dictionary. Accessed on 7 February 2020 at https://www.merriam-webster.com/dictionary/psychiatry

Mueller, A. S., Abrutyn, S., Pescosolido, B. and Diefendorf, S. (2021) The social roots of suicide: theorizing how the external social world matters to suicide and suicide prevention. Frontiers in Psychology Review, 31 March 2021

NISRA (2018) Northern Ireland multiple deprivation measure A 2017 (NIMDM). Accessed on 8 February 2021 at https://www.nisra.gov.uk/statistics/deprivation/northern-ireland-multiple-deprivation-measure-2017-nimdm2017

O'Connor, R. C. and Kirtley, O. J. (2018). The integrated motivational-volitional model of suicidal behaviour. Philos. Trans. R. Soc. Lond. B Biol. Sci. 373, 20170268. doi: 10.1098/rstb.2017.0268

O'Keeffe, P. (2001) Suicidology, counselling and identity exploration: an investigation of postvention strategies for suicide survivors. Unpublished MSc dissertation. University of Ulster

O'Keeffe, P. (2010) Client suicide and clinician identity: an investigation of identity development in clinician survivors of client suicide. Unpublished PhD dissertation. University of Ulster

O'Neill, S., Ferry, F., Murphy, S., Corry, C., Bolton, D. et al. (2014) Patterns of Suicidal Ideation and Behaviour in Northern Ireland and Associations with Conflict Related Trauma. PLoS ONE 9(3): e91532. doi:10.1371/journal.pone.0091532

O'Reilly, D. and Rosato, M. (2015) Religion and the risk of suicide–longitudinal study of over 1 million people. British Journal of Psychiatry, 206(6), 466-470

Patterson, O. (2014). Making sense of culture. Ann. Rev. Sociol. 40, 1–30. doi: 10.1146/annurev-soc-071913-043123

Rasmussen, M. L. (2013) Suicide among Young Men: Self-esteem regulation in transition to adult life. Dissertation submitted for the degree PhD at Univ of Oslo, Norway

Rasmussen, M. L., Diersrud, G., Dyregrov, K. and Haavind, H. (2014) Warning signs of suicide among young men. Nordic Psychology, 66(3), 153-16

Rees, T. (2015) Suicide in Northern Ireland is not linked to religious affiliation. Accessed on 8 February 2021 at https://www.patheos.com/blogs/epiphenom/2015/03/suicide-in-northern-ireland-is-not-linked-to-religious-affiliation.html

Shahtahmasebi, S. (2015) Editorial: What is suicide prevention? Dynamics of Human Health, 2(2). Retrieved from http://journalofhealth.co.nz/?page_id=830

Shneidman, E. S. (1985) Definition of suicide. Northvale, NJ: Jason Aronson

The H Wars: aitch or haitch (2016) Accessed on 7 February 2021 at https://www.abc.net.au/radionational/programs/archived/booksandarts/the-h-wars-aitch-or-haitch/7541200

Tomlinson, M. (2012) War, peace and suicide: The case of Northern Ireland. International Sociology, 27(4), 464-482. https://doi.org/10.1177/0268580912443579

Tonge, J. (2020) Beyond Unionism versus Nationalism: the Rise of the Alliance Party of Northern Ireland. Political Quarterly, 15 May 2020

Vaisey, S. (2009). Motivation and justification: a dual process model of culture in action. Am. J. Sociol. 114, 1675–1715. doi: 10.1086/597179

\* \* \*

## Chapter 8
# Psychological autopsy – a flawed concept of limited value?

**Introduction**

The opening sentences of the preface, and closing remarks in a conclusion, to a recent textbook by Northern Irish authors about suicide, and suicidal behaviour, stated:

'There are no quick or easy solutions to the complex problem of suicide, but ... regarding suicide as the product of an insane mind, fails to explain why people kill themselves [while] the view [exists] that suicide is profoundly abnormal and a case for medical treatment' (O'Connor & Sheehy, 2000: vii) ... 'but it is important to bear in mind that suicidal behaviour is not abnormal [but] is the result of a multitude of risk factors – psychological, social and clinical – and that there is no single pathway to suicide' (O'Connor & Sheehy, 2000: 131).

Both authors were eminent psychologists, who appeared reluctant to concede that any and every suicide, i.e. the lethal outworking of an individual's feelings, thoughts, choices, decisions and actions, could be compressed, abbreviated and translated into a medical matter, viz. 'a case for medical treatment'.

These authors set down a number of investigative approaches to the scientific study of suicidal behaviour that 'apply rigorous, systematic and analytic methodologies in the pursuit of knowledge and understanding' (O'Connor and Sheehy, 2000: 23). These included analysis of official suicide statistics; coroners' inquest papers and records; longitudinal cohort analysis; suicide note analysis; interviews with parasuicides [non-fatal acts of self-harm or self-injury that are intentional but not necessarily with suicidal intent] and high risk groups; and randomized controlled trials. However they found that these six endeavours were variously flawed, biased, time-consuming, expensive, and/or problematic. It is also clear that all six of these approaches are closely aligned with nomothetic or quantitative methods which traditionally seek to establish and test hypotheses that may be applicable across a total population.

The seventh approach, psychological autopsy, was described as 'useful for third-party analysis including: psychological, clinical and psychosocial factors' but also 'time-consuming, tends to be expensive, retrospective analysis, subject to relations' own suicide schema (i.e. subjective knowledge and experience)' (O'Connor and Sheehy, 2000: 24). Yet this albeit imperfect approach, may be better able to consider these factors than the above mentioned alternatives.

Foster's (1997: xi, 10, 25) 'case control psychological autopsy study of suicide' aimed to 'achieve a better understanding of suicide ... especially the strength and nature of the link between suicide and mental disorder'. He described psychological autopsy, hereafter referred to as PA, as:

'the cornerstone of suicide research ... which involves detailed interviews with bereaved relatives and friends of suicides (sic); interviews with general practitioners, psychiatrists and other mental health professionals; and pooling of information from a variety of documentary sources ... described as an interview with the deceased by proxy (Black and Winokur, 1990) ... a procedure for determining the most appropriate certification of equivocal [viz. uncertain or ambiguous] deaths (Litman et al., 1963)'.

Foster (1997: 115) concluded that 'suicide prevention ought to be accompanied by ... social policy and governmental measures to reduce socioeconomic deprivation ... emphasis on the strong link between suicide and treatable mental disorder and the enduring suffering of bereaved relatives and friends of suicides (sic); investment in ... suicide research... and harnessing the protective effect of religious commitment'. His cautious but realistic end piece stated: 'Some (not all) suicides ought to be preventable' (Foster, 1997: 115).

[Re 'sic' above: Referring to a person who died by self-destruction as 'a suicide' focuses exclusively on the way a person met their death, to the total exclusion of their personhood, their humanity, their whole life before their death, and their entitlement to dignity and respect, as are all of humanity, alive or deceased.]

Foster's (1997) deployment of PA as a research tool brings to mind Maslow's (1966) well-known remark: 'I suppose it's tempting, if the only tool you have is a hammer, to treat everything as if it were a nail that links suicide ("the nail") and mental disorder ("the hammer")' (Joiner, 2005). Further, Foster's (1997) conclusions emphasise the macro-aspects of suicide while largely avoiding each suicide's personal, individual, idiosyncratic, and catastrophic micro-outcomes. [Incidentally, Foster's study was part-funded inter alia by Eli Lilly & Co Ltd and Duphar Laboratories Ltd (Foster, 1997: x)].

The evident uniqueness of each death by suicide – its victim, its situation, its circumstances, viz. existential, relational, societal and demographic, its pathway from beginning to end and its lethal consequences for the victim and, potentially, her/his survivors – are plain and obvious. None of these key, discrete data appear to be regarded as either necessary or worthy of detailed, discrete consideration by nomothetic analysts in their search for 'knowledge and understanding'. Hence, in this writer's view, the idiographic, case-study, qualitative method may be a more appropriate approach to accrue, by analysis and scientific study of this data, 'knowledge and understanding' about the whole life and their pathway to death by suicide of a fellow human. This seems more closely aligned with psychological autopsy.

## Suicide's blind spot

On reflection, this writer considers that, if appropriately deployed, important aspects of the psychological autopsy method can contribute to shedding some light upon 'the blind spot that is the incomprehensibility at the core of suicide' (Sands, 2009). In this regard, Sands (2008) in her doctoral research considered a proposition that 'meaning making processes are activated to help individuals to make sense and coherence of events that disrupt existing meaning structures' (Sands, 2009: 10). Her investigation relied on a case study approach that 'used hermeneutic interpretive methodology' to analyse the spoken and written words of 16 participant adults, women and men, referred to as 'experiential experts on ... suicide grief', who 'voluntarily attended a suicide bereavement group of 30 hours over three months' and included 'a range of relationships of loss [by] participants ... between six months and 3 years bereaved'.

This study eschewed individual differences choosing to assemble 'a representative cross-section of bereavement group participant data' (Sands, 2009: 12). Audio-recorded conversations with, and the writings of study participants, complemented this data. Sands (2008) proposed a tripartite process of adaptation – understanding, reconstructing and repositioning – by survivors of bereavement by suicide of their relationship with the deceased, their relationship with self, and their relationship with others outside and within grief groups, consisting of:

Trying on the shoes: understanding the relationship - the bereaved engages with the intentional nature of a suicide death

Walking in the shoes: reconstructing the relationship – the death story is reconstructed by the bereaved involving themes that focus on the pain of the life and death of the deceased

Taking off the shoes: repositioning the relationship – the bereaved have 'differentiated from the deceased and negotiated the incomprehensibility of the blind spot at the centre of suicide' (p14) (Sands, 2009: Figure 1, p12).

Sands (2009) cautioned that some risk, sometimes called 'retraumatisation', was present during the 'reconstruction' phase for the bereaved who 'can become so immersed in walking in the shoes of the deceased and imagining their mindset that they experience similar hopelessness and suicide ideation' (p13). Essential support for the bereaved during this phase involved building up their realisation towards acceptance of the fact that 'you are different and want to live' (p13) while, for reasons that only the deceased was aware of, they – the deceased – were unwilling or unable so to decide. Work during the final 'repositioning' phase involved adjustment from 'the death event and pain of the deceased's life [that] are separated from more nurturing memories' such as to 'validate the suffering of the deceased but not their decision to kill themselves' (p14).

The writer is not aware whether Sands (2009) suicide grief model, or a similar approach, is deployed by Northern Irish suicide bereavement groups – statutory, community and/or voluntary – or local coroner's office bereavement support staff. Unfortunately, it seems unlikely that the level of expert resources that might be required to organise and manage the Sands (2009) or similar approach would be publicly financed in Northern Ireland unless it was already deployed and centrally funded in the three other UK regions and/or Ireland.

## Psychological autopsy in Northern Ireland

It might be quite an error to believe that in Northern Ireland all non-suspicious deaths, where death was not the result of a crime, are the subject of a pathologist's report, a post-mortem examination, a psychological autopsy or a coroner's inquest. Why? Because it all depends: unfortunately finding out what criteria determine the state's practice in this regard is beyond the scope of this study.

This chapter focuses on one of these potential responses by government or its agencies, viz. the appropriateness and value of psychological autopsy post-suicide in Northern Ireland. The author therefore sought from relevant organisations, information about their involvement, or otherwise, in psychological autopsy post-suicide.

Invitations were issued to the Chief Constable, Police Service of Northern Ireland (PSNI), the Northern Ireland Ambulance Service, the Northern Ireland Coroners' Service, the Northern Ireland Departments of Health and Justice, the NI Fire and Rescue Service, the NI Prisons Service, the NI Probation Service, and the NI Social Workers Association, to comment on:

i) Their procedures and practices, if any, in relation to suicide-related psychological autopsy

ii) To note information from the American Association of Suicidology (AAS) about that organisation's training programmes in relation to certification, as Psychological Autopsy Investigators, and its relevance, if any, to our Northern Irish public service human resources, including inter alia police officers, ambulance/fire and rescue service officers, social workers, probation officers, prison warders and staff, coroners and coroners' office, NI Department of Justice staff, and NI Department of Health staff, including medical and psychological staff and bereavement counsellors.

Their various responses confirmed that training courses for PA investigators, that are de rigueur in the US, seem absent currently from UK/Irish training curricula for Northern Irish public servants.

## American Training Courses For Psychological Autopsy Investigators

Currently American Association of Suicidology (AAS) offers a one day, nine hour virtual training module, via ZOOM, with an option to schedule the course over four days, for a current fee of $350. A leaflet on the AAS website states:

'Developed in 1960 by AAS's founding president, Dr. Edwin Shneidman, as well as Robert Litman, MD, and Norman Farberow, PhD, and refined over the years since, the psychological autopsy has become a best practice post-mortem procedure to reconstruct the proximate and distal causes of an individual's death by suicide or to ascertain the most likely manner of death where that manner of death is equivocal and left undetermined by a medical examiner or coroner. The psychological autopsy, furthermore, helps promote understanding of the often asked "why?" question raised by survivors regarding the suicide of their loved one, is used in case-control research studies to better ascertain risk factors for suicide, and helps to answer questions of causation in both individual suicide cases (e.g. where negligence may be alleged) and interconnections between cases (as in clusters of suicides): hence lessons may be learned to inform prevention efforts' (AAS, 2021).

This training was approved by relevant USA professional associations for certified counsellors, psychologists and social workers.

## Equivocal suicides and psychological autopsy

As enthusiasts of television crime dramas know well, it's reasonably simple and does not require more than a moment of Inspector Poirot's consideration (or that of a police constable or other first responder) to decide on discovering a corpse, whether death was natural, accidental, suicide or homicide (NASH, 2017). Any crime drama typically themed as a 'who-dun-it' invariably requires either a suicide or a homicide.

Real life is different. As mentioned above, early in his career as a medical examiner in the US, Robert Litman MD et al. (1970, 1976, 1983) identified and attempted to resolve the complex issue of a death that did not fit 'normal criteria' for determination as natural, accidental, suicide or homicide (NASH, 2017). They said that such a classification 'obscures the fact that individuals may make a considerable contribution toward their own deaths under circumstances not ordinarily considered suicide' (Litman et al., 1970, 1976, 1983: 485). These practitioners devised the psychological autopsy approach inter alia 'to ascertain the most likely manner of death where that manner of death is equivocal [viz. uncertain or ambiguous] and left undetermined by a medical examiner or coroner' (AAS, 2021).

The following paragraphs summarise the ongoing debate in suicidology among researchers, including Litman (1989), regarding the value, relevance and practicality of psychological autopsy in understanding human self-destruction, during almost six decades, to date, since Litman et al's (1963) seminal article.

## 500 Psychological Autopsies

Twenty-five years after their ground-breaking 1963 article, Litman (1989) reviewed 500 consecutive equivocal [viz. uncertain or ambiguous; suicide or accident] cases from 1977 to 1985. He classified most of these cases as deaths by ingestion, by gunshot or by hanging while finding that 'mental incompetence (caused for example by serious mental illness) interfering with the ability of the deceased to understand that his or her action would result in death, did not emerge as an issue' (p 645). Writing in relation to his own bailiwick of Los Angeles, he was in no doubt that local coroners 'have had no difficulty in finding clear and convincing evidence for making a decision (suicide or accident) in the great majority of self-inflicted deaths'. This was quite clear in relation to suicide by self-inflicted gunshot wounds 'which account for about half of the suicides and very few accidents' (p 645). However, in up to 10%

of cases, 'the initial evidence is equivocal, usually because the available evidence is insufficient or incomplete' (p 645). Most of these involved 'lethal ingestion, usually of multiple substances' although some traffic fatalities and drownings could pose difficulty. He described the 'data-gathering and decision-making process' for overcoming evidential shortcomings so as to determine 'the most appropriate certification of the death, whether suicide or something else, such as accident or undetermined [as] a 'psychological autopsy' (p 638).

In an earlier paper (Litman, 1984: 88) he described this as:

'a procedure which involves the reconstruction of the life style and circumstances of the victim, together with details of behaviours and events that led to the death of that individual (Farberow and Neuringer, 1971)...obtained through interviews with persons who were close to the deceased, including family, friends, business associates and physicians (Rudestam, 1979) [such that] the final judgment as to the mode of death is based upon a review of all known facts and circumstances; including the anatomical autopsy, police reports at the scene of the death and the psychological reconstruction (Shneidman, 1977)'.

Litman (1984: 89) added pointedly that 'coroner's opinions and death certificates are not necessarily decisive in disputes over insurance benefits. Because insurance policies are civil contracts, only a court can decide'.

## Therapeutic Effects of Psychological Autopsies

Henry and Greenfield (2009) observed a therapeutic effect, helpful or otherwise, for interviewees participating in psychological autopsy. They reviewed 35 interviews with parents, siblings, friends and a grandmother to 'better understand adolescent/young adult suicide' (p20). Beneficial outcomes ranged across reconsidering self-blame, 'discovering other meanings to the suicide (e.g. relationship break-up, employment loss, psychiatric disorder, etc.), diminishing their own sense of responsibility' (p21), feeling their participation was useful for research/prevention, reducing negative feelings such as taboo, stigma and isolation, accepting the reality of their loss and enhanced self-understanding and insight into the 'why' of their own feelings (p22).

Negative effects were reported by 20% of participants including one becoming 'clinically depressed', and another becoming 'delusional' linked to painful insights they experienced. One felt 'let down', one launched a lawsuit alleging neglect by health professionals 'to protect the deceased' (p22) while several disliked the interviewer's perceived focus on negative aspects of the deceased, without reference to their emotional strengths. Limitations mentioned by the authors included absence of a comparison group in relation to variable time spent – from 6 to 8 hours – with survivors; variable duration between suicide and interview – from 6 to 18 month and the use of a single individual in three roles: to interview respondents, to provide support as appropriate and to assess respondents' feedback.

## The Validity of the Psychological Autopsy (PA)

Homand (2010; 2015) discussed the validity of the psychological autopsy and its role in forensic psychology. She described the 'idea that we can [learn] about what a person was feeling and going through prior to their death from secondary sources is both extraordinary and debatable'. The PA process, she said, was a way to give those left behind answers based on their own input about the deceased, through interviews, and other evidence including medical records, personal items of the deceased and a forensic examination of the body/corpse. This positive intent and potential insights were not, Homand said, what was being questioned by psychologists. They are saying it was the method employed to collect the information that was debatable.

Since no uniform guidelines existed for data collection and interpretation, there was no way to compare them or their results empirically. Without a set structure for identifying, contacting, and receiving consent from appropriate survivor interviewees, each autopsy stood alone without any way to confirm its relevance, material accuracy or authenticity. Homand (2010; 2015) agreed that the choice of interviewer and their level of training and experience, the location of interview, 'the emotional state of the informants' (Pouliot and De Leo, 2006), the time elapsed since the death and the duration of the interview could affect the PA's outcome. Crucially, the use of suitable case controls that match socioeconomic factors and cultural differences are vital 'to make a PA a more objective and empirical part of forensic psychology, instead of just descriptive data and subjective' (Homand, 2010; 2015).

Homand (2010; 2015) was convinced that uniform and objective PAs could benefit all concerned, including the bereaved, and 'that studying of the causes of suicide can profit psychologists all over the world': left unchanged, this aspect of psychology is 'barely valid or reliable' (Homand, 2010; 2015)

## Personal psychological autopsy

Jordan (2011) held that a central task for most survivors is 'to understand the life of the person who ended their life' (p90). He referred to this as their need to conduct their own kind of personal psychological autopsy (PA) in order to learn to live with the 'blind spot' (Sands, 2009), 'realising they will never fully understand the internal experience of the person who has died (Sands, 2009)'. In his review of her late mother's literary obituary (Rappaport, 2009), Jordan (2011) complimented Dr Rappaport's 'remarkable book that will be of help to anyone who seeks to understand the complexity of suicide and its multilayered impact on those left behind' (p91). He described how she explored the factors contributing to her mother's death from the perspectives of her mother, her father, her siblings and herself – as a child and as an adult. He noted her exceptional ability to integrate her professional knowledge with these personal insights about her mother and her mother's life. Thus she avoided 'reducing suicide to the simplistic explanations offered by the mental health establishment (suicide is the result of a psychiatric disorder), religious institutions (suicide is a moral failing) or families and communities (suicide is someone's fault)'. Jordan (2011) believed that Rappaport's compassionate biography 'honours her mother's spirit and allows her to live on in the lives of following generations' (p92).

## Adverse life events and suicide: a synthesis of psychological autopsy studies

Foster (2011) had 13 years earlier stated that PA was 'the cornerstone of suicide research' (1997: 115). In the current study, he ranged across and summarised findings regarding potentially suicidal influences of adverse life events, from peer-reviewed PA literature in Europe (England, Sweden, Finland, Northern Ireland, Estonia, Germany, Italy), Asia (Taiwan, India, China, Pakistan, Hong Kong), the Americas (USA [4 studies], Canada, Columbia), and Australasia (Australia, New Zealand /Aotearoa). The large number of life events, cited by Foster (2011) that were regarded as 'adverse', was not located either contextually or culturally other than geographically. Interestingly, as a consultant psychiatrist, Foster (2011) acknowledged that:

'some of the risk associated with interpersonal events, forensic events, physical illness, major debt, unemployment and loss events is independent of mental disorder' (p 11).

In his commentary on multiple publications, he did not fully address the major limitations in PA methodology except to list recall bias, informants' possible ignorance of life events that affected the deceased and difficulty ascertaining the authentic opinion of the deceased about the contribution of specific events to her/his suicide, aka the 'blind spot' (Sands, 2009). Meanwhile over 5 years earlier, two major peer-reviewed studies had examined PA's methodological deficiencies that compromised its reliability, in particular regarding lack of standardisation (Snider et al., 2006) and lack of equivalence in study design and inconsistencies in findings (Pouliot and De Leo, 2006).

## Meaning-making through Psychological Autopsy interviews: the value of participating in qualitative research for those bereaved by suicide

Dyregrov et al. (2011) investigated how participation in research projects was experienced by perceived vulnerable populations, including those bereaved by suicide. Their conclusions divided participants into 3 groups:

62% - overall positive; 10% - unproblematic; and 28% - positive and painful (p685).

Positive experiences were linked to meaning-making processes, gaining new insight and a hope to help others. These outcomes were found to be unrelated to participant gender, relationship with deceased, and time elapse since loss. These authors preferred qualitative interviews with survivors rather than quantitative methods, where the latter relied upon medical charts, suicide notes, death certificates, autopsy records or post-death pathological examinations, questionnaires by 'proxies', analysed by statistics.

Qualitative interviews were less controlled by interviewer/researcher, permitting 'emotional topics' to arise. Hence primary evidence emerged regarding potential distress and harm that the bereaved may/may not experience. Researchers/interviewers needed to be skilled, sensitive, and experienced regarding bereaved participants' needs in order to minimize harm (p686): also empathic, caring, understanding, gentle, humane, interested and sincere (p706). In contrast with the potential rigidity of parallel quantitative research findings, qualitative work in this field (p706/707):

i) Has been shown to derive material that is transferable
ii) Can, in principle, lead to valid scientific knowledge
iii) Arrives at conclusions that are anchored in the interview material
iv) Relies upon the craftsmanship, empathy, and knowledge of the researcher/interviewer to reinforce interview findings
v) Requires that researchers/interviewers should be trained in suicidology and qualitative research methods.

Participants' difficulties in bereavement research may be outweighed by the qualitative approach, when it is conducted by competent, compassionate, skilled researchers/ interviewers. It was noted that survivors of totally unexpected 'out of the blue' suicide were likely to have a different experience of research participation than those 'bereaved by more expected suicides' (p708).

Participants reported benefits that included:

i) Remedied feelings of confusion and emptiness
ii) Valued talking with a professional with insights into reasons and processes around suicide
iii) Meaning-making (viz. some insights and improved understanding) about the death due to interview structure that private/random talks do not have

iv) Survivors who had avoided dealing with the suicide felt relief and gratitude that they had been able to talk about the traumatic event

v) Both those who had, and those who had not previously talked about their loss by suicide said it was 'good to talk'.

It was shown in this study that, 'although some of the bereaved may face some difficulties when participating in research, our research clearly shows that the interview participation is, overall, very highly evaluated' (Dyregrov et al., 2011: 708).

## Sociological autopsy: an integrated approach to the study of suicide in men

Scourfield et al. (2012) borrowed or mimicked the psychological autopsy (PA) approach in attempting to inform its 'avowedly sociological purpose ... encompassing the construction of knowledge about suicide cases and also aiming towards reasonably objective judgments about the circumstances of suicidal individuals' (p472). They added that 'suicide is certainly a topic of enduring sociological interest' but concluded that 'we can only address suicide prevention through sociological research to a very limited extent, given the problems that there are with knowledge about suicide cases' (p467). They concluded also that there are clearly limitations to the sociological autopsy (p472).

They accepted the complexity of individual cases while ranging widely across factors relevant to the suicidal act, evidenced in a study of 100 suicide case files from a UK coroner's office. These factors included money/work/employment issues, relationship breakdown, debt and criminal activity (more frequent in male suicide), isolation, alcohol dependency, diagnosis of mental illness (unspecified) and problems related to children (more frequent in female suicide).

Worryingly, these authors remarked that data on social class, ethnicity and sexual orientation was absent from coroners' files. Some features of abusive behaviour were noted, where all but one, out of a total of 23 cases found, related to males. It is perhaps also concerning, given the unrivalled decision power of the coroner, that these writers:

'note the silences there can sometimes be in coroners' files. There are some very thin files in which the contextual social information that we might expect to find is absent and few data are available beyond reports on pathology and location of the corpse' (p468).

Finally, these authors found that, as first responders, local police officers emerge as key professionals in generating evidence about suicide, although in the UK including Northern Ireland, it is exclusively coroners who make the crucial judgment about how a death should be categorised (p467).

## Understanding causes of suicide: psychological autopsies (PA) should not be our only resource

Walter and Pridmore (2013) assert that 'no single method can confidently and reliably be used to identify the factors associated with a suicide'. They go on to say that the methods and findings of PA merited critical analysis. In particular, they say, PA studies have variously reported that while all (Dorpat and Ripley, 1960) or almost all (Bertolote et al., 2004) suicides are associated with mental disorder, more recent autopsies (Phillips, 2010), systematic autopsy reviews (Milner et al., 2012) and opinions (Braithwaite, 2012) have challenged this notion.

They argued that 'it comes as no surprise that many researchers, including Snider et al. (2006), have voiced concern about the validity and reliability of psychological autopsies' (Walter and Pridmore, 2013).

They said PA's deficient methodology, including ill-defined instruments and retrospective nature have pointed to post-mortem diagnoses of mental disorder that were frequently invalid. Further, they opined that the medicalisation of suicide largely ignored Durkheim's (1897/2002) widely accepted position regarding the primacy of social and cultural drivers. They suggested that 'other sources of information [including] longitudinal studies of various patient groups and descriptions of suicide in the popular press ... have a potentially valuable role to play'. They said that journalists, in addition to family members and coroners [may] have important potentially useful data to contribute.

The intervention by these two medical professors, G. Walter and S. Pridmore, questions the long-standing, traditional standpoints of their profession, regarding the pre-eminence of mental ill-health as a prerequisite for understanding suicidal behaviour. They asserted that 'we cannot afford to invest all our energies in one method of enquiry into the cause of suicide, such as psychological autopsy'. They added that 'we must not ignore other investigative methods that may yield valuable, relevant data'.

## How to integrate proxy data from two informants in life event assessment in psychological autopsy

Zhang et al. (2018) attempted by statistical analysis to test the validity of an interviewee's proxy data, that is personal reflections on the deceased that might complement evidence from health records.

This technical study was of limited value herein although it did identify limitations that were commonly found in PA evidence gathering including:

i) Living subjects / interviewees / informants were different from people with suicidal behaviour

ii) They were most likely to be in grief or with different characteristics

iii) Living subjects self-reports were regarded as 'gold-standard' criteria, yet they may not have been totally truthful

iv) Recall bias existed

(Zhang et al., 2018: 17,18).

## Psychological autopsy (PA): the psychological assessment of the dead individual's role in the death (Vasudevan et al., 2020)

An excellent paper by two Indian professors and an Australian psychologist presented in a cogent straightforward way, the benefits and potential limitations of PA particularly when questions arose regarding the mental state of the deceased prior to death. They suggested that mental health professionals and behavioural scientists were best placed to investigate, and to provide evidence to the coroner / medical examiner to aid their conclusions as to all the ascertainable information concerning the deceased's life up to and including their death, including its psychological aspects.

**Psychological versus Sociological perspectives on suicide (Stack and Gundlach, 1994)**

There is an interminable argument about suicide between sociology ('it's a societal thing') and psychology ('it's an individual's self-destructive act): this article from 1994, almost three decades ago, exemplifies some aspects of this long-running debate. More recently, Scourfield et al. (2012) – see above – were open-minded enough, as sociologists, to try to understand psychology's perspective on suicide and to concede that sociology's contribution to suicide prevention was, at best, limited. However Stack and Gundlach (1994) were less accommodating.

Describing the sociological method, they cited Durkheim's (1897/2002) dogmatic, underpinning principle, that sociology 'is fundamentally based on groups and group statistics' (p1257/1258). They added that Durkheim:

'demonstrated that even the most private and personal behaviours, such as suicide, are subject to group-level processes such as modernisation, secularisation, the breakdown of extended family systems, the development of free enquiry and other social forces' (p1258).

They also cited work on the societal or group level of alcohol consumption and suicide (Wasserman, 1989) and the impact of economic development on suicide rates (Girard, 1993) (p1258). Meanwhile these writers noted that 'the psychological autopsy (PA) championed by [psychologists] has serious problems' including the critical and crucial issue of the victim's unavailability for interview (p1259). Determined to torpedo the PA concept, they listed other weaknesses including accessing the victim's 'significant others [who] in some cases are non-existent given that many suicidal individuals are socially isolated' (p1259). When located, they may 'not [be] well informed about the lonely victim ... some refuse to be interviewed ... and [if] long after the victim is dead, this poses recall problems' (p1259).

Both of these sociologist authors contrasted these perceived, blocking issues in PA with 'standard sociological survey research where objects of the interview, the respondents, are still living and where their significant others do not typically have to be interviewed' (p1259).

## A Psychological Autopsy of the Suicide of an Academically Gifted Student: Researchers' and parents' perspectives

In its introduction, this unique PA study by Cross et al. (2002), conducted over 4 years (1997-2001), represented the then widely-held and accepted view of suicide that dates back to the 1990's and before in the US. This focused upon 'significant risk factors associated with adolescent suicide', headlined by psychiatric disorders such as depression / anxiety; drug and alcohol abuse; genetic factors; family loss, disruption; friend or family member of suicide victim; [sexual identity issues]; rapid socio-cultural change; media emphasis on suicide; impulsiveness /aggressiveness; ready access to lethal methods (Davidson and Linnoila, eds., 1991: 248).

The nature of suicide is 'rooted in a most personal experience base ... one that is rarely knowable by others' (Cross et al., 2002: 247). Their study 'uses the methods and procedures of PA to describe the life of a gifted college student who completed suicide ... it follows the subject ["Reed Ball"] across his 21 years of life looking at milestones, stages, and significant events through the eyes of both the researchers and parents of the deceased child' (p251). The parents [one of three study's co-authors, P. B. Ball, was Reed's mother] provided a detailed 5 page 'timeline of significant events in Reed's lifespan' from birth in 1973 to death in 1994: sources included parents' journals, Reed's essays and notes, including 'suicide notes', diaries, school-teachers communications, and medical / psychological assessments.

The authors appear to have agreed to use a 'phenomenological lens' to examine Reed's life rather than classifying him as a casualty of a psychological malady. In conjunction with the above-mentioned 'timeline', several prominent psychological theories were used to offer a range of interpretations of what might have influenced Reed's ultimately lethal behaviour (p251). Extracted from timeline data, eight relevant themes were observed from Reed's psychological case history. These included a litany of negative attributes (p252):

i) Mood swings from 7 years of age
ii) Periods of depression/hopelessness and impaired judgment
iii) Difficulty in adjustment to new school/country (family emigrated from US to Canada when Reed was 8 years old)
iv) Interpersonal difficulties with peers, including romantic relationships
v) Low self-esteem
vi) Engaged in escapist behaviours
vii) Suicidal ideation present for 8 or more years and over 12 attempts at self-harm
viii) Felt a loss of control, impairment of judgment, and lost trace of reality prior to final attempt (some psychotic features present).
ix) Theories applied to Reed's case study included Golombek's Theory (Sargent, 1984); Shneidman's Theory (1981); Psychodynamic Theory (Holmes, 1991); Existential Theory (Frankl, 1963); Cognitive Theory (Beck et al. 1985); and Suicide Trajectory Model (Stillion & McDowell, 1996). Some, but not all of these 'explanations' for Reed's life and death by suicide, matched his parent's perceptions of their son's life.

Few would dispute that there is ever a simple, straightforward statement that can fully represent the life and death of any individual. This is especially true where death was by suicide. In this exceptional PA study, several insights emerged:

i) Importance of understanding the interaction between the psychological make-up of a person in interaction with her/his environment
ii) Parents, teachers, counsellors and peers should always be aware of 'signs of suicide' identified in the general youth population, and should not consider that aberrant behaviour, belief systems, or both are a typical part of being a gifted person

iii) Reed Ball's suicide demonstrated that the field of gifted and talented education needs to attach high priority to the study and prevention of suicide

iv) Most importantly, communication and intervention are the key to preventing loss of life to suicide. Even if there is some resistance in the 'at risk' individual, it is essential that professionals, parents and peers support each other in intervening and preventing such a death [Cross et al. (2002: 258)].

## Standardising the psychological autopsy: addressing the Daubert Standard

Pouliot and De Leo (2006) in a lengthy paper concluded that psychological autopsy lacked a standardised procedure leading to methodological shortcomings, lack of equivalence in design and inconsistencies in findings. Taking up this challenge, Snider et al. (2006) set out technical arguments for recommending a standardised protocol / template for psychological autopsy when used evidentially in US legal cases. They sought to address the issue of admissability of psychological autopsies in legal cases that had been questioned under the Daubert standard of evidence.

In short, the so-called Daubert Standard was derived from a US Supreme Court ruling, in 1993, that must be met to be accepted by a US federal court. This stated that to be admissible, evidence must be 'founded on scientific knowledge' meaning that any testimony 'must be grounded in the methods and procedures of science and possess scientific validity to establish evidentiary reliability' (p512). The court listed five factors to be used as guidelines for admissibility, by a federal judge as the final gate-keeper, to decide upon admissibility of expert testimony:

i) Whether the theories and techniques employed by the witness have been tested

ii) Whether they have been subjected to peer review and publication

iii) Whether the techniques employed have a known error rate

iv) Whether they are subject to standards governing their application

v) Whether the theories and techniques employed enjoy widespread acceptance.

The protocol suggested by Snider et al. (2006) was based upon feedback from 13 suicidologists (unnamed) regarding questions that may arise concerning 15 essential areas of enquiry in a psychological autopsy. These are headlined below, with an indication of how many aspects within each heading might be interrogated further:

i) Recommended documentation/archival records – 9 sub-headings
ii) Site of death – 3 sub-headings
iii) Demographics – 10 sub-headings
iv) Recent symptoms / behaviours – 19 sub headings
v) Precipitants to the death – 11 sub-headings
vi) Psychiatric history – 7 sub-headings
vii) Physical health – 5 sub-headings
viii) Substance abuse – 5 sub-headings
ix) Family history – 7 sub-headings
x) Firearms history – 5 sub-headings
xi) Attachments / social supports – 8 sub-headings
xii) Emotional reactivity – 3 sub-headings
xiii) Lifestyle / character – 5 sub-hearings
xiv) Access to care – 2 sub-headings
xv) Other areas of enquiry – 4 sub-headings.

The authors conclude that, as the Daubert Standard was a guideline for the judiciary, the admissibility of this suggested protocol rests more with the judge than any other individual. However, they infer that unless forensic suicidology made a conscious effort to standardise and test this, or a similar procedure, then any claim regarding the robust reliability of psychological autopsy in determining 'whether or not an equivocal death is suicide or not' would continue to be in dispute (p517).

## Qualitative evidence in suicide: findings from qualitative psychological autopsy studies

Hjelmeland and Knizek (2016) focused on qualitative psychological autopsy (PA) studies that attempted to answer the "why?" question in suicide. Based on the medical model (symptoms/diagnosis/treatment/monitor) PA became a prime approach in the study of risk factors for suicide (Cavanaugh et al., 2003) through interviews with one or two bereaved relatives in addition sometimes to analysis of other data (suicide notes, medical/psychiatric records, police records, coroners' findings). Psychiatric illness was found in 90% of suicides, particularly 'depressive disorders'. Hjelmeland and Knizek (2016) strongly challenged these findings: 'there is reason to question both the "truth" that almost all those who die by suicide suffer from one or more mental disorders and the causal implication between the two' (p357). They noted 'the fact that many of the questions asked to assign a psychiatric diagnosis to the deceased by means of interviewing some of the bereaved ... cannot be answered reliably by anyone other than the person to be diagnosed' (p357). Therefore they recommended that 'such quantitative PA studies, at least as diagnostic tools, now should be abandoned' (p357).

These writers questioned studies that fail to disclose the source of their data. For instance, it may be 'problematic' to rely on information from closest relatives since those 'closest in kin' may not be 'closest in terms of confidence or intimacy'. The nature of the informants' relationship can contribute 'very different information ... due to difference in interests and expectations ... or differences in access to relevant information'. They contrasted, for example, information from a mother and from a mother-in-law where relationship issues were assumed to be relevant for the suicide. Hjelmeland and Knizek (2016) believed it was 'crucial to know who provided the information obtained in PA studies ... but very few, if any, quantitative PA studies where psychiatric diagnoses have been assigned, have discussed or mentioned such issues' (Hjelmeland et al., 2012: 358).

Hjelmeland and Knizek (2016) cited several qualitative PA studies – suicide in the elderly, suicide in young men, suicide in internally displaced peoples' camps in Northern Uganda and suicide in women – that demonstrated the multidimensional, multifactorial nature of each suicide. They stressed that 'it is important to interpret the suicides in relation to the whole life history of the deceased' (p366). They assert that qualitative PA studies offered both a deeper and wider, as well as a different, understanding of suicide than what quantitative PA studies have been able to' (p368). However, they accepted Shneidman's (1985) view that every suicide is unique, and uniquely complex, and that 'it is high time to take some of this complexity into consideration in suicide research and prevention' (p368). They called for a change of focus so as to move away from domination of risk factors, particularly mental disorders, towards more qualitative research that examined and took into careful consideration the context, culture and complexity of perceived suicidal behaviour.

They concluded that PA studies rooted in the biomedical illness model have drifted far away from what Shneidman (1981) conceived them to be. Hence they believed psychological autopsy, that largely disregarded social and cultural factors, was now a 'tainted' concept that needed to be called something else if it were to integrate qualitative methodology with consideration of context, culture and complexity (Hjelmeland and Knizek, 2016: 368).

## Concluding remarks

The comprehensive, albeit meandering research journey from O'Connor and Sheehy (2000) and their understanding of suicide as 'a result of a multitude of risk factors – psychological, social and clinical – and that there is no single pathway to suicide' (p131) to Hjelmeland and Knizek (2016) and the latter's view of the uniqueness, complexity, and cultural, contextual relevance of suicidal behaviour, has been documented in suicidology's extensive published output over two decades. Radical change in suicide prevention practice may take some time, though, because the allied, vested interests of psychiatry and psychopharmacology, may be as slow to amend their 'cash cow' status-quo as Vladimir Putin might also be to embrace Amnesty International.

**Myth:** (fictitious popular idea) Responsibility for their suicide rests entirely with the deceased individual in every part of the world.

**Fallacy:** (misleading argument) Mental disorder is the predominant, precipitating factor in almost every suicide.

## Afternote

### A Northern Irish solution to statistics-based high suicide rates

This issue arose in Northern Ireland in late 2020 when the Northern Ireland Statistics and Research Agency (NISRA) and the NI Coroner's Office decided to look again at a number of deaths, by 'drug overdoses or drug-related deaths' (BBC, 2020) that had been classified as 'undetermined deaths' and were thus included as 'probable suicides' in the annual suicide statistics count for 2019. The interim mental health champion for N Ireland, Professor Siobhan O'Neill commented:

'... the suicide statistics comprised two groups of deaths – suicides where the coroner has declared a verdict (sic) of suicide and undetermined deaths... [She said] undetermined deaths would traditionally have been included in the suicide statistics because they were probable suicides. Those included drug overdoses or drug-related deaths, and the review that happened [in 2019] analysed those. It was following that analysis that they (the Coroner and NISRA) decided the majority of those were not suicide deaths. So when those deaths were taken out of our suicide rate last year, the number goes down substantially, compared with previous years. With previous years, they're now undergoing the same exercise, to examine those undetermined deaths in more detail, so that we can get more accurate suicide statistics for the region' (BBC, 2020).

What remained unclear about this purported 'review' was exactly what the 'additional scrutiny of undetermined deaths' (BBC, 2020) amounted to, in relation to 2019 that is currently being applied, apparently, to suicide statistics for the four years 2015 to 2018. This writer enquired from NISRA on 19 October 2020 and received an informative response two months later (18 December 2020), including a link to an explanatory 'Guidance Note' reporting the most recent data (17 February 2021) issued by NISRA, including the following:

"Where a person has died from any cause other than natural illness for which they have been seen and treated by a registered medical practitioner within 28 days prior to the death, the death must be referred to the Coroner. A death which is suspected to be suicide must therefore be referred to the Coroner and can only be registered after the Coroner has completed his/her investigation. The information provided by coroners at registration of the death is used to code the underlying cause of death. In some instances, it can be difficult to establish whether the cause of death was suicide. If it is not clear, or the Coroner has not specifically stated that it is a suicide, these are coded as 'Undetermined'.

"Prior to 2015 ICD 10 coding of deaths was done ... by a dedicated coder which allowed for case by case scrutiny, including a process by which further information could be sought from the Coroner in relation to 'undetermined deaths'. [After] coding was transferred to ONS (UK Office for National Statistics), working in conjunction with the NISRA Vital Statistics Unit ... all drug related deaths registered after being referred to the Coroner were statistically classed as 'undetermined', unless NISRA received specific documentation from the Coroner which indicated that the death was the result of self-inflicted injury or was an accident and therefore not within the definition of suicide.

"Following a quality exercise (sic) between NISRA and the Coroners' Service, to better understand drug related deaths and intent, improvements have been made in order to reduce the number of deaths coded as 'undetermined':

1. Since 2019, all documentation received by NISRA and going back to Q3 2018, which involved a drug-related death without an indication of intent, was flagged to the Coroners Service, in order for a verdict of accidental / suicide or undetermined intent to be provided. Of 86 cases reviewed, 66% were deemed accidental.
2. In late 2019, the Coroners' Service introduced a new I.T. system within which all drug-related deaths must be assigned as either accidental death, suicide or undetermined intent at point of processing. Together, these changes have resulted in a discontinuity in the statistical series, with the number of 'undetermined' deaths reducing from 132 in 2017 to 10 in 2019.

There has also been a small impact in 2018 due to checks carried out at (1) above" (NISRA, 2021).

What is clear in this writer's opinion, is that in the absence in Northern Ireland of mandatory public inquests for each death by suspected suicide, a limited, bureaucratic, paper-based, administrative process, allied to the 'opinion of the Coroner', continues to be a major source of information on NI suicide, including statistics. A revised investigatory approach, taking account of relevant social and cultural factors, and employing an appropriate, qualitative methodology to examine context, culture and complexity, should be seriously considered by the NI Coroners' Service, to address equivocal deaths, including suspected suicides, as a common sense alternative to the current, resource-light, largely desk-based process.

## References

AAS (2021) Psychological Autopsy Training Program. Accessed on 15 February 2021 at https://suicidology.org/wp-content/uploads/2020/03/Program-Description-2020-PACT-updated-2.18.20.pdf

BBC (2020) NI suicide rate expected to fall following review. Karen Atkinson. 7 October 2020. Accessed on 15 October 2020 at https://www.bbc.co.uk/news/uk-northern-ireland-54436324

Beck, A. T., Steer, R., Kovacs, M. and Garrison, B. (1985) Hopelessness and eventual suicide: a 10 year prospective study of patients hospitalised with suicidal ideation. American Journal of Psychiatry, 142, 559-563

Bertolote, J., Fleishmann, A., De Leo, D. et al. (2004) Psychiatric diagnoses and suicide: revisiting the evidence. Crisis, 25: 147-155

Black, D. W. and Winokur, G. (1990) Suicide and psychiatric diagnosis. In S.J. Blumenthal and D. J. Kupfer, (eds.) Suicide over the life cycle. P 136. Washington: American Psychiatric Press

Braithwaite, R. (2012) Suicide prevention and mental illness. BMJ, 345:e8201

Cavanaugh, J. T., Carson, A. J., Sharpe, M. and Lawrie, S. M. (2003) Psychological autopsy studies of suicide: a systematic review. Psychological Medicine, 33, 395-405

Cross, T. L., Gust-Brey, K. and Ball, P. B. (2002) A psychological autopsy of the suicide of an academically gifted student: researchers' and parents' perspectives. Gifted Child Quarterly, 46(4), 247-264

Davidson, L. and Linnoila, M. (eds.) (1991) Risk factors for youth suicide. New York, NY: Hemisphere

Dorpat, T. & Ripley, H. (1960) A study of suicide in the Seattle area. Compr Psychiatry, 1: 349-359

Durkheim, E. (1897/2002) Suicide: a study in sociology. London: Routledge

Dyregrov, K.M., Dieserud, G., Hjelmeland, H., Straiton, M., Rasmussen, M. L., Knizek, B. L. and Leenaars, A. A. (2011) Meaning-making through psychological autopsy interviews: the value of participating in qualitative research for those bereaved by suicide. Death Studies, 35, 685-710, 2011

Farberow, N.L. and Neuringer. C. (1971) The social scientist as coroner's deputy. Journal of Forensic Sciences, 16:15-39

Foster, T. J. (1997) A retrospective case control study of suicide in Northern Ireland. A thesis submitted to the Faculty of Medicine at Queen's University of Belfast for the degree of Doctor of Medicine. 29 November 1997

Foster, T. J. (2011) Adverse life events proximal to adult suicide: a synthesis of findings from psychological autopsy studies. Archives of Suicide Research, 2011, 15: 1, 1-15

Frankl, V. E. (1963) Man's search for meaning: an introduction to logotherapy (I. Lasch, Trans.). Boston, MT: Beacon Press

Girard, C. (1983) Age, gender and suicide: a cross-national analysis. American Sociological Review, 58: 553-74

Henry, M. and Greenfield, B. J. (2009) Therapeutic effects of psychological autopsies. Crisis, 30(1), 20-24

Hjelmeland, H. and Knizek, B.L. (2016) Qualitative evidence in suicide: findings from qualitative psychological autopsy studies. In K.Olsen et al. (eds.) Handbook of qualitative health research for evidence-based practice. New York, NY: Springer Science + Business Media

Hjelmeland, H., Dieserud, G., Dyregrov, K., Knizek, B. L. and Leenaars, A. A. (2012) Psychological studies as diagnostic tools: are they methodologically flawed? Death Studies, 36, 605-626

Holmes, D. (1991) Abnormal psychology. New York, NY: HarperCollins

Homand, D. (2010; 2015) The validity of the psychological autopsy. Danielle Homand, St Mary's College of California. Completed 10 November 2010. Uploaded to Researchgate 8 September 2015.

Jordan, J. R. (2011) The aftermath of a suicide: a review of 'In her wake: a child psychiatrist explores the mystery of her mother's suicide' by Nancy Rappaport. 2009. New York, NY: Basic Books. Death Studies, 35: 90-96, 2011

Litman, R. E., Curphey, T., Shneidman, E.S., Farberow, N. L. and Tabachnick, N. (1963) Investigations of equivocal suicides. JAMA. 1963. 184(12). 924-929

Litman, R. E., Curphey, T., Shneidman, E. S., Farberow, N. L. and Tabachnick, N. (1970, 1976, 1983) The psychological autopsy of equivocal deaths. In E. S. Shneidman et al., The Psychology of Suicide, Ch 30, pages 485-496. New York, NY: Jason Aronson, Inc

Litman, R. E. (1984) Psychological autopsies in court. Suicide and Life-threatening Behaviour, 14(2), Summer 1984

Litman, R. E. (1989) 500 Psychological autopsies. Journal of Forensic Sciences JFSCA. Vol. 34, No. 3, May 1989, pp 638-646

Maslow, A. H. (1966) The psychology of science. University of Wisconsin. Madison, WN: Harper & Row.

Milner, A., Sveticic, J., and De Leo, D. (2012) Suicide in the absence of mental disorder? A review of psychological autopsies across countries. Int J Soc Psychiatry, 2012 [Epub ahead of print]

NASH (2017) The four manners of death. Jack Claridge, Exploring Forensics. Accessed on 14 March 2021 at http://www.exploreforensics.co.uk/the-four-manners-of-death.html

NISRA (2021) Guidance note to users on suicide statistics in Northern Ireland: Updated February 2021. Accessed on 4 March 2021 at https://www.nisra.gov.uk/sites/nisra.gov.uk/files/publications/

Guidance%20Note%20to%20Users%20on%20Suicide%20Statistics%20in%20Northern%20Ireland.pdf

O'Connor, R. and Sheehy, N. (2000) Understanding suicidal behaviour. Leicester, UK: BPS Books

Phillips, M. R. (2010) Rethinking the Role of Mental Illness in Suicide. American Journal of Psychiatry, 167: 7, July 2010

Pouliot, L. and De Leo, D. (2006) Critical issues in psychological studies. Suicide and Life- Threatening Behaviour, October 2006, 36(5), 491-510

Rappaport, N. (2009) In her wake: a child psychiatrist explores the mystery of her mother's suicide. New York, NY: Basic Books

Rudestam. K.E. (1979) Some notes on conducting a psychological autopsy. Suicide and Life- Threatening Behaviour, 9;141-144.

Sands, D, (2008) A study of suicide: meaning making and the griever's relational world. Unpublished PhD dissertation. Accessed on 9 March 2021 at https://opus.lib.uts.edu.au/handle/10453/20269

Sands, D. (2009) A tripartite model of suicide grief: meaning-making and the relationship with the deceased. In Grief Matters, the Australian journal of grief and bereavement Autumn 2009 vol 12 (1), pages 10-17

Sargent, M. (1984) Adolescent suicide: studies reported. Journal of Child and Adolescent Psychotherapy, 1(2), 49-50

Scourfield, J., Fincham, B., Langer, S. and Shiner, M. (2012) Sociological autopsy: an integrated approach to the study of suicide in men. Social Science and Medicine, 74 (2012) 466-473

Shneidman. E.S. (1977) The psychological autopsy guide. Guide to the Investigation and Reporting of Drug-Abuse Deaths, U.S. Department of Health, Education and Welfare, 6: 42-56.

Shneidman, E. S. (1981) Suicide thoughts and reflections. Suicide and Life-threatening- Behaviour, 11, 198-231

Shneidman, E. S., Farberow, N. L. and Litman, R. E. (1970, 1976, 1983) The psychology of suicide. New York, NY: Jason Aronson, Inc

Snider, J. F., Hane, S. and Berman, A. L. (2006) Standardising the Psychological Autopsy: addressing the Daubert standard. Suicide and Life-Threatening Behaviour, October 2006, 36(5), 511-518

Stack, S. and Gundlach, J. (1994) Psychological versus Sociological Perspectives on suicide: a reply to Mauk et al. (1994) In Social Forces, June 1994, 72(4), 1257-1261

Stillion, J. M. and McDowell, E. E. (1996) Suicide across the lifespan. Washington, DC: Taylor & Francis

Vasudevan, A. K., Hanumantha, and Eccleston, L. (2020) Psychological autopsy: the psychological assessment of the individual's role in the death. Medico-Legal Update, July-September 2020, v20(3)

Walter, G. and Pridmore, S. (2013) Understanding the causes of suicide: psychological autopsies should not be our only resource. Letter to the editor, Turkish Journal of Psychiatry, January, 2013

Wasserman, I. (1989) The effects of war and alcohol consumption patterns on suicide: United States, 1910-1933. Social Forces, 68: 513-30

Zhang, J., Wang, Y. and Fang, L (2018) How to integrate proxy data from two informants in life event assessment in psychological autopsy. BMC Psychiatry, 2018, 18: 115, 13-18.

* * *

## Chapter 9
# Theories about Suicide – 15 and counting ...

**Introduction**

For every death by self-destruction, a theory may be constructed, erected and confirmed, or otherwise, by a coroner's inquest. The reality of a suicide, or as a pathological exercise, the anatomy of a suicide will always remain incomplete, eluding even the most diligent, forensic examination. Why? The reason is self-evident: the deceased must, beyond dispute[1], have intended to die by their own hand for suicide to match its basic, dictionary definition, yet s/he will remain unavailable sine die for interview about what they thought they were doing, that is, what their intention was before, during and after their lethally, fatal self-harming behaviour.

This unbreakable, evidential barrier has neither deflected, nor prevented, suicidology's attempts by way of investigative enquiry, involving careful weighing of available evidence, and perhaps also by extensive speculation, to construct, erect and apply theories, albeit in the unending absence of primary evidence, that explain, and/or aid the understanding of, the uncommon, human behaviour called death by suicide. [In Northern Ireland, deaths by suicide annually were most recently around 1.3% (2019) of all registered deaths (NISRA, 2021)].

This chapter surveys the landscape, and reviews the architecture of the several extant theories about suicide [that numbered 15 the last time I looked (Lester, 1994)]. First, it is necessary to examine the motives underpinning the efforts of theorists, that range from identification of perceived flaws or weaknesses in existing theories, all the way through combinations or frameworks of aspects of existing theories, to the creation more recently of new models of human suicide that seek to address the acknowledged complexity, contextual nature and cultural relevance of deaths by suicide across the countries of the world.

Before proceeding, it is important to note that this presentation excludes consideration of, historically based, cultural notions about deaths by suicide that precede Freud (1856-1939). We shall focus on theoretical prognostications on suicide during the period before and after its deletion[2] from criminal statutes in GB (1961), Northern Ireland (1966) and Ireland (Irish Republic) (1993). So-called 'assisted suicide' or 'euthanasia' is discussed at Chapter 14 below.

[1]The UK Supreme Court, decided, on 13 November 2020, that the standard of proof for the coroner's conclusion was the civil standard, viz. the balance of probabilities.

[2]A person commits an offence under Section 2 of the Suicide Act 1961 if he or she does an act capable of encouraging or assisting the suicide of another person, and that act was intended to encourage or assist suicide or an attempt at suicide. The offence is referred to in this policy as 'encouraging or assisting suicide'. The consent of the Director of Public Prosecutions (DPP) is required before an individual may be prosecuted. The offence of encouraging or assisting suicide carries a maximum penalty of 14 years' imprisonment. This reflects the seriousness of the offence (CPS, 2010).

## The motives of the theorists

Most recently, two theorists, both eminent psychologists, namely Thomas Joiner (2005; 2010) and Rory O'Connor (2011) have published, following peer-review, their contrasting models or theories of suicide. Joiner is quite candid regarding the origins and development of his occupational interest in suicidology: the death by suicide in Atlanta, Georgia, of his father, Thomas Sr., aged 56, in August, 1990 when Joiner, aged 25, was a graduate student in Austin, Texas. As I write, Joiner is now 55, one year younger than his father at death. O'Connor's interest is more professional than personal, although in 2016, he acknowledged he had 'lost important people to suicide' (O'Connor, 2016). [The writer shares this catastrophic loss experience that may in part explain his motivation for ongoing research and practitioner interest in suicidology.]

These hypothetical approaches are indeed 'contrasting', perhaps even opposed to each other. Rory O'Connor 'conceptualises suicide as a behaviour (rather than a by-product of mental disorders)' (O'Connor and Nock, 2014:75) while Thomas Joiner opines that 'virtually everyone, approaching if not 100% who dies by suicide had a mental disorder ... at the time of death' (Joiner, 2010: 188). Klonsky and May (2015: 116) proposed a theory of suicide positioned within an ideation-to-action framework, similar to the theories of Joiner and O'Connor. They offered separate explanations for (a) the development of suicidal ideation and (b) the progression from suicidal ideation to attempts, in terms of just four factors: pain, hopelessness, connectedness, and suicide capacity.

A key condition for suicide, according to Joiner, was one's 'ability to endure pain and provocation ... to increase your capability to take your life' (Hjelmeland and Knizek, 2019: 5). On the contrary, it was elsewhere argued that 'most suicide methods, including violent ones, may not be physically painful at all, at least not in all cases' for example, a gunshot to the head or jumping from a tall building on to concrete (Hjelmeland and Knizek, 2019: 6), as exemplified in the lyric: "Suicide is painless, it brings on many changes ..." (MASH, 1970/72). Joiner challenged this in his tripartite – perceived burdensomeness, a sense of low or thwarted belongingness, and acquired capability and desire for suicide – risk-factor theory (Joiner, 2005), recast as the interpersonal theory of suicide or the Interpersonal-Psychological Theory of Suicide (IPTS). Some believed this misrepresented human self-destruction, that they held to be a 'complex, multifactorial and highly contextual phenomenon' (Hjelmeland and Knizek, 2019: 2). Although Joiner did not acknowledge that others might not fully accept his groundbreaking 'explanation of why people die by suicide' (Joiner, 2005: 15), one skeptical voice echoed across the years from over a century ago:

'Explanations exist; they have existed for all time; there is always a well-known solution to every human problem—neat, plausible, and wrong' (Mencken, 1920).

Hjelmeland and Knizek (2019) rejected Joiner's (2005) claim that the 'Interpersonal Theory of Suicide (IPTS) not only will explain all suicides everywhere but also the conditions under which they occur [adding] that the IPTS does not even come close to back up its significant claim [and hence] its dominating role in today's suicidology is unwarranted' (p 2).

A worrying issue related to Joiner's theoretical essentials for every suicide, namely 'a mental disorder' (Joiner, 2010: 188) underpinning the above-mentioned tripartite elements, viz. attitudes towards others (burdensomeness and social alienation / isolation) and attributes of self (capability to suicide), was its wide-ranging nature. Numerous mental disorders – as listed symptomatically in the Diagnostic and Statistical Manual of Mental Disorders, Fourth Edition, DSM-IV (1994) – were linked by Joiner to, and associated with, risk for suicidality (Joiner, 2005: 191- 202). These included anxiety disorders, substance use disorders, borderline personality disorder, anorexia nervosa, bulimia, major depression, bipolar disorder, mood disorders, and anti-social personality. However suicidology's most challenging unknown, previously articulated by O'Connor and Sheehy (2000: vii), viz. predicting when someone will kill themselves, remained while 'the risk of suicide after a suicide attempt persists for up to 32 years after the index attempt (Probert-Lindström et al., 2020). Previously, O'Connor and Nock (2014) addressed the issue of suicide and 'psychiatric disorders', aka mental disorders:

'Perhaps the most widely studied risk factor for suicidal behaviour is the presence of a previous psychiatric disorder. Findings from psychological autopsy studies suggest that more than 90% of people who die by suicide have a psychiatric disorder before their death. On balance, however, most people with a psychiatric disorder never become suicidal (i.e. experience suicidal thoughts, make suicide attempts, or die by suicide). For instance, less than 5% of people admitted to hospital for treatment of an affective disorder die by suicide; most people with a psychiatric disorder will not die by suicide, nor will they experience suicidal behaviour. Thus, although the presence and accumulation of psychiatric disorders are risk factors for suicidal behaviour, they have little predictive power, and perhaps more importantly do not account for why people try to kill themselves.' (O'Connor and Nock, 2014: 74).

In the remainder of this section, the author will refer to other suicide theorists' motives and views from Freud and Jung to Alvarez ['closed world of suicide' (1971/74: 293)], Shneidman (1993) and Wenzel & Beck (2008), arriving back again to the above-mentioned Joiner and O'Connor. He will then argue that each self-destructive event is 'a law unto itself', that remains forever known about only in part, and never ever fully understood by survivors, psychological autopsy investigators, coroners or society.

## Freud

Freud (1856-1939) made several written contributions over the years about his understanding of suicide. He had experienced at least one client/patient suicide (Hamilton, 2005) but did not comment in detail upon this tragedy nor about how it affected or influenced him (O'Keeffe, 2010). See Litman (1967) at 'Psychodynamic' in '13 Fields Contributing to Suicidology' below.

## Shneidman

Shneidman's work on understanding suicide excludes consideration of psychiatry's questionable contribution:

'A proponent of the psychological and sociological causes of suicide, Shneidman pushed back against the view of suicidal behaviour as a symptom of mental illness to be medicated. "Ed really worked to humanise the issue of suicide, to consider what's happening psychologically with folks who are suicidal, rather than neurochemically or otherwise", says James R Rogers, professor of education at the University of Akron in Ohio, USA' (Harding, 2009).

Nor did he believe that so-called suicide notes might offer previously unknown insights. This emerged from a 'masked comparison of genuine suicide notes with simulated ones solicited from non-suicidal people' that proved inconclusive (Harding, 2009). He proposed that 'unbearable psychological pain' was a key source of suicidal feelings:

'Shneidman argued that suicide is not a drive towards death, but an escape from unbearable pain; for him, the therapist's goal was not to forbid suicide, but to work with the suicidal person to find other ways to ease their pain. Shneidman also used his knowledge and understanding to help people who had lost a loved one to suicide' (Harding, 2009).

Shneidman's Cubic Theory of Suicide (1993b) represented suicide on three perpendicular axes ('x' – Perturbation; 'y' – Pain; and 'z' – Press) of a cube with three visible facets, representing these three components of this model, the severity of each varying from "1" ("little pain," "low perturbation," and "positive press") to "5" ("intolerable pain," "high perturbation," and "negative press") (Baryshnikov and Isometsä, 2022). His theory incorporated and combined common psychological features of human self-destruction, aka his ten commonalities of suicide (Shneidman, 1985):

i) The common purpose of suicide is to seek a solution
ii) The common goal of suicide is cessation of consciousness
iii) The common stimulus of suicide is intolerable psychological pain
iv) The common stressor of suicide is frustrated psychological needs
v) The common emotion of suicide is hopelessness-helplessness
vi) The common cognitive state of suicide is ambivalence
vii) The common perceptual state in suicide is constriction
viii) The common action in suicide is egression
ix) The common interpersonal act in suicide is communication of intention
x) The common consistency in suicide is with lifelong coping patterns

(Shneidman, 1993: 34).

Shneidman (1993: 42, 43) described 'pain' as 'psychological pain' that emanated from thwarted psychological needs' (p43), that progressed from little or no pain, through some bearable pain to intolerable psychological pain. He conceived of 'perturbation' as the feeling of being upset or perturbed. His wordy description tracked the effect of this state of mind from open-mindedness and relatively clear thinking, through constriction of thought, tunnel vision and narrowing of focus to few options, towards cessation, death and egression as one (and ultimately the only) solution to the problem of pain and frustrated needs. He linked this to 'something akin to impulsiveness – a tendency to get things over with, to bring them inappropriately to a quick resolution; to have little patience and low tolerance for open and stressful situations; to jump to conclusions; and to jump at opportunities for more immediate resolution [towards] lethal impulsivity' (p44). As for 'press' (or pressure), Shneidman (1993) is less clear about this entity except to identify its negative influence in relation 'to things done to an individual (and the way they are incorporated and interpreted), and to which s/he reacts' (p44). These could include 'conditions or events that perturb, threaten, stress, or harm the individual' (p44). These might include 'both actual and imagined events, in the sense that everything is mediated by the mind' (p44).

Shneidman (1993: 56) coined the term 'psychache' to represent a level of psychological pain experienced, perhaps exclusively, by an individual en route to suicide:

'From the view of psychological factors in suicide, the key element in every case is psychological pain; psychache. All affective states (such as rage, hostility, depression, shame, guilt, affectiveness, hopelessness, etc.) are relevant to suicide only as they relate to unbearable psychological pain. If, for example, feeling guilty or depressed or having a bad conscience or an overwhelming unconscious rage makes one suicidal, it does so because it is painful. No psychache, no suicide' (Shneidman, 1993: 56).

In a later paper, Shneidman (1999) accepted that psychological pain can accompany physical pain adding that 'there can be psychological pain in the absence of physical pain' (p287). He created a Psychological Pain Assessment Scale (PPAS) for use in clinical psychotherapy, that listed over 20 'feelings that were prominent in your worst pain', such as 'abandonment', 'betrayal', 'emptiness', 'helplessness', 'hopelessness', 'powerlessness', 'rejection', 'self-hate' and 'worthlessness'. Joiner (2005) had developed Shneidman's approach by borrowing from this 'feelings' list for his 'essentials for every suicide', viz. negative 'attitudes to self and others' while adding lethality to 'attributes of self', by including 'capability to suicide', as noted above.

[As I write this, I recall a recent radio broadcast (BBC, 2021) of an interview with the widower of a 63 year-old wife, and mother of three adult children who died by suicide in June 2020. Both partners were reasonably well-known public figures in the British political and sports worlds. The widower said he had no indication that anything was amiss with his wife with whom he said he had daily contact, personally or by phone. Apparently, the deceased had used internet searches related to suicide on several occasions less than a month before her death but left no written note. The word 'depression' was used in the interview. One friend was reported at the inquest to have noticed that the deceased 'was not her usual self' a few days before her death – the inquest also heard that deceased had issues with anxiety and depression.]

Shneidman (1993) noted that vast numbers of people suffer from minor and major depressions, adding that suicide is a nervous dysfunction not a mental disease (p55). However he could not have been clearer about depression and suicide. He noted that depression is not a legitimate cause of death on the death certificate 'but many people, too many people have died of suicide' (p55).

Shneidman (1993: 45-47) listed 13 'fields contributing to suicidology' that he presented to locate his 'psychological approach in a wider perspective'. These 13 fields, involving 40 odd writers and one organisation, the American Psychiatric Association, whose endeavours ranged across four centuries, from Graunt (1662) to Leenaars (1988), might be diagrammatically represented by concentric circles. The outer circle would, like a clock-face, locate the 13 various fields, from 'life history', to 'philosophical/theological', 'sociological' and 'psychiatric' through 'psychological' to 'biological/biochemical'. The inner circle would be formed by 40 studious onlookers, each within their own 'field', focused upon a centre spot occupied by an isolated, deceased-by-suicide human corpse. Unfortunately, despite long-standing investigations and explorations, no one has come close to developing a reliable way, accurately to predict, foresee, forecast or anticipate an individual suicide (Pokorny, 1983, 1993; Shneidman, 1993: 61-91). It seems that knowledge about any individual suicide may always be destined to be retrospective.

## 13 Fields Contributing to Suicidology

It is important to emphasise that Shneidman (1993) was invariably professionally respectful in relation to the arguments and propositions of colleague students and researchers in suicidology. Accordingly, it is worth summarising in brief his comments upon the work of others that Shneidman (1993: 45, 46) was familiar with and that he took into account as he further developed his Cubic Theory (see discussion above).

### Life History

Three writers (Allport, 1937; Murray, 1967; and Runyon, 1982) understood suicide as an end-point that may have been evident, in retrospect, 'in previous patterns of response to comparable life situations' (p45). It remained unclear what the predominant self-destructive trigger may have been within the mind of the deceased.

### Personal Documents

Four writers (Allport, 1942; Shneidman and Farberow, 1957; and Leenaars, 1988) understood suicide 'through the analysis of such personal documents as letters, diaries, autobiographies and ... suicide notes' (p45). The retrospective nature of this perspective, which inter alia informs psychological autopsy, is all too obvious.

### Demographic / Epidemiological

Five writers (Graunt, 1662; Sussmilch, 1741; Dublin, 1963; and Hollinger and Offer, 1986) seemed to concentrate upon 'census data, including statistics for sex, age, race, religious affiliation, marital status, socioeconomic status, etc.' (p45). This approach continues to be popular with many of today's researchers given the interest and reliance of some upon 'big data'.

### Systems / Theoretical

Three writers (Blaker, 1972; Miller, 1978; and Tyler, 1984) understood suicide 'as an act within a living system; both the individual and the individual-within-the-society are considered as living systems' (p45). This somewhat obscure perspective may be loosely related to an updated version of Durkheim's societal viewpoint.

## Philosophical / Theological

Four writers (Pepper, 1942; Fowles, 1964; Choron, 1972; and Battin, 1982) appeared to take an existential stance in presenting suicide in relation to and 'in terms of answers to questions such as these: What is the purpose of life? Are there forces beyond ourselves? What is our relation to the universe? Is there life after death?' (p46).

## Sociocultural

Five writers (Hendin, 1964; Lifton, Kato and Reich, 1979; and Iga, 1986) widened their perspective to consider sociocultural data accessible by way of 'knowledge of various countries and cultures such as Sweden, Japan, etc' (p46).

## Sociological

Three writers (Durkheim, 1897/1951; Douglas, 1967; and Maris, 1981) believed suicide was best understood 'in terms of an individual's relationship to her/his society, estrangement from it, ties to it' (p46).

## Dyadic and Family

Two writers (Pfeffer, 1986; and Richman, 1986) located suicide 'in terms of the stressful interaction between two people or within a family nexus' (p46). In Northern Ireland, researchers have identified 'relationship issues' as central to understanding suicide:

'The largest category of adverse events, experienced by a third of those who died by suicide, is that of relationship breakdown or discord. Efforts to support people with relationship difficulties and to help people manage conflict in relationships are therefore to be encouraged in terms of suicide prevention' (Bunting et al., 2014).

## Psychiatric

One writer (Kraepelin, 1883/1915) and one organisation (American Psychiatric Association (APA), 1987) have asserted that suicide was best understood 'in terms of mental illnesses (e.g. depression, schizophrenia, alcoholism). More recently, the latter has stretched this narrow, arguably self-interested perception to include serious consideration of 'suicidal behaviour' as a diagnostically unique mental disorder. Silverman and Berman (2020) have categorically dismissed this initiative that sought to classify 'suicide risk' as a symptom of a mental disorder, as follows:

'... we have a great deal yet to learn about near-term risk for suicide, no less the trajectories and pathways of the suicidal process. Until such time as we can do a much better job of characterizing this process, its components, how these components develop and express themselves at the individual level, and how to assist patients to navigate an acute suicidal state, we see little value in labelling these thoughts and behaviours as diseases, disorders, disturbances, or syndromes' (Silverman and Berman, 2020: 245).

## Psychodynamic

Four writers (Freud, 1910/1967; Zilboorg, 1937; Menninger, 1938; and Litman, 1967) proposed that suicide was best understood in terms of unconscious conflicts, especially unconscious hostility towards the father; suicide was seen as unconscious murder. Litman (1967) noted that Freud 'never synthesized his views into an organised presentation. There is no paper on suicide comparable to Freud's dissertations on war' (p325). It would be presumptuous to attempt briefly to summarise Freud's 'clinical observations, inferences and speculations which illuminate multiple aspects of suicide ... scattered through numerous papers concerned primarily with other issues and other goals' (p 325) across 58 years of writing (1881-1939). We shall therefore simply note Litman's (1967) conclusions:

'The following evaluative comments are based on my several years' experience as chief psychiatrist in a multidisciplinary project of research, training, and clinical service for suicide prevention. My experience is in agreement with Freud's general schematic view. Deep down there is a suicidal trend in all of us. This self-destructiveness is tamed, controlled and overcome through our healthy identifications, ego-defences, and constructive habits of living and loving. When the ordinary defences, controls and ways of living and loving break down, the individual may be forced into a suicidal crisis. At such times s/he feels helpless, hopeless and abandoned and may or may not be aware of a great deal of unexpressible, aggressive tension ... most therapeutic actions of therapists ... are aimed at reinforcing the ego-defences, renewing the feeling of hope, love, and trust and providing emergency scaffolding to aid in the eventual repair and healing of the splits in the patient's ego' (Litman, 1967: 339).

## Psychological

Two writers (Murray, 1938; and Shneidman, 1985) argued that suicide is best understood in terms of psychological pain, produced by the frustration of psychological needs. As stated earlier (see above), Shneidman had coined the term 'psychache' to describe the psychological pain that he believed was a key element, a predisposing factor, in each suicide: 'no psychache, no suicide' (Shneidman, 1993: 56).

## Constitutional / Genetical

Two writers (Roy, 1986; and Kety, 1986) held that suicide was best understood primarily as an expression of inborn (constitutional or genetic) factors.

## Biological / Biochemical

Five writers (Bunney and Fawcett, 1965; and Asberg, Nordstrom, and Traskman-Bendz, 1986) asserted that suicide was best understood as a result of biochemical imbalances in the body fluids (blood) and organs (brain).

## How theories about suicide might help the person at risk of suicide

The above crucial issue appeared rhetorical since there is no single theory or approach or model that offered a comprehensive basis for understanding the human suicide phenomenon. Understanding and prevention are mirror images – without understanding, there cannot be prevention; prevention presupposes understanding. O'Connor and Nock (2014) listed 11 post-Freud attempts to analyse and explain the phenomenon in detail. Two of these – Shneidman's Cubic Theory (1985) was outlined above and Joiner's Interpersonal-Psychological

Model (2005) will be further examined later. Eight of the remaining predominant models merit mention herein:

i) Diathesis–stress–hopelessness model of suicidal behaviour. Schotte and Clum (1987). Cognitive vulnerability (eg. social problem solving) accounts for the association between stress and suicide risk.

ii) Suicide as escape from self. Baumeister (1990). Main motivation of suicide is to escape from painful self-awareness.

iii) Clinical model of suicidal behaviour. Mann and colleagues (1999). Stress–diathesis model, wherein suicide risk is caused not only by psychiatric disorder (stressor) but also by a diathesis (i.e. tendency to experience more suicidal ideation or impulsivity).

iv) Suicidal mode as cognitive behavioural model of suicidality. Rudd and colleagues (2001). Based on the ten principles of cognitive theory, the model describes the cognitive, affective, behavioural, and physiological system characteristics associated with the development of suicide risk.

v) Arrested flight model. Williams (2001). Suicide risk is increased when feelings of defeat and entrapment are high and the potential for rescue (eg. social support) is low.

vi) Schematic appraisal model of suicide. Johnson and colleagues (2008). An appraisal model which proposes that risk is caused by the interplay between biases in information processing, schema, and appraisal systems.

vii) Cognitive model of suicidal behaviour. Wenzel & Beck (2008). Diathesis–stress model with three main constructs: dispositional vulnerability factors, cognitive processes associated with psychiatric disturbance, and cognitive processes associated with suicidal acts.

viii) Differential activation theory of suicidality. Williams and colleagues (2008). Associative network model, in which the experience of suicidal ideation or behaviour during a depressive episode increases the likelihood that it will re-emerge during subsequent episodes (O'Connor and Nock, 2014: 74).

The Integrated Motivational-Volitional Model of Suicidal Behaviour, was that presented by O'Connor (2011): this approach is summarised next, together with O'Connor's own thoughts about its practical application in helping those at risk of suicide.

## The Integrated Motivational-Volitional Model of Suicidal Behaviour (IMVM)

As mentioned earlier, Rory O'Connor (2011) 'conceptualises suicide as a behaviour (rather than a byproduct of mental disorders)' (O'Connor and Nock, 2014: 75) while Thomas Joiner opines that 'virtually everyone, approaching if not 100%, who dies by suicide had a mental disorder ... at the time of death' (Joiner, 2010: 188). I have accessed Rory O'Connor's latest iteration of his IMVM of suicidal behaviour (O'Connor and Kirtley, 2018). My immediate response is to acknowledge its complexity, and to be somewhat concerned as to the possibility of adequate comprehension of its ramifications by non-specialists in suicidology. Its contrast with Joiner's straightforward interpersonal-psychological theory of suicide (IPTS) is considerable. I attempt below to present the IMVM approach with minimum complexity.

The basic model (as illustrated below, in O'Connor and Nock, 2014: 76) presents three phases:

Phase 1 – Background factors and triggering events - Pre-motivational phase

Phase 2 – Development of suicidal thoughts - Motivational phase – ideation / intention formation

Phase 3 – Attempting suicide - Volitional phase – Behavioural enaction.

In simple words, these 'phases' or stages represent i) where the individual is in the world; ii) what's going on in the individual's mind before and during that time period; and iii) how the individual acts when self-destructive behaviour begins. Each phase is then described in words, (See Figure 4 below) linked by plus-signs or linking arrows, that attempt to represent a dynamic, psychological process within the individual, from the arrival of suicide-related factors and events (aka situations and circumstances), to development of 'threat to self', 'motivational' and 'volitional' drivers (or motivators), that may or may not translate into a lethal trajectory towards suicidal behaviour.

The IMVM iteration (2018) embellished the basic model (2011) with 15 'refinements', after noting that a failed attempt may 'not manifest in the same way' if and when a repeat is attempted. Eight of these are termed 'key volitional moderators' ranging from i) access to means, ii) planning, iii) exposure to suicide or suicidal behaviour, iv) impulsivity, v) physical pain sensitivity / endurance, vi) fearlessness about death, vii) mental imagery, and viii) past suicidal behaviour. A further seven (7) refinements, referred to as 'key premises', are worth noting in full:

| | Premise |
|---|---|
| 1 | Vulnerability factors combined with stressful life events (including early life adversity) provide the backdrop for the development of suicidal ideation. |
| 2 | The presence of pre-motivational vulnerability factors (e.g. socially prescribed perfectionism) increase the sensitivity to signals of defeat. |
| 3 | Defeat/humiliation and entrapment are the key drivers for the emergence of suicidal ideation. |
| 4 | Entrapment is the bridge between defeat and suicidal ideation. |
| 5 | Volitional phase factors govern the transition from ideation/intent to suicidal behaviour. |
| 6 | Individuals with a suicide attempt or self-harm history will exhibit higher levels of motivational and volitional phase variables than those without a history. |
| 7 | Distress is higher in those who engage in repeated suicidal behaviour and over time, and intention is translated into behaviour with increasing rapidity. |

Table 1: Key Premises of IMVM (O'Connor and Kirtley, 2018: 3)

## Practical Application of IMVM in therapy with clients at suicide risk

O'Connor and Kirtley (2018) offered brief suggestions specifically linked to identification of a client's psychological locus vis-a-vis their model's phases:

'If an individual is distressed and feeling trapped but they are not suicidal, then clearly interventions that reduce the likelihood that suicidal ideation emerges could offer benefit. To this end, targeting factors within the motivational phase of the model should be highlighted.

For example, given that entrapment is a potentially modifiable predictor of suicide attempts over time ... this is an important treatment target. It would also make sense to incorporate the assessment of entrapment into routine clinical care alongside depression and suicidal ideation. The challenge, though, is that there are not yet any evidence-based treatments to reduce entrapment ... theoretical models such as the IMVM model should be a starting point for the development of interventions, because they specify the potential mechanisms that should be targeted, thereby increasing the likelihood of interventions being effective. Finally, at the macro-level, suicide prevention efforts need to urgently tackle inequality, poverty and disadvantage, key drivers of suicide (pre-motivational phase)' (O'Connor and Kirtley, 2018).

It seemed that the development and designation of this novel, comprehensive model (IMVM) for suicidal behaviour, represented an early stage in transition of theory into effective practice for supporting clients at risk of suicide. A similar difficulty – transition from theory into therapeutic practice – existed in Joiner's (2005) Interpersonal Theory of Suicide (IPTS).

[NB Definitions are needed for: diathesis (aka predispositional vulnerability), defeat, humiliation, feeling trapped, entrapment, etc. for deeper understanding regarding clinical psychotherapy in real world client interactions.]

Figure 1. The integrated motivational–volitional (IMV) model of suicidal behaviour

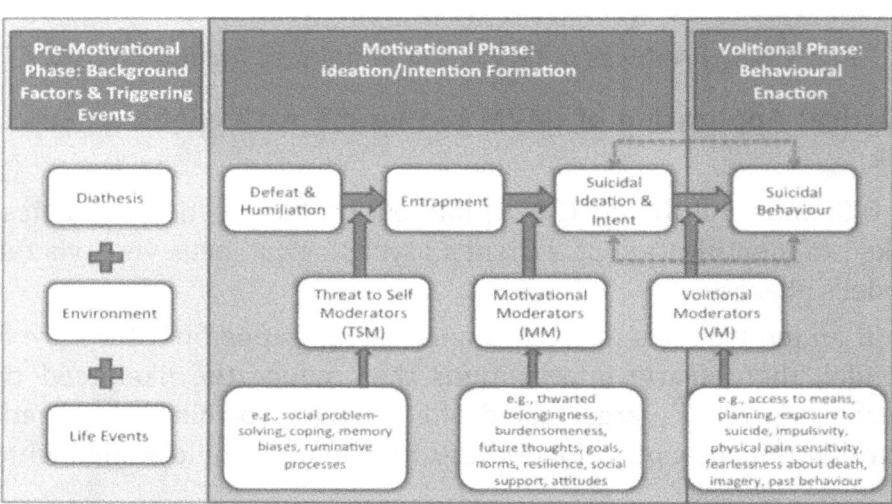

Fig. 4: The Integrated Motivational-Volitional Model of Suicidal Behaviour (IMVM (O'Connor and Kirtley, 2018:2) from The Integrated Motivational-Volitional Model of Suicidal Behaviour. Philosophical Transactions of the Royal Society B. 373: 20170268, gratefully acknowledged.

## Thomas Joiner's (2005) Interpersonal Theory of Suicide (IPTS)

The diagram below encapsulates Joiner's radical approach to unravelling, once and for all, the suicide enigma. In presenting this theory's tripartite essentials for suicide – any and all suicide – in the concluding part of this section, this is not a parallel with 'keeping the good wine to the last'. Rather, Joiner's approach merited close examination not least because of its significant influence over a couple of decades.

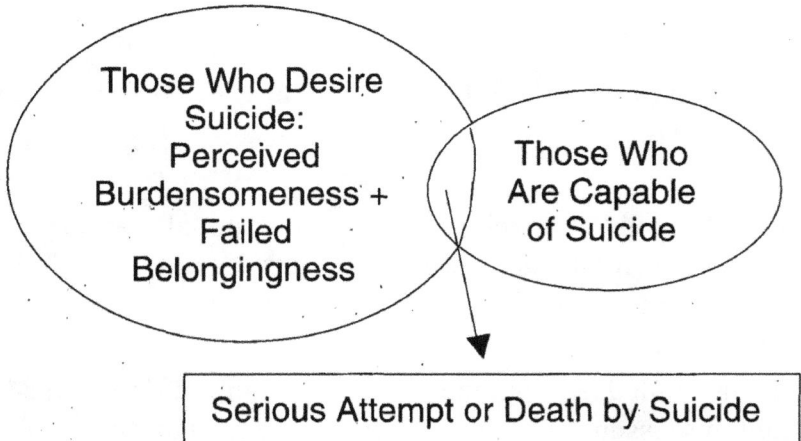

Fig 5: The Interpersonal-Psychological Theory of Suicide from Joiner, T. E. (2005:138) Why people die by suicide. Cambridge, Mass: Harvard University Press (HUP license R12826 granted).

Joiner (2005) argued that, if brevity was his goal, he would answer the question: 'why do people die by suicide?' by saying 'Because they can and because they want to' (Joiner et al., 2009: 4). He then spent some time setting out his three essential conditions for suicide. What he called 'acquired capability in suicidality' was a learned attribute, necessary for self-killing but which was likely to be dormant without the desire to die by suicide, i.e. to want to do so. He connected such 'desire' with two Americanisms: 'perceived burdensomeness' and 'failed belongingness' (viz. isolation). Joiner was unable to find a synonym for the former term, relying on examples from the literature to convey 'this is what I mean by it'. Perhaps the nearest standard English terms might be onerousness or oppressiveness or heaviness (https://www.freethesaurus.com/burdensomeness). These words missed Joiner's point: he wanted to suggest a sense of their state of mind that might emerge from questionnaire responses, by a person at risk of suicide, to statements like:

'These days the people in my life would be better off if I were gone

These days the people in my life would be happier without me

These days I think I have failed the people in my life

These days I think I am a burden on society

These days I feel like a burden on the people in my life

These days I think I make things worse for the people in my life

These days I feel disconnected from other people' (Joiner et al. 2009: 58).

Clearly, this quiz over-relied upon an individual's 'external frame of reference' which was at odds with a more psychologically healthy 'internal frame of reference', based upon one's own high valuation of one's unique self.

Regarding 'failed belongingness' or 'isolation', Joiner (2009: 13, 14) associated this 'essential' condition for suicide with undisputed axioms regarding humans as social animals and their related need to belong to and to be valued by social groups (families, tribes, clans, etc.), in order to survive. Whether one can rely upon 'isolation', or 'failed belongingness' as an essential precondition for suicide, is another matter entirely.

As discussed earlier, Hjelmeland and Knizek (2019) demolished Joiner's assertion 'that the IPTS not only will explain all suicides everywhere but also the conditions under which they occur', and declared it 'unwarranted' not least because 'he seems to have cherry-picked a few studies that may be interpreted to support the theory'. They cannot accept his – at face value – nonsensical laboratory-like conditions for suicide to occur, such that 'people are stripped of their contextual biography'.

## Challenges

Joiner (2005, 2009, 2010) was not formally (i.e. using the normal challenges of peer review and/or public discussion/debate) invited to respond to arguments presented politely and professionally by Paniagua et al. (2010). These writers summarised their failed attempt to publish their comments as a peer-reviewed contribution to a professional journal despite strong support from several respected expert suicidologists. Ultimately, they decided to publish their line of reasoning privately, in a widely available 64 page AuthorHouse pamphlet.

Hjelmeland and Knizek (2019) identified multiple problems with Joiner (2005) and mentioned five major additional issues highlighted by Paniagua et al. (2010), in their peer-reviewed article in Death Studies, published online 29 January 2019. They detailed one of these as follows.

Many of the studies claimed by Joiner et al. (2017) to support the IPTS:

i) Address the issue of suicide ideation instead of suicide and serious suicide attempts

ii) Also fail to 'test' whether all three IPTS components (perceptions of burdening others, social alienation and the capacity to 'commit' suicide) are present simultaneously: many 'tests' only include one or two of them and therefore can at best be considered partial tests (Hjelmeland and Knizek, 2019).

Hjelmeland and Knizek (2019) added that in their view, the IPTS is virtually impossible to test, and that it would be relatively easy to show that suicide indeed may occur without all three components being present.

It is to their considerable credit that Panaigua et al. (2010) were able to accept Joiner's (2005) important contribution to unifying some 'carefully selected' (p13) existing theories about suicide (e.g. Durkheim, Shneidman, Beck, Baumeister and Linehan), while rejecting his claim to have created a new theory of suicide. It is important to continue to challenge, politely but robustly, suicidology's strangely silent, submissive response to the IPTS's extravagant claim 'to have something to say about all deaths by suicide worldwide, across all cultures, by employing three simple concepts [constructs]' (Joiner, 2005: 226). After their literature review, they concluded:

'... no single article was found that questioned the core assumptions of the theory ... This suggested that something was wrong, in that either leading theoretical experts on suicide ... were more interested in dealing with theories that are multifactorial (which is the opposite of Dr Joiner's theory) or they do not want to spend time with a theory that is essentially reductionist in terms of being the final theoretical explanation of all suicidal acts' (Paniagua et al., 2010: xi).

Joiner's continuing silence is troubling, not least for practitioners in suicidology but also for survivors of bereavement by suicide.

## Conclusions

Joiner's (2005, 2009, 2010) idiosyncratic view of suicide theory is mirrored in his rejection of qualitative research studies when acting as editor-in-chief of Suicide and Life-threatening Behaviour (SLTB), the 'house' magazine of the American Association of Suicidology (AAS). However, this reluctance to engage with the idiographic 'case study' approach in favour of the nomothetic 'statistical' approach was often overlooked by Joiner in his three books.

As noted by Philip Connors, Newsday, on the rear cover of the 2005 book, Joiner 'offers a dizzying array of studies to shore up his argument'. Many of these are qualitative / idiographic in nature. For example, he relied extensively upon a quasi-psychological autopsy of his father's death by suicide (2005: 1-15). Later, he referred to two cases of clients at risk of suicide, 'Gayle' and 'Sharon' (p21-25). He then used multiple examples from the literature to illustrate his contention that 'acquired capability to suicide' was a prerequisite for suicidal behaviour (p46-93). Joiner was careful not to mention Freud's psychoanalytic theory of instincts, viz. the libido [aka Eros, the life instinct] and self-preservation drives and the death instinct (Litman, 1967: 331): 'To Freud, suicide represented a symptom we suffer from, a product of man and his civilization, a consequence of mental trends that can be found to some degree in every human being' (Litman, 1967: 337). Joiner (2005: 94-136) did however emphasise that to die by suicide required the deceased to overcome the extraordinarily powerful life instinct. He preferred to invent the term 'the desire for death' and then to conceive of the essential (to his theory) situational circumstances that activated it, viz. burdening others and social isolation. Joiner's Chapter 3, 'The desire for death' (2005: 94-136 incl) is replete with illustrative excerpts from case studies including 'Steve', Joiner's father, Yuit Eskimos, a Malaysian couple, Kurt Cobain, Sylvia Plath, David Reimer, and Charles Bishop, as well as appropriate references to findings in quantitative studies.

In their 2009 textbook, Joiner and colleagues again used examples harvested from published, qualitative case studies to bolster use of a therapeutic approach, derived from the IPTS. Examples include 'Beatrice', Knipfel, Tina Zahn, and others already referred to in his 2005 book.

In his later 2010 textbook, in challenging 'myths about suicide', Joiner again deployed case study examples, including Meriwether Lewis, Rosellini, Hart Crane, David Foster Wallace, Joiner's father, Cesare Pavese, Jeong Dabin, Primo Levi, Shneidman's 'Arthur', Vince Foster, Christine Chubbuck, Matsuoka, Korshunova and others referred to above.

It remains to be seen whether, when and if, suicidology is prepared respectfully to acknowledge the importance of Dr Thomas Joiner's original and creative work not least as a unifier of several existing theories and views on suicide, so that suicidology research can reach beyond the medicalisation of suicide accepting that:

"... mental illness does not explain all deaths by suicide ... that suicide is motivated by pain and hopelessness, and that pain and hopelessness can be caused not only by mental illness but by other factors such as overwhelming interpersonal struggles or loss, seemingly insurmountable financial problems, chronic medical conditions, and systematic discrimination and persecution" (Klonsky and Dixon-Luinenburg, 2022).

The complexity of suicide's essential multifactorial and multidimensional nature may not be capable of further and deeper levels of understanding, until everyone committed to this desirable goal can begin again actively to listen to each other and to co-operate and collaborate together with empathy and mutual regard on our research journey.

**Myth:** (fictitious popular idea) Joiner's Interpersonal Psychological Theory of Suicide (IPTS) is the last word on explaining every suicidal behaviour.

**Fallacy:** (misleading argument) Qualitative theory does not meet the standards necessary for scientific validity.

**Addendum:** Shneidman (1993: 34) notes Kelly's (1961) unique view of each suicide, that is both philosophical and psychological: Kelly 'views suicide by proposing that each individual has his or her own private (unique, idiosyncratic) epistemology – his or her personal construct of the world – and that a suicide is to be understood as that individual's efforts to validate that personal construct' (p34).

## References

Alvarez, A. (1971/74) The savage god. London: Penguin Books Ltd

Allport, G. (1937) Personality. A psychological interpretation. New York, NY: Holt, Rinehardt & Winston

American Psychiatric Association (1987/2013) Diagnostic and Statistical Manual of Mental Disorders. 3rd Edition/5th Edition. Washington, DC: American Psychiatric Association

Asberg, M., Nordstrom, P. and Traskman-Bendz, L. (1986) Biological factors in suicide. In Suicide, (ed.) A. Roy, pp 47-71. Baltimore: Williams & Wilkins

Baryshnikov, I. and Isometsä, E. (2022) Psychological pain and suicidal behaviour: a review. Front Psychiatry, 2022, 13: 981353

Battin, M. P. (1982) Ethical issues in suicide. Englewood Cliffs, NJ:Prentice-Hall

Baumeister, R. (1990). Suicide as escape from self. Psychological Review, 97(1), 90-113.

BBC (2021) Interview by Emma Barnett with Owen Paterson. Accessed on 16 April 2021 at https://www.bbc.co.uk/sounds/play/m000v2pt

Blaker, K. P. (1972) Systems theory and self-destructive behaviour. Perspectives in Psychiatric Care 10: 168-172

Bunney, W. E. and Fawcett, J. A. (1965) Possibility of a biochemical test for suicide potential. Archives of General Psychiatry, 13: 232-239

Bunting, B., Corry, C., O'Neill, S., Moore, A., Benson, T. and McFeeters, D. (2014) Death by suicide: a report based on the Northern Ireland coroner's data base. Ulster University, HSC Research and Development Division, NI Public Health Agency

Choron, J. (1972) Suicide. New York, NY: Scribner's

CPS (2010) Suicide: Policy for Prosecutors in Respect of Cases of Encouraging or Assisting Suicide. Accessed on 1 April 2021 at https://www.cps.gov.uk/legal-guidance/suicide-policy-prosecutors-respect-cases-encouraging-or-assisting-suicide

Diagnostic and Statistical Manual of Mental Disorders (DSM IV) (1994) Washington, DC: American Paychiatruc Association

Douglas, J. D. (1967) The social meaning of suicide. Princeton, NJ: Princeton University Press

Dublin, L. I. (1963) Suicide: A sociological and statistical study. New York, NY: The Ronald Press Company

Durkheim, E. (1897/1951) Suicide: A study in sociology. Trans. J. A. Spaulding and G. Simpson. Glenoe, IL: Free Press, 1951

Fowles, J. (1964) The Aristos. Boston: Little, Brown

Freud, S. (1910/1967) Comments on suicide. In On Suicide, ed. P Friedman, trans. E. Fitzgerald, pp. 140 -141. New York, NY: International Universities Press, 1967

Freud, S. (2021) The Ethics of Suicide Digital Archive. Accessed on 1 April 2021 at https://ethicsofsuicide.lib.utah.edu/selections/freud/

Graunt, J. (1662) Natural and political annotations ... upon the bills of mortality. London

Hamilton, J. W. (2005) Freud and the suicide of Pauline Silberstein. The Psychoanalytic Review, Vol 89(6) June 2005. Extract accessed on 20 April 2021 at https://guilfordjournals.com/doi/10.1521/prev.89.6.889.22099

Harding, A. (2009) Obituary: Edwin Shneidman. The Lancet, Vol. 374, 25 July 2009

Hendin, H. (1964) Suicide in Scandanavia. New York, NY: Grune & Stratton

Hjelmeland, H. and Knizek, B. L. (2019) The emperor's new clothes? A critical look at the interpersonal theory of suicide. Death Studies, 29 Jan 2019.

Hollinger, P. C. and Offer, D. (1986) Sociodemographic, epidemiologic and individual attributes of youth suicides. Bethesda, MD: Department of Health and Human Services

Iga, M. (1986) The thorn in the chrysanthemum: suicide and economic success in modern Japan. Berkeley: University of California Press

Johnson, J., Gooding, P., and Tarrier, N. (2008) Suicide risk in schizophrenia: explanatory models and clinical implications, The Schematic Appraisal Model of Suicide (SAMS). Psychol Psychother 2008; 81: 55–77

Joiner, T. E. (2005) Why people die by suicide. Cambridge, Mass: Harvard University Press

Joiner, T. E. (2010) Myths about suicide. Cambridge, Mass: Harvard University Press

Joiner, T. E., Van Orden, K. A., Witte, T. K. and Rudd, M.D. (2009) The interpersonal theory of suicide: guidance for working with suicidal clients. Washington, DC: American Psychological Association

Joiner, T. E., Buchman-Schmitt, J. M., Chu, C. and Hom, M. A. (2017) A sociobiological extension of the interpersonal theory of suicide. Crisis, 38(2), 69-72

Kelly, G. A. (1961) Suicide: the personal construct point of view. In The Cry for Help, (ed.) N. Farberow and E. S. Shneidman, pp. 255-280. New York, NY: McGraw-Hill

Kety, S. (1986) Genetic factors in suicide. In A. Roy, Suicide (ed.) pp. 41-45. Baltimore: Williams & Wilkins

Klonsky, D. E. and May, A. M. (2015) The Three-Step Theory (3ST): A New Theory of Suicide Rooted in the "Ideation-to-Action" Framework. International Journal of Cognitive Therapy, 8(2), 114–129

Klonsky, E. D. and Dixon-Luinenburg, T. (2022) Mental Disorders and Beyond in the Quest to Understand Suicide: A Reply to Joiner and Robison. Archives in Suicide Research. Published online on 4 Jan 2022. Accessed on 26 September 2022 at https://www.tandfonline.com/doi/full/10.1080/13811118.2021.2005726?scroll=top&needAccess=true

Kraepelin, E. (1983/1915) Textbook of psychiatry. 1915

Lifton, R. J., Kato, S. and Reich, M.R. (1979) Six lives / Six deaths. New Haven, CT: Yale University Press

Leenaars, A. A. (1988) Suicide notes. New York, NY: Human Sciences

Lester, D. (1994) A comparison of 15 theories of suicide. Suicide and Life-threatening Behaviour, 24(1), pp80-88

Litman, R. E. (1967) Sigmund Freud on suicide. In Essays in Self-destruction, ed. E. S. Shneidman pp. 324-344. New York, NY: Science House

Mann, J. J., Waternaux, C., Haas, G.L., and Malone, K. M. (1999) Toward a clinical model of suicidal behavior in psychiatric patients. Am J Psychiatry 1999; 156: 181–89

Maris, R. (1981) Pathways to suicide: a survey of self-destructive behaviours. Baltimore: John Hopkins University Press

MASH (1970/1972) Lyrics 'Suicide is painless'. Johnny Mantel. Accessed on 6 April 2021 at https://genius.com/Johnny-mandel-suicide-is-painless-lyrics

Mencken, H. L. (1920) Prejudices: Second Series, Volume 2. Page 158. New York, NY: Alfred A. Knopf. Accessed on 6 April 2021 at https://books.google.co.uk/books?id=hy47AAAAYAAJ&q=well-known&redir_esc=y&hl=en#v=snippet&

Menninger, K. A. (1938) Man against himself. New York, NY: Harcourt, Brace and World

Miller, J. G. (1978) Living systems. New York, NY: McGraw-Hill

Murray, H. A. (1938) Explorations in Personality. New York, NY: Oxford Universities Press

NISRA (2021) Deaths by suicide: intentional self-harm and undetermined intent, 2019. Accessed on 30 April 2021 at https://www.nisra.gov.uk/publications/registrar-general-annual-report-2019-cause-death

O'Connor, R. and Sheehy, N.P. (2000) Understanding suicidal behaviour. Leicester, UK: BPS Books

O'Connor, R.C. (2011) Towards an integrated motivational–volitional model of suicidal behaviour. In R. C. O'Connor, S. Platt, J. Gordon (Eds) International Handbook of Suicide Prevention: Research, Policy and Practice. Chichester: John Wiley & Sons, 2011: pp181–98.

O'Connor, R. C. and Nock, M. K. (2014) The Psychology of Suicidal Behaviour. Lancet Psychiatry, Vol. 1, 73-85. Accessed on 8 April 2021 at http://dx.doi.org/10.1016/ S2215-0366(14)70222-6

O'Connor, R. C. (2016) Blog: Youth Suicide prevention needs more than social media regulation. Posted Feb 12, 2019, 243 pm by Karen Wetherall [updated Feb 14, 2029, 8:29am]. Accessed on 4 April 2021 at http://wwwsuicideresearch.info/news1/youthsuicidepreventionneedsmorethansocialmediaregulation

O'Connor, R.C., and Kirtley, O.J. (2018) The Integrated Motivational-Volitional Model of Suicidal Behaviour. Philosophical Transactions of the Royal Society B. 373: 20170268.

O'Keeffe, P. (2010) Client suicide and clinician identity: an investigation of identity development in clinician survivors of client suicide. Unpublished doctoral dissertation. Jordanstown, N Ireland: University of Ulster

Paniagua, F. A., Black, S. A., Gallaway, M. S. & Coombs, M. A. (2010) The interpersonal-psychological theory of attempted and completed suicide. Bloomington, IN: AuthorHouse

Pepper, S. (1942) World Hypotheses. Berkeley: University of California Press

Pfeffer, C. (1986) The suicidal child. Berkeley: University of California Press

Probert-Lindström, S., Berge, J., Westrin, Å. et al. (2020) Long-term risk factors for suicide in suicide attempters examined at a medical emergency in patient unit: results from a 32-year follow-up study. BMJ Open 2020; 10:e038794. doi:10.1136/ bmjopen-2020-038794

Richman, J. (1986) Family therapy for suicidal individuals. New York, NY: Springer

Roy, A., (ed.) (1986) Suicide. Baltimore: Williams & Wilkins

Rudd, M. D., Joiner, T. and Rajab, M. H. (2001) Treating suicidal behaviour: an effective, time-limited approach. New York, NY: Guilford Press

Runyon, W. M. (1982) Life Histories and Psychobiography: Explorations in Theory and Method. New York, NY: Oxford Univ Press

Schotte, D. E. and Clum, G. A. (1987) Problem-solving skills in suicidal psychiatric patients. J Consult Clin Psychol 1987; 55: 49–54

Shneidman, E. S. (1985) Definition of suicide. New York, NY: Wiley

Shneidman, E. S. (1993) Suicide as psychache: a clinical approach to self-destructive behaviour. Northvale, NJ: Jason Aronson Inc

Shneidman, E. S. (1993b) Figure 3-1. A theoretical cubic model of suicide. From "A psychological Approach to Suicide" E. S. Shneidman, 1987, in G. R. Vandenbos and B. K. Bryant (eds.), Cataclysms, Crises and Catastrophes: Psychology in Action. Washington, DC: American Psychological Association. Copyright©1987 by the American Psychological Association. Reprinted by permission.

Shneidman, E. S. (1999) Conceptual contribution: the psychological pain assessment scale. Suicide and Life-threatening Behaviour, 29(4), Winter 1999, 287-291

Shneidman, E. S. and Farberow, N. (eds.) (1957) Clues to suicide. New York, NY: McGraw-Hill

Silverman, M.M. and Berman, A. L. (2020) Feeling ill at ease with a new disease: labeling suicide-related behaviours as a DSM-5 diagnosis. Crisis, 41(4), 241-247

Sussmilch, J. (1741) Die GottlicheOrdnung in den Veranderungen des MenschlichenGeschlechts, aus der Geburt, dem Tode und der Fortflanzugdessenbenerwiesen. Berlin: J. C. Spenser

Tyler, L. (1984) Thinking creatively. San Francisco: Jossey-Bass

The UK Supreme Court (2020) R (on the application of Maughan) Appellant v Her Majesty's Senior Coroner for Oxfordshire (Respondent) [2020] UKSC 46. On appeal from [2019] EWCA Civ 809

Wenzel, A. and Beck, A. T. (2008) A cognitive model of suicidal behaviour: theory and treatment. Applied and Preventive Psychology. 12(4). 189-201. October 2008.

Williams, J. M. G. (2001) The cry of pain. London: Penguin

Williams, J. M. G., Van der Does, A. J. W., Barnhofer, T., Crane C. and Segal, Z. S. (2008) Cognitive reactivity, suicidal ideation and future fluency: preliminary investigation of a differential activation theory of hopelessness/suicidality. Cognit Ther Res 2008; 32: 83–104.

Zilboorg, G. (1937) Considerations in suicide with particular reference to that of the young. American Journal of Orthopsychiatry 7:15-31

\* \* \*

## Chapter 10
# Camus – the only problem

**Introduction**

Dorothy Rowe (1991: 205), an Australian child psychologist, wrote that a person contemplating suicide should not overlook the fact that to die by suicide involved both choice and action: 'We have to choose to die and we have to take powerful actions in order to kill ourselves.'

A decade and a half later, Joiner (2005) stated that any person will die by suicide because they want to and because they can – in short because they develop, simultaneously, both the desire and the capability to do so (Joiner et al., 2009: 4). Since 2005, these few words have intrigued suicidology, not least because they re-stated as an undisputed fact, what was the staringly, logically obvious, not least since Rowe (1991). The only issue then appeared to be, in Northern Ireland for example, why deaths by suicide hover between 1.3% and 2% of all deaths? It's almost as if the issue of suicide – allegedly a major public health issue (Black & McKay, 2019), 2019) – has been reduced to two questions: why suicide? and how suicide? Choice and Action? So according to Joiner (2005), that's what the suicide prevention conundrum boils down to - why? and how? – and what are we to do about that?

The Northern Ireland government's attitude to suicide was summed up in their latest strategy document:

'It is important that we acknowledge that suicide is a major problem in our society and, also, that it is preventable. The feelings that drive suicide are often temporary. With the right help, people can get through a suicidal crisis and recover' (Protect Life 2, 2019: 2).

O'Neill, S. et al. (2016: 13), writing in a Northern Ireland context, were more circumspect, not to say realistic:

'Suicide is an important and *potentially* preventable cause of mortality' (italics added).

Whether optimism or realism inform the state's motivation, regarding suicide prevention, it is back to the beginning in several ways: a person will be unable to die by suicide, if and when 'the feelings that drive suicide', that is their 'desire' and their 'capability' are unavailable. The inverse will also be true: if and when 'desire' is stimulated and 'capability' is close at hand, then – in the absence of a life-saving, external intervention – suicide will occur. The complexity of human suicidal behaviour, according to Joiner (2005, 2009, 2010) rests within that desire-capability nexus, concealed from others within the individual consciousness of each person.

An alternative analysis by one of the founders of modern suicidology, that purports to be the scientific study of human self-destruction, was articulated persuasively by Shneidman (2005) who held that:

'suicide is *not* a disease of the brain, like senility, but rather has a very different formula, specifically that suicide *is* rather extreme [unbearable] psychological pain coupled with the idea that death [cessation] can provide a solution to the problem of seemingly unacceptable [psychological] distress' – italics in original (Shneidman, 2005: 7).

It seemed that for Joiner et al. (2009) 'desire to die by suicide' translated for Shneidman (2005) into 'intolerable psychological pain' or psychache, while for Joiner et al. (2009) 'capability to kill myself' was rendered for Shneidman (2005: 10) into lethally self-destructive action that resulted in 'cessation of consciousness'.

The question then arises, regarding the libraries that have been, and are being, written considering how to prevent suicide: why as yet has no effective, efficient, economic psychotherapeutic methodology been devised, proven and promulgated. As yet, nobody knows, although Joiner et al. (2009: 110) conceded that, regarding outpatient treatment 'several psychotherapies have been shown to be effective in preventing suicide attempts'. They listed the following as 'promising':

'cognitive therapy, dialectical behaviour therapy, problem-solving therapy, multisystem therapy, and partial hospitalization with a psychoanalytic focus as well as interpersonal psychotherapy and mindfulness-based cognitive therapy' (Joiner et al., 2009: 110).

The most recent published attempt to locate conclusive evidence of an effective psychotherapy was a meta-analysis by Swift et al. (2021) that compared the Collaborative Assessment and Management of Suicidality (CAMS) approach with several other commonly used interventions for the treatment of suicide and other suicide related variables, including 'medication, cognitive therapy, cognitive-behavioural therapy, and dialectical behaviour therapy [DBT]' (p2). This study concluded that 'the results of this meta-analysis provide strong evidence for CAMS as an intervention for suicidal ideation' (Swift et al., 2021: 12).

**Camus 1**

Where does Camus come in? A Nobel literature prize winner, he died in 1960, aged 47, in a car accident. Hence he was limited in being able only to access suicidological analyses extant at the time, including inter alia those of Freud, Jung, Durkheim, Zilboorg, Murray, Menninger, Foucault and Allport. He was thus unable to experience the explosion of studies in suicidology during the following six decades to date. Indeed his attitude to suicide may therefore have been conditioned and programmed primarily by his personal, experiential, developmental, philosophical and existential explorations that inter alia produced the Myth of Sisyphus (Camus, 1942/2005). This short work featured a single sentence that expressed his idiosyncratic perspective:

'There is but one truly serious philosophical problem and that is suicide' (Camus, 1942/2005: 1).

Shneidman (2005: 7) discussed briefly 'some philosophical aspects of suicide' in his consideration of anodyne psychotherapy for suicide. Earlier he defined 'an anodyne' as 'a substance that, or a person who, relieves *pain*' (italics in original). The psychotherapist's main function is to be anodynic; to lessen pain ... for anyone' (Shneidman, 1996: 151). Shneidman (2005: 7) said Camus held that 'the central problem for philosophy was the enigma of suicide – wrestling with the complicated question (often asked in the midst of pain): Why stay alive?' Shneidman added that 'two historic philosophic forces were engaged in an ongoing territorial fight for ownership of suicide' (p7). These forces he labelled *'brain'* and *'mind'* – italics in original:

'... whether suicide is to be understood primarily in psychiatric terms as a biological disorder in the brain, as a mental disease called depression (and treated with anti-depressive medications) or whether it is to be best understood as a psychological drama in the mind related to psychological pain and suffering and best addressed by focusing on the reduction of the person's psychache, [and] treated in terms of the sufferer's own vocabulary' (Shneidman, 2005: 7).

He added that in philosophic terms, it is a choice between the 'mechanistic' Rene Descartes (1596-1650) and the 'humanistic' David Hume (1711-1776) and thus choosing between:

'the notions of German psychiatrist Emile Kraepelin (1856-1926) who believed there were diseases of the personality comparable to diseases of the perineum – or a fealty to the notions of French sociologist Emile Durkheim (1858-1917) who related suicide to inner feelings (like estrangement or loneliness or anomie) and to their ties to the larger society' (Shneidman, 2005: 7).

Not being medically qualified, I am drawn to Shneidman's (2005: 11) reasoning that among 'many patterns of frustrated psychological needs that [can] lead to suicide ... about half a dozen can be differentiated' including:

'Thwarted *love,* acceptance, belonging – related to frustrated needs for succorance and affiliation.

*'Fractured control* – related to frustrated needs for achievement, autonomy, order, and understanding.

'Assaulted self-image and avoidance of *shame*, defeat, humiliation, disgrace, related to frustrated needs for affiliation, defendance and shame-avoidance.

'Ruptured key relationships and the attendant *grief* and bereftness – related to frustrated needs for affiliation and nurturance.

'Excessive *anger,* rage and hostility – related to frustrated needs for dominance, aggression and counteraction.'

(italics in original) (Shneidman, 1996: 25).

Although Shneidman (2005: 8) was not medically qualified he acknowledged 'several intellectual disciplines...that touch on suicidology' namely philosophy, history, sociology, biochemistry/medicine, psychiatry, psychoanalysis, biography, survivorship and volunteers. Although he did not advocate suicidology qua suicidology as a distinct, self-standing scientific discipline, a recent consideration of suicidology as a 'social practice' examined its distinctiveness:

'Suicidology, we argue, can be conceived of as a social practice which is i) directed towards an overall purpose, ii) shaped by particular traditions, iii) dependent upon processes of learning and socialisation to sustain it, iv) in possession of an internal authority structure which governs particular ways of seeing and doing, and v) embedded socially, culturally, historically, and politically' (Fitzpatrick et al., 2014).

These five aspects of intellectual and/or research endeavour were believed to be present in the study and practice of suicidology:

'Suicide has long been the subject of philosophical, literary, theological, and cultural-historical inquiry. But despite the diversity of disciplinary and methodological approaches that have been brought to bear in the study of suicide, we argue that the formal study of suicide, that is, suicidology, is characterised by intellectual, organisational, and professional values that distinguish it from other ways of thinking and knowing ... considering suicidology as a 'social practice' offers ways to usefully conceptualise its epistemological, philosophical, and practical norms' (Fitzpatrick et al., 2014).

The absence of recognised, scientific credentials for suicidology has unfortunately resulted in open season in relation to evidence-free publication of anything and everything about suicide and its prevention, in mainstream and social media. Hence Alvarez's concession (1971/74: 14) that nearly everyone (and presumably anyone) had their own uncontested views about suicide.

Camus the philosopher, and Frankl the psychiatrist were two exceptionally able writers on human self-destruction whose views on suicide were somewhat more worthy of examination and consideration than many.

## Camus 2

Alvarez (1971/74) stated 'I offer no solutions. I don't in fact believe that solutions exist, since suicide means different things for different people at different times' (p13), before acknowledging the very many who offered him 'references, ideas and suggestions' while he was writing his book (p14). He included Camus' 'The Myth of Sisyphus' – 'a beautiful philosophical essay' – as an important influence (p12). When Camus wrote The Myth of Sisyphus – in 1940, after the fall of France, a serious illness and some kind of depressive crisis – he began with suicide as 'but one truly philosophical problem' (Camus, 1942/2005: 1) and ended with an affirmation of individual life, in itself and for itself, desirable because it is 'absurd', without final meaning or metaphysical justification (Alvarez, 1971/74: 151).

Alvarez noted that in relation to suicide, a 'large mass of material on the topic grows larger every year ... little of [which] is of much interest to anyone except the specialist, and even less has to do with what the layman personally knows of suicide' (p12). Yet, the vast majority of suicide victims and survivors bereaved by suicide are concentrated in the latter category. In my experience, as a survivor, researcher, teacher and writer on suicide, I can confirm the ongoing 'taboo' applied to the phenomenon by media in Northern Ireland, although most available outlets schedule an occasional article or broadcast as and when a 'story in the public interest' comes their way.

Camus, born in Algeria, then a French colony, became a prolific writer of novels, plays and essays. He was active in the Resistance during the Nazi occupation of France (1940-45), and later called for a non-violent resolution of the Algerian war (1954-62), advocating a federal Algeria where Algerian Arabs and his own people, the European pied noirs, could live in peace. Throughout his life he wrestled with the existential notion of the meaninglessness of human life: 'Though he showed lust for life and a Mediterranean oneness with nature, happiness was an unrelenting quest' (Marlowe, 2013).

Lara Marlowe added that Camus in his literature presented his characters addressing their various experiences and interactions in what he believed to be an absurd universe. He dramatised his notion of the absurdity of life when, writing in the first person via stream of consciousness, he specifically characterised Meursault's murder of an innocent Arab in 'The Outsider' (1946/73) as the act of a 'man condemned [to death] because he does not play the game ... an outsider to the society in which he lives, wandering on the fringe, on the outskirts of life, solitary and sensual' (Drazin, 2012). Cyril Connelly, cited in the introduction to Camus (1946/73: 9), excoriated the corrupt, colonial power structure: 'The Bourgeois Machinery with its decaying Christian morality and bureaucratic self-righteousness which condemns the Outsider [to death] just because he is so foreign to it ... is typical of a European code of Justice applied to a non-European people'. He added that 'a few hundred miles farther south [of French Algeria] and a "touch of the Sun" would have been recognised, no doubt, as a cause for acquittal, in the case of a white man accused of murdering a native (sic), but part of the rigidity of the moribund French court is the pompous assumption that Algiers is France' (Camus, 1946: 9).

While being closely associated with the existentialism of Sartre and de Beauvoir for several years, his book 'The Rebel' (Camus, 1951/2000) denounced the totalitarianism of the Soviet Union, and created a permanent rift with these pro-Soviet communist intellectuals. Although Hendricks (2018) said Camus 'preferred not to be called a philosopher' following 'The Rebel': he wished to be considered separately from 'the existential school of thought'. However, Yalom (1980a) described Camus as one of several 'leading existential thinkers' (p16) for whom the quest for meaning, as represented inter alia in goals, values, and ideals, could be a matter of life or death:

'I have seen many people die because life for them was not worth living. From this I conclude that the question of life's meaning is the most urgent question of all' (Camus, cited by Yalom, 1980b: 420).

Alvarez (1971/74: 114) quoted Camus' view that 'what is called a reason for living is also an excellent reason for dying'. Camus' attitude to suicide – 'the only philosophical problem' – was a logical outworking of his claim that, since there was no more 'meaning' in death than in life, then searching for what made life worth living was not an unreasonable activity. In short, suicide would conclude prematurely what Camus held was an interesting, even if ultimately – in his view – a futile task. Alvarez (1971/74) concluded his masterly work, citing Camus:

'There is only one liberty, wrote Camus in his Notebooks, to come to terms with death. After which, everything is possible' (p283).

Hendricks (2018) believed Camus had 'some great insights on the meaning of life, why you should look to this life and not the next, and why suicide is a poor choice'. He argued that Camus' view, although somewhat disturbing and challenging, contained potentially valuable insights about how to cope with 'our existential dread', offering some suggestions on 'how to live our meaningless lives'. However, there was no shifting Camus from his firm conviction that all and any attempts by science, philosophy, society or religion to find an answer to the question of the meaning of life would be 'immune to the problem of the *absurdity* of life'. Wikipedia offered a definition of this seldom used term:

'An absurdity is a thing that is extremely unreasonable, so as to be foolish or not taken seriously, or the state of being so' (Wikipedia, 2021).

In his The Myth of Sisyphus, Albert Camus offered four roles for people who recognised the absurdity of life. The first was to take Don Juan as an example: reject the notions of sin, damnation, and salvation, and seek the enjoyment of sex and other sensations. The second would use the actor as a paradigm: seek to enjoy every part you play with intensity as you encounter new people and experiences. The third looked at the conqueror: know that conquests are impermanent, but enjoy the pleasure of the quests. The last was the creative artist who knew that he can't change the world, but enjoyed what he could do. In short, an intelligent person who saw the absurdity of life should seek what pleasures he can obtain while alive, without feeling guilt (Drazin, 2012).

Camus attempted to lift readers out of their existential gloom by suggesting that the 'meaninglessness' and 'absurdity' of life and living should be addressed by humanity just like any other problem. Hendricks (2018) implied that Camus may have edged a bit close to the 'do as I say not as I do' camp when he compared the meaninglessness of life with 'background fact, like gravity, that must be reckoned with' by humanity. Although Yalom (1980a: 15) recognised Kierkegaard's important contribution to existential philosophy, Camus was less kind, criticising the Danish philosopher, who 'understood that life was absurd but fled towards God rather than embracing the fact' (Hendricks, 2018). Camus' answer was to 'embrace the meaninglessness', become an exemplar [like Camus] and 'get through it with a smile'. Undoubtedly, Camus may be more fully understood as a man of his times by what he wrote.

J. M. Coetzee, like Camus, a recipient of the Nobel Prize for Literature, considered that all literature mirrored the experiential life of the author:

"In a larger sense, all writing is autobiography: everything that you write, including criticism and fiction, writes you as you write it" (Professor Wu, 2016).

Jorge Luis Borges, a highly regarded Argentinean author, expressed the same view more colourfully:

"I wrote a story once about a man who began a very large picture, and therein was a kind of map – for example, hills, horses, streams, fishes, and woods and towers and men and all sorts of things. When the day of his death came, he found he had been making a picture of himself. That is the case with most writers" (Professor Wu, 2016)'.

Harper Lee, Emerson and Samuel Butler expressed similar sentiments (Professor Wu, 2016). If we apply these opinions to Camus' writing, then Hendricks (2018) argued that:

'Across his body of work, he (Camus) praises sunshine, women, the beach, kissing, dancing, and good food. He loved sports and was a champion soccer player in his youth. He took great enjoyment in the little things and encourages us to do so as well. Just because life is meaningless doesn't mean it can't be enjoyable!'

Camus concluded that our inability – as he believed – to find a meaning in life that can satisfy our needs, ought not to drive us 'into the loving arms of religion, science, society or even producing meaning ourselves' (Hendricks, 2018).

Viktor Frankl endured years of unspeakable horror in four Nazi death camps, including Auschwitz: he expressed a view that was radically different to Camus' as to the meaning of life and the meaning of the world.

## Viktor Frankl

Dr Viktor Frankl (1905-1997) was a psychiatrist whose interests bridged the boundary between philosophy and psychotherapy. His life experience, particularly his response to incarceration as prisoner number 119104 in the Auschwitz concentration camp by the Nazis, and his response to its barbaric cruelty, formed the basis of his book, 'Man's Search for Meaning', that he wrote over nine days in 1945 (Frankl, 1959/85: 16). He described how his own 'deep desire ... striving and struggling for a worthwhile goal, a freely chosen task' (p126-127) to reconstruct a ready for publication manuscript confiscated from him on arrival at Auschwitz, enabled him to survive both serious physical disease, viz. typhus fever and the risk of cardiovascular collapse. As noted by Nietzsche, and cited by Frankl: 'S/he who has a *why* to live for can bear almost any *how*' (p126) – italics in original.

Mark Dawes (2020), introduced Frankl's book in a YouTube video #1 (2020), by citing Frankl's opening response to his psychotherapy patients after they listed the problems and dilemmas that brought them to therapy. That response was 'Why do you not commit suicide?' Allport (1959/1985) revealed, in relation to 'the suicide question', that:

'from their answers he (Frankl) can often find the guide-line for his psychotherapy. In one life, there is the love for one's children to tie to; in another life, a talent to be used; in a third, perhaps only lingering memories worth preserving. To weave these slender threads of a broken life into a firm pattern of meaning and responsibility is the object and challenge of logotherapy ... Dr Frankl's own version of modern existential analysis' (Allport, cited in Frankl, 1959/85: 9).

Logotherapy was devised by Frankl in response, as a practicing psychiatrist, to his insights into how those incarcerated by the Nazis, including himself, survived concentration camp brutality. 'Logos' is a Greek word for 'meaning'. The Viktor Frankl Institute of Logotherapy in Israel (VFILI) represents the current, practical application of the 'Logotherapy in a Nutshell' chapter of Frankl's book (1959/85).

What has occurred to me (this writer), as a reason not to die by suicide, is different to those cited by Allport – see above, which I acknowledge and appreciate – but rather an ego-driven desire to 'see what happens next' or 'to find out how it all works out' rather than choosing to close the curtains on my life prematurely – given that death, my death, is the certainty that I live with daily.

Frankl described inter alia three examples of highly unlikely transitions that, for him, illustrated and exemplified 'one of the main features of human existence [being] the capacity to rise above' (p154) seemingly impossible, unbearable situations, when these are able to be perceived and understood in the context of their existential meaning and purpose:

i) An elderly GP consulted Dr Frankl because of his severe depression, two years after the death of his much-loved wife. Frankl reframed the GP's predicament by asking him 'What would have happened, Doctor, if you had died first, and your wife would have had to survive you?' He replied 'Oh, for her this would have been terrible; how she would have suffered!' Dr Frankl then replied, 'You see, Doctor, such a suffering has been spared her, and it was you who have spared her this suffering – to be sure at the price that now you have to survive and mourn her'. The GP said nothing, shook Dr Frankl's hand and calmly left his office. Frankl's lesson here was that suffering ceases to be suffering the moment it finds a meaning, such as the meaning of a sacrifice (p135).

ii) An Eastern European rabbi told Dr Frankl that he'd lost his first wife and six children in Auschwitz where they were gassed. He survived, but it turned out his second wife was sterile. Although Dr Frankl observed that procreation was not the only meaning of life, the rabbi 'evaluated his plight as an orthodox Jew in terms of despair that there was no son of his own who would ever say Kaddish [prayer for the dead] for him after his death.' Relying on the therapeutic effect of the rabbi's religious conviction, and thus his spiritual resources, Dr Frankl enquired of him did he not hope to see his children again in Heaven. The rabbi's response was that since his children died as innocent martyrs, they merited the highest place in heaven, but 'as for himself, he could not expect, as an old, sinful man to be assigned the same place'. Dr Frankl then suggested that, perhaps, the meaning of the rabbi's surviving his children was that he might be purified through his years of suffering, and though not innocent, that he might become worthy of joining them in Heaven. This new point of view was sufficient to offer the rabbi relief from his suffering (p142-143).

iii) A young mother attempted to die by suicide, alongside her older son, who was disabled by infantile paralysis and in a wheelchair, following the sad death of her younger son, aged 11. Her son prevented this – he liked living, life remained meaningful for him. The therapist's task was to explore why this was not the case for his mother, how could she be supported so that her life could still have a meaning. Dr Frankl invited this mother to imagine being 80 years old, on her death-bed and looking back on her life, as a childless woman but full of financial success and social prestige. Dr Frankl asked her 'What will you think of it? What will you say to yourself?' Her tape recorded response was: 'Oh, I married a millionaire, I had an easy life full of wealth, and lived it up! I flirted with men; I teased them! But now I am eighty; I have no children of my own. Looking back as an old woman, I cannot see what all that was for; actually I must say my life was a failure!' Dr Frankl then asked her to look back at age eighty on her own life. Her recorded response reflected her wish to have children, how one boy had died and a second was [disabled] and would have been sent to an institution if she had not taken over his care. She then said: 'Though he is [disabled] and helpless, he is after all my boy. And so I have made a better human being out of my son'. Then in tears, she added that she could look back peacefully on her life, realise that it was full of meaning, and that she had done her best for herself and for her son. 'My life was no failure!' she added (p139-140).

Allport's reference to Dr Frankl's 'suicide question' resonates with Dr Orbach's (2001) use of 'therapeutic empathy' in psychotherapeutic work with a client at risk of suicide. He said that he would invite his client, to 'actually "convince" me [his therapist] that suicide is the only solution left' (Orbach, 2001: 174). Orbach said he would then 'participate in the consideration of suicide as an actual alternative without pressing against the suicidal decision.'

The next paragraph briefly considers Frankl's logotherapy in relation to existential principles.

## Victor Frankl's Existentialism

Magrini (2020) examined Frankl's key ideas associated with logotherapy and their relationship – if any – with existential principles in order to illuminate the related philosophical elements of logotherapy. He concluded that Frankl was more of an 'existentialist' than he would care to admit and that his psychotherapeutic approach could be called 'existential psychology'. Yalom (1980a: 15) referred to existential psychotherapy as the exploration of themes related to existence including being, choice, death, freedom, isolation and absurdity. Frankl's life experience after surviving Auschwitz had concentrated upon the power of man's search for meaning (or purpose or goal or objective) as a vital therapeutic change agent. He concocted the phrase 'will to meaning', as a kind of differentiation from Adler's 'will to power' or Freud's 'will to pleasure' (or pleasure principle), emphasizing that 'striving to find a meaning in one's life is the primary motivational force in man' (Frankl, 1959/85: 121).

Yalom (1980a) was not fully persuaded that logotherapy was a valid therapeutic approach although he stated that Frankl was 'an eminently pragmatic thinker' (Yalom, 1980a: 17). He did consider further how 'meaning or purpose of life' might be assessed psychometrically. In a preliminary remark, he cited Erik Erikson's suggestion that 'one must ... solve the task of establishing self-worth and personal identity before being able to develop a satisfying sense of life meaning' (Yalom, 1980a: 459). Yalom (1980a) offered the following summary of relevant research results:

i) The less the sense of meaning, the greater the severity of psychopathology

ii) A positive sense of meaning is associated with deeply held religious beliefs

iii) A positive sense of meaning is associated with self-transcendent values [The quintessential example of self-transcendence is undoubtedly Viktor Frankl's experience in the concentration camps of World War II. Despite his great personal suffering (and frequently having few or none of Maslow's 'hierarchy of needs' met)—or perhaps because of it—Frankl found a higher purpose in his life.]

iv) A positive sense of meaning in life is associated with membership in groups, dedication to some cause, and adoption of clear life goals

v) Life meaning must be viewed in a developmental perspective: the types of life meaning change over an individual's life; other developmental tasks must precede development of meaning (Yalom, 1980a: 459-460).

## Conclusion

I found no evidence that Camus was aware of or familiar with Frankl's work – or vice versa. Their lives overlapped in part – Camus (1913-1960) and Frankl (1905-1997) – but their professional lives, one a philosopher–author the other a psychiatrist–author, were somewhat diverse. As outlined above, each was aware of the existence of suicide as a powerful influence over human thought and action. Unfortunately, because of his tragic, early death we cannot know how Camus might eventually have engaged with Frankl on an intellectual, philosophical or psychotherapeutic level.

**Myth:** (fictitious popular idea) Suicide as a public health issue can be effectively addressed without improved access to effective counselling and psychotherapy

**Fallacy:** (misleading argument) Suicidology does not merit consideration as a discrete discipline in college and university syllibi

## References

Allport, G. W. (1959/85) Preface, to V. E. Frankl 'Man's Search for meaning', pp 9-13. New York, NY: Washington Square Press

Alvarez, A. (1971/74) The savage god: a study of suicide. London: Penguin Books Ltd

Black, L.A. & McKay, K. (2019) Suicide statistics and strategy in Northern Ireland: Update. 28 November 2019. A blog from the Northern Ireland Assembly Research and Information Service

Camus, A. (1942/2005) The Myth of Sisyphus. London: Penguin Books

Camus, A. (1946/73) The Outsider. London: Penguin Modern Classics

Camus, A. (1951/2000) The Rebel. London: Penguin Books

Dawes, M. (2020) Response to Viktor Frankl re 'why not suicide'. Accessed on 22 May 2021 at https://www.youtube.com/watch?v=DTvYZz1Cxg8

Dattilio, F. M. (2003) When life calls out to us: the love and lifework of Viktor and Elly Frankl. American Journal of Psychotherapy, Vol 57, 1. 140-142

Drazin, I. (2012) Camus' understanding of the meaning of life: The Outsider. Accessed on 26 May 2021 at https://booksnthoughts.com/camus-understanding-of-the-meaning-of-life/

Fitzpatrick, S. J., Hooker, C. and Kerridge, I. (2014) Suicidology as a social practice. Social Epistemology. Online first 12 March 2014. Accessed on 27 May 2021 at http://www.imhlk.com/wp-content/uploads/2019/09/suicidology-as-social-practice-PP-2014.pdf

Frankl, V. E. (1959/1985) Man's search for meaning. New York, NY: Washington Square Press

Hendricks, S. (2018) The meaning of life: Albert Camus on faith, suicide, and absurdity. Accessed on 30 April 2021 at https://bigthink.com/scotty-hendricks/the-meaning-of-life-albert-camus-on-faith-suicide-and-absurdity

Jaffe, A. (1970) The myth of meaning in the work of C. J. Jung. London: Hodder & Stoughton

Joiner, T. E. (2005) Why people die by suicide. Cambridge, MA: Harvard University Press

Joiner, T. E., Van Orden, K. A., Witte, T. K. and Rudd, M. D. (2009) The interpersonal theory of suicide: guidance for working with suicidal clients. Washington, DC: American Psychological Association

Joiner, T. E. (2010) Myths about suicide. Cambridge, MA: Harvard University Press

Magrini, J. M. (2020) Frankl's logotherapy and the existentialism of Camus, Jaspers and Sartre. Accessed on 25 May 2021 at https://www.academia.edu/42990290/Frankls_Logotherapy_and_the_Existentialism_of_Camus_Jaspers_and_Sartre

Marlowe, L. (2013) How absurd: the world as Albert Camus saw it. The Irish Times. Monday 7 November 2013

O'Neill, S., Corry, C., McFeeters, D., Murphy, M. and Bunting, B. (2016) Suicide in Northern Ireland – an analysis of gender differences in demographic, psychological and contextual factors. Crisis, 2016, Vol. 37(1), 13-20

Orbach, I. (2001) Therapeutic empathy with the suicidal wish: principles of therapy with suicidal individuals. American Journal of Psychotherapy, 2001, 55(2), pp 166-184

Professor Wu (2016) Writing as autobiography – is there no difference between fiction and non-fiction? Accessed on 18 May 2021 at https://nothingintherulebook.com/2016/02/19/writing-as-autobiography-is-there-no-difference-between-fiction-and-non-fiction/

Protect Life 2 (2019) A strategy for preventing suicide and self-harm in Northern Ireland 2019-2024. Department of Health. NI Government, Stormont, Belfast

Rowe, D. (1991) Breaking the bonds: understanding depression, finding freedom. London: Fontana, HarperCollins

Shneidman, E. S. (1996) The suicidal mind. New York, NY: Oxford University Press

Shneidman, E. S. (2005) Anodyne psychotherapy for suicide: a psychological view of suicide. Clinical Neuropsychiatry, 2005, 2(1), 7-12

Swift, J. K, Trusty, W. T. and Penix, E. A. (2021) The effectiveness of the Collaborative Assessment and Management of Suicidality (CAMS)

compared to alternative treatment conditions: A meta-analysis. Suicide and Life-threatening Behaviour, 2021; 51-5, 882-896 https://doi.org/10.1111/sltb.1276

Wikipedia (2021) The meaning of 'absurdity'. Accessed on 18 May 2021 at https://en.wikipedia.org/wiki/Absurdity

Yalom, I. D. (1980a) Existential psychotherapy. US: Basic Books (Perseus Books Group)

Yalom, I. D. (1980b) Camus, in Aniela Jaffe (1970) The myth of meaning in the work of C. J. Jung. Title page. London: Hodden& Stoughton. Cited in I. D. Yalom (1980a) Existential psychotherapy, p420. US: Basic Books (Perseus Books Group)

YouTube video #1 (2020) Mark Dawes. Accessed on 22 May 2021 at https://www.youtube.com/watch?v=DTvYZz1Cxg8

Viktor Frankl Institute of Logotherapy in Israel (VFILI) (2021) Suicidal ideation. Accessed on 22 May 2021 at https://themeaningseeker.org/suicidal-ideation

\* \* \*

## Chapter 11
# Suicide – justice for the deceased

**Introduction**

In chapter 15 (below) on the vocabulary or language of suicide, I note the multiple 'reported definitions of suicide' from Durkheim (1897/2002) to the World Health Organisation (WHO, 2022). In the current chapter, I rely upon the conventional or everyday meaning of the term, i.e. the act of taking one's life, although Shneidman's (1994: 6) 'fairly slim book', entitled 'Definition of Suicide', that states this preliminary definition, extends to a total of 257 pages of analysis and discussion.

I refer to this matter because in Northern Ireland in 1981, 10 men died during their 'hunger strike' protest in prison, in relation to their demand for perceived status as political prisoners, viz. 'prisoners of war', rather than 'ordinary decent prisoners' jailed on conviction and sentence for criminal offence/s. Over 30 years later, Tomlinson (2012) noted that:

'while Irish Republicans saw the deaths as tantamount to "murder", Unionists ... saw the deaths as "self-inflicted" and a matter of free choice. These deaths were in fact classified as "suicides" by the [Northern Ireland] Registrar General's office, a label avoided by the Catholic church at the time' (Tomlinson, 2012).

It appears that coroner's inquests for the ten deceased prisoners recorded verdicts (sic) of "starvation, self-imposed" (O'Keeffe, T., 1984). So, in the current chapter, what would 'justice for the suicide deceased' mean, when we include deaths where the 'suicide' label was, for whatever reason, disputed?

Justice for the murdered deceased is a rudimentary historical notion that recognises murder's criminal, punishment, preventative, restorative and reformative aspects: identify, locate, detain, and try the person/s suspected of the crime, in a legally constituted court of the accused's peers, and give a fair and equitable sentence. None of these aspects are relevant to the suicide deceased. For decades, since suicide was decriminalized – 1961 in Britain, 1966 in Northern Ireland, 1993 in Ireland (RoI), while suicide was never a crime in Scotland – state justice agencies took no legal or other action in its aftermath. In Ireland (RoI) decriminalisation had no effect upon suicide rates (Osman et al., 2017). This chapter examines the 'justice for the suicide deceased' conundrum.

Although mentioned in passing elsewhere in this study, investigation and exploration of the predicament that culminated in both choice and action (Rowe, 1991) and/or desire and capability (Joiner, 2009) in suicide by any deceased individual, has not been given the attention it merits in ongoing efforts to understand the enigma of suicide. By 'predicament', we mean 'the reason why'. A recognised 'reason why' is the deceased's attempt to contend with unbearable psychological pain, viz. psychache (Shneidman, 1996: 4). This might be regarded as an essential condition for suicide, necessary albeit perhaps not sufficient. But it does not take us much further regarding 'justice for the suicide deceased' conundrum.

Of course, in order for a coroner to conclude that a death was the outcome of an intentional, self-destructive act by the deceased, with zero active involvement of third parties, there must be a statutory investigation. But postvention (Shneidman, 1973: 33), that is caring for the survivors of bereavement by such a sudden, catastrophic death, and ensuring that they continue living their lives well, invariably becomes the focus of interest and activity in the immediate and continuing aftermath of a suicide. And our unfortunate brother or sister who, 'before their time', have chosen to absent themselves from us, are left alone - as alone as in the moment of their sad, isolated death.

So what would 'justice for the deceased' by suicide amount to? Homicide's aftermath offers a clue. In Northern Ireland, this justice-related aftermath of our recent sectarian, bigoted history, continues unabated as families shattered by political murder, for example on

Bloody Sunday (1972) in L'derry, or in Ballymurphy (1971) in Belfast, or at the La Mon Restaurant (1978) in County Down, or at Greysteel, L'derry (1993) or in an uncounted litany of scenes of human desecration and destruction, campaign with unflagging determination for fuller explanations of their loved one's killing.

This urgent need for justice for those deceased by unlawful killing, viz. murder, contrasts starkly with the uncomfortable, societal forgetfulness that with few exceptions descends, cloud-like upon family members and colleagues, bereaved by suicide. These latter mourners are normally left to 'get on with their lives' and to 'try to get over it' as best they can. But as for the suicide deceased themselves, little more is ever heard about them – who they were, what caused their lethal psychache, what might have been done to ease it and what lessons might the rest of us learn from each suicidal calamity. All we can be reasonably sure of is the mode of their sudden, untimely demise. Paraphrasing Shelley's (1817) Ozymandias: for the suicide deceased, 'nothing beside remains', except 'the decay ... of lifeless things'.

In the following, I propose to highlight this yawning gap in communal recognition and insightful acknowledgement of the catastrophic, premature loss of fellow humans' lives while suffering lethal psychache, and unable or unwilling to remain with the rest of us in the land of the living. Their families, friends, neighbours and colleagues continue sine die to endure the never-ending costs and execrable benefits of an antediluvian legacy from times past when a suicide death, and specifically its actor, was invariably regarded as attacking both community and society, and suitable only for condemnation and excoriation (De Leo et al., 2006: 7).

There are many exceptions, including the above-mentioned Irish hunger-strikers' deaths, where some limited life history related information exists, including coroners' inquest reports, published books and media stories. But, to begin at the beginning: inquested or not, sensitively investigated and analysed or passed over, a complete narrative of 'the reason why ' any death by suicide has occurred will usually remain, and continue to remain unavailable, since the victim's autobiography, by definition, remains essentially unknown, and the deceased is unavailable for interview. That awful conundrum is the subject of this chapter.

Some suicides are remembered, most are forgotten

## Arthur, son of Mrs Hannah Zukin

In a unique psychological autopsy, Shneidman (2003), investigated, at her specific request, the death by suicide of Mrs Zukin's physician-lawyer son, Arthur, aged 33 years, using his 11 page handwritten suicide note as primary evidence. Within a six month period and a few months after Arthur's death, he interviewed Arthur's mother, father, brother, sister, best friend, ex-wife, girl friend, psychotherapist, and attending physician/psychiatrist. He shared his interview notes and Arthur's suicide note with eight experts in suicidology. Each of these gentlemen – Morton Silverman, Robert E. Litman, Jerome Motto, Norman L. Farberow, John T. Maltsberger, Ronald Maris, David Rudd and Avery D. Weisman – offered their 'unique perspective on Arthur's tragic fate' (Shneidman, 2003: inside wrapper) and inter alia 'what might have been done to save his life' (ibid. xiv).

Shneidman (2003: xiv) said this detailed case study 'has features that are unique and features that are ubiquitous'. He said that 'in essence, this [case study] report is my special letter to [Mrs Zukin] who shared her son's death, his suicide note and his friends and relatives with me' (ibid. xiv).

In her foreword, Judy Collins – whose son Clark, aged 33 also died by suicide – suggested that other survivors of bereavement by suicide might benefit hugely from finding out as much as they can about what happened and why it happened:

'Dr Shneidman ... shatters the secrets, opens the door to forgiveness of Arthur by his family, and to healing of each family member's own wounds. To be able to celebrate the life of our departed loved one and stop the crushing secrecy that can destroy us if we let it, we must go through the pain' (Shneidman, 2003: x).

It seems to me that there can be no justice for our deceased loved ones without reconciliation, and this may only be possible by finding out, understanding, acknowledging and commemorating as much of the actualité of their life as we reasonably can, on our journeys of healing towards acceptance and peace.

## Dr David Ross

Five years after the above-mentioned Northern Ireland 'hunger strikes', on 13 June 1986, a further death-by-suicide linked to that period, was reported. In 1981, Dr David Ross, a former general practitioner (GP) in Ballyclare, Co Antrim, was a prison doctor in charge of the medical treatment of prisoners in the Maze Prison (formerly Long Kesh). He oversaw inter alia the care of republican prisoners who had decided to starve themselves to death to secure 'political status'.

Carswell (2021) described the life, death and aftermath of Dr Ross's death from gunshot wounds in a carefully researched article on the 'forgotten hunger strike victim'. The coroner concluded that while he 'suffered from "recurrent depressive illness" and was taking anti-depressants and anti-anxiety medication prescribed by his doctor and a psychiatrist ... his [gunshot] wounds were consistent with self-infliction' (Carswell, 2021). Carswell (2021) said the late Dr Ross was remembered fondly by his professional colleagues and prison staff and also by many, though not all, former prisoners who knew him during their incarceration. One of Dr Ross's former colleagues, a deputy governor, said:

'[his] "exceptional" role in the hunger strikes, which had been relegated to a footnote or passing reference in histories of the period, has never been properly recognised. We all thought he was such a nice guy and a very, very good doctor ... [he] had considerable difficulty in accepting the role he was playing as doctor "shepherding" the hunger strikers to painful deaths, an act that challenged the "do no harm" pledge of his Hippocratic oath, sworn as a doctor to preserve life. It was a conflict in him: he was trying to keep his patients alive and to look after them and they were trying to kill themselves. His job was to try to save their lives but they were committed to taking their own lives' (Carswell, 2021).

As regards the question of justice for Dr Ross, it hardly seems sufficient 35 years after his death by suicide, aged 57 years, merely to reverse Shakespeare's (1599/1623) dictum, and to recall with something deeper than mere respect, that in Dr David Ross's life:

"The good that men do lives after them, the evil is oft interred with their bones."

## Jeffrey Edward Epstein

On 10 August 2019, a prisoner was found dead in his cell, allegedly by suicide, while on remand on sex-trafficking and related charges in a Manhattan (New York) federal prison. Jeffrey Epstein, a 66 year old convicted sex offender and a wealthy financier, was on 'suicide watch' following a suspected suicide attempt 18 days earlier. Unfortunately, prison guards did not, for whatever reason, check on Epstein every 30 minutes, as prison rules demanded. In fact, on the evening before his death, CCTV evidence showed he was last seen alive in his cell at 1030pm by a guard, before 8 hours later being found dead the following morning, at 630am by guards routinely distributing breakfast to prisoners. Two days before his death, on 8 August 2019, Epstein had signed his last will and testament in the presence of two attorneys (Epstein, 2019).

In the US, any celebrity shenanigans, including a famous (or in this example infamous) character's demise in suspicious circumstances, generates a media avalanche of tsunami proportions. Epstein's prison demise was no different:

'New York City's Chief Medical Examiner Barbara Sampson conducted a four-hour autopsy on Epstein's body on August 11, 2019. Epstein's lawyers sent pathologist Michael Baden to observe the autopsy. Following the autopsy, the medical examiner's office reported that Epstein had hanged himself with a sheet from his bed' (Epstein, 2021a). Almost two years on, it was reported, on 21 May 2021, that "The circumstances of Epstein's death remain the subject of an investigation by the DOJ's Office of the Inspector General" (Epstein, 2021b).

On 27 June 2023, the US Dept of Justice Inspector General M. E. Horowitz issued a highly critical report on the circumstances leading up to Epstein's death by suicide:

"Numerous and serious" instances of misconduct and dereliction of duty contributed to a setting that allowed "arguably one of the most notorious inmates" in the Federal Bureau of Prison's custody the opportunity to take his own life, Horowitz said.

"While the [Office of the Inspector General] determined [Metropolitan Correctional Center] New York staff engaged in significant misconduct and dereliction of their duties, we did not uncover evidence contradicting the FBI's determination regarding the absence of criminality in connection with Epstein's death," the report said.

'Horowitz called the Bureau of Prisons' failures troubling not only because staff did not keep watch over a person in their custody, but also because Epstein's death prematurely ended the process of criminal justice. The staff's failures "effectively deprived Epstein's numerous victims of the opportunity to seek justice through the criminal justice process," the report said' (Solis, 2023).

The almost four year hiatus in certifying and clarifying with precision the circumstances of Jeffrey Epstein's death by suicide may have contributed to widespread media (and social media) speculation on a huge scale – now effectively concluded – regarding whether Epstein's death was indeed by suicide or by homicide or otherwise. The innocent victims of Epstein's alleged depredations however retain the possibility of some form of redress, from society perhaps, but more likely from financial compensation in view of Epstein's reputed great wealth.

**Ordinary decent suicides**

As mentioned in chapter 4 – 'Counting suicides but disregarding the lessons – one by one', above, in Northern Ireland, any death in prison custody is subject to investigation by our Prisoner Ombudsman, in addition when relevant to a coroner's inquest. The Prisoner Ombudsman is accountable to the Northern Ireland Assembly through the Minister of Justice, is independent of the NI Prison Service and 'meets regularly with the South Eastern Health and Social Care Trust [NI Dept of Health] in respect of deaths in custody investigations' (Ombudsman, 2019). In relation to public inquests, in Scotland and Northern Ireland (with a family's agreement) a public inquest after suicide is not held if it is not deemed to be in the public interest and if the relevant authorities agree the death was suicide (The Irish Times, 2014).

However, most 'ordinary decent suicides' are normally unreported by local/Irish or national/British media unless a 'public interest' motivation, or excuse, is acted upon editorially. This practice is in stark contrast to deaths that occurred in Northern Ireland or elsewhere that were believed to be related to 'The Troubles' (1968-1998). Detailed reporting on a daily basis of these criminal /conflict-related /political outrages was regarded by print and broadcast news managers and editors as mandatory. Three major publications,

Lost Lives (McKitterick et al., 1999), Bear in Mind these Dead (McKay, 2008) and more recently, Children of the Troubles (Duffy and McClements, 2019), record the names, circumstances and stories of many conflict-related 'Troubles' deaths.

As for the thousands of 'ordinary' deaths by suicide before and since the Good Friday / Belfast Agreement (1998), little is known beyond intermittent news reports, occasional largely statistically-based academic papers and related media comment, not least because case files are normally unavailable to researchers, being locked away in the Northern Ireland Court Service Coroner's Office premises. Tomlinson (2013: 10) was particularly critical concerning:

'the limited data routinely published on deaths by suicide [that] restrict(s) the full appreciation of social factors behind completed suicides ... individuals who have been in contact with mental health services [constitute] under a third of suicides ... there is much that could be done to improve the sociological autopsy of suicide thereby sharpening the understanding of risk and the disconnect between mental health services and those in psychological crisis' (Tomlinson, 2013: 10).

## Some Northern Irish suicides that are remembered

A rare insight into the Northern Irish suicide phenomenon was offered in an exceptional article by Lyra McKee (2016b), a 29 year old journalist, who was later murdered on 18 April 2019 by gunfire, aimed vaguely, randomly and ruthlessly at a police cordon during a Derry/ L'derry riot. Lyra was present in the company of journalist colleagues observing proceedings when she was shot dead by gunfire from a group of Irish republican paramilitary dissidents. Her article, three years before, addressed the upsurge in suicide statistics in the 16 years from 1998 to 2014, following the Good Friday / Belfast Agreement (1998).

Lyra described the reported death by suicide, having made earlier attempts, of her erstwhile childhood friend Jonny, aged 17 years, in 2008. Lyra said she learned from a mutual friend, Mick, that Jonny's stepfather had told him Jonny was found dead in 'the grounds of a mental institution where he was staying after a previous suicide attempt' (p2). She said that she learned later that Jonny was indeed alive and well having survived an overdose. Some time afterwards, along with friends, she met him at a pub where Jonny told her that:

'after he was taken to a mental health facility, several more failed suicide attempts followed: "It was always very opportunistic – it was never planned out" he says, "If I saw an opportunity, I took it." Since then, though, his life has changed. With the help of medication to keep him stabilized, he has his own flat, and is going back to school ... But the problem hasn't gone away and there are plenty more friends and acquaintances who never made it into adulthood ... The tragic irony of life in Northern Ireland today is that peace seems to have claimed more lives than war ever did' (p7, 8).

Lyra relied inter alia upon work by Tomlinson (2012, 2013) who wrote:

'Since 1998 the suicide rate in Northern Ireland has almost doubled, following a decade during which the rate declined from a low level of 10 per 100,000 of the population to 8.6. The overall rate is now 16.25' (Tomlinson, 2013: 4).

Tomlinson (2013) identified several possible explanations of this upward post-Good Friday/Belfast Agreement (1998) surge, including changes in reporting and recording, changes in mental illness and/or service provision, changes in behaviour: alcohol and drugs, changes in protective factors: religion, family life and normative expectations, and economic change: recession and unemployment. But what he described as 'the most neglected explanation [and what] may be the decisive factor in raising suicide rates in recent years ... is associated in some way with [Northern Ireland's] violent conflict' (Tomlinson, 2013: 9). He believed that there was a Northern Ireland province-wide conflict-related effect:

'the cohort of children and young people who experienced the worst period of violence from 1970 to 1977 is the cohort experiencing the highest and most rapidly increasing suicide rates in the decade after 1998' (Tomlinson, 2013: 9).

He linked the damaging impact of conflict-related, extreme situations upon combatants, security personnel, civilians and, specifically upon 'children caught up in adverse, violent situations [who] will be less psychologically resilient in later life'. He went further:

'... children that grew up in the conflict were the most acculturated to division and conflict, and the externalized expressions of violence. The consequence of peace is that such expressions of aggression and violence are no longer socially or politically approved and arguably, become internalized instead' (Tomlinson, 2013: 10).

McKee (2016a) questioned what might explain the fact that of 3,709 people who lost their lives to suicide during the 15 years between 1999 and 2014, 676 of them – nearly a fifth – were younger than 25. Most of these unfortunate youngsters were in all probability too young to have been active participants in the conflict. She accepted that while middle-age suicide might, in part, be explained by the trauma of the conflict, she wondered 'what could account for the deaths by suicide of young people who'd never seen the war' (p5). She referred to a study by O'Neill, S. et al. (2014) that established a link between suicidal behaviour and having experienced a traumatic event, including those related to conflict. They discovered that World Health Organisation (WHO, 2008) research found that out of 28 countries, including Israel, South Africa and the Lebanon, Northern Ireland had the highest rates of post-traumatic stress disorder (PTSD): 39% of the population here had experienced a traumatic event related to the conflict. The most frequently reported event was 'civilian in a place of ongoing terror' (19.5%').

McKee (2016a) said that Prof O'Neill explained how survivors of traumatic experiences could, sub-consciously, 'pass down to their children and grandchildren, a phenomenon known as "intergenerational transmission of trauma"'. In essence, when someone saw something horrible, and were traumatized, this affected how they related to everyone else, including their children and grandchildren. Hence McKee's so-called 'ceasefire babies' – who were too young to have been actors in the conflict – were likely to be dealing with the added stress of the conflict, even though most of them never witnessed it directly (p5).

It is indeed ironical in the extreme, that Lyra McKee's assassin is believed to have been aged 18 or 19 years, a 'post-ceasefire baby', groomed from innocence to murder by older, Irish republican paramilitary dissidents.

The next paragraph will examine the contrast in Northern Ireland society between the attention and concern regarding the survivors of bereavement by suicide and our frequent disregard of the victims, deceased by suicide.

## Focus on the bereaved versus neglect of the deceased

Shneidman (1972: ix) coined the term 'postvention' meaning 'working with survivor-victims of a committed suicide to help them with their anguish, guilt, anger, shame and perplexity'. He described 'the anguish of the survivor's bereavement [as] nearly always special: sharp, prolonged and inimical' (p x):

'I believe that the person who commits suicide puts his psychological skeleton in the survivor's emotional closet – he sentences the survivor to deal with many negative feelings and more, to become obsessed with thoughts regarding his own actual or possible role in having precipitated the suicidal act or having failed to abort it. It can be a heavy load' (Shneidman, 1972: x).

The elevated risk of suicide for survivors bereaved by suicide cannot be underestimated. But due to suicide's complexity – related in part to absence of evidence – there is no cause/effect relationship between a parent's suicide and their offspring's subsequent self-destruction. This does nothing to mitigate the agony of family suicide and its related mystery.

The enigma of suicide, was expressed succinctly by a mother, whose son Jody, aged 19, 'with everything to live for', killed himself using the same means as his father, John O'D White, used when the boy was 14 years of age:

'The truth of suicide dies with the victim. The survivor can only guess. They must put the pieces of a life together to try to come up with reasons for an unreasonable death' (White-Bowden, 1985: 12).

No one appeared to have advised Susan White-Bowden that her son might be at increased risk of suicide following his father's suicide. It was unclear whether her family had accessed or benefitted from specialised help in the five year period following the father's death. Yet, unless survivors are forewarned, and forearmed, by competent, compassionate post-suicide helpers, then effectively all family members may be at enhanced risk. Firestone (1997) said:

'It is almost impossible for an individual not to be psychologically impaired by a loved one's suicide ... (T)he self-inflicted death of a family member or close friend reinforces destructive thought processes in the survivors. Suicide strengthens the anti-self system [viz. self-destructive aspect of the personality] of those left behind; the act of self-destruction is almost always used in the survivors' defence system, which causes emotional damage' (Firestone, 1997: 248).

Hence Susan White-Bowden's mourning family, bereaved by John O'Donnell White's suicide, seemed not to have availed of any therapeutic intervention, but to 'get on with their lives' and to 'try to get over it' as best they could – with the catastrophic consequence of Jody's suicide.

I recall a consultant psychiatrist in 1990 cautioning my two brothers and myself following the suspected death, the second in our family, of our younger sibling by suicide some months earlier. His words, 30 plus years on, continue to echo in my brain: 'The taboo has been broken – you're all at risk now', he said before abruptly concluding our brief conversation.

Firestone (1997: 251) cited Leenaars (1994: 58) who stated 'there is no universal formulation regarding how to respond to a highly lethal person'. Given the known complexity of suicide, it was unsurprising that 'suicide intervention is optimally practiced in co-operation with a number of colleagues, representing various disciplines, and even individuals outside the helping professions' (Leenaars, 1994: 58). The apparent absence of such 'optimal practice' in supporting citizens at risk of suicide in Northern Ireland may unfortunately be related to our ongoing level of suicide attrition where 'around 70% of people who die by suicide in Northern Ireland are not known to mental health services' (Black, 2021).

## So who were the suicide deceased?

Only family members, close friends, colleagues and perhaps some professionals, including medical/psychological/religious practitioners are likely to possess anything approaching intimate knowledge of the deceased, prior to their demise. At an inquest, the coroner's remit is so narrow – the 'who/where/when/how' death event agenda – and the public nature of this scenario is necessarily so restrictive, that only a limited, inevitably skewed presentation of the victim is likely to emerge. Its focus is on the victim's death: their life, their identity, their lived experience and who they were, is largely if not totally disregarded.

A delay of up to 24 weeks elapsed during 2018 between the date of a death and its registration as a suicide (Black and McKay, 2019). This means that a lag will exist in relation to suicide data as reported by the N I Research & Statistics Agency. A total of 263 suicide victims were registered in Northern Ireland in 2020 (Black, 2021). Brief notices, paid-for by the bereaved, in the 'Deaths' columns of three local newspapers – Belfast Telegraph, The Irish News and News Letter – will normally state the deceased's name and age / date of death, occasionally adding the qualifier 'sudden', or 'surrounded by her/his loving family' but excluding additional information other than details of forthcoming funeral arrangements. Brief items reporting deaths by suspected suicide of a handful of these fellow citizens may be mentioned in local news reports, if a 'story' that meets 'public interest' criteria is regarded as 'newsworthy' and at the editor's discretion.

Most of our unfortunate 263 suicide deceased will not merit any editorial mention. Some summarised examples of recent, randomly-selected media reports, may help to illustrate how much, or how little, people living here know about the gory details of this 'major public health issue that devastates families and communities' (Black and McKay, 2019).

## Examples of news reports about some suicide deceased
### Case #1 – Unagh

A 55 year old mother of three children, Unagh Gallogly, died after a drowning incident in June 2019. This example of a potentially avoidable suicide death was the subject of a public inquest that was reported in local media in January 2021. Two print media reports (Young, 2021; Deeney, 2021) described extraordinary efforts by members of the public, police and an RNLI volunteer to rescue this woman. The inquest heard that she had contacted both her brother, John and her husband, Michael around 1030pm on the night that she later drove her car into Lough Erne, at Kesh, Co Fermanagh. A text to her husband said: 'Just about to head into the river, good to go' while in a short phone conversation with her brother, the deceased said: 'John, John, I love you. I am away, bye, bye'. When John said 'What do you mean, where are you?' she repeated: 'Bye, bye. I'm going. I'm away I love you'. John said 'Stop ... mammy's watching, would you just stop, where are you?' John told the inquest 'All I heard her saying was "Lough Erne" ... the phone went dead. The coroner recorded her death 'formally' as suicide 'fresh water drowning which caused swelling of the brain caused by lack of oxygen and multi-organ failure' (Deeney, 2021).

Tragically, the heroic efforts of police, public and volunteers were not enough to save poor Unagh's life. We learned very little about who Unagh was or about the pathway (O'Keeffe, 2017) to her self-inflicted demise. An inquest in Northern Ireland appears to be precluded from investigating this. Hence we are unable even to speculate about what might have been said, not said, done or not done and by what person or agency, up to about 1030pm on 15 June 2019 that might have spared her life.

### Case #2 - Kloe

A print media article (McGonagle, 2018) reported that a 16 year old schoolgirl, Kloe Aiken-Smith, was found dead on Friday 2 November 2018 in a wooded area on the outskirts of Belfast. She was believed to have been reported missing the previous day. In a statement issued on 5 November 2018 a police spokesperson said: 'A postmortem has been carried out following the sudden death of a 16 year-old girl in the Four Winds area on Friday 2 November 2018. The death is not being treated as suspicious'. An online news outlet, Belfast Live, stated on 20 November 2018: 'The Our Lady and St Patrick's College [student] was found on wooded ground at Burnside Park in the Four Winds area of South Belfast. Her death has been linked to prescription medication' (Fitzmaurice, 2018). In the same report, this news outlet announced a special fund-raising event:

'Friends of a young girl who died suddenly will celebrate her life next month at a special fundraising event. The event [on 9 December 2018] is also hoped to raise awareness with a member of the Addiction NI team [to] speak to the young people at the start of the evening. Money raised will go to the charity. [Ms S.D.], a cousin of Kloe's mother D and general manager of the [event venue] visitor attraction, is organising the night.

'She told Belfast Live: "We just wanted to give Kloe's friends a safe space to come and remember her. Local musicians have volunteered to do it so all the money will be going to Addiction NI. Sadly she has passed away, but it's important people get to celebrate her life.

"At the start of the night there's a fella from Addiction NI who's going to talk to the young people there. He knows what he's doing and is going to keep it brief as we don't [want] it to come across like they're being lectured.

"But it's important to get the message across about the dangers out there and what can happen. If we can get something positive from what's happened that would be good. If just one person there takes on board what's been said then that'll be something positive."' (Fitzmaurice, 2018)

We know very little about Kloe's life or any detail about the pathway to her death. It remained unclear if Kloe's death was ruled accident or undetermined or suicide, in the absence of a coroner's investigation. Inquests in Northern Ireland are held at the discretion of the coroner.

## Case #3 - Lewis

A print media article (Harte, 2021) reported that a 34 year old man, employed as a facilities manager, died in Leeds, England and an inquest in 2013 concluded that the death was as a result of a gambling addiction. The article's theme and content related to proposed changes to gambling laws in Northern Ireland, in the context of the death of Lewis Keogh, aged 34, who 'was £50,000 in debt and leading a double life that eventually drove him to suicide' (Harte, 2021). Lewis was from Fermanagh, Northern Ireland, a Teesside University sports science graduate, and at his death was living in Leeds. His parents, Peter and Sadie, said they believed 'Lewis developed a taste for gambling aged just nine when he played on arcade machines during ferry trips to France and back ... our son's gambling journey began while he was at school and things spiralled from there' (Harte, 2021).

Some information about Lewis was found on websites via an internet search. This offered some limited insights into Lewis's life including phrases from his suicide note: 'addiction is cruel' and 'I want some peace'. It was not until after Lewis died that Peter and Sadie discovered that he had in fact run up debts of £50,000 through credit cards and bank loans as he fed an addiction that had held him in its grip for six or seven years. He is thought to have made occasional visits to a casino but, in the main, gambled on internet roulette and poker games. His father said: 'Lewis took his own life because he was ill and he couldn't see a way out of his addiction. He couldn't see a way of stopping.' His mother added:

'I'm not angry with Lewis, he was obviously too ashamed to tell us and couldn't cope on his own. His suicide note emphasised that the debt was nothing to do with it. Suicide is a direct result of gambling addiction, not the debt. He said "addiction is cruel", he didn't say he couldn't cope because of his debt. We need to get that through to people. It's addiction and what it does to your head and what it does to your brain, it's like being on crack cocaine' (Yorkshire Evening Post, 2019).

We learned little here about Lewis's death journey except its apparently lengthy duration and his death's direct link to his lethal response to his admitted addiction.

## Case #4 - Callum

An unattributed article on the front page of 'The Irish News' (2021c) newspaper dated 5 June 2021 reported the 'sudden death' of a 23 year-old civil engineering graduate on 1 June 2021. It was presumed that poor Callum Fitzpatrick may have died by suicide as his grieving family asked for donations to the Public Initiative for the Prevention of Suicide and Self-harm (PIPS). In 2014, when he was just 16, Mr Fitzpatrick became one of Northern Ireland's youngest ever lottery winners after he won £390,000. Online media stories focused on Callum's big win but said little about him except that he was a member of the GAA's Ballymartin GAC, worked in a bar and helped out in his family's shop.

We learned little of note about Callum's identity, nothing about his death pathway, nor the circumstances of his demise or any information about a public inquest.

## Case #5 - Francis

Francis Toner, aged 65, was reported in a 'Lives Remembered' column in 'The Irish News' newspaper, dated 5 June 2021. This article, contributed by and attributed to 'The Toner family', was in effect a first anniversary obituary for Francis, offering some detail of his life history from 1964 until his death on 4 June 2020. The fourth of eight children, he was described as a 'larger-than-life figure by personality as well as physical presence.' Francis, from Magherafelt, Co L'derry, Northern Ireland had worked as a helper in the Samaritans and then trained and worked full-time as a 'mental health counsellor'. The article presented Francis as the life and soul of the party who 'was always at the centre of any gathering of family or friends ... if there was a wake on, and Francis was sitting up, everybody would want to join him to enjoy the craic and company'. The article concluded with the shockingly disturbing and sad news that:

'Unfortunately, Francis had his own internal war that no-one was aware of and on June 4 2020 he decided to end that battle' (The Irish News, 2021a)

Counselling vulnerable clients, which appeared to be Francis's working life, is a highly challenging and potentially risky occupation that can lead to psychological burnout and compassion fatigue:

"[Counselling] practitioners may be hesitant to discuss their strains and struggles as therapists when they worry that such disclosures could threaten their livelihood. This fear of exhibiting distress or vulnerability, so at odds with what [their] work is all about, is implanted early in professional training and reinforced at every turn ... What is fostered is a greater concern with how one looks than with who one is ... There can be little doubt that this state of alienation from self and others contributes to such important problems as burnout, addiction, boundary violations and suicide among practitioners" (Sussman, 1995: 6, 7).

Professional counsellors are duty bound to work under the skilled supervision of a qualified clinician. One online 'sympathy notice' (Funeral Times, 2020) on 5 June 2020, attributed to James Gallagher, described Francis as 'an exceptional clinical supervisor and an even better human being'. No further information was available about this aspect of Francis's life and work nor any inquest information.

## Case #6 – Conchur

Two local newspaper articles reported on 17 November 2020, the recovery of 20 year old Conchur Doherty's body from the River Foyle, L'derry four days after he had been seen entering the river (Murray, News Letter, 2020; McKinney, The Irish News, 2020). Conchur was described as an extremely pleasant pupil with an infectious sense of humour. He was also known as an Irish language enthusiast and founding pupil at Irish medium school Gaelscoil na Daroige. One reporter cited social media as follows:

'On social media on November 12 a family member posted: "Our wee son Conchúr (Doherty) took his own life in the early hours of Wednesday morning jumping from the Peace Bridge" ' (Murray, 2020).

This calamity, principally for poor Conchur and no less catastrophic for his family and friends, and as reported by local and social media, offered next to nothing about who this young man was and what his pathway to death by self-destruction was. The reason why remained inscrutable and beyond any understanding. It was not known if and when a public inquest might be convened.

**Case #7 – Tony**

A local newspaper article, on 19 January, 2019, reported the death on Friday 11 January by suicide of Anthony 'Tony' O'Toole, aged 45 years, a father of five and a grandfather, who managed a Belfast pizza establishment. Tony was found dead at home by his mother who lived next door when he did not arrive at work. Tony's brother said he was 'caring', had a 'big heart', 'never had mental health problems and never talked about feeling low'. He pleaded with other men to reach out for help and talk about their feelings (McConville, 2019). The article described Tony's community involvement in running three marathons for cancer and suicide awareness charities. As a teenager, he had jumped into the water at a pier in Ballycastle, Co Antrim to rescue a young friend, helping to drag him to safety and to resuscitate him. Years later he subdued a knifeman who was targeting a friend and disarmed him. The newspaper's editorial on 19 January 2019, entitled 'Reach out to the vulnerable', referred to Tony's suicide in relation to 'the issues faced by those trying to help people with depression', adding:

'Our page-one story carries an appeal from the brother of a man who died by suicide. He urges people to reach out and talk about their worries. It sounds simple but there are obviously many victims of suicide who felt they could not step forward to discuss their issues' (The Irish News, 2019).

Suicide benefits no one. It is one of the most complex of human behaviours that is conventionally but inaccurately linked to 'depression': instead suicide, meaning the permanent extinction of consciousness, might be better understood as relating to the victim's unbearable, psychological pain, known as psychache, that is almost invariably totally concealed from others. The unfortunate victim may believe, wrongly, that suicide represents their only option. In reality, however, suicide may indeed extinguish their pain but it also kills the victim while generating multiple, painful, long-lasting consequences for innocent survivors: that is any individual who remains alive following the suicide death of someone with whom they had a significant relationship or emotional bond (AAS, 2021). No information was found to date regarding a coroner's inquest.

## Case #8 - Aaron

Aaron Laverty, aged 15, was reported in a newspaper article, dated 1 January 2019, to have died by suicide, on 28 December 2018. The article quoted a social media message from 'Aaron's heartbroken mother who described how her "beloved son ... has grew (sic) his wings way too soon". She also said her "heart is shattered into a million pieces" adding that "my son will never be forgotten; he lives on in my heart forever' (McGonagle, 2019). Their neighbour who set up a GoFundMe page wrote: 'I'm currently fundraising for my neighbour who recently lost her beautiful son ... to suicide 28.12.18 – 15 years old. I'm helping to raise money in order to help with funeral costs for the family ... to relieve a stress [they] shouldn't have to worry about after this deeply saddening news'. Young people who knew Aaron posted sympathetic messages on social media while a local elected politician 'expressed his condolences to the teenager's family and friends. This is a young life tragically lost with a devastated family left behind ... this will be a sad and devastating time for ... family, siblings ... and for his large group of friends, there will also be much sadness'.

There is little in the article, besides a small photograph, about who Aaron was or what his pathway to early death might have been: however, his grieving friends described him on social media as 'a loving, caring lad ... Aaron was caring to anyone that knew him always helped with what he could help with' (McGonagle, 2019).

Any search for even a microscopic glimmer of light in this story will fail utterly. However, in the absence of any new information that might emerge from a coroner's inquest, a ticking time-bomb may have unwittingly and unintentionally been created leading to the risk of similar episodes in the future. One can only hope that everything possible will be done by Northern Ireland state and local community and voluntary agencies and resources to ameliorate and hopefully minimize this by the provision of ongoing effective psychotherapeutic support for the survivors of Aaron's death.

### Case #9 – Shane

Two articles, on the first page, with a large photograph, and on an inside page, with two photographs, described the aftermath of the death by suicide on 15 December 2018, of Shane Brennan, aged 29, a father of two children (McConville, 2018 a & b). The front page article represents a plaintive appeal by Shane's fiancée, and mother of one-year old Teddy. She said there had been no indication that anything was wrong, describing Shane as 'an amazing character ... he always gave his true self that was his caring, honest, generous, fun-loving personality'. And to those in need of support, she added: 'It's OK not to be OK. I would just say if there is any sort of feeling in your body and head that you don't want to be around any more, don't think about it, go and get help' (McConville, 2018a). The second longer article, described Shane's footballing career and his fiancée's loving admiration of her partner. However, two key remarks by his partner are of note. First: 'There was nothing to indicate why he did it,' his partner said. Second: 'Shane was one of those people who put other people's happiness in front of his own. Whatever he had he would give, the clothes off his own back. If he had 50 pence in his pocket to last a week, he would have given it to them,' she added (McConville, 2018b). The 'riddle, wrapped in a mystery, inside an enigma' of suicide emerged here when Shane's lethal, self-destructive behaviour was seen in the context of his otherwise positive lifestyle, as observed by his fiancée.

In the absence of a coroner's inquest, and the possible emergence of new information, it seemed that nothing more will be known about Shane's pathway to an early death by his own hand.

### Case #10.1 – Reece

A newspaper article, dated 7 October 2017, reported that a 21 year-old father of three, and former amateur boxer, Reece McAlorum, died suddenly at home (Monaghan, 2017). Almost 3½ years later, a second article, dated 2 January 2021, stated that Reece took his own life in October 2017, at the age of 21. This article described how his family 'are devastated' after being told they must exhume his remains and move them to another grave. No further explanation for the reburial was available other than 'a change in circumstances within the family circle' (McConville, 2021).

We learned almost nothing about Reece's life, other than references to his sporting endeavours and his three children, and there was no information about his pathway to an early death by suicide. As before, in the absence of a coroner's inquest and new information emerging, nothing more will become known about his short life and tragic death.

## Case 10.2 – Annaleece

A front page article, dated 14 April 2022, including three photographs, and headlined "Family left 'numb' over death of second child to suicide" (McConville, 2022), reported the death of 17 year-old Annaleece McAlorum by (suspected) suicide, in hospital three days after 'attempting to take her own life in a mental health unit'. This death followed the loss, also by suspected suicide, of poor Annaleece's brother, Reece (RIP), then aged 21, five years earlier in 2017, as noted at Case 10.1 above. A government agency, the Belfast Health and Social Care Trust, which offered 'heartfelt condolences to the family' said it would be conducting 'a full investigation with the family's involvement'. The Trust is the public health organisation covering Belfast, one of five Trusts, created in April 2007 by the then Department of Health, Social Services and Public Safety (DHSSPS), now known as the Department of Health (DoH). The Belfast Trust employs 22,000 staff and has responsibility for services to over 340,000 patients, provided at various hospitals and health units, including Belfast City Hospital, the Royal Victoria Hospital, the Mater Hospital and Musgrave Park Hospital as well as the Beechcroft Child and Adolescent Mental Health Unit, where Annaleece was found dead. The latter is a Belfast Trust facility that 'helps teenagers aged under 18 who are experiencing difficult thoughts, feelings, experiences and behaviours' (Belfast Trust, 2022).

At the time of writing, I have no information about inquests for Reece (RIP) and Annaleece (RIP) nor of the Belfast Trust's promised investigation.

## Comment on media reports of suicide deaths

The opportunity to learn from the actualité of these suicide deaths, as an additional point of entry into effective reduction of suicidal deaths, is blocked by our society's acceptance of the status quo regarding lack of access to, investigation of, and presentation to the public, of the hidden facts of Northern Ireland suicide that are held by the Northern Ireland Courts Service and its agencies.

## Suicides that turned out not to be suicides

### Colin Howell

One notorious example in Northern Ireland of misidentification as a suicide pact by both police and coroner, was the double murder of Trevor Buchanan and Lesley Howell, by Colin Howell and Hazel Buchanan (later Stewart), in May 1991.

'Police originally believed they had died in a suicide pact after discovering their partners were having an affair. Nearly two decades passed before dentist Howell (58) suddenly confessed to both killings. He pleaded guilty to the murders in 2010 and was ordered to serve at least 21 years behind bars. Howell also implicated his former lover [Hazel Buchanan Stewart] in the plot and gave evidence against her at her trial. In March 2011 she was unanimously convicted of both killings by a jury at Coleraine Crown Court' (The Irish News, 2021b).

The question of justice for these two innocent murdered citizens had to wait for almost two decades. One further example of a 'staged' suicide being used in a futile attempt to cover up a murder was the Potter case (Morris, 2018).

### Derek Potter

A short article (Morris, 2018) in The Guardian newspaper, on 9 November 2018, described the murder conviction and imprisonment, at Swansea Crown Court (Wales) of 64 year old Derek Potter, who strangled his 66 year-old wife, Lesley Potter, on 7 April 2018. Potter staged a hanging to suggest she had killed herself and her death was not initially treated by police as suspicious (Morris, 2018). As in the Howell case (above) the police bungled the initial investigation.

Potter phoned emergency services telling them he had found his wife hanging in a bedroom and had tried to revive her. On 25 April, two weeks before Lesley's cremation that was arranged for 8 May, Potter disclosed to a colleague, Natalia M-K: 'I love my wife very much but she was doing my head in, so I had to strangle her'. Natalia told the police and a detailed post-mortem followed, when a pathologist found that Lesley had 30 rib fractures, and over 30 bruises on her neck, face, arms, back, legs and feet. He concluded that manual strangulation had contributed to her death.

Shortly afterwards, Potter was arrested, charged with murdering his wife and convicted. Jailing him for life, with a minimum term of 17 years, the judge said it was clear Potter strangled Lesley 'in a sudden and furious burst of temper [and] that you [tried] to cover it up by the pretence – a shameful and despicable charade – that she had committed suicide' (Soole, 2018). The victim impact statements make for sad reading as families had to tell children their granny had taken her own life only to have later to tell them that she had been killed (Morris, 2018). Justice for poor Lesley was delivered by the court but a complicated grief response by her loving family members was likely, that may require specialist caring support. It is unknown whether this was provided to them.

## Conclusions

The issue addressed in this chapter – justice for the suicide deceased – does not appear, on any evidence I can find, to rate as being other than of secondary importance in our society in the aftermath of a death by suicide. A dignified funeral appears to be considered adequate while public inquests are discretionary. Priority seems to be given to alleviation of the grief of survivors, those left alive who were close to the deceased. The provision of caring, compassionate support for those bereaved by suicide, fits well with conventional notions of fairness and justice. This helping process – known as postvention – has come to mean not only assistance to the bereaved but also assistance to anyone whose risk of suicide might be increased in the aftermath of someone else's suicide (Action Alliance, 2015). Indeed Shneidman (1972: x) argued that 'postvention is prevention for the next decade and for the next generation'. He added that 'postvention probably represents the largest problem and thus presents the greatest area for potential aid'. Thus postvention might be regarded as key to reducing the incidence of suicide in those bereaved by the suicide. Perhaps this should be seen to be of primary importance – to employ a political cliché – if it can contribute to ensuring that the tragedy is not repeated within the constituency of post-suicide survivors. In the meantime, regarding justice for the deceased, 'the yawning gap' in communal recognition and insightful acknowledgement including 'a complete narrative of "the reason why" any death by suicide occurred' (see above) continues to be ignored, unaddressed, and ultimately unknown.

**End-note**

One 'justice for the suicide deceased' campaign was proposed in 2019, in relation to suicide deaths that might be 'linked with Northern Ireland's violent past' (Edwards and Young, 2019). This was an attempt by the father of a man, James Wilson, aged 27 years, who died by suicide in 1989, to have his son added to the official 'Troubles' death toll :

'Ernie Wilson, a former part-time UDR soldier, was driving a bus in Lisnaskea (Co Fermanagh) in 1988 when an IRA bomb exploded. Arlene Foster [later a prominent Northern Ireland politician] was one of the schoolchildren on board the bus. Although no one was killed in the explosion, a year after the bombing Mr Wilson's 27-year-old son James died by suicide. Mr. Wilson believes that his son blamed himself for what happened to the bus, as he helped check it every morning before his father left for work. Mr Wilson said there is no way his son could have spotted the device, which had been concealed by IRA terrorists aboard the bus. Mr Wilson said he had "no doubt" his son took his own life because of the Troubles and that his death should be recognised on the official death toll. He said that similar deaths by suicide linked to the conflict in Northern Ireland should also be recorded, but only with the agreement of each family' (Edwards and Young, 2019).

The status of this new campaign was unknown at the time of writing.

**Myth:** (fictitious popular idea) Sometimes suicide is the only option.

**Fallacy:** (misleading argument) Suicide can happen to anyone, like a bolt from the blue.

# References

Action Alliance (2015) Responding to Grief, Trauma, and Distress After a Suicide: U.S. National Guidelines Survivors of Suicide Loss Task Force, April 2015. Accessed on 13 May 2022 at The National Action Alliance for Suicide Prevention (action alliance for suicide prevention.org)

AAS (2021) American Association of Suicidology. Clinician Survivor Task Force. Accessed 29 June 2021 at https://jmcintos.pages.iu.edu/therapists_mainpg.htm

Ballymurphy Massacre (1971) See factual narrative, accessed on 9 June 2021, at https://en.wikipedia.org/wiki/Ballymurphy_massacre

Belfast Trust (2022) Belfast Health and Social Care Trust, the government agency responsible inter alia for the Beechcroft Child and Adolescent Mental Health Unit. Accessed on 12 May 2022 at https://belfasttrust.hscni.net/hospitals/beechcroft/

Black, L-A., and McKay, K. (2019) Suicide statistics and strategy in Northern Ireland: Update, 28 November 2019. Research Matters, a blog from the Northern Ireland Assembly Research and Information Service

Black, L-A. (2021) Suicide: research and information. Research Paper, 14 April 2021. Research and Information Service, Northern Ireland Assembly

Bloody Sunday (1972) See factual narrative, accessed on 9 June 2021, at https://en.wikipedia.org/wiki/Bloody_Sunday_(1972)

Cain, A. C. (ed.) (1972) Survivors of suicide. Springfield, Illinois: Charles C Thomas

Carswell, S. (2021) The forgotten hunger strike victim. The Irish Times. 12 June 2021.

Collins, J. (2003) Foreword. In Edwin S. Shneidman (2003) Autopsy of a suicidal mind. Page x. Oxford: Oxford University Press

Deeney, D. (2021) Inquest told of 'heroic efforts' to save woman. Donna Deeney. Belfast Telegraph, 14 January 2021

De Leo, D., Burgis, S., Bertolote, J. M., Kerkhof, A. J. F. M. and Bille-Brahe, U. (2006) Definitions of suicidal behaviour: lessons learned from the WHO/EURO multicentre study. Crisis, 2006, 27(1), 4-15

Duffy, J. and McClements, F. (2019) Children of the Troubles: the untold story of the children killed in the Northern Ireland conflict. Dublin, Ireland: Hachette Books Ireland

Durkheim, E. (1897/2002) Suicide. A study in sociology. London: Routledge Classics 2002

Edwards, M. and Young, D. (2019) Call for Troubles death toll to also include suicides backed by Foster. Mark Edwards & David Young. Belfast Telegraph, 11 January, 2019. Accessed on 30 June 2021 at https://www.belfasttelegraph.co.uk/news/northern-ireland/call-for-troubles-death-toll-to-also-include-suicides-backed-by-foster-37701027.html

Epstein (2019) Reference to his last will and testament. Accessed on 9 June 2021 at https://en.wikipedia.org/wiki/Death of Jeffrey Epstein

Epstein (2021a) Jeffrey Epstein's autopsy. Accessed on 18 June 2021 athttps://en.wikipedia.org/wiki/Death_of_Jeffrey_Epstein#Autopsy_report_and_criticism

Epstein (2021b) Investigation of circumstances of Epstein's death. Accessed on 18 June 2021 at https://www.cnbc.com/2021/05/25/judge-approves-deferred-prosecution-deal-for-epstein-jail-guards.html

Firestone, R. W. (1997) Suicide and the inner voice: risk assessment, treatment, and case management. London: Sage Publications

Fitzmaurice, M. (2018) Kloe Aiken-Smyth pals to celebrate teenager's life at fundraising event. Accessed on 27 June 2021 at https://www.belfastlive.co.uk/news/belfast-news/kloe-aiken-smyth-pals-celebrate-15440713

Funeral Times (2020) Francis (Frank) Toner (RIP) Sympathy notice from James Gallagher on 5 June 2020. Accessed on 12 May 2022 at https://www.funeraltimes.com/francis-franktoner374356504

Good Friday/Belfast Agreement (1998) Underpins the Northern Ireland peace process, its constitutional settlement and its institutions. Published 10 April 1998. Northern Ireland Office, Belfast

Greysteel Massacre (1993) See factual narrative, accessed on 9 June 2021, at https://en.wikipedia.org/wiki/Greysteel_massacre

Harte, L. (2021) Gambling reforms 'a step in the right direction'. Lauren Harte. Belfast Telegraph, 28 May 2021

Joiner, T. E. (2009) The interpersonal-psychological theory of suicide: current empirical status. American Psychological Association. Psychological Science Agenda. Science Briefs, June 2006

Kessler R. C. and Ustun, B. (eds.) (2008) The WHO world mental health surveys. Global perspectives of mental health surveys. pp. 14-32. New York: Cambridge University Press

La Mon Restaurant Bombing (1978) See factual narrative, accessed on 9 June 2021, at https://en.wikipedia.org/wiki/La_Mon_restaurant_bombing

Lanigan, R. (2020) The suicide epidemic among Northern Ireland's 'Ceasefire babies'. New Statesman, London. 22 January 2020

Leenaars, A. A. (1994) Crisis intervention with highly lethal suicidal people. In A. A. Leenaars, J. T. Maltsberger and N. A. Neimeyer (eds.) Treatment of suicidal people (pp 45-59) Washington DC: Taylor & Francis

McConville, M. L. (2018a) Think of who you have ... so many people care about you – seek help. Marie Louise McConville. The Irish News, page one, 19 December 2018

McConville, M. L. (2018b) You want to know why and we will never know why. Marie Louise McConville. Page 11, The Irish News, 19 December 2018

McConville, M. L. (2019) Dad-of-5 takes his own life: brother says suicide was 'complete shock' as he urges other men to talk ... never hold anything in. Marie Louise McConville. The Irish News, 19 January 2019, front page 'splash' with photo

McConville, M. L. (2021) Family left 'devastated' by news they must exhume and re-bury son. Marie Louise McConville. The Irish News. 2 Jan 2021

McConville, M. L. (2022) Family left 'numb' over death of second child to suicide. Marie Louise McConville. The Irish News, 14 April 2022

McGonagle, S. (2018) Funeral for teenage girl after body find. Suzanne McGonagle. The Irish News, 6 November 2018

McGonagle, S. (2019) Devastation as teenager dies days after Christmas. Suzanne McGonagle. The Irish News, 1 January 2019

McKay, S. (2008) Bear in mind these dead. London: Faber and Faber

McKee, L. (2016a) Suicide of the Ceasefire Babies. Mosaic. 19 January 2016. 16 pages. Accessed on 17 June 2021 at Suicide of the Ceasefire Babies | Mosaic (mosaicscience.com)

McKee, L. (2016b) Suicide among the Ceasefire Babies. The Atlantic. 20 January 2016. 9 pages

McKinney, S. (2020) Missing man's body recovered from river. Seamus McKinney. The Irish News, 17 November 2020

McKitterick, D., Feeney, B., Thornton, C., McVea, D. and Kelters, S. (1999) Lost Lives: The Stories of the Men, Women and Children who Died as a Result of the Northern Ireland Troubles. Edinburgh, Scotland: Mainstream Publishing Company Ltd

Monaghan, J. (2017) Tributes paid to 'gentleman' Reece McAlorum after 21 year old dies suddenly. John Monaghan. The Irish News, 7 October 2017

Morris, S. (2018) Husband who staged wife's suicide jailed for murder. Steven Morris. The Guardian, 9 November 2018

Murray, G (2020) Body of NI man discovered after search – family thank voluntary based search and rescue charity who recovered his body – GoFundMe campaign raised thousands. News Letter, 16 November 2020

O'Connor, R. C. (2021) When it is Darkest: why people die by suicide and what we can do to prevent it. London: Vermilion

O'Keeffe, Terence (1984) "Suicide and Self-Starvation". Philosophy. 59 (229): 349–363. Cited in Wikipedia, accessed on 22 June 2021 at https://en.wikipedia.org/wiki/1981_Irish_hunger_strike

O'Keeffe, Philip (2001) Suicidology, counselling and identity exploration: an investigation of postvention strategies for suicide survivors. Unpublished master's degree dissertation. Jordanstown, Co Antrim: Ulster University [Accessible at 'completed projects' via www.identityexploration.com]

O'Keeffe, Philip (2010) Client suicide and clinician identity: an investigation of identity development in clinician survivors of client suicide. Unpublished doctoral dissertation. Jordanstown, Co Antrim: Ulster University [Accessible at 'completed projects' via www.identityexploration.com]

O'Keeffe, Philip (2017) Individual approach needed. VIEW digital, Social Affairs Journalism, issue 40, page 22, 2016 [published 15 Sept 2017] Accessed on 27 June 2021 at https://viewdigital.org/issue-40-suicide

Ombudsman (2019) Prisoner Ombudsman for Northern Ireland Annual Report, 2018-19. Stormont Estate, Belfast, N. Ireland

O'Neill, S. M., Ferry, F., Murphy, S., Corry, C., Bolton, D., Devine, B., Ennis, E. and Bunting, B. (2014) Patterns of suicide ideation and behaviour in Northern Ireland and associations with conflict-related trauma. 19 March 2014. PLoS one. www.plosone.org.

Osman, M., Parnell, A. and Haley, C. (2017) "Suicide shall cease to be a crime": suicide and undetermined death trends 1970 – 2000 before and after the decriminalization of suicide in Ireland 1993.Ir J Med Sci (2017) 186: 201–205

Rowe, D. (1991) Breaking the bonds: understanding depression and finding freedom. London: Fontana

Rowe, D. (1991) Suicide is not a solution. In Dorothy Rowe, Breaking the Bonds: understanding depression and finding freedom. Chapter 14, pp 205-210. London: Fontana

Shakespeare, W. (1599/1623) Quotation from Marc Antony in Act III, Scene 2 of The Tragedy of Julius Caesar. First performed 1599 in The Globe, London. Published in the First Folio 1623

Shelley, P. B. (1817) Ozymandias: a sonnet, written in iambic pentameter. London: The Examiner

Shneidman, E. S. (1972) Foreword. In Albert C. Cain (ed.) (1972) Survivors of Suicide. Springfield, Illinois: Charles C Thomas

Shneidman, E. S. (1973) Deaths of Man. New York, NY: Quadrangle/The New York Times Book Co.

Shneidman, E. S. (1994) Definition of suicide. London: Jason Aronson Inc

Shneidman, E. S. (1996) The suicidal mind. Oxford, UK: Oxford University Press

Shneidman, E. S. (2003) Autopsy of a suicidal mind. Oxford, UK: Oxford University Press

Solis, N. (2023) How did Jeffrey Epstein die? New report details suicide, major lapses by prison officials. Nathan Solis. Los Angeles Times, 27 June 2023. Accessed on 1 April 2024 at https://www.latimes.com/world-nation/story/2023-06-27/watchdog-report-finds-negligence-mismanagement-at-n-y-jail-where-jeffrey-epstein-died

Soole, Mr Justice (2018) Potter Murder: The full sentencing remarks from the Honorable Mr Justice Soole. Accessed on 30 June 2021 at https://www.walesonline.co.uk/news/wales-news/live-updates-husband-who-murdered-15386624

Sussman, M. B. (ed.) (1995) A perilous calling: the hazards of psychotherapy practice. Introduction, pages 6, 7. New York, NY: John Wiley & Sons Inc.

The Irish News (2019) Reach out to the vulnerable. Editorial, 19 January 2019 – see McConville, 2019. Accessed on 12 May 2022 at https://www.irishnews.com/news/northernirelandnews/2019/01/19/

The Irish News (2021a) Mental health counsellor spent his life helping others. The Toner Family. Lives Remembered, 5 June 2021. Additional information accessed on 28 June 2021 at https://www.funeraltimes.com/francis-franktoner374356504

The Irish News (2021b) 'I was very naïve', Hazel Stewart says of relationship with killer dentist Colin Howell. Unattributed. 28 June 2021

The Irish News (2021c) Man who won lottery as a teen laid to rest after sudden death. Unattributed. Page 1, 5 June 2021

The Irish Times (2014) Legal requirement for an inquest after a suicide needs to be reviewed. Ciaran Austin. Accessed on 23 June 2021 at https://www.irishtimes.com/news/social-affairs/legal-requirement-for-an-inquest-after-a-suicide-needs-to-be-reviewed-1.1894929

Tomlinson, M. (2012) Transition to peace leaves children of the NI troubles vulnerable to suicide. Note: Personal view of author. Posted on the British Politics and Policy blog, London School of Economics

Tomlinson, M. (2013) Dealing with suicide: how does research help? Knowledge Exchange Seminar Series, Northern Ireland Assembly, October 2012 – May 2013, 11 April 2013

Torney, K. (2014) Suicide kills as many as the Troubles. The Detail, 10 February 2014. Funded by the NI Community Relations Council

Young, C. (2021) Coroner praises rescuers who tried to save woman. Connla Young. The Irish News, 14 January 2021

Yorkshire Evening Post (2019) Bereaved couple's moving message on gambling addiction as Leeds football club remembers their son - To the outside world, Lewis Keogh seemed to have it all. The Newsroom. 12 January 2019. Accessed on 12 May 2022 at https://www.yorkshireeveningpost.co.uk/news/bereaved-couples-moving-message-gambling-addiction-leeds-football-club-remembers-their-son-159606

White-Bowden, S. (1985) Everything to live for. New York, NY: Poseidon

WHO (2008) The WHO World Mental Health Survey Initiative. Geneva: WHO

WHO (2022) Suicide. World Health Organisation. Information accessed on 10 May 2022 at http://www.emro.who.int/health-topics/suicide/feed/atom.html

\* \* \*

## Chapter 12
# Suicide, murder and accidental death – allocation of state investigative resources

## Introduction

The theme of this chapter is an exploration of how scarce, tax-payer funded, government investigative resources are deployed in Northern Ireland in relation to the deaths, in particular deaths by suicide, of our citizens. These resources are principally controlled and exercised initially by the Police Service of Northern Ireland (PSNI) and ultimately by the Northern Ireland Courts Service. Both are accountable, as appropriate, to the Northern Ireland Justice Department, although the Policing Board has an ex-post oversight role regarding the PSNI. In short, we are discussing the economics of suicide.

Natural deaths, as their name suggested, were not regarded as a matter for actions by the state other than for bureaucratic reasons, registration and so on. However, a moment's reflection – although somewhat longer for me – revealed stark contrasts regarding how the Northern Ireland state addressed deaths by murder, suicide and/or accident.

## Murder

A murder could be deemed to have occurred when any person of sound mind and discretion, unlawfully kills another human being, outside of wartime (i.e. not an enemy combatant, for example), and they clearly intended to either cause grievous bodily harm (GBH) or death (Compensation, 2021). This is a Northern Ireland study: a variety of fanciful epithets – the Troubles, the conflict, our sectarian dispute, the armed struggle, our fight for freedom, et al. – were variously deployed – meeting linguists' wide range of political and propaganda objectives – to refer to thousands of murders, woundings and assaults, destruction of property and unmitigated mayhem here from c.1969-1998. One external viewpoint was represented by a former titular head of a major world religion, when His Holiness Pope John Paul II stated on 28 September 1979 during his Irish visit:

'I pray with you that the moral sense and Christian conviction of Irishmen may never become obscured and blunted by the lie of violence, that no one may ever call murder by any other name but murder, that the spiral of violence may never be given the distinction of unavoidable logic or necessary retaliation. Let us remember that the word remains forever, "All who take the sword will perish by the sword"' (The New York Times, 1979).

Almost three decades later, an exceptional insight into the mind of an archetypal Northern Irish republican revolutionary was captured for all time on Irish television (RTE) on 17 January 2005 when, Mitchell McLaughlin, then a leading member of the political 'wing', Sinn Fein, of a brutal terrorist organisation, the Provisional Irish Republican Army (PIRA), revealed his thinking, that may or may not reflect that of his comrades, when it was reported, and not contested, as follows:

'Mr McLaughlin's remarks were made on RTÉ's Questions & Answers programme on Monday night. Asked by the Minister for Justice, Mr McDowell, if he would classify the shooting of Ms McConville as a crime, he said: "I think it was wrong". Asked again if he thought it was a crime, he replied: "No, I do not". Jean McConville, a widowed mother of 10, was abducted and killed by the IRA in 1972. Her remains were found on Shelling Beach, Co Louth, [on 26 August 2003]. The McConville family has always said she was killed because she went to the aid of an injured British soldier. The IRA said she was an informer, a charge the family has always rejected' (Brennock, 2005).

Extracts from a report by the Police Ombudsman for Northern Ireland (2006) stated:

i) 'A post-mortem examination was carried out [on Mrs McConville's remains] by Dr Richard Shepherd on 28 August

2003. He identified the cause of death as a "firearm wound to the back of the head." On 1 September 2003 a second examination was carried out by Dr Marie Cassidy, Deputy State Pathologist. She identified the cause of death as "a gunshot wound to the head"' (page 9)

ii) 'In March 1999 the PIRA admitted that they had killed a number of people, including Mrs McConville and alleged that some of them had been informants. The PIRA have consistently stated since that date that Mrs McConville was abducted because she was an informant' (page 11)

iii) 'There is no evidence, information or intelligence of any kind which refers to or emanated from Mrs Jean McConville prior to 2 January 1973. She is not recorded as having been an agent ["informer"] at any time. She was an innocent woman who was abducted and murdered' (page 15).

Although the dirty word 'war' has occasionally been used, only a few retired, former paramilitary activists and their political apologists, have so far publicly and on the record, described the killing of their Northern Ireland neighbours as being other than the crime of 'murder':

'Of approximately 3,600 killings during the conflict, which started in 1969, more than 3,000 remain unsolved. The cold case backlog has tangled policing and politics and produced just a handful of prosecutions' (Carroll, 2021).

Regarding murder, a most serious criminal offence under any/all legal systems – only treason was more serious – the state's response was ex post facto, meaning 'after the fact', that is after a death by natural or accidental causes or by suicide was ruled out, only then would a full criminal inquiry into murder / homicide be initiated. In police-speak, murder investigation files normally remained 'open' until concluded by the conviction and sentence of the culprit/s. As I write, addressing the legacy of Northern Ireland's political murders remained a live but heavily contested issue across Northern Ireland:

'Under former chief constable Sir Hugh Orde, the PSNI's Historical Enquiry Team (HET) chronologically dealt with (sic) more than 1,600 cases between its formation in 2005 and 2014 when effectively it folded. Figures issued by the PSNI late in 2019 showed that the [successor] PSNI Legacy Investigation Branch had 1,130 cases on its books, touching on the deaths of 1,421 people over decades. Of these, 583 deaths were attributed to republicans, 294 deaths to loyalists, 289 deaths to the British army, 51 to police, 69 were of unknown attribution and 135 were non-paramilitary related deaths' (Moriarty, 2021).

Importantly, a murder victim's Northern Ireland dependents were entitled to financial compensation from the state, under a scheme administered by the Criminal Injuries Compensation Authority (CICA).

## Suicide

Regarding suicide, defined in brief as 'self-inflicted death', no criminal offence was committed by a person deceased by suicide since suicide was decriminalised decades ago, although potential criminal offences still existed where any third party encouraged or facilitated a person to take their own life. Therefore, it was clear that no compensation for bereaved survivors of suicide deaths was possible under the CICA scheme.

Holt (2011) described some of the reasons deployed then for ceasing to consider suicide to be a criminal offence. The key driver for this groundbreaking revision of England's long standing anathema towards suicide was not related to suicide as such. Rather it was about removing a criminal sanction against attempted suicide. One statistic mentioned by Holt (2011) spoke volumes: in 1956, 5,387 failed suicide attempts were 'known to the police'; of these 613 (or 11.4%) were prosecuted, most 'offenders' were discharged, fined or put on probation, but 33 (or over 5%) were sent to prison.

Prof Nav Kapur, head of research at Manchester University's Centre for Suicide Prevention, cited by Holt (2011) said:

'Attitudes to suicidal behaviour have changed over time and at different times in different places. What was happening in the late 50s and early 60s was that attitudes shifted from suicide as wrongdoing or sin to the medicalisation of suicide, recognising that the majority of individuals attempting suicide or dying [from suicide] were in a great deal of distress'.

## The aftermath of suicide

However, there was considerable evidence of potentially long-lasting, deleterious effects upon post-suicide, bereaved survivors, estimated at up to 135 people for each suicide death (Cerel et al., 2018). In England, a complex array of support services and organisations existed to offer, facilitate and provide practical ongoing help to survivors (Public Health England, 2016). In Northern Ireland, many of these were replicated, in addition to a new province-wide support service.

The National Health Service (NHS) Western Health and Social Care Trust (WHSCT) in Northern Ireland in partnership with the Police Service of Northern Ireland (PSNI) developed this local support service over a decade ago. It was important to understand how this happened:

'In 2006, a team from WHSCT visited the Baton Rouge Crisis Intervention Centre (BRCIC), USA and were so impressed with the early intervention work they did with people bereaved by suicide that they designed and established a similar service in the then Foyle and Sperrin Lakeland Trusts. This service became known as the Family Liaison Service where people bereaved by suicide were proactively engaged by the team.

'Crucial to the timely delivery of the service has been a partnership with the Police Service of Northern Ireland (PSNI), leading to the development of the sudden death form (SD1) completed by the officer in charge after a suspected death by suicide. Once the form is received, the team makes telephone contact with the family within 24-48 hours of the death. The purpose of this initial contact is to introduce the staff member of the service, outline the aim of the service and to arrange a home visit where anyone (not just family members) who has been impacted by the death can attend. The purpose of the first meeting is to start the process of talking about suicide to reduce stigma.

'Further one to one meetings are held to enable the bereaved to talk about their own personal grief. They are also introduced to the Bereaved by Suicide Support Group that meets monthly. The team also run an open referral system and referrals are received from GPs, mental health services, non-governmental organisations (NGOs) and self-referrals. Referrals are accepted whether the bereavement is recent, or at any time in the past' (Public Health England, 2016: 21).

The comprehensive information collated in the sudden death (SD1) form mentioned above, by the PSNI investigating officer on behalf of the Family Liaison Service, includes:

Police district; date of death; deceased's marital status, gender; age, date of birth; are children/vulnerable adults at risk? Yes/No; deceased's name/address; nationality/ethnic background; GP, if known; location of incident; suspected method of [suspected] suicide; suspected alcohol or drugs taken? Yes/No/Unknown; attending mental health services? Yes/No/Unknown; (a) Next-of-kin or significant other informed of death? Yes/No/Unknown; (b) Next-of-kin or significant other aware that suicide is suspected? Yes/No/Unknown; Has next-of-kin or significant other given permission that their contact details can be passed on to the Support Services [Family Liaison Service] Yes/No/Unknown – if YES supply contact details incl name, landline/mobile numbers, relationship to deceased, and address; address of next-of-kin / significant other; Any other relevant information. Completed forms to be emailed using restricted sensitivity to relevant authority.

Since its inception, 'the Family Liaison Service's experiences across the UK have highlighted the importance of partnership working (particularly with police) and proactive contact with bereaved families to overcome the stigma and associated feelings surrounding a death by suicide' (Public Health England, 2016: 21).There was little doubt that this scheme represented a vitally important resource for hundreds, if not thousands, of people here, bereaved by suicide. Given an estimated 263 suicides in 2020 (Black, 2021: 3), a mathematical calculation revealed a huge number, in excess of 35,000 potential service users.

However, in Northern Ireland, I can find no evidence that the state offered financial support (over and above existing natural death grants, where applicable) to family, friends, colleagues and/or others bereaved by the loss of a person to suicide.

**Natural & Accidental**

A state-funded welfare payment system existed to help people bereaved after natural deaths. In relation to accidental deaths, additional compensation might be available if a court found that negligence by third parties contributed to the death.

## Accidental & Undetermined Cause

Although there has been an eons-long ongoing debate, certainly since Gautama Siddharta became the Buddha, about when 'death' qua 'death' actually occurs in humans, our doctors who sign death certificates and our funeral directors who embalm, etc. human corpses prior to burial, are our experts. Exceptionally, the reasons for a particular death are challenged, by survivors, and others.

For example, the Howell and Potter cases (see Chapter 11 above) involved a change, following legal challenges, in initial designations from 'suicide pact' and 'suicide', respectively, to murder. Rarely was such a challenge made or upheld: hence the NASH classification, that distinguished natural, accidental, suicide and homicide deaths, had some credibility. But exceptions occurred, as described for example, by Shneidman (1981) and Litman (1963), when it was unclear, beyond a reasonable doubt, whether a death was accidental or by suicide:

'It so happens that a considerable number of deaths - the estimate is between 5 and 20 percent of all deaths which need to be certified - are not clear as to the correct or appropriate mode. These unclear or uncertain deaths are called equivocal deaths. The ambiguity is usually between the modes of suicide or accident, although uncertainty can exist between any two or more of the four modes' (Shneidman, 1981).

A recent illustrative example occurred in Northern Ireland in mid 2020 when a significant number of deaths, principally drug-related, that were registered in 2019 as by 'undetermined cause' were re-investigated by the Northern Ireland Coroner, in conjunction with the Northern Ireland Statistics and Research Agency (NISRA). The previous statistical protocol considered and registered the cause of such deaths, on the balance of probabilities, to be suicide. The issue here revolved around the intent of deceased: did s/he deliberately overdose intending to die or was their death unintended, that is 'accidental'?

The outcome of this exercise was to re-classify a number of these 'undetermined cause' deaths as being 'by accident'. Hence 57 previously 'undetermined' deaths, were removed from the 'suicide' category, resulting in a significant reduction of the 'deaths by suicide' statistic for 2019 (Atkinson, 2020). Data for earlier years were currently under investigation. NISRA issued a revised 'Guidance Note', in February, 2021, in an attempt to explain and to justify their decisions and the resulting statistical alterations (NISRA, 2021).

There remained, at the date of writing, a need for further information in the public domain about who these deceased individuals were, what was known about the circumstances of their pathways to death and how and why the Northern Ireland Coroners' Office erred in initially assigning an incorrect cause of death.

For survivors of bereavement from whatever cause, the statistical gymnastics alluded to above were cold comfort indeed. What was demonstrated, however, was that public inquests were essential for all deaths where the epithet 'natural' has not been correctly and appropriately attached, and where an undisclosed risk existed of a death being wrongly classified under NASH or 'undetermined' descriptors. Currently, the Northern Ireland Coroners' Office had total discretion in this regard.

In the next paragraphs, we briefly consider the economics of homicide in Northern Ireland, in the context of the costs of crime, and the economics of youth suicide in Ireland, in the context of some societal factors related to indices of human development in several countries.

**The Economics of Murder in Northern Ireland**

Government statistics did not permit extraction of the overall costs of murder, its investigation by police and prosecution of actors by the Public Prosecution Service in Northern Ireland. However, some insights were available in one relevant report (Cost of Crime in NI, 2010). This disclosed that 'the costs [as a consequence] of homicide to individuals, business and government in 2006/07' (p 31) totalled £37.1 million, made up of 'physical/emotional impact on victims' (£24.6 million), 'cost of lost output' (£10.5 million), 'victim support costs' (£0.2 million), and 'response: police, prisons, courts' costs (£2.4 million). Official recorded homicide data were used to determine the number of homicides in NI in 2006/07, when 23 cases of murder (and one case of manslaughter) were registered in that year' (Cost of Crime, 2010: 46). In recent years, murders have ranged from 17 (2016/17), to 27 (2017/18), 29 (2018/19), 21 (2019/20) and 22 (2020/21) (Homicides NI, 2021).

Murder investigations were post-murder, that is events driven, with access by state agencies to potentially unlimited, supplementary budgets. Estimated outlays were known only after investigations were completed or in progress. Suicide was not subject to investigation, as such, except to secure evidence for the coroner that death was self-inflicted, without any third-party involvement whatsoever. Hence suicide investigations incurred nil or negligible outlays.

**The Economics of Youth Suicide**

Northern Ireland was part of the UK which did not meet the criteria of the United Nations Development Programme (UNDP) to be designated as a 'country' with the highest human development index. The UK was not ranked in the top ten countries, but Ireland was: so for our purposes, we shall regard Irish, viz. Irish Republic, data as a 'near-enough' proxy for Northern Ireland.

These UNDP criteria are threefold:

i) Life expectancy at birth

ii) Mean years of schooling

iii) Gross national income per capita

Research by Doran and Kinchin (2020) examined the 'economic and epidemiological impact of youth suicide mortality [for youth aged between 15 and 24] in countries with the highest human development index.' These countries were Norway, Australia, Switzerland, Germany, Denmark, Singapore, Netherlands, the Republic of Ireland, Canada and the United States. Doran and Kinchin (2020) measured the economic impact of youth suicide using three criteria:

i) Years of life lost

ii) Years of productive life lost

iii) Present economic value of lost productivity.

Their analysis was hedged around with their view that 'suicide is preventable', referencing the oft-repeated, considered opinion of the

World Health Organisation (2014). O'Neill, S. et al. (2016: 13) were more realistic when they opined that: 'Suicide is an important and *potentially* preventable cause of mortality' (italics added). Doran and Kinchin (2020) supplied some additional flesh to the bones of suicide prevention stating that 'there is now strong evidence to suggest that restricting access to lethal means can prevent suicide and that school-based awareness programmes play a role in reducing suicide attempts and suicide ideation' (p2). One is reminded of similar UK policies regarding removal of lethal coal gas from the domestic supply (1975) and the restriction of over-the-counter sales of lethal quantities of paracetamol (1998).

Doran and Kinchin (2020) mentioned that a 'systems-based approach' to suicide prevention was proposed in Australia (Black Dog Institute, 2016), that built on nine strategies:

i) After care and crisis care
ii) Psychological and pharmacotherapy treatments
iii) Building the capacity and support of general practice teams
iv) Frontline staff training
v) Gatekeeper training
vi) Schools programmes
vii) Community campaigns
viii) Media guidelines
ix) Means restriction

They also offered the view that there was increasing evidence of the cost-effectiveness [or return on investment] of suicide prevention strategies. However a reality check was called for given the actualité of current economic costs of each youth suicide revealed in their study. In Ireland / Northern Ireland average years of life lost were estimated at 59.6 years (males) and 63.8 years (females), years of productive life lost were estimated at 47.5 years, (both males and females), value of average earnings foregone: $1,872,954 (males) and $1,428,782 (females). They concluded their study of the costs of youth suicide in the 10 countries mentioned above that:

'Economic evidence can assist public health-care decision-makers to understand the magnitude of adverse outcomes associated with suicide and the potential benefits to be achieved by investing in effective strategies to address suicidal behaviour. This research has attempted to quantify the economic and epidemiological impact of youth suicide in countries with the highest human development index. The results are staggering – almost 7,000 young lives are lost each year to suicide representing a loss of 406,730 years of life at a cost of over $5.53 billion. Reducing youth suicide requires a multifaceted approach and significant investment by governments' (Doran and Kinchin, 2020).

## Prevention Blues

Comparisons between the respective roles of the state in relation to the investigation of murder and suicide, involved some risk of an unenlightening 'apples v oranges' debate. As noted above, in 2006/07, the cost of murder in N Ireland, including its investigation, totalled £37.1 million, in relation to 23 murders, and one case of manslaughter. In 2020/21 a total of 22 murders were investigated. In 2014, the costs of youth suicide in Ireland were estimated at just under £800,000 for each death: in that year a total of 51 young people – 42 males and 9 females, aged between 15 and 24, died by suicide (Doran and Kinchin, 2021: 5). Mathematics converted these data to a total cost of youth suicide in the Irish Republic in 2014 at £40.8 million.

## Economic cost of suicide and deliberate self-harm in N Ireland

Comparable data for Northern Ireland was located in an occasional paper written by NI civil service economists (Department of Health NI, 2019). This data did not discriminate on the basis of the deceased's age, stating that a total of 305 suicides were recorded in the calendar year 2017 while financial data related to the 2017/18 financial year. The paper's authors conceded that 'economic costs [were] broad estimates ... as calculating these costs is not an exact science'.

They also noted, under 'Direct Costs', but without further comment, that 'police service and coroner service attendance costs at suicides and follow-up investigations [and] NI Fire & Rescue Service (NIFRS) [costs] to retrieve remains' were excluded due to lack of data.

They estimated the **Total Economic Costs of Suicide** at **£473,864,181 (2017/18).**

They identified three cost categories:

i) **Direct Costs** – These are costs associated with health service interventions such as ambulance costs and other costs associated with conducting post-mortems and funeral costs: £3,460,225.

ii) **Indirect Costs** – These are made up mainly of lost – by suicide – output or earnings from an absent labour force over an expected lifetime. The calculation also involves an estimate for unpaid work (e.g. housework, volunteering in community etc.): £178,438,958.

iii) **Intangible Costs** – These costs relate to human grief and suffering including that experienced by family and friends. These costs are the most difficult to measure in monetary terms as they consist of notional costs with no market existing for valuing them directly: £291,964,997.

At the time of writing, a new draft Northern Ireland programme for government (PFG) awaited political action following an election in May 2022. An earlier (draft) PFG (2016-2021) under Outcome 4 – "we enjoy long, healthy, active lives" (NI Govt. PFG 2016-2021, 2016: 23) included a performance indicator: 'reduce preventable deaths'. This was reflected in the aims of the NI Suicide Prevention Strategy, Protect Life 2 (2019: 16):

1. Reduce the suicide rate in Northern Ireland by 10% by 2024.
2. Ensure suicide prevention services and support are delivered appropriately in deprived areas where suicide and self-harm rates are highest.

The economists' paper (Department of Health NI, 2019) illustrated the aspirational 'positive outcome of a measure ... to reduce suicide' by 10%, by estimating that up to 30 lives might be saved, and up to approx £47m economic cost avoided. (Cost per suicide £1,553,653)

The current Northern Ireland Suicide Prevention Strategy, Protect Life 2 (2019), stated:

'£8.7m is currently invested annually in suicide prevention by the Department of Health through the Public Health Agency which, in turn, supports community led suicide prevention services and funds Health and Social Care Trusts to provide local suicide prevention co-ordinators, family liaison officers (who work with bereaved families), training officers (suicide prevention and mental health promotion), and self-harm resources. A range of suicide prevention and emotional health and wellbeing programmes have also been funded separately under the transformation programme' (Protect Life 2, 2019: 34).

A range of services, 18 in all, were also delivered under Protect Life 2, including:

i) **Lifeline**, a crisis telephone helpline
ii) **Training** in suicide awareness & intervention skills, and primary care depression awareness
iii) **Counselling** by voluntary and community groups
iv) **Self-harm registry** – detailed recording and collating of information on every self-harm injury presentation to Emergency Departments
v) **Self-harm intervention** project
vi) **Sudden Death Notification** & process to gather "real time" data on suspected suicide deaths and to facilitate support services to the bereaved
vii) **Reducing access to means of suicide**
viii) **Place of Safety** – improved protocols between Health and Social Care (HSC) and the police service (PSNI)
ix) **Media Reporting** – guidelines produced to support sensitive reporting of suicide, including monitoring media reporting
x) **Safe Place** – consideration of temporary supportive environment for someone in emotional crisis
xi) **Safer Custody**
xii) **North/South Collaboration** on island of Ireland
xiii) **Public Information Campaigns** – information on services
xiv) **Community Capacity Building & Support** – mental health promotion

xv) **Emergency community response plans** – for identifying & responding early to emerging suicide clusters

xvi) **Research & data collection** including UK National Confidential Inquiry into Suicide & Homicide by people with mental illness

xvii) **Flourish – Churches initiative**

xviii) **Bereavement support & guidance** (Protect Life 2: 35).

What was excluded was any reference to consideration by the NI government, of establishing an organised, systemic process of examination, after any statutory, coronial investigation was concluded, of potential life-protecting, life-preserving actions – when and by whom – that might have saved the life, protem, of any person deceased by suicide. It seems to me that continuously overlooking this learning opportunity is a grave, long-standing error.

Given the huge economic cost of suicide in N Ireland – in 2017, £474 million – justification for investment in education for prevention by such a learning endeavour must be a no-brainer.

## A suicide prevention non-sequitur

Much diligent, well-informed and well-intentioned effort by many good people was devoted over several years to preparing and publishing suicide prevention strategies for Northern Ireland since an inaugural edition in 2006 (Black and McKay, 2019). A broad range of persons, agencies, organisations, and oversight bodies, including ultimately the Northern Ireland Assembly, regarded the current strategy document – Protect Life 2 – as key to guiding their sincere efforts in suicide reduction.

Chandler (1962) authored the organizational principle 'structure follows strategy', meaning that unless the enterprise's structure supported its strategy, outcomes would not meet expectations. In spite of a strategic approach to prevention, suicide continues to destroy individuals, families, communities and neighbourhoods across our land. The question remains: does our suicide prevention structure support our strategy?

In my view, it really is time to apply basic principles of organizational development to our plethora of suicide prevention resources and their activities so that a recognisable structure emerges that all players are content with. An appropriate name comes to mind for this new dedicated organisation, shaped and structured to deliver its remit: to implement the agreed suicide prevention strategy for our people, efficiently, effectively and economically, and to report its performance regularly to us all through our elected Assembly : The Northern Ireland Suicide Prevention Authority. How much longer must we wait?

## Conclusions

As a society, we must face up to the issue of accountability for suicide. Instead of allocating 100% responsibility to the deceased-by-suicide citizen, we, the living must investigate what contribution we / society / our political-social systems / academe et al. made and continue to make to suicide's destruction of citizens here, day by day. As we demonstrated earlier, the economic costs of suicide are massive. One wonders what the outcome might be if the state's unacknowledged contribution to suicide were tested in law. An existing insight related to medical negligence claims in the Northern Ireland health service that are currently running at £30 million annually (Madden, 2021).

The 'staggering' costs of suicide, in particular of youth suicide, have not been reflected in the levels of public investment that might be expected from the state, in exercising its responsibilities to protect the lives of its citizens from suicide (Article 2, Human Rights Act, 1998).

As far as I can tell, analysis of the facts of any death by suicide in Northern Ireland is limited to the following:

i) To secure factual evidence from the police service (PSNI) for the Coroner's office, regarding identity of the deceased, date, location and method of their death, and confirmation that cause of death was by suicide, with no third party involvement whatsoever

ii) Consideration of and decision regarding convening an inquest, including as appropriate, consultation with key, bereaved survivors

iii) Convening, organising, and holding of a public inquest, if appropriate, by the Coroner.

I have found no evidence, apart from occasional and infrequent academic studies – with limited public circulation – involving consultation with the Coroner's office, that any public information whatsoever is available regarding:

iv) What, if anything, might have been done, and by which actor – person or organisation - to prevent any individual death by suicide

v) What, if anything, has been learned from the coroner's investigation regarding any individual death by suicide that might be valuable, and worth promulgating widely, in relation to the prevention of future deaths by suicide

vi) The fact that each death by suicide has unique features that distinguish it from all others and that may be worthy of wider promulgation in the public interest, after consultation with, and agreement of key, bereaved survivors.

**Myth:** (fictitious popular idea) Every death by suicide is preventable

**Fallacy:** (misleading argument) There is little to be gained by public inquests into deaths by suicide

# References

Article 2 (2021) Human Rights Act, 1998. Accessed on 14 July 2021 at https://www.equalityhumanrights.com/en/human-rights-act/article-2-right-life

Atkinson, K. (2020) NI suicide rate expected to fall following review. Karen Atkinson. BBC News NI. 7 October 2020. Accessed on 8 July 2021 at https://www.bbc.co.uk/news/uk-northern-ireland-54436324

Black Dog Institute (2016) An evidence based systems approach to suicide prevention : guidance on planning, commissioning and monitoring. Canberra, ACT: COA

Black, L-A. (2021) Suicide: Northern Ireland. Dr Lesley-Ann Black. NI Assembly Research and Information Service. Research Paper. 14 April 2021. Accessed on 17 July 2021 at http://www.niassembly.gov.

uk/globalassets/documents/raise/publications/2017-2022/2021/health/2321.pdf

Black, L-A., and McKay, K. (2019) Suicide statistics and strategy in Northern Ireland: update. Lesley-Ann Black and Keara McKay. Research matters, Northern Ireland Assembly, Research and Information Service. 28 November 2019. Accessed on 16 July 2021 at https://www.assemblyresearchmatters.org/2019/11/28/suicide-statistics-and-strategy-in-northern-ireland-update/

Brennock, M. (2005) SF remarks on woman's killing widely criticised. The Irish Times, 19 January 2005

Carroll, R. (2021) Northern Ireland victims' families condemn plan to end prosecutions. The Guardian. 14 July 2021

Cerel, J., Brown, M., Maple, M. et al. (2018) How Many People Are Exposed to Suicide? Not Six. Suicide and Life-Threatening Behaviour. 2018. doi:10.1111/sltb.12450

Chandler, A. D., Jr. (1962) Strategy and Structure: Chapters in the History of the American Industrial Enterprise. Cambridge, MA: MIT Press

Compensation (2021) Murder compensation claims. Accessed on 13 July 2021 at https://www.advice.co.uk/criminal-injuries-compensation/how-families-of-a-murder-victim-could-claim-compensation/

Cost of Crime in NI (2010) Cost of Crime in Northern Ireland: DOJ Research and Statistical Series: Report No. 1. Oxford: Oxford Economics

Department of Health NI (2019) Economic cost of suicide and self-harm in Northern Ireland September 2019. Accessed on 18 May 2022 at https://niopa.qub.ac.uk/handle/NIOPA/11697

Doran, C. M. and Kinchin, I. (2020) Economic and epidemiological impact of youth suicide in countries with the highest human development index. PLoS ONE 15(5): e0232940. Accessed on 8 July 2021 at https://doi.org/10.1371/journal.pone.0232940

Gawande, A. (2020) Why Americans are dying from despair. The New Yorker. 16 March 2020

Holt, G. (2011) When suicide was illegal. Accessed on 5 July 2021 at https://www.bbc.co.uk/news/magazine-14374296

Homicides NI (2021) Number of homicides: offences recorded in Northern Ireland from 2002/03 to 2020/21. Accessed on 12 July 2021 at https://www.statista.com/statistics/916727/homicides-in-northern-ireland/

Human Rights Act (1998) Article 2: Right to life. https://www.mind.org.uk Accessed on 15 March 2024

Litman, R.E., et al. (1963) Investigations of equivocal suicides. J.A.M.A. 184: 924-29

Madden, A. (2021) Northern Ireland trusts facing medical negligence cases going back to the 1960s as payouts reach £30m annually. The Belfast Telegraph, 25 January 2021. Accessed on 17 July 2021 at https://www.belfasttelegraph.co.uk/news/northern-ireland/northern-ireland-trusts-facing-medical-negligence-cases-going-back-to-1960s-as-payouts-reach-30m-annually-40005971.html

Moriarty, G. (2021) Britain's stance on Troubles killings brings more anguish to victims. The Irish Times, 14 July 2021. Accessed on 19 May 2022 at https://www.irishtimes.com/news/politics/britain-s-stance-on-troubles-killings-brings-more-anguish-to-victims-1.4620301

NI Govt PFG 2016-2021 (2016) Draft Northern Ireland Programme for Government Framework 2016-2021. 26 May 2016. Stormont, Belfast.

NISRA (2021) Guidance Note to Users on Suicide Statistics in Northern Ireland, updated February 2021. Northern Ireland Statistics and Research Agency. [First published July 2020, last updated 19th October 2021]

O'Neill, S., Corry, C., McFeeters, D., Murphy, S. and Bunting, B. (2016) Suicide in Northern Ireland: an analysis of gender differences in demographic, psychological and contextual factors. Crisis, 2016, 37(1), 13-20

Police Ombudsman for Northern Ireland (2006) Report into the complaint by James and Michael McConville regarding the police investigation into the abduction and murder of their mother Mrs Jean

McConville. August, 2006. Police Ombudsman for Northern Ireland, New Cathedral Buildings, St. Anne's Square, 11 Church Street, Belfast BT1 1PG. Website: www.policeombudsman.org

Protect Life 2 (2019) Protect Life 2: a strategy for preventing suicide and self-harm in Northern Ireland 2019-24. NI Department of Health. Stormont, Belfast. Accessible from NI Dept of Health at https://www.health-ni.gov.uk/sites/default/files/publications/health/pl-strategy.PDF

Public Health England (2016) Support after a suicide: a guide to providing local services, a practical resource. Supported by the National Suicide Prevention Alliance (NSPA). Surrey, England: NSPA

Shneidman, E. S. (1981) The psychological autopsy. First published in Louis A.Gottschalk et al. (eds.) Guide to the Investigation and Reporting of Drug-Abuse Deaths (edited by Louis A. Gottschalk et al., 1977, pp. 42–56.) Reprinted in Suicide and Life-threatening Behaviour (SLTB), Winter, 1981. Accessed on 7 July 2021 at https://onlinelibrary.wiley.com/doi/full/10.1111/j.1943-278X.1981.tb01009.x

Solis, N. (2023) How did Jeffrey Epstein die? New report details suicide, major lapses by prison officials. Nathan Solis. Los Angeles Times, 27 June 2023. Accessed on 1 April 2024 at https://www.latimes.com/world-nation/story/2023-06-27/watchdog-report-finds-negligence-mismanagement-at-n-y-jail-where-jeffrey-epstein-died

The New York Times (1979) Excerpts from homilies Pope John Paul II delivered in Drogheda and at Dublin, Ireland. New York, NY: Publishers The New York Times

United Nations Development Programme (2024) Role: to eradicate poverty while protecting the planet in 170 countries. https://www.undep.org Accessed on 15 March 2024

Youth suicide myths (2021) The myths & facts of youth suicide. Accessed on 16 July 2021 at https://suicideprevention.nv.gov/Youth/Myths/

World Health Organisation (2014) Preventing suicide: a global imperative. Geneva: WHO 2014

\* \* \*

# Chapter 13
# Suicide, freedom and individual human rights

## Introduction

By now, if you've got this far, we have a fair idea about what human suicide means. As for 'freedom' and 'individual human rights', we shall go back to the beginning.

## Freedom – individual liberty

In our 100 year-old, representative albeit imperfect but democratically elected jurisdiction, 'freedom' has a specific meaning, viz. individual liberty, with a conditional qualifier, 'under the law'. Where we live, 'freedom' does not mean liberty to behave whatever way we like. Experience being a teacher par excellence, I still remember clearly my 'freedom lesson' of half-a-century ago. I recall, back in the summer of 1969, as an underpaid probationer teacher, I worked for a season with some teacher colleagues as an assistant barman in Lynch's Bar, in Bangor, Co Down.

The 'Twelfth Day' [12 July 1969] was being celebrated in a nearby 'Field' by local and visiting Orange Order members, their families and friends with much music, marching, craic and picnicking. Around lunchtime, a large group of brethren and their families, including young children came into the bar for relaxation and refreshment. Nothing unusual happened until a youngster approached me and asked for potato crisps and lemonade. I put the order together on a tray and indicated the price to the kid. "Naw, mister. It's the Twelfth. We can do whatever we like today." The youth then gathered up the crisps and drinks and walked off back to his family group. I quickly realised that no payment was likely to be forthcoming from that 'freedom-loving' customer. Of course, as a neophyte Twelfth Day barman – I'd never before worked behind a bar on this significant Northern Ireland calendar day – I was not au fait with the curiously elastic, cultural expectations of some customers. A teacher-barman colleague had observed the scene and, in a low voice said 'Just let it go – make sure you get the cash first next time'. Thus one of the multiple meanings in Northern Ireland of the 'umbrella term' freedom was revealed to me.

Liberty doesn't come naturally to humans – hence the development globally of enforcement mechanisms of liberty's conditions and limitations, across the whole range of human activities, individual, group, national and international. And who created these policing outfits? Power holders in positions of authority, democratically or more often by way of the force of dictatorship, to preserve their status quo and/or because they were fearful of political or cultural revolution.

Freedom under statute law to die by suicide – as mentioned earlier – was confirmed in N Ireland in 1966, following sheepishly and robotically a decriminalizing initiative in England & Wales in 1961. Not that our sisters and brothers, estimated at 263 poor souls in 2020 (Black, 2021: 3), who chose to end their life by suicide were likely to be either affected or influenced one way or another by statute law.

## Autonomy – individual human rights

There is a related aspect of freedom, referred to as autonomy, defined as 'independence or freedom, as of the will or of one's actions' otherwise 'self-determination' (Dictionary.com). Szasz (2011) seriously criticised what he believed was the flawed relationship between human autonomy and coercive approaches to suicide prevention:

'Laws that enable some persons to lock up other persons whose behaviour they find upsetting [known as 'sectioning' in UK/Ireland] have nothing to do with health, medicine or treatment: they are a system of extralegal social controls without the due-process safeguards of the criminal justice system. Calling this arrangement 'suicide prevention' is deception and self-deception. The non-coercive prevention of death may, under certain circumstances, be a noble end. The coercive prohibition of it is, a priori, ignoble and unworthy of modern people in secular societies' (Szasz, 2011: xiii).

## Right to life and our suicide prevention strategy

In considering issues related to individual human rights, we now examine legalistic notions of 'the right to life' in relation to our 'Protect Life 2' suicide prevention strategy.

## The Human Rights Act 1998 and the European Convention of Human Rights (ECHR)

In Chapter 12, above, I alluded to the state's Article 2 responsibilities to protect citizens' lives from suicide. Clearly this duty is seriously limited and massively constrained, as explained below.

What follows is a discussion of the protection offered, or withheld, by UK statute law, viz. the ECHR, in relation to any person at serious risk of suicide. Its Article 2 as enacted in the UK by the Human Rights Act, 1998, is the relevant clause, which reads as follows:

1. Everyone's right to life shall be protected by law. No one shall be deprived of his life intentionally save in the execution of a sentence of a court following his conviction of a crime for which this penalty is provided by law.
2. Deprivation of life shall not be regarded as inflicted in contravention of this Article when it results from the use of force which is no more than absolutely necessary:

(a) In defence of any person from unlawful violence

(b) In order to effect a lawful arrest or to prevent the escape of a person lawfully detained

(c) In action lawfully taken for the purpose of quelling a riot or insurrection.

Per item #1 above, death sentences on 'conviction of a crime for which this penalty is provided by law', viz. treason, was ultimately, in 2004, outlawed by the ECHR's 13$^{th}$ Protocol. Many states, including the UK (GB/NI) and Ireland, have now removed the death sentence, including for treason:

**Capital punishment in the United Kingdom** was used from ancient times until the second half of the 20th century. The last executions in the United Kingdom were by hanging, and took place in 1964, before capital punishment was suspended for murder in 1965 and finally abolished for murder in 1969 (1973 in Northern Ireland). Although unused, the death penalty remained a legally defined punishment for certain offences such as treason until it was completely abolished in 1998. In 2004 the 13th Protocol to the European Convention on Human Rights became binding on the United Kingdom, prohibiting the restoration of the death penalty for as long as the UK is a party to the convention[1] (Wikipedia, 2021).

In Ireland, the death penalty was abolished in 1964 for all but the murder of Gardaí, diplomats and prison officers. It was abolished by statute for these remaining offences in 1990 and was finally expunged from the Constitution of Ireland by a referendum in 2001 (Wikipedia, 2024).

But the UK state's duty of care, under the ECHR, in relation to a citizen at risk of suicide is limited and constrained by the citizen's perceived 'custodial' status, as 'free' or 'detained by the state'. Curtice and Sandford (2009) revealed this yawning gap between the state's duty of care – in the context of quality of treatment and issues of clinical negligence – for those detained by the state and the absence of any duty of care in relation to everyone else, viz. citizens not detained by, or in the custody of state agencies:

'It is important that clinicians remain focused on patients and the wider community both inside and outside the prison walls. Support for inmates must be reviewed and all cases of completed suicide or near misses (sic) must be investigated in accordance with the appropriate procedure. Any enquiry will look closely at issues of quality of treatment and issues of clinical negligence. The message is clear: those detained by the state must be safeguarded from murder, suicide and neglect' (Curtice and Sandford, 2009: 450).

Hence, freedom to take your own life, in Northern Ireland, was acknowledged by the state as an event beyond any statutory 'duty of care'. This perhaps explained the absence of any formal state involvement in protecting the life of any citizen from suicide, unless that citizen is in state custody. But, you will argue, Northern Ireland's Department of Health published six separate suicide prevention strategy policy documents since 'Protect Life 1' in 2006 (Black and McKay (2019). However, a cursory examination of the current 'suicide prevention' strategy policy document, Protect Life 2 – a strategy for preventing suicide and self harm in Northern Ireland, 2019-2024, confirmed this long-standing hands-off approach.

In Northern Ireland, therefore, the state currently has no statutory duty to prevent suicide except as outlined above.

**Protect Life 2 – a strategy for preventing suicide and self harm in Northern Ireland 2019-2024 and beyond**

The stated purpose of the strategy was:

to set the priorities and define the key actions for reducing the prevalence of suicide and self-harm over the period 2019 – 2024.

The stated aims of the strategy were:

1. Reduce the suicide rate in Northern Ireland by 10% by 2024.
2. Ensure suicide prevention services and support are delivered appropriately in deprived areas where suicide and self-harm rates are highest.

[In September 2024, an 'Action Plan, Report and Recommendations', was published by the NI Dept of Health, based upon a review of Protect Life 2:

In September 2023, the Department of Health Permanent Secretary, Peter May, announced the extension of the Protect Life 2 Strategy (2019) for a further three years to the end of 2027, with the potential for an additional extension to 2029.

It was recognised that whilst solid progress has been made in delivering on the strategy's objectives since it was published in September 2019, challenges in relation to the budget and the impact of the COVID-19 pandemic have prevented full delivery. The three-year extension is to allow more time for fuller implementation and for the existing actions to be delivered.

As part of the Strategy extension, the Department agreed to undertake a Review of the Protect Life 2 Action Plan. This Review is to inform the future Action Plan and its implementation. The aims and objectives of the Protect Life 2 Strategy are not being reviewed and will not change at this point (Protect Life 2 Review, 2024).]

The 2019 document continued to rely upon 'mental health' as an essential sine qua non in understanding and reducing suicide. Unfortunately, there was no unanimity among all or indeed any of the stakeholders in suicidology as to what 'mental health', or its opposite, viz. 'mental illness' meant.

My antipathy to the term 'mental health' related back to a range of school playground articulations of how this hearsay concept was perceived by youngsters, inter alia:

'Your head's cut'

'You're away in the head'

'Your head's a marley (marble)'

'You're a head-case'

'You're mental'

'Head problems, eh?'

'You need your head examined'

'You need to see the head doctor'

'The men (sic) in white coats are coming to take you away'.

So that my personal antipathy to the use of the term did not intrude unduly, I cited the World Health Organisation's published definition of 'mental health'.

The WHO (2018) offered the following description of what 'mental health' meant:

**'Key facts**

- Mental health is more than the absence of mental disorders.
- Mental health is an integral part of health; indeed, there is no health without mental health.
- Mental health is determined by a range of socioeconomic, biological and environmental factors.
- Cost-effective public health and intersectoral strategies and interventions exist to promote, protect and restore mental health.

Mental health is an integral and essential component of health. The WHO constitution states: "Health is a state of complete physical, mental and social well-being and not merely the absence of disease or infirmity." An important implication of this definition is that mental health is more than just the absence of mental disorders or disabilities.

Mental health is a state of well-being in which an individual realises his or her own abilities, can cope with the normal stresses of life, can work productively and is able to make a contribution to his or her community.

Mental health is fundamental to our collective and individual ability as humans to think, emote, interact with each other, earn a living and enjoy life. On this basis, the promotion, protection and restoration of mental health can be regarded as a vital concern of individuals, communities and societies throughout the world.' WHO (2018)

72% of people who died by suicide in Northern Ireland had not been under the care of statutory mental health services in the 12 months prior to death (Protect Life 2, 2019: 13). What were these 'statutory mental health services', what 'care' did they offer and what statute/law legitimised them? The NI government website entitled 'Mental Health Services' (2021) did not specifically refer to suicide or suicide prevention. Nor did it use the term 'mental illness': instead it mentioned 'mental health problems'. The site identified the general practitioner (GP) as the initial contact for citizens regarding mental health services. An immediately obvious part-solution to the disconnected 72% suicide deceased mentioned above might be a GP initiative 'to reach out' by inviting all registered patients to an annual cup of tea, or the like, at the surgery.

Our current suicide prevention strategy mentioned statute law only twice (see Appendix below) but excluded any reference to the Human Rights Act, 1998, the ECHR or the Mental Health Northern Ireland Order, 1986: the latter is discussed below.

I could find no information that estimated how many of the above-mentioned 'disconnected 72% suicide deceased' were 'mentally ill but undiagnosed'. However, the Protect Life 2 strategy document stated:

'Research, commissioned under the Protect Life Strategy, involving in-depth analysis of records on almost 1,600 deaths by suicide, highlights the known associative factors of mental illness (almost 60% of those who died had been diagnosed with a mental health condition; a substantial proportion of the rest would likely have had an undiagnosed mental disorder), unemployment, alcohol (particularly in young people), and a history of prior suicide attempts. In addition, experience of an adverse incident prior to suicide was common. These experiences centred on relationship difficulties and family discord but also included bereavement, financial difficulties and employment concerns, and physical illness diagnoses' (Protect Life 2, 2019: 30).

A serious, but obvious difficulty existed, however, because there were no comparable data relating to the unquantified number of citizens who were 'diagnosed with a mental health condition', but who chose NOT to kill themselves. Hence we continued to ponder the 'blind spot' or 'blind spots, one for each suicide', that might begin to explain, or even hint at, what actually tipped the scales of life versus death for our unfortunate suicide deceased.

Sands (2008) referred to a post-suicide grief process involving a bereaved person's ability to reconstruct beneficial meanings and memories about the deceased, after having 'negotiated the inexplicability of the blind spot at the centre of a death by suicide ... and [being] no longer intensely focused on intentionality and reconstruction of the death story' (Sands, 2008: 162). Conventionally, that 'blind spot' is occupied by some aspect of mental illness, that cannot but be perceived by the bereaved as pejorative, in view of the continuing stigma attached to 'head problems'.

## Mental Health Northern Ireland Order (1986)

Over three decades ago, a government Order, the Mental Health (Northern Ireland) (MHNI) Order, 1986 – equivalent to a statute – articulated the state's duty towards citizens with 'mental health problems'. Almost a quarter of a century later, as summarised below, this 'duty' in relation to 'mental health problems' was elaborated in an explanatory publication, 'Guidelines on the Use of the MH(NI) Order,

1986' (2011), extending to 112 pages, that seemed consciously and deliberately to adopt psychiatric terminology throughout.

The Mental Health (Northern Ireland) Order (1986) addressed the 'care, treatment and protection of people who experience mental disorder', defined in the legislation as 'mental illness, mental handicap (viz. learning disability), and any other disorder or disability of mind' (Guidelines, 2011: 5). In short, the law provided for the care of citizens diagnosed by psychiatry as mentally ill. The Guidelines (2011) listed a large number of statutes, including the Human Rights Act (1998) that should be taken into consideration in relation to implementing the 1986 Order (Guidelines, 2011: 8, 9 & 10). A mental health strategy document followed a decade later.

## Mental Health Strategy (2021b)

More recently, Northern Ireland's Department of Health published a Mental Health Strategy 2021-2031, including an 'Easy Read Summary' (Mental Health Strategy, 2021b). This opened with some plausible if somewhat over-simplified, explanatory remarks:

'What is mental health? Your mental health is how you think and feel about things in your mind. If your mental health is good, you feel well and happy. If you have mental health problems, you might feel sad, angry or worried' (p1).

It continued:

'Northern Ireland has more people with mental health problems than other parts of the United Kingdom. People with less money may have more mental health problems. People with mental health problems may have more money problems. Northern Ireland has more mental health problems because of our history of fighting, called the "Troubles"' (p2).

Linking and/or associating poor mental health with poverty and our recent civil conflict inadvertently acknowledged that in Northern Ireland, poor mental health could be considered to be a political issue, not least in relation to inadequate government investment in addressing the issue:

'Less money is spent on mental health services in Northern Ireland compared to the UK and Ireland' (p3).

The strategy summary then articulated its vision, its priorities, its themes and its ideas, all of which were encapsulated in the form of 35 actions: 'These are things we want to do to change mental health services in Northern Ireland' (p7). Those with clear political ramifications included:

'Action 10: More money for children and young people's mental health services. Better care when they move to adult services' (p10).

'Action 24: Build good hospitals for when people need to go into hospital' (p13).

'Action 26: Make sure there are safe services in Northern Ireland for people getting treatment who might hurt themselves or others. This is called low secure in-patient care' (p14).

'Action 27: All services in Northern Ireland need to have one plan. They need to talk to each other to help people who are having great difficulty with their mental health or are in danger' (p14).

'Action 31: Have a whole Northern Ireland mental health service (p16).

'Action 35: Have a Centre for mental health research with money to pay for the research. Research looks at problems very carefully to answer questions. We need everyone to work hard together to make this plan work' (p16).

[A caveat was entered regarding the money that the Northern Ireland state has had to spend on Covid -19 [since 2020 and ongoing]. It has 'less money for other services ... [and will] need to do work to find the money needed to make all the [35] actions happen' (p17)].

Only two of the above 'Actions' could be linked, indirectly, to suicide and/or self-harm – Actions 26 & 27.

## Monitoring & measuring strategic outcome

Self-evidently a strategy, or plan of action, designed to achieve a long-term or overall goal(s), that merits serious consideration must incorporate objectives that are specific, measurable, achieveable, realistic and timely, otherwise SMART objectives (Doran, 1981). It seems particularly important that a decade long Mental Health Strategy 2021-2031 (2021a) should include credible mechanisms to assess periodically its level of performance. These might be usefully complemented within a key-results framework (Doerr, 2017).

As mentioned above in Chapter 12, under 'Economic cost of suicide and deliberate self-harm in N Ireland', the current Northern Ireland Suicide Prevention Strategy, Protect Life 2 (2019: 16) includes a performance indicator to 'reduce the suicide rate in Northern Ireland by 10% by 2024'.

**Mental illness and suicide – close to an oxymoron?**

Joiner (2010) estimated that 100% of suicide deceased were mentally ill. Make of that what you will. A more frequently cited figure, that 90% suicide deceased were mentally unwell, offered little ambiguity:

'it is now generally accepted that 90% or more of suicides have one or more psychiatric disorders at the time of suicide' (Roy, 2001: 60)

Roy (2001) relied upon postmortem psychological autopsies, whose methodology was disputed by some (Hjelmeland et al., 2012) as being seriously flawed. But this did not cause the author/s of our Protect Life 2 strategy (p30) to question this 'simple answer to the complex problem' of 'Why suicide ' As Mencken (1917) postulated:

'Explanations exist; they have existed for all time; there is always a well-known solution to every human problem — neat, plausible, and wrong' (Mencken, 1917).

Salvatore (2015) eloquently relocated this '90% of suicides were mentally ill' paradigm to its more appropriate unproven category in his comprehensive 'discussion draft' on the questionable contribution of psychological autopsy studies to understanding suicide. He cited the WHO (2014) caution 'that despite a strong link between mental illness and suicide, no single cause has been found and many factors play a role in a suicide'. But the mathematical / statistical approach to management of global human suicidal behaviour necessarily ignored the lessons inherent in the uniqueness of each suicide. This 'passing over' of 'why' any one person took their own life, could be ascribed to

Durkheim's (1897/2002) invention of sociology's macro-statistical approach. Currently, Durkheim (1897/2002) was understood to intend 'his theory to explain variation among social environments in the incidence of suicide, not the suicides of particular individuals' (Berk, 2006: 60):

'Durkheim believed there was more to suicide than extremely personal, individual life circumstances: for example, a loss of a job, divorce, or bankruptcy. Instead, he took suicide and explained it as a social fact instead of a result of one's circumstances. Durkheim believed that suicide was an instance of social deviance. Social deviance being any transgression of socially established norms' (Wikipedia, 2021).

Salvatore (2015) carefully critiqued the flawed methodology that underpinned psychological autopsy (PA), thus rendering unreliable some, at least, of its outcomes in many if not most cases:

i) <u>Informants:</u> The PA relied upon interviews with those who knew the deceased in life but whose information was limited to what they remembered of what they had observed. Issues included bias and hearsay (Lichter, 1981), the traumatic loss effect on near relatives, added to time elapse (Jacob and Klein-Benheim, 1993), the 'emotional and stressful' effect of the interview experience that caused up to 25% of informants to be 'upset' (Hawton et al., 2003), and the questionable ethics of 'using' traumatised, recently bereaved relatives (Beskow et al., 1990; Cvinar, 2005).

ii) <u>Interpretation by psychiatry:</u> The 'reliability of suicide survivors in identifying signs and symptoms of possible mental illness in someone they cared about' was complicated by a) informants' struggle to understand why the suicide happened, b) feelings of responsibility for not preventing the suicide, and c) negative sentiment towards the victims (Jordan, 2001). Informants' remarks about the deceased required quite a 'leap of faith' by psychiatry to bridge from those opinions directly to the deceased's state of mind prior to and immediately before their lethal behaviour.

iii) <u>Standardisation:</u> Although the American Association of Suicidology (AAS) offered training courses for psychological autopsy investigators, national or international accreditation protocols did not appear to be enforced.

My own enquiries in N Ireland yielded negligible information about the use of psychological autopsy here.

Salvatore (2015) cited the so-far unanswered question, posed over 9 years ago:

'Is it really possible to assign a psychiatric diagnosis to someone who is dead by interviewing someone else?' (Hjelmeland et al., 2012).

Recently, a 'top psychiatrist' claimed, in an ongoing lawsuit, that she was dismissed from her Yale University teaching role for 'linking a lawyer's psychology to Donald Trump's'. The lawyer, 'who contributed defence arguments to Trump's first impeachment trial', complained that:

'the forensic psychiatrist's public diagnosis had violated ethics rules. "The idea that you can diagnose me without ever having met me is unprofessional, irresponsible and unacademic" he wrote' (Helmore, 2021).

These contrasting deployments of psychiatric evaluations and diagnoses in absentia – of the deceased and of public, 'celebrity' figures – did not enhance psychiatry's shaky reputation as an evidence-based discipline.

Another debatable PA aspect included its vulnerability to confirmatory bias: if PA's purpose was to make a psychiatric diagnosis, researchers might focus on responses indicating signs of mental illness rather than on those that did not (Rogers and Lester, 2010). The risk of diagnostic imprecision was evident, when 'plumping' for mental illness resembled professional guesswork. McCready and Waring (1986) held that ex-post psychiatric diagnosis was suspect since absence of a face-to-face interview screened out both the patient's perspective and direct observation of interpersonal behaviour: neither was capable of being supplied by third parties.

Salvatore (2015) suggested that even when all essential elements of the mental status examination existed, inter alia, personal appearance, speech, affect, behaviour, and stream of thought, and the diagnosis is done 'by the book', it was still a clinical judgment call.

Autopsy meant 'to see for one's self' but in PA the deceased's experiences, behaviours, feelings, beliefs and motivation were seen by the investigator and the psychiatrist through the recall of others (Salvatore, 2015).

Salvatore (2015) referred to a 2008 study of 9,276 suicides by the US Centers for Disease Control and Prevention's National Violent Deaths Reporting System (NVDRS) that concluded that mental health problems were the most common circumstances among suicide deceased. However, only 45.4% had a diagnosed mental illness at death. The incidence of mental health problems in a very large population of victims was half (50%) that routinely reported by PA studies.

Salvatore (2015) did not dispute that mental illness was a 'strong risk factor' for suicide but he held that several studies (Harris and Barraclough, 1997; Chesney et al., 2014; Bertolete, J. et al., 2002 & 2004) did not confirm that almost every suicide victim had a diagnosable mental illness.

Salvatore (2015) concluded his important discussion by noting that despite the issues he raised, PA remained a practical and viable research strategy for information gathering about suicide victims. But he insisted that PA should be 'untethered from the mental illness model of suicide' so that a wider range of factors, such as the victim's social behaviour and interactions, should not be overridden by mental illness. He noted, for instance, that the Interpersonal Theory of Suicide (Joiner, 2005) saw lack of social connectedness and similar variables, including acquired capability for self-harm, as raising the risk of suicide. Salvatore concluded that the chances of any radical development occurring – particularly in relation to the mental illness model – relied upon researchers, academics and policy makers understanding and acknowledging the limitations of research and exercising caution in repeating generalisations, including the '90% of suicides were mentally ill' paradigm.

Thomas Szasz was unique in psychiatry in sustaining for over five decades (1960-2012) his challenge to the validity of the thinking that sustained the 'mental illness' model of suicide. As mentioned earlier, Szasz argued that each human being, in the absence of brain disease –

that he clearly distinguished from 'mental illness' – had the ability and the duty to take responsibility for her/his own behaviour, including in relation to suicide (Benning, 2016: 293).

## Dr Thomas Szasz's Challenge to the Mental Illness Model for Suicide

For a multiplicity of reasons (and excuses), including the vested interests of big pharma and the deadweight of psychiatry's professional associations, Szasz's major ideas and legacy remained outwith accepted policy and practice in the West, in relation to understanding suicide. This resistance might to an extent be explained by society's preference for convention, aka the status quo ante. Particularly when it is locked in by reputation and income, convention will tend to continue unopposed. An American populist politician, William Jennings Bryan (1893) was reported, in a Lincoln, Nebraska newspaper, to have observed:

'It is useless to argue with a man whose opinion is based upon a personal or pecuniary interest; the only way to deal with him is to outvote him' (Bryan, 1893).

Of course, this disposition worked both ways: Szasz's stubborn 'opinion' remained largely unaltered throughout his professional life in psychiatry. He held that 'mental illness was a harmful myth without a demonstrated basis in biological pathology and with the potential to damage current conceptions of human responsibility' (Kelly et al., 2010). Szasz's doubts about the purported (by medicine) similarities between physical and mental illnesses remained but Kelly et al. (2010: abstract) maintained that 'a failure to describe a biological basis for mental illness does not mean there is none':

'Szasz did not deny that humans have difficulties but he preferred to conceptualise them not as mental illnesses but as "problems in living" (Szasz, 1961/2010) ... psychiatrists could have a legitimate role ... in assisting individuals with problems [in an] ideal relationship between psychiatrist and patient ... based on consensual contact rather than coercion' (Benning, 2016: 292/3).

Kendell (2004) rebutted Szasz's claim that mental illnesses failed to meet the definition of disease, since his argument 'understated the extent to which suffering and incapacity were fundamental attributes of disease' (cited in Benning, 2016: 293).

Szasz's withering criticism highlighted the interplay between diagnosis, and political and social power:

'medicalisation gives a pre-eminent role to [medical] doctors, it privileges the role of medication as a therapeutic intervention and so the pharmaceutical industry stands to profit much by stretching the boundaries of the concept of mental disorder [leading to] this ever-widening reach of psychiatric diagnosis and to the pharmaceutical industry's complicity in this phenomenon not only by supporting "new" categories of psychiatric disorder (such as adult attention deficit disorder) but by endorsing the lowering of diagnostic thresholds for a host of established psychiatric disorders such as bipolar disorder' (Benning, 2016: 293)'

In relation to the current study, the DSM's (APA, 2013) developing interest in categorising 'suicidal behaviour' as a mental disorder, offered untold profiteering opportunities for psychiatry to pathologise this ultra-complex human behaviour. This represented an ongoing confirmation of Szasz's opinion regarding psychiatry's colonising tendency, implicit in what he repeatedly argued was its apparent urge to medicalise everyday life (and death):

'Suicide Behaviour Disorder (SBD) was introduced in DSM-5 as a disorder for further consideration and potential acceptance into the diagnostic system. There are numerous positive developments that would arise from the addition of a suicide-related diagnosis ... SBD presents with several significant limitations, however, and possible alternative additions to future DSMs are highlighted' (Fehling and Selby, 2021).

Fehling and Selby (2021) have written a lengthy article that purports to offer evidence in favour of adding Suicide Behaviour Disorder to the DSM's burgeoning encyclopedia of behavioural symptoms, citing no fewer than 176 references. They listed five 'essential diagnostic criteria' that were remarkably similar to typical areas for psychotherapeutic exploration by an expert clinician with a client/patient perceived at risk of suicide. It then listed ten 'validators', or areas for client/patient evaluation, including 'antecedent (4)', 'concurrent (3)', and 'predictive (3)' – that resemble client/patient family history, current disposition, previous medical history and possible treatment options. These authors conceded that effective suicide risk assessment underpinned existing approaches to this client/patient work and concluded:

'Overall, more research is needed to confirm the validity, reliability, clinical utility, and ethical soundness of SBD or any of the alternative additions introduced in this manuscript. Any suicide-related addition to the DSM, however, would improve the field by aiding clinicians in making the best decisions for their clients and ensuring clients at risk for suicide receive appropriate treatment' (Fehling and Selby, 2021: 11).

Szasz (1963) also queried the interface between psychiatry and legal orthodoxy in relation to individual agency and personal responsibility where, in some cases, an individual with mental illness was assumed not to be responsible for their actions, particularly alleged criminal acts. The 'mental illness and suicide' question was specifically addressed by Szasz (2011), only a short time before his death. If 'mental illness' was indeed a myth, then much of the psychiatric architecture erected to prevent suicide by 'healing mental illness' would rest on the most unstable foundations imaginable.

So how would Szasz address the undoubted catastrophe of suicide, that takes up to a million lives annually (WHO, 2021)? His attitude was perhaps best summarised in his 'Suicide Prohibition – The Shame of Medicine' (2011):

'Everyone knows that preventing the death of a person intent on killing him/herself is impossible, except perhaps by the most extraordinary means (p98). The sense that our life is no longer worth living – the condition we sometimes call a "mental illness" – is without doubt one of the most "painful" of all human experiences. Such suffering is however, not per se an illness or medical problem. It is a philosophical and moral problem. In so far as we communicate our suffering to persons close to us, our suffering becomes a problem for them as well. Any attempt to *forcibly* (italics in original) interfere with the life of such a sufferer converts their private personal problem into a public, political one (p100). If suicide be deemed a problem, it is not a medical problem. Managing it as if it were a disease, or the result of a disease, will succeed only in debasing medicine and corrupting the law (cover notes)' (Szasz, 2011).

Thomas Szasz was nothing if not consistent in both 'talking the talk' and 'walking the walk' about suicide. After a fall at home, sustaining a serious back injury, aged 92 years, and suffering excruciating pain, he chose not be hospitalised and on a morphine drip, and decided against proposed surgery on his fractured thoracic vertebrae. Returning home with pain-relieving medication, he ended his suffering and his life a few days later 'by his own hand', as reported by his friend of over 24 years, Jeff Schaler:

'Tom's view on suicide was simple: The right to life includes the right to death. He always opposed "assisted suicide," and he was extremely critical of people ... who advocated assisted suicide, especially as some twisted practice of medicine. Suicide is an ethical issue. It is not a medical issue ... Tom always valued autonomy, and I knew there was no way he would ever end up in a nursing home, depending on others to take care of him, if he had any control over the matter. Obviously, he could have had a stroke, or some illness that would have rendered suicide impossible. I suppose he would have found a way even in that kind of situation. People often commit suicide by refusing to eat and drink, so where there is a will, there is a way' (Schaler, 2012).

**The humanitarian impulse**

I have heard that in Central Park in New York, there used to be benches where anyone could engage in the daylight hours, at no financial cost, with a trained counsellor about what was troubling them, or in Szasz-speak their 'problems in living'. Dr Google (online) was unable to confirm whether this service still exists.

My original thought, close to concluding this chapter, is therefore about how to utilize the humanitarian impulse that continues to function, certainly in UK/Ireland, as represented in the financial contributions that many make to charitable causes, particularly in the aftermath of natural or accidental disasters.

Helplines and lifelines have been around since the Samaritans began their 'helping by listening' work over six decades ago. Social media is ubiquitous. But these communication channels do not offer the intimate, face-to-face contact and interaction that, in my opinion as a practitioner in psychotherapy/suicidology, may be essential for effective, humane, compassionate, non-judgemental helping of one human by another human.

So why don't our local authorities, funded by those same generous charitable citizens mentioned above, not consider locating discrete contact points, staffed by volunteers - skilled, trained, registered counsellors – where anyone and everyone might, when they need to, seek and obtain neighbourly, confidential help. After all, lighthouses offered a similar service for centuries to mariners on the high seas, whether in trouble or just passing by.

Just a thought.

# Appendix

## Northern Ireland Act 1998

Section 75 of the Northern Ireland Act 1998 (the Act) required designated public authorities [including the Department of Health] to comply with two statutory duties:

Section 75 (1) – In carrying out the functions as they relate to Northern Ireland there is a requirement to have due regard to the need to promote equality of opportunity between:

- Persons of different religious belief, political opinion, racial group, age, marital status, or sexual orientation
- Men and women generally
- Persons with a disability and persons without
- Persons with dependants and persons without.

Section 75 (2) – In addition, without prejudice to the obligations above, in carrying out the functions as they relate to Northern Ireland, the Department is required to have regard to the desirability of promoting good relations between persons of different religious belief, political opinion or racial group.

In line with the Department's Equality Scheme, the Department has completed an Equality Screening and updated this following consultation. The Department has concluded that a full Equality Impact Assessment is not required (Protect Life 2, 2019: 74)

## The Rural Needs Act NI (2016)

The Rural Needs Act (NI) 2016 (the Act) provides a statutory duty on public authorities to have due regard to rural needs when developing, adopting, implementing, or revising policies, strategies and plans, and when designing and delivering public services. Accordingly the Department of Health has completed a Rural Needs Impact Assessment Template which has been published with this Protect Life 2 Strategy (2019: 74).

**Myth:** (fictitious popular idea) Adding 'Suicide Behaviour Disorder' to the Diagnostic and Statistical Manual of Mental Disorders (DSM) will ensure clients at risk of suicide receive appropriate treatment.

**Fallacy:** (misleading argument) The UK state's duty of care, under the ECHR, in relation to citizens at risk of suicide applies to everyone.

## References

APA - American Psychiatric Association (2013) Diagnostic and Statistical Manual of Mental Disorders, DSM 5 (5th ed.). Arlington, VA: American Psychiatric Publishing

Benning, A. B. (2016) No such thing as mental illness? Critical reflections on the major ideas and legacy of Thomas Szasz. BJPsych Bulletin (2016), 40, 292-295

Berk, Bernard B. (2006). "Macro-micro relationships in Durkheim's analysis of egoistic suicide". Sociological Theory. 24 (1): 58–80

Beskow, J., Runeson, B. and Asgard, U. (1990) Psychological autopsies: methods and ethics. Suicide and Life-threatening Behaviour, 20(4), 307-323

Bertolote, J. and Fleischman, A. (2002) Suicide and psychiatric diagnosis: a worldwide perspective. World Psychiatry, 1(3), 181-185

Bertolete, J., Fleishmann, A., De Leo, D. and Wasserman, D. (2004) Psychiatric diagnoses and suicide: Revisiting the evidence. Crisis, 25(4), 147-155

Black, L-A. (2021) Suicide: Northern Ireland. NI Assembly Research and Information Service, Research Paper 23/21. 14 April 2021

Black, L-A. and McKay, K. (2019) Suicide statistics and strategy in Northern Ireland: update. NI Assembly Research and Information Service (RaISe), Stormont, Belfast. Accessed on 3 August 2021 at https://www.assemblyresearchmatters.org/2019/11/28/suicide-statistics-and-strategy-in-northern-ireland- update/

Bryan, W. J. (1893) Opinion and self-interest. Accessed on 14 August 2021 at https://quoteinvestigator.com/2017/11/30/salary/

Chesney, E., Goodwin, G. and Fazel, S. (2014) Risks of all-cause suicide mortality in mental disorders: a meta-review. World Psychiatry, 13, 153-160

Curtice, M. and Sandford (2009) Article 2 of the Human Rights Act 1998 and the treatment of prisoners. Advances in Psychiatric Treatment, vol 15, 444-450

Cvinar, J. (2005) Do suicide survivors suffer social stigma? A review of the literature. Perspectives in Psychiatric Care, 41(1), 14-21

Dictionary.com (2021) Definition of 'autonomy'. Accessed on 28 July 2021 at https://www.dictionary.com/browse/autonomy

Doerr, J. (2017) Measure what matters. Brentford, England: Portfolio Penguin

Doran, G. T. (1981) There's a S.M.A.R.T. way to write management's goals and objectives. Accessed on 7 October 2022 at https://community.mis.temple.edu/mis0855002fall2015/files/2015/10/S.M.A.R.T-Way-Management-Review.pdf

Durkheim, E. (1897/2002) Suicide - a study in sociology. London: Routledge Classics

ECHR (2021) European Convention of Human Rights. https://www.echr.coe.int Accessed on 15 March 2024

Fehling, K. B. and Selby, E. A. (2021) Suicide in DSM-5: Current Evidence for the Proposed Suicide Behaviour Disorder and Other Possible Improvements. Frontiers in Psychiatry, Feb 2021

Guidelines (2011) Guidelines and Audit Implementation Network, October, 2011. On the use of the Mental Health (Northern Ireland) Order (1986)

Harris, E. and Barraclough, B. (1997) Suicide as an outcome for mental disorders: a meta-analysis. British Journal of Psychiatry, 170, 205-228

Hawton, K., Houston, K., Malmberg, A. and Simkin, S. (2003) Psychological autopsy interviews in suicide research: the reaction of informants. Archives of Suicide Research, 7, 73-82

Helmore, E. (2021) Top psychiatrist fired for public diagnosis of Trump's mental state. Edward Helmore. The Guardian, 28 March 2021

Hjelmeland, H., Dieserud, G., Dyregrov, K., Knizek, B. and Leenaars, A. (2012) Psychological autopsy studies as diagnostic tools: Are they methodologically flawed? Death Studies, 36, 605-626

Human Rights Act (1998) Article 2: Right to Life. https://www.mind.org.uk Accessed on 15 March 2024

Jacobs, D. and Klein-Benheim, M. (1993) The expanding role of psychological autopsies. In A. A. Leenaars (Ed.) Essays in honour of Edwin Shneidman. Northvale, NJ: Jason Aronson

Joiner, T. E. (2005) Why people die by suicide. Cambridge, Mass: Harvard University Press

Jordan, J. (2001) Is suicide bereavement different? A reassessment of the literature. Suicide and Life-threatening Behaviour, 31(1), 91-102

Kelly, B. D., Bracken, P., Cavendish, H., Crumlish, N., MacSuibhne, S., Szasz, T., and Thornton, T. (2010) The myth of mental illness: 50 years after publication: What does it mean today? Irish Journal of Psychological Medicine, March 2010, 27(1), 35-43

Kendell, R. E. (2004) The myth of mental illness. In J. A. Schaler (ed.) Szasz Under Fire: The Psychiatric Abolitionist Faces his Critics, pp. 29-55. Chicago and La Salle, IL: Open Court, 2004

Lichter, D. H. (1981) Diagnosing the dead: The admissibility of the psychiatric autopsy. American Criminal Law Review, 18, 617-635

McCready, J. R. and Waring, E. M. (1986) Interviewing skills in relation to psychiatric residency. Canadian Journal of Psychiatry, 1986 May; 31(4): 317-22

Mencken, H. L. (1917) Simple solution to complex problem – wrong. Source: "The Divine Afflatus" in New York Evening Mail (16 November

1917); later published in Prejudices: Second Series (1920) and A Mencken Chrestomathy (1949). Accessed on 8 August 2021 at https://quotepark.com/quotes/1473292-hl-mencken-explanations-exist-they-have-existed-for-all-time/

Mental Health Strategy (2021a) Mental Health Strategy 2021-2031 [Complete document]. Department of Health, Stormont, Belfast, N Ireland

Mental Health Strategy (2021b) Mental Health Strategy 2021-2031 [Easy Read Summary]. Department of Health, Stormont, Belfast, N Ireland

Mental Health Services (NI) (2021) NI Direct Government Services. Accessed on 3 August 2021 at https://www.nidirect.gov.uk/articles/mental-health-services

Protect Life 2 (2019) Protect Life a strategy for preventing suicide and self-harm in Northern Ireland 2019-2024. Department of Health. Stormont, Belfast

Protect Life 2 – Review (2024) Action plan: Report and recommendations. September 2024. NI Dept of Health, Stormont, Belfast

Rogers, J.R. and Lester, D. (2010) Understanding suicide: why we don't and how we might. Cambridge, MA: Hogrefe Publishing

Roy, A. (2001) Consumers of mental health services. Suicide and Life-threatening Behaviour, 31-1, Supplement 60-83

Salvatore, T. (2015) Do 90% of suicide victims really have serious mental illness? Psychological autopsy studies, psychopathology, and ... Montgomery County Emergency Services, PA, USA. Downloaded on 27 January 2017 from https://www.researchgate.net/publication/274710108

Sands, D.C.C. (2008) A study of suicide grief: meaning making and the griever's relational world. A dissertation awarded a doctorate of philosophy (PhD) from the University of Technology Sydney, New South Wales, Australia

Schaler, J. A. (ed.) (2004) Szasz Under Fire: The Psychiatric Abolitionist Faces his Critics.Chicago and La Salle, IL: Open Court

Schaler, J. A. (2012) Kaddish for Thomas Szasz. Accessed on 18 August 2021 at http://www.szasz.com/szaszdeath.htm

Szasz, T. (1961/2010) The myth of mental illness: Foundations of a theory of personal conduct. Rev. ed. 1961. Reprint, New York, NY: HarperCollins, 2010

Szasz, T. (1963) Law, liberty and psychiatry: an enquiry into the social uses of mental health practice. New York, NY: Macmillan

Szasz, T., (2011) Suicide prohibition: the shame of medicine. Syracuse, NY: Syracuse University Press

Wikipedia (2021) Capital punishment in the United Kingdom. 9 July 2021. Accessed on 8 August 2021 at https://en.wikipedia.org/wiki/Capital_punishment_in_the_United_Kingdom

Wikipedia (2021) 27 July 2021. Emile Durkheim. Accessed on 11 August 2021 at https://en.wikipedia.org/wiki/%C3%89mile_Durkheim#Suicide

Wikipedia (2024) Capital punishment in Ireland. Accessed on 13 August 2024 at https://en.wikipedia.org/wiki/Capital_punishment_in_Ireland#Abolition

World Health Organisation (WHO) (2014) Prevent suicide: a global imperative. Geneva, Switzerland

World Health Organisation (WHO) (2018) Mental health: strengthening our response. 30 March 2018. Accessed on 3 August 2021 at https://www.who.int/news-room/fact-sheets/detail/mental-health-strengthening-our-response

World Health Organisation (WHO) (2021) WHO guidance to help the world reach the target of reducing the suicide rate by one third by 2030. News Release 17 June 2021

\* \* \*

## Chapter 14
# Suicide – assisted suicide and murder

**Introduction**

A deluded if naively patriotic Northern Ireland citizen joins an oath-bound terrorist organisation, acquires a gun and kills a fellow citizen, ostensibly as a 'political act' to either a) advance his organisation's united Ireland campaign by 'armed struggle' or b) to defend and protect Northern Ireland's locus as a constitutional element of a multi-nation United Kingdom, viz. England, Northern Ireland, Scotland and Wales.

According to UK/Irish criminal law, such an action, regardless of any outrageous label in mitigation, is murder:

'Murder is an offence under the common law of England and Wales. It is considered the most serious form of homicide, in which one person kills another with the intention to cause either death or serious injury unlawfully' (Wikipedia, 2021b).

On conviction, a lawfully constituted court will impose a sentence of imprisonment for life. None of the 'alphabet soup' of Northern Ireland's oath-bound terrorist organisations – inter alia PIRA, UDA, UFF, UVF, INLA, 'Red Hand Commando' and their many splinter groups, e.g. IPLO – has ever conceded that their members' murderous actions were crimes, viz. unlawful. The legendary Northern Ireland hunger strikes (1980, 1981) that killed 10 men were regarded by their terrorist organisation sponsors (PIRA-7 and INLA-3) as premeditated acts of murder, by the British State. The Northern Ireland Registrar of Births, Marriages and Deaths ruled that these tragic, avoidable, deliberate, self-inflicted deaths were suicides. (See Wikipedia, 2021a, for the full horrible story.)

## Killing neither murder nor manslaughter

However, this chapter is not about 'killing' that is defined as 'murder': no one nor any of the 'dogs in the street' in Northern Ireland needed to consult a lawyer or a dictionary to understand fully the enormity of 'man's inhumanity to man' in this place during 1966-2010, and that continued sporadically afterwards. These dates were aligned with the publicly funded Troubles Permanent Disablement Payment Scheme, otherwise, a pension scheme for people who were badly injured as a result of terrorist violence that opened for applications in September 2021:

'The scheme covers violence related to the Troubles between 1966 and 2010, including incidents in Great Britain and Europe' (BBC News NI, 2021).

Citizens here know about this scheme having survived over 3,500 'Troubles' murders and an estimated 40,000 injured. In what follows, we explore murder's blood(y) brothers known under multiple disguises as euthanasia, physician-assisted suicide, mercy killing, assisted suicide, and assisted dying. There are more pseudonyms – termination of life without specific request, intensified treatment of pain and symptoms, withholding / withdrawing treatment, and terminal sedation (Woodruff, 2019).

In my 83$^{rd}$ year as I write, you could say I have more than an academic interest herein.

## So when did it all begin

In modern times, it all began in Switzerland in 1937 (Stefan, 2016). But it has been around since Greek and Roman times. A historical timeline for euthanasia and assisted suicide was available online from 500 BCE to 2020 (Procon, 2020). This tracked a doleful journey from the 'tolerant' attitude of Greeks and Romans to infanticide, active euthanasia and suicide (500 BCE) to the current legalising of physician-assisted suicide for terminally ill adults in Aotearoa/New Zealand in October, 2020. The better, more difficult question is: does the world, including Northern Irish humanity need it now – yet another version of suicide – more than it needs high quality, compassionate end-of-life care, including as appropriate, expert palliative care? Currently, in the UK, including Northern Ireland, encouraging or assisting a person to take their own life, is a criminal offence for which the penalty on summary conviction is a term of imprisonment for up to 14 years:

'In Northern Ireland, suicide ceased to be a crime by virtue of section 12 of the Criminal Justice (Northern Ireland) Act 1966, an Act passed by the then Stormont Parliament.

Section 13(1) of the Act provides:-

"A person who aids, abets, counsels or procures the suicide of another shall be guilty of an offence and shall be liable on conviction on indictment to imprisonment for a term not exceeding fourteen years."

Prosecution for this offence requires the consent of the Director of Public Prosecutions for Northern Ireland' (Public Prosecution Service Northern Ireland, 2009).

The subject was not mentioned in Protect Life 2 (2019). It seemed as if assisted suicide was an unrelated 'something else'. There were no assisted suicide rates or trends, first, because there were no successful or any relevant prosecutions, and second, because, presumably, the treating doctor's death certificate would not use the term: a 'cause of death' entry on the certificate would presumably refer to an underlying, terminal, physical illness. Has anyone examined this issue – is it an 'issue' in Northern Ireland? Has it 'begun' yet? Was it already here, in some quasi-legal form that did not contravene the statute in Northern Ireland? A casual enquiry online located a two-decades old research paper that revealed some anonymous, self-disclosed data in relation to the practice of euthanasia in Northern Ireland by our family doctors.

## Research evidence on GPs' attitudes to euthanasia

McGlade et al. (2000) asked over a thousand Northern Ireland general practitioners (GPs) to complete a questionnaire on their attitudes to the issue of patient requests for euthanasia, their nature and doctors' experiences of such requests. Just over 400 valid questionnaires were completed, a 38% response rate, after a first and only mailing, that was considered representative and within researchers' reasonable expectations. This research suggested definitions of three distinct approaches to euthanasia:

i) Passive euthanasia means withdrawing or withholding life-sustaining or life-prolonging treatment

ii) Physician-assisted suicide means intentionally providing the means or instruction by which a person could kill her/himself, e.g. writing a prescription for a lethal dose of drugs

iii) Voluntary active euthanasia means taking active steps yourself to bring about the patient's death, e.g. administering an overdose (McGlade et al., 2000: 795).

Just under a third (n=118) of responding GPs said they had 'received an explicit or tentative request in the past five years from a patient to hasten death' (p795):

'54 doctors received requests for passive euthanasia of whom 39 complied. Twelve of these doctors supplied data about their actions: three stated they had withheld fluids, three had withheld antibiotics, two had withheld other medication, and four said they complied by 'minimal intervention'.

'19 doctors received requests for physician-assisted suicide of whom one doctor complied.

'38 doctors received requests for active euthanasia of whom four complied' (McGlade et al., 2000: 796).

103 of the GPs surveyed offered some insights into patients' motives for requesting euthanasia. One fifth of these involved repeated requests while 8% of these patients were aged 50 or less. Their concerns ranged from 'loss of dignity' (64.7%), 'a burden to others' (54.9%), 'pain' (47.1%), 'physical and mental dependency' (41.2%), 'loss of control' (37.3%), and other reasons including 'tired of life', a sense of hopelessness, fear, exhaustion, and the death of a friend' (McGlade et al., 2000: 795).

None of the 400+ GPs supplied any 'details ... about actions taken in relation to physician-assisted suicide or active euthanasia'. Presumably one stark reason may have included their fear of the risk of prosecution, under the 1966 statute, although McGlade et al. (2000) do not address this. Their research offered evidence of a gulf between GPs 'moral position' on euthanasia and their degree of willingness to 'endorse physician-assisted suicide or active euthanasia':

'Even if a doctor has no moral objections to a particular course of action, the extent of his or her willingness to participate in such an action may be limited ... asked if they would participate in passive euthanasia only 67% said they would. Only 28% and 33% of those declaring support for [physician-]assisted suicide and active euthanasia, respectively, said they would be willing to participate in the respective behaviour' (McGlade et al., 2000: 796).

This research highlighted the indeterminate, inconsistent and problematic nature of GPs' attitude to end-of-life decisions:

'It may be, in time, that doctors may feel a need to declare to patients where they stand on sensitive moral issues if for no other reason than to minimize potential conflict in the conduct of [end-of-life] treatment ... Further research is needed on the pressures engendered and on the training doctors may require to cope with the possibility of increasing requests from patients for euthanasia' (McGlade et al., 2000: 796).

One recent, notorious criminal trial and a subsequent public enquiry offered vital evidence of the need two decades ago for reform in medical practice in relation to end-of-life care in GB/Northern Ireland in view of existing, untested statutes that prohibited GPs, along with every other citizen, from encouraging or assisting in suicide. This involved the outrageous, wilful misbehaviour of a British family GP, Dr Harold Shipman, who over the course of 20 years, colluded in multiple, serial murders, by hastening the deaths of hundreds of his patient.

## Dr Harold Shipman, GP & serial killer

Harold Shipman qualified in 1970 to be a doctor at Leeds University's School of Medicine and worked as a hospital doctor in Pontefract General Infirmary until 1974 when he continued his murderous career as a GP in Todmorden, a market town in West Yorkshire. By then he was suffering blackouts, had developed an addiction to pethedine / 'demerol', a pain-killer, and was forging patient prescriptions for his own use.

On being detected, he was arrested and convicted in 1975, on eight charges (32 cases were taken into consideration) of illegally obtaining controlled drugs by forging prescriptions. He was fined £600, attended a brief drug rehabilitation clinic but, crucially and inexplicably, he was not 'struck off' by the General Medical Council (GMC), the body responsible for regulating UK doctors. Meirion (2021) said that a West Yorkshire drug squad police detective George McKeating attended the GMC's disciplinary hearing, but was not called to give evidence. Detective Sergeant McKeating's devastating report – that Shipman was a danger to the public and should be struck off the medical register – was not filed, and was thus ignored by the GMC.

This fatal blunder, that Meirion (2021) called 'a grave error', liberated Shipman to practice again without his patients' awareness of his criminal record. In 1977 Shipman obtained a GP post in Hyde, Manchester and continued working as a GP in Hyde throughout the 1980s. He established his own surgery at 21 Market Street in 1993, becoming a respected member of the community (Wikipedia, 2021c). Evidence presented to the Smyth Enquiry suggested that during his 21 years as a GP in Hyde, Shipman murdered 250 or more of his patients: had he been struck off or even monitored, these killings could have been prevented (Meirion, 2021).

**The Shipman Enquiry**

In July 2002 the Smyth Enquiry concluded that Shipman killed at least 215 of his patients and possibly more. Most of his victims were elderly women – in all 171 were women and 44 were men – but it was believed his youngest victim was just four years old, a girl called Susie Garfitt (Finnis, 2020). In her sixth and final report, issued on 24 January 2005, the Enquiry Chair reported that she believed that Shipman, during the early stage of his medical career at Pontefract General Infirmary, had killed three patients, and she had serious suspicions about four further deaths, including that of the four-year-old girl (Wikipedia, 2021c).

A key outcome of the Enquiry related to the health status of his victims. Most of these unfortunate people did not require and were not receiving end-of-life care from Shipman. There was little need further to rehearse his murderous crimes, but more importantly, we now review lessons learned and to what extent, if any, end-of-life care was influenced and/or reformed during, and in the decades-long aftermath of the public enquiry that followed Shipman's conviction.

Although only (sic) convicted of 15 murders and of altering one patient's will in January, 2000, it was accepted by Dame Janet Smyth, the Public Enquiry Chair, that he had unlawfully killed [up to] 260 of his patients (Baker, 2004: 303):

'He committed these murders by injecting his patients with lethal doses of diamorphine, a strong painkiller related to heroin which has legitimate and widespread use in the treatment of the terminal stages of cancer and in other medical conditions' (Overview: Shipman Enquiry, 2007: 7).

The public enquiry 'was tasked with investigating the extent of Shipman's unlawful activities, enquiring into the activities of the statutory authorities and other organisations involved, and making recommendations on the steps needed to protect patients for the future. The Enquiry published a total of six reports' (Overview: Shipman Enquiry, 2007: 3).

## What changes were proposed in end-of-life care following the Shipman Enquiry?

Many administrative and procedural changes appear to have been made in relation to medical practice. These were referred to as the Shipman Effect (Wikipedia, 2021c):

a) Changes in dispensing practices
b) Reluctance to over-prescribe pain medication that may have led to under-prescribing
c) Death certification practices were altered
d) Movement away from single-doctor general practices to multiple-doctor general practices – ostensibly to enhance safeguarding and monitoring doctors' decisions.

The documentation needed for a cremation (in Britain but emulated in Northern Ireland) was altered post-Shipman to ensure greater confidence that nothing untoward had occurred in relation to the deceased. Cremation organisers now had to confirm this in their responses to two questions in a six page 'application for cremation of a person who has died':

"Do you know or suspect that the death of the person who has died was violent or unnatural? Do you consider that there should be any further examination of the remains of the person who has died?" (Cremation 1, 2017)

Baker (2004) focused on three implications for general practice of Shipman's home-based murders. Firstly, he believed that in spite of Shipman's disgraceful behaviour, patient trust in their family doctor had been largely maintained, and that this might merit more openness in patient interactions. Secondly, closer monitoring of general practice was needed for prevention of murder and lesser misdeeds that were concealed by poor record keeping, including fabricated entries in cremation and death certificates, misappropriation of diamorphine, failure to keep a controlled drugs register, and repeated lying both to relatives and to colleagues (p305). Thirdly, trust between general practitioners, so damaged by Shipman's criminal deceptions, needed to be restored and renewed so as to move beyond a general attitude of mistrust.

Baker (2004) pointed to five specific action points relating to implementing an effective method of monitoring clinicians, and other medical professionals and their attitudes and behaviours at work. These were outlined below:

i) General practitioners' national and local professional leadership was not successful in implementing reform and in helping doctors to respond positively. GPs may therefore have been too acquiescing in going along with the old established but broken systems that contributed to weaknesses in health care, for example in relation to cremation certification and the neglected procedures for monitoring controlled drugs

ii) Revalidation - otherwise acceptance by medical doctors of their responsibility to demonstrate continued competence – needed to be formally implemented by requiring GPs to hold membership of the Royal College of General Practitioners so as to draw every practitioner into a community of peers 'to provide both practical support and a continuing challenge to maintain and improve performance' (Baker, 2004: 305)

iii) The survival of patients was unquestionably the most important aspect of medicine. Yet the absence of monitoring mortality rates of patients of general practice allowed Shipman over a 20 year period to murder undetected until greed – forging a patient's will – exposed his catastrophic crimes. This seemed an appalling lapse, rooted in an unquestioning attitude expressed currently with heavy irony - but fatally for Shipman's innocent patients - in the remark 'Trust me I'm a doctor'

iv) Oversight of GPs professional activities was paramount. Serial killing of patients must be rendered close to impossible if patient trust was to be fully restored. But no monitoring system was capable of providing total oversight of GPs' patient interactions. 'While the difficulties have to be recognised, everything possible must be done to make sure that Shipman remains unique' (p306)

v) Patients should be able to check their doctor's performance or advice if they wish. Shipman manipulated and distorted the idealised image of the doctor/patient relationship, by adopting a paternalistic 'doctor knows best' attitude, that his patients accepted and that protected him from detection. Putting doctor and patient on an equal footing was unrealistic but … 'openness will be a key element … [including] sharing records with patients, copying referral letters to them, and the provision of increasingly detailed information about illness and treatments [allied with] information about the doctor's performance … [that] might include summaries from audits and reports of objective assessments of clinical competence' (p306).

## What were the results of implementing Shipman Effect reforms?

The extent to which this proposed revolution in general practice, and more widely in medicine, was or was not implemented was the subject of a January 2021 letter by a member to the Royal College of Surgeons (RCS) (Meirion, 2021).

Meirion (2021: 13) noted that Judge Dame Janet Smyth identified 'the fundamental flaw' that facilitated Shipman in condemning over 260 of his patients to early deaths: 'the professional loyalty among doctors and their instinct to put their own interests ahead of the welfare of patients'. In her enquiry report/s, she made over 100 recommendations although not all have so far been implemented. Importantly the former, lethally incompetent General Medical Council and its disciplinary panels now have lay members and doctors are in a minority. Also 'an effective hotline system is in place for patients to raise a complaint about a doctor' (Meirion, 2021: 13).

Meirion (2021: 13) criticised a new annual 'lengthy and stressful' appraisal process along with a five-yearly revalidation exercise – both mandatory – that each of the UK's 250,000 doctors would now have to successfully undergo to maintain their licence to practice. He inferred that the assumption that surveillance of doctors would identify the occasional 'rogue' doctor – like Shipman – was over-optimistic. He explained why he believed this 'time-consuming, face-saving invention by a then discredited GMC [that] has created yet another NHS related, bureaucratic industry costing millions' was unlikely to work (Meirion, 2021: 13). He held that while the overwhelming majority is moral with scrupulous integrity, the 'tiny minority of doctors with something to hide can easily outwit the appraisal system' (p13).

Meirion (2021: 13) cited the extraordinary case of a fake psychiatrist - Zholia Alemi – who had never qualified in medicine but was able to gain GMC registration with forged papers after which she achieved the Royal College of Psychiatrists 'gold medal standard' specialist qualification. During her 22 years in fraudulent NHS employment, she detained at least 24 patients under the Mental Health Act. Like Shipman, greed exposed her multiple crimes: she was detected forging an 83 year old patient's will in order to inherit a £1.3 million estate. Convicted of fraud and theft in October 2018, she was given a 5 year prison sentence by Judge James Adkin who told her 'This was despicable, cruel criminality motivated by pure greed' (Taylor, 2019 a & b).

It was a salutary lesson indeed to reflect upon excerpts from Meirion's (2021: 13) medical calendar, revealing appalling examples of human wickedness and pure evil:

i) 'Child porn doctor struck off': Meirion said he was astonished that a Google search revealed pages of cases. He asked: Did these doctors declare their criminality in the compulsory 'probity' section of their annual appraisals? (p13)

ii) Dr Andrew Wakefield: Would this charlatan ever have declared at appraisal that he was deliberately falsifying research [data] to prove an association between MMR vaccine, gut problems and autism? (p13). [Wakefield subsequently deceived the 'Lancet' editor and thus an unknown number of that highly regarded journal's readership of medical practitioners.]

iii) Ian Paterson: This disgraced Birmingham surgeon performed unnecessary breast surgery on hundreds of unfortunate women. He was detected, not by the appraisal system, but by patient complaints. He received a 20 year prison sentence (p13)

iv) Average of 80 doctors struck off annually by the GMC: Meirion believed that they were rarely (if ever) identified by the appraisal system.

Meirion (2021) was convinced, as many doctors have said before, that Shipman 'would have skipped through the appraisal system without difficulty'. He recommended that 'this failed monolithic epitaph to the scrutiny of doctors needs to be abolished and the money [it consumes] reallocated to patient care' (p13).

In these times of Covid-19 and while honouring and celebrating the remarkable heroism of the medical and other 'essential' services, it was necessary to remain rooted in accepting the reality of our flawed human nature. Meirion's conclusions therefore restored the medical profession's imperfect reputation, as merely and mostly comprising our pretty ordinary fellow citizens, who possessed some specialist knowledge, skills and experience but who, like every one of us, were liable 24/7 to the unremitting and cloying motivation of self-interest:

'The Hippocratic Oath include(s) two categoric statements that demand the physician's beneficent intervention: 1. "I will apply the regimens of treatment according to my ability and judgment for the benefit of my patients and protect them from harm and injustice," and 2. "Into whatever house I enter, I will do so for the benefit of the sick ..."' (BMJ, 2019)

The likelihood of corruption of this ancient medical practitioner's 'do no harm' oath could be restrained only by the certainty – if, when and where it existed, or was suspected – of detection and retribution.

## Learning about how post-Shipman, lethal ageism kills

A BBC documentary 'The Shipman Files' (Wilson, 2021) concluded that the late 20th century trashing in UK/Ireland of older citizens, by ignoramuses in politics and wider society, as useless consumers of scarce resources, who contributed little in return, created a cultural context for Shipman's 20 year killing spree. These unchallenged youth-focused, tabloid-driven, evidence-free, populist attitudes arguably contributed more recently, indeed currently, to the 'before their time' destruction by the Covid-19 virus of thousands of older residents of UK/Irish care homes. Some avoidable deaths were now believed to have been due to relocation of aged, unwell patients from NHS hospitals to privately managed care homes, inadequately staffed by unprotected, low-paid care workers. Maishman (2021) reported from Scotland that:

'Thousands of elderly patients were discharged from hospitals to care homes in the early months of the pandemic to free up hospital beds in a move the Scottish Government later admitted was a "mistake".

'In a report, 'Authority to Discharge', the Mental Welfare Commission for Scotland has analysed around 10 per cent of these moves – 457 patients – and found 20 were unlawful. The "disappointing" findings expose "endemic examples of poor practice", the Commission said, some of which pre-date the pandemic. A lack of understanding of the law, power of attorney and good practice mean many more than 20 patients are likely to have been moved unlawfully, said Julie Paterson, chief executive of the Commission.

'Jackie Baillie, Scottish Labour health spokesperson, called the moves "scandalous". Scottish Care, which is a representative body for independent social care, said the report made for "disturbing reading". A previous report from Public Health Scotland found that it "could not rule out" a link between hospital discharges and later Covid-19 outbreaks in care homes. Thousands of patients were moved without Covid-19 tests and some were moved even after testing positive' (Maishman, 2021).

In Northern Ireland, this 'slaughter of aged care home residents' pattern appeared to be repeated during the first year (March 2020 to March 2021) of the pandemic with appalling evidence of the lethal outcomes of a slow learning syndrome that seemed to have impeded state action to save the lives of our treasured older citizens:

'The Covid-19 death toll among care home residents in Northern Ireland has reached 1,000. Statistics from the Northern Ireland Statistics and Research Agency (NISRA) show that up to the week ending March 12 [2021] 764 coronavirus linked deaths had occurred in care homes, while 236 residents had died in hospital having been moved there for treatment. Care home residents make up about 35% of deaths linked to Covid-19 in Northern Ireland according to NISRA ... The total number of coronavirus-related deaths in Northern Ireland reported by the agency up to March 12 [2021] stood at 2,877.' (Young, 2021).

These awful death statistics in the context of 'care' homes – the clue is in that adjective – raised important questions about whether – how well or how badly – the state's societal responsibilities to ensure that Article 2 (EHRC, 2021) human rights of our older citizens were recognised and exercised. An online news release, updated October 2020, offered an insight into a key element of what may have contributed to a major failing by the state:

'Care home residents are more at risk because of individual vulnerabilities, shared living space and frequent close contact with others who can unwittingly spread COVID-19 within and between settings' (NI-HSE Health & Care Board, 2021).

The attrition in Northern Ireland care homes due to the coronavirus therefore cannot but be linked – directly to care home owners/managers and indirectly to the overseeing agencies of the NI Department of Health – to their failure inter alia to provide necessary protection from Covid-19 infection, presumably by adequate, effective personal protective equipment (PPE), to both care home staff and care home residents ... This was particularly the case during the pre-vaccine period until the early months of 2021.

A UK government guidance (Public Health England, 2020) appeared to consider that 'professionals' working in 'health and social care settings' were at greater risk of lethal coronavirus infection than vulnerable, and/or aged care home residents:

'Those most at risk within the UK are professionals working in health and social care sectors. This [is] because these sectors are responsible for providing essential treatment and care for those who are confirmed to have COVID-19, are symptomatic or are highly vulnerable. They are in prolonged close contact with individuals who are symptomatic or particularly vulnerable to infection' (Public Health England, 2020).

It was accepted that 'professionals', viz. uninfected staff looking after home residents, were essential for residents' well-being and welfare but the principle that 'the customer comes first' seemed to have been breached. Why the needs of vulnerable citizens, especially the aged unwell, but also those with learning difficulties, and those unable to care adequately for themselves, were considered secondary to those of their 'professional' carers, is examined next in an end-of-life context.

## Saving lives right up to the moment of natural death

The global Covid-19 pandemic since March 2020, and the ongoing M-pox outbreak, declared in August 2024 by WHO (2024) to be a public health emergency of international concern (PHEIC), highlighted for over 7 billion humans what value, if any, was placed by their governments – democratic, authoritarian, autocratic and theocratic – on each individual citizen's life. Coincidentally, the dawning of the climate emergency, so long denied by political and scientific naysayers, has reinforced humanity's developing awareness of the fragility and irreplaceable uniqueness of each life. This double pronged assault – worldwide, deadly, physical disease and an approaching ecological calamity of tsunamic proportions, too often disguised in its tabloid description as 'global warming' – may or may not be confronted and defeated, and human life as we know it may continue. Or not. How is all of this related to end-of-life policy and practice, including euthanasia?

UK/Irish hospitals and care homes, both NHS and independently managed, relied almost exclusively on career medical practitioners to advise and deliver medical treatment up to and including end-of-life care. Their lengthy, largely publicly funded, training and career development extended over several years: 4 to 6 years as an undergraduate in a university medical school; then a 2 year foundation programme of postgraduate medical training; then general practice or specialty training – there were up to 60 medical specialties – for three to seven years. Each medical doctor would have enjoyed between 9 to 15 years of education, training and supervised practice (BMA, 2021a).

This lengthy period of programming and conditioning in the mores, traditions, values, standards and traditions of the UK/Irish medical professions would be expected to generate strong, behavioural boundaries for doctors, engendering in patients an implicit trust in their doctor's diagnoses and treatments. And yet Meirion (2021: 13) opined that this probationary, educational pathway, followed by annual appraisals and quinquennial evaluations was not proof against the depredations through human wickedness and pure evil of an unknown number of individual 'rogue' doctors.

Many of us will die in hospital or in a care or nursing home. Expert, compassionate, end-of-life medical and social care, alongside the services of colleagues with practical, palliative abilities, therefore becomes a necessary and indispensible resource, in a range of venues, including but not limited to a patient's home. A complicating factor in recent times was a developing cacophony across Ireland/UK, including Northern Ireland, of near-enthusiastic support for legalising medical regimes involving assisted dying, or assisted suicide, amounting in essence to the selective culling of our treasured, vulnerable citizens – the vulnerable elderly, those with learning difficulties and those with perceived, terminal, medical diagnoses and prognoses – call it as you will. In the current climate, how to achieve total safety for vulnerable patients continued to elude UK/Irish medicine.

## A warning from history

German history's blood-stained message offered a learning opportunity. The ghosts of innumerable, defenceless, innocent, murdered victims of Nazi medicine's policy of state-sponsored 'forced' euthanasia – Aktion T4 – from 1939 until the war's end in 1945, continued to cry out for justice and needed to be heard and heeded by today's generation of the UK/Irish medical professions. Those German doctors, lawyers, police officers and administrators who organised and executed the mass slaughter of hundreds of thousands of vulnerable human beings were almost all Nazi Party careerists who, in this instance and exceptionally – fascist dictator Adolf seldom committed 'policy' to paper - carried out Hitler's written instructions:

'The legal basis for the programme was a 1939 letter from Hitler, not a formal "Führer's decree" with the force of law. Hitler bypassed Conti, the Health Minister and his department, who might have raised questions about the legality of the programme and entrusted it to Bouhler and Brandt:

"Reich Leader Bouhler and Dr. Brandt are entrusted with the responsibility of extending the authority of physicians, to be designated by name, so that patients who, after a most critical diagnosis, on the basis of human judgment [menschlichenErmessen], are considered incurable, can be granted mercy death [Gnadentod]'.

— Adolf Hitler, 1 September 1939" (Wikipedia, 2021d)

Key implementers of Atkion T4 included Philipp Bouhler (Head), Hitler's personal physician Dr Karl Brandt, a physician's son Viktor Brack, psychiatrist Prof Werner Heyde (Organisers), and Dr Ernst-Robert Grawitz, German Red Cross leader. Dr Gerhard Wagner, a surgery professor's son, later leader of the Reich Doctors Chamber, died in 1939 and was succeeded by Dr Leonardo Conti. Wagner was jointly responsible earlier for euthanasia and sterilization carried out against Jews and the handicapped, and showed himself at the Nuremberg Party Congress in 1935 to be a staunch proponent of the Nuremberg Laws, and thereby also of Nazi Germany's race legislation and racial politics. Under Wagner's leadership, the Nazi killing institution at Hadamar Euthanasia Centre was established (Wikipedia, 2021e; 2021f).

Only after the International Military Tribunal convicted and sentenced the major Nazi war criminals on 1st October 1946 was a special court – Military Tribunal #1 – established by the US Military

Government for Germany to try 23 physicians charged with war crimes and crimes against humanity. Paragraphs 9 & 14 of the indictments before the Tribunal that convicted Nazi physicians, K. Brandt and Brack and 14 others, included references [edited] to the Atkion T4 euthanasia programme:

'9. Between September 1939 and April 1945 the defendants Karl Brandt, Brack, [and two others] unlawfully, wilfully, and knowingly committed war crimes, as defined by Article II of Control Council Law No. 10, in that they were principals in, accessories to, ordered, abetted, took a consenting part in, and were connected with plans and enterprises involving the execution of the so-called "euthanasia" program of the German Reich in the course of which the defendants herein murdered hundreds of thousands of human beings, including nationals of German-occupied countries. This program involved the systematic and secret execution of the aged, insane, incurably ill, of deformed children, and other persons, by gas, lethal injections, and diverse other means in nursing homes, hospitals, and asylums. Such persons were regarded as "useless eaters" and a burden to the German war machine. The relatives of these victims were informed that they died from natural causes, such as heart failure. German doctors involved in the "euthanasia" program were also sent to Eastern occupied countries to assist in the mass extermination of Jews.

'14. Between September 1939 and April 1945 the defendants Karl Brandt, Brack, [and two others] unlawfully, wilfully, and knowingly committed crimes against humanity, as defined by Article II of Control Council Law No. 10, in that they were principals in, accessories to, ordered, abetted, took a consenting part in, and were connected with plans and enterprises involving the execution of the so called "euthanasia" program of the German Reich, in the course of which the defendants herein murdered hundreds of thousands of human beings, including German civilians, as well as civilians of other nations' (Linder, 2009).

On 21 August 1947, 16 physicians were convicted and sentenced of whom 7 – including Dr Karl Brandt and Viktor Brack – were hanged on

2 June 1948 (Linder, 2009). Bouhler, Grawitz, Conti and Heyde all died by suicide in 1945 while Wagner died suddenly on 25 March 1939.

The Shoah Resource Centre believed 'one of the most heinous aspects of the Euthanasia Programme was the fact that its staff members were trained medical doctors, sworn to help care for their patients not destroy them ... At its inception, the program was even illegal – and yet the Euthanasia practitioners seemed to have no moral, religious or legal doubts about what they were doing' (Shoah Resource Centre, 2021).

Current UK/Irish human rights and equality laws and culture, offered some protection in relation to the perceived inestimable value, located in statute that both UK/Irish states placed on promoting and defending the welfare and well-being of each and every citizen's human life (Hamilton, 2021). The question remained about the risk, if any, of 'a slippery slope' towards dilution of this current reasonably satisfactory situation, that might be created by the current, allegedly widespread, public clamour for legalising 'assisted dying', however that ambiguous term and its various synonyms was defined.

It was important therefore to re-iterate the research evidence of McGlade et al. (2000: 796) who identified a gulf between UK/Irish GPs 'moral position' on euthanasia and their degree of willingness to 'endorse physician-assisted suicide or active euthanasia'. However, a recently publicised change in the disposition of UK doctors' trade union (BMA) towards its members' attitudes in relation to assisted dying invited careful examination and consideration. This became even more pertinent in the light of proposals for legalising assisted suicide in Ireland – a 'Dying with Dignity Bill', and in the UK – an 'Assisted Dying Bill', currently under consideration in each jurisdiction.

## UK Doctors' Trade Union changed its policy on euthanasia

The British Medical Association changed its policy in September 2021 on euthanasia – that opposed any change in British law outlawing 'mercy killing' – to a position of neutrality. Announcing this radical shift and having taken into consideration survey responses in 2020 by under 20% (n=28,986) of their membership (n=149,799), the BMA seemed to have decided to 'climb up and sit on the euthanasia fence'. This novel 'observer status' was evident in their somewhat contradictory statement, part of which stated:

'On 14 September 2021 our policy-making body (the representative body) voted in favour of a motion changing the BMA's policy from opposition to a change in the law on assisted dying, to a position of neutrality.

'This means we will neither support nor oppose attempts to change the law. We will not be silent on this issue, however ... Representatives also reiterated their call for robust protection for conscientious objection should the law change in the future' (BMA, 2021b).

In this matter of life and death, the BMA's stance was now akin to that adopted by the medieval executioner just before they chop off your head: 'Sorry mate but it's my job'.

This is the same doctors' trade union that during 1945/47, held out to the bitter end against the establishment of Aneurin Bevan's UK National Health Service (NHS) (Foot, 1975). Then, as now, they asserted their 'responsibility to represent our members' interests and concerns in any future legislative proposals' (BMA, 2021). On that occasion, Bevan articulated in 1946 the fundamental principle that underpinned his proposed National Health Service and that must continue to motivate and empower today's NHS medical practitioners:

'I have determined that what we must keep before us all the time is the welfare of the patient, the individual citizen, and not the vested interests of corporate bodies' (Foot, 1975: 152).

Bevan's words could not mean anything other than his overwhelming conviction that medical treatment must always respect the primacy of the patient, the individual citizen. The overriding issue, therefore, in relation to any involvement by doctors in euthanasia, was whether any conflict existed between their 'interests and concerns' and 'the welfare of the patient, the individual citizen' that could be detrimental to the latter. And that dilemma represented the real crux of the assisted dying debate. It seemed obvious that end-of-life care and palliative care, separately or in combination, represented a life-preserving approach to a resolution of the above mentioned 'conflict':

'End of life care is support for people who are in the last months or years of their life. They should have been seen by a doctor regularly. If a doctor believes you will die very soon, they must explain this to you and the people close to you' (NHS, 2021a):

'Palliative care is an approach that improves the quality of life of patients and their families facing the problem associated with life-threatening illness, through the prevention and relief of suffering by means of early identification and impeccable assessment and treatment of pain and other problems, physical, psychosocial and spiritual. World Health Organisation' (The Palliative Hub, 2021).

Approximately 16,000 Northern Ireland citizens died each year (NISRA, 2021). It could safely be assumed that currently the question of assisted dying did not arise, not least because no prosecutions related to an alleged breach of the law outlawing 'encouraging or assisting a suicide' have been reported.

In February 2020, the BMA Physician Assisted Dying Survey Report (BMA, 2021b) included the following 'Trends in the results', in members' support/opposition to changing the BMA's assisted dying policy:

1. Members in Northern Ireland were generally more opposed than those in other [UK] nations (no significant differences were found between members in England, Scotland and Wales)
2. Overall, medical students were generally more supportive and GPs generally more opposed, than most other branches of practice
3. These specialties tended to be generally more supportive: anaesthetics, emergency medicine, intensive care, and obstetrics & gynaecology
4. These specialties tended to be more opposed: clinical oncology, general practice; geriatric medicine; and palliative care.

## Concluding remarks

### Effect of physician-assisted suicide on palliative care

The jury was out as to whether assisted dying was detrimental to palliative care. Two important studies – samples from a growing literature – were summarised below, illustrating some remaining as yet unresolved difficult and complex developmental and organisational challenges.

**Study #1 – Gerson et al. (2020)**

Gerson et al. (2020) carried out qualitative research in three jurisdictions (Quebec, Canada; Oregon, USA; and Flanders, Belgium) with 29 respondent professionals, including 19 physicians, and 10 other professionals including organisational leaders, nurses, social workers, psychologists, and spiritual care counsellors involved in both assisted dying and palliative care. Its objective was to explore the relationship of palliative care with assisted dying in these settings, from the perspective of palliative care clinicians and other professionals involved in assisted dying and palliative care. Interview extracts cited by Gerson et al. (2020) revealed the inevitable cognitive dissonance generated in some respondents in their conflicted efforts to bridge the circle between preserving and ending their patients' lives:

'The cultural aims and cultural drivers for palliative care and for euthanasia, for me, it's the same - Professional 1'.

The authors' worrying conclusions (presented below) to this excellent study merited close attention and reflection in UK/Ireland since, 27 years after Oregon legalised euthanasia, they represented the ongoing underlying conflict between the aspirations of physicians and the various auxiliary professionals, given their respective superior (viz. physicians) and subordinate (viz. professionals) standing in exercising their parallel but distinct patient caring activities:

'We find that no clear or uniform relationship between palliative care and assisted dying can be identified in any of the three locations. Indeed, our analysis indicates that when a field of practice such as palliative care is potentially seen as threatened by another field, such as assisted dying, several patterns emerge that go beyond simple characterisation of the relationship between the two. The relationship between assisted dying and palliative care is influenced by legal regulations that are subject to change (p49-50), variable and sometimes inconsistent institutional policies and support systems, the type of assisted dying offered (medically or self-administered), and structures of healthcare funding (p51). Cooperation or integration between the two practices may also be perceived by some as dependent upon whether palliative care professionals' views of assisted dying are compatible with their views about 'care'.

'An overarching concern which unites the three jurisdictions is a lack of public knowledge, recognition and understanding of appropriate palliative care, as well as obtaining access to it. The context and practicalities of how assisted dying is being implemented alongside access to palliative care, need to be attended to in order to inform any future laws. We seek a better understanding of whether and in what ways assisted dying presents a threat to palliative care. There is a clear need for more attention to how palliative care and assisted dying can co-exist, where both are available (Gerson et al., 2021).

**Study #2 – Doerflinger (2017)**

In 2016, the Hemlock Society (rebranded by way of a terminological lurch as 'Compassion & Choices' - C&C), promoters and advocates of physician-assisted suicide, leafleted some US state legislatures with a paper entitled 'Medical Aid in Dying Fact Sheet'. Doerflinger (2017) carefully but comprehensively demolished the pamphlet's major but selectively evidenced proposal, comprising several published studies, seeking legislative approval of medical-aid in dying, aka physician-assisted suicide. His conclusions were:

1. The studies cited by C&C generally do not show what it claims, and their conclusions have been corrected or modified by other studies.
2. There is no convincing evidence that laws allowing physician-assisted suicide improve palliative and end-of-life care, and there is significant evidence that such laws can have the opposite effect – and that the laws, and the campaign promoting them, have a disturbing impact on overall suicide rates.
3. If these laws have a deleterious effect on palliative and end-of-life care, and on suicide prevention efforts in the general population of the states enacting them, the number of people (including seriously ill people) adversely affected by them vastly

exceeds the number of patients who actually make use of the "aid in dying" option. (Doerflinger, 2017).

**A humanistic outlook**

A humanist history academic, Kevin Yuill (2021) wrote about 'the disturbing campaign to legalise assisted dying' in the UK. Polling suggested, he said, that eight out of ten people in Britain favour a change in the law. He was concerned that although popular support for assisted dying might be rooted in relieving distress, others may have 'a more worrying goal: the use of assisted dying to create a more efficient society' (Yuill, 2021). He also noted that medically assisted death, that was intended to be reserved solely for the terminally ill and the mentally competent, was legally extended, respectively, in Canada to include 'disabled people'; in Belgium to include terminally ill children, and the Netherlands to include those suffering from blindness, tinnitus, autism, dementia and 'mental illness'.

Even before the outbreak of Hitler's aggressive war, Ponsonby, the founder of the British Voluntary Euthanasia Society – rebranded in 2005 as the short-stay Swiss hoteliers 'Dignity in Dying (DiD)' – targeted as candidates for euthanasia in 1936, those identified as 'being a burden', and those who 'are no longer of any use'. Although nominally a Labour Peer, Ponsonby's 'rhetoric reflected a society where the brutal utilitarianism of eugenics had not yet been discredited by the Nazi horrors' (Yuill, 2021).

Yuill (2021) suggested that DiD's claimed membership of 25,000 reflected societal worries about the consequences of an aging society, including far from unusual, though somewhat over-pessimistic fears of 'spending our last years with an ever-diminishing quality of life'. But he cautioned that assisted dying campaigners pushed for eligibility to be extended beyond the terminally ill to anyone suffering from a debilitating condition. The logical outcome of legalisation, Yuill believed, would be to categorise 'the elderly, sick or disabled as burdens for simply wanting to continue to live.' He added that 'politicians should hesitate before their sympathetic intentions push society even closer to this nightmare' (Yuill, 2021).

## The Doctrine of Double Effect

The practicalities of end-of-life care may involve doctors in administering pain-relieving medications that, in some circumstances, can have the unintended effect of their patient's earlier death. Tuckey and Slowther (2009) considered the ethical dilemma for clinicians when their legitimate attempts to relieve their patients' pain and suffering may produce this so-called 'double-effect'. In short, treatment and/or medication may be intended for pain relief, viz. a good purpose, while simultaneously leading to an unintended outcome, viz. the patient's demise. These writers stated that, in the aftermath of the Shipman case – see above – some 'doctors may be reluctant to prescribe high doses of opiates necessary to treat severe pain fearing that their intentions will be misconstrued' (Tuckey and Slowther, 2009). They added that [while] critics of the so-called doctrine of double-effect (DDE):

'cited the ambiguity surrounding the interpretation of intention as a flaw ... others see this as beneficial, maintaining that it protects the proper image of medicine which holds that doctors heal and do not kill ... [while] DDE prevents us from sliding down the slippery slope into a general acceptance of active euthanasia' (Tuckey and Slowther, 2009).

## Valuing human life

Going back to the beginning might aid deeper understanding of the complex issue of the taking of human life. Hamilton (2021) asked: 'What responsibility do we have to protect our own and others' lives? What values, if any, would outweigh that responsibility and entitle us to risk our lives?' He said our answers would reveal the value we gave to human life: 'All societies will place a high value on human life ... if people are entitled to kill at will and with impunity, all social bonds will be precarious, placing the economic and cultural development of society and its survival at risk'.

Hamilton (2021) added that in most cultures the value of human life was grounded more deeply than that pragmatic argument. Life had commonly been seen as sacred, whether set in a religious [or other philosophical] framework. The sacredness of life was evident in the respect accorded to the deaths of soldiers and civilians in the service of a higher cause, to save the lives of others or in martyrdom for refusal to renounce their convictions and principles, including religious practices, in the face of torture. The industrial scale of killing in the trenches of the 1914-1918 war, in the pattern bombing of cities, such as Dresden, and in the atrocious horrors of Hiroshima and Nagasaki, diminished the sacred character of life and death in Western culture (Hamilton, 2021). In his conclusions, Hamilton (2021) asked whether:

'the discrediting of higher values that might govern our attitudes to human life ... encouraged a ... calculus ... in making decisions about life and death ... in such issues as abortion and assisted dying [that] is increasingly individual choice, supported by an appeal to compassion. All of us have an interest in asking whether [this trend] will be conducive to a humane society in which the lives and integrity of the most vulnerable of its members are respected' (Hamilton, 2021).

## Endpiece

Dr Herbert Hendin (1997, 1998) merits the final few words in this chapter, citing the last paragraph from the final page of 'Seduced by Death', the classical, nonpareil text on the subject by Herbert Hendin, M.D. :

'Dying patients are themselves often revolted by their condition. It is remarkable how their perceptions change when they encounter caregivers who accept their humanity and do not perceive them this way. Such caregivers are harder to find in a cultural climate that encourages the easier option of euthanasia. Within a culture that provides no vision for making the last phase of life more meaningful, an attitude of revulsion becomes part of a cultural narrative moving both doctors and patients towards euthanasia. That attitude in turn reflects what happens when medicine is used to hasten death rather than to relieve suffering' (Hendin, 1997, 1998: 268).

**Myth:** (fictitious popular belief) Doctors can always be trusted to act in the best interests of their patients.

**Fallacy:** (misleading argument) Euthanasia and palliative care are two sides of the same solution to the problem of extreme human suffering.

# References

Baker, R. (2004) Implications of Harold Shipman for general practice. Postgrad Med J 2004; 80; 303-306

BBC News NI (2021) Troubles pension scheme opens for applications. Accessed on 2 September 2021 at https://www.bbc.co.uk/news/uk-northern-ireland-58388323

BMA (2021a) British Medical Association. Medical training pathway. 1 September 2021. Accessed on 18 September 2021 at https://www.bma.org.uk/advice-and-support/studying-medicine/becoming-a-doctor/medical-training-pathway

BMA (2021b) Physician assisted dying survey. Accessed on 22 September 2021 at https://www.bma.org.uk/advice-and-support/ethics/end-of-life/physician-assisted-dying/physician-assisted-dying-survey

BMJ (2019) First do no harm: the impossible oath. Dr Spyros Retsas FRCP. 19 July 2019. Accessed on 23 September 2021 at https://www.bmj.com/content/366/bmj.l4734/rr-2

Cremation 1 (2017) Application for cremation of the body of a person who has died. Accessed on 3 September 2021 at https://assets.publishing.service.gov.uk/government/uploads/system/uploads/attachment_data/file/697075/cremation-form-1-app-for-cremation-of-body.pdf

Doerflinger, R. (2017) The effect of legalising assisted suicide on palliative care and suicide rates: a response to 'Compassion and Choices' (formerly The Hemlock Society). 3 March 2017. Accessed on 24 September 2021 at https://lozierinstitute.org/the-effect-of-legalizing-assisted-suicide-on-palliative-care-and-suicide-rates/

EHRC (2021) Article 2: Right to Life. Equality and Human Rights Commission. Updated 3 June 2021. Accessed on 18 September 2021 at https://www.equalityhumanrights.com/en/human-rights-act/article-2-right-life

Finnis, A. (2020) Harold Shipman's victims, how many people he murdered, who they were and when they were killed. Accessed on 2 September 2021 at https://inews.co.uk/culture/television/

harold-shipman-victims-list-how-many-people-killed-doctor-murders-665833

Foot, M. (1975) Aneurin Bevan, Vol 2: 1945-1960. Herts., England: Paladin/Granada Publishing Limited

Gerson, S. M., Koksvic, G. H., Richards, N., Materstvedt, L. J. and Clark, D. (2020) Assisted dying and palliative care in three jurisdictions: Flanders, Oregon and Quebec. Accessed on 24 September 2021 at https://apm.amegroups.com/article/view/57549/pdf

Hamilton, A. (2021) Valuing human life. Accessed at Eureka on 10 September 2021 at https://www.eurekastreet.com.au/article/valuing-human-life [Thursday 9 September 2021]

Hendin, H. (1997, 1998) Seduced by death. New York, NY: W.W. Norton & Company

Linder, D. O. (2009) The Nuremberg Trials: The Doctors Trials. In Famous Trials, Professor Douglas O. Linder. Accessed on 21 September 2021 at https://famous-trials.com/nuremberg/1903-doctortrial#defendants

Maishman, E. (2021) Patients moved unlawfully from hospitals to Scottish care homes during first wave, report finds. The Scotsman, 20 May 2021. Accessed on 17 September 2021 at https://www.scotsman.com/health/patients-moved-unlawfully-from-hospitals-to-scottish-care-homes-during-first-wave-report-finds-3243315

McGlade, K. J., Slaney, L., Bunting, B. P. and Gallagher, A. G. (2000) Voluntary euthanasia in Northern Ireland: general practitioners' beliefs, experiences and actions. British Journal of General Practice, 2000, 50, 794-797

Meirion, T. (2021) Letter to Royal College of Surgeons Bulletin. January, 2021. Accessed on 7 September 2021 at https://publishing.rcseng.ac.uk/doi/pdf/10.1308/rcsbull.2021.23

NHS (2021a) What to expect from end-of-life care. 20 June 2021. Accessed on 22 September 2021 at https://www.nhs.uk/conditions/end-of-life-care/what-to-expect-from-care/

NI-HSE Health & Care Board (2021) Care homes and COVID 19. Updated October 2020. Accessed on 18 September 2021 at http://www.hscboard.hscni.net/coronavirus/covid-19-care-homes/

NISRA (2021) Northern Ireland death statistics. Accessed on 24 September 2021 at https://www.nisra.gov.uk>publications>monthlydeaths

Overview: Shipman Enquiry (2007) Learning from tragedy, keeping patients safe: Overview of the Government's action programme in response to the recommendations of the Shipman Enquiry. February, 2007. London: HMSO

Procon/Encyclopaedia Brittanica, Inc. (2020) Historical timeline – euthanasia and assisted suicide. Accessed on 23 August 2021 at https://euthanasia.procon.org/historical-timeline/

Protect Life 2 (2019) Protect Life 2: a strategy for preventing suicide and self-harm in Northern Ireland 2019 – 2024. Northern Ireland Department of Health. Stormont, Belfast.

Public Health England (2020) Guidance about coronavirus (COVID-19) personal protective equipment (PPE). Published April, 2020; Updated July, 2020. Accessed on 18 September 2021 at https://www.gov.uk/government/collections/coronavirus-covid-19-personal-protective-equipment-ppe

Public Prosecution Service Northern Ireland (2009) PPS publishes interim guidance on prosecuting cases of assisted suicide and launches public consultation. 23 September 2009. Belfast: Public Prosecution Service

Public Prosecution Service Northern Ireland (2010) Policy on prosecuting the offence of assisting suicide. February 2010. Belfast: Public Prosecution Service

Shoah Resource Centre (2021) Euthanasia Program. Accessed on 20 September 2021 at https://www.yadvashem.org/odot_pdf/Microsoft%20Word%20-%206303.pdf

Smyth, Dame Janet (2002) Chairman, The Shipman Enquiry. First Report. Volume one. Death disguised. Manchester: The Shipman Enquiry

Stefan, S. (2016) Rational suicide, irrational laws. New York, NY: Oxford University Press

Taylor, R. D. (2019a) Bogus psychiatrist's patients given electroshock therapy. 18 May 2019.

The Herald (Glasgow). Accessed on 16 September 2021 at https://www.heraldscotland.com/news/17648743.bogus-psychiatrists-patients-given-electroshock-therapy/

Taylor, R. D. (2019b) Background: 'Zholia Alemi didn't have a clue what she was doing'. 18 May 2019. The Herald (Glasgow), Accessed on 16 September 2021 at https://www.heraldscotland.com/news/17648744.background-zholia-alemi-didnt-clue-doing/

The Palliative Hub (2021) About palliative care. Accessed on 22 September 2021 at https://adultpalliativehub.com/about-adult-palliative-care/

Tuckey, L. and Slowther, A. (2009) The doctrine of double effect and end-of-life decisions. Clinical Ethics, 2009, 4 : p12-14.

WHO (2024) World Health Organisation: WHO Director-General declares mpox outbreak a public health emergency of international concern. News Release, 14 August 2024

Wikipedia (2021a) 1981 Irish hunger strike. Accessed on 19 August 2021 at https://en.wikipedia.org/wiki/1981_Irish_hunger_strike

Wikipedia (2021b) Murder in English law. Accessed on 23 August 2021 at https://en.wikipedia.org/wiki/Murder_in_English_law#:~:text=Murder%20is%20an%20offence%20under,death%20or%20serious%20injury%20unlawfully-and /

Wikipedia (2021c) Harold Shipman. Accessed on 2 September 2021 at https://en.wikipedia.org/wiki/Harold_Shipman

Wikipedia (2021d) Aktion T4. 25 August 2021. Accessed on 19 September 2021 at https://en.wikipedia.org/wiki/Aktion_T4

Wikipedia (2021e) Karl Brandt. 25 July 2021. Accessed on 19 September 2021 at https://en.wikipedia.org/wiki/Karl_Brandt

Wikipedia (2021f) Viktor Brack. 18 September 2021. Accessed on 19 September 2021 at https://en.wikipedia.org/wiki/Viktor_Brack

Wilson, C. (2021) The Shipman Files: a very British crime story. Chris Wilson. BBC Documentary film. BBC2 & BBC iPlayer, 28 September 2021.

Woodruff, R. (2019) Euthanasia and physician assisted suicide: are they clinically necessary or desirable? International Association for Hospice and Palliative Care, 2019. Accessed on 23 August 2021 at https://hospicecare.com/policy-and-ethics/ethical-issues/essays-and-articles-on-ethics-in-palliative-care/euthanasia-physician-assisted-suicide-are-they-clinically-necessary-or-desirable/

Young, D. (2021) Covid death toll among NI care home residents reaches 1,000. David Young. Belfast Telegraph. 19 March 2021. Accessed on 18 September 2021 at https://www.belfasttelegraph.co.uk/news/northern-ireland/covid-death-toll-among-ni-care-home-residents-reaches-1000-40215589.html

Yuill, K. (2021) The disturbing campaign to legalise assisted dying. Dr Kevin Yuill. The Spectator, 4 July 2021. Accessed on 21 September 2021 at https://www.spectator.co.uk/article/the-disturbing-campaign-to-legalise-assisted-dying

\* \* \*

# Chapter 15
# Suicide or penacide – terminology and importance of language

## Introduction

Suicide and Suicide Grief: "'Pena' is from the Latin 'poena' (punishment or torment), the root of the word 'pain'. 'Cide' is from 'cedere' (to strike down). Penacide is 'the killing of pain.' It incorporates the reason, wanting to terminate one's pain. It eliminates the notion that 'wanting to die' has anything to do with killing oneself. Penacide is not a kind of suicide. It's what causes the deaths recorded as suicides. It is the true name of the beast" (DMR-Dark My Road, 2008).

'Suicide …' s/he muttered, 'sure it's just somebody killing themselves – what more is there to it?' This might be a fairly typical response by anyone to an enquiry by a neophyte reporter, clutching a liveried mike, on a downtown Belfast city centre street, asking: 'What do you think the word 'suicide' means?' The possibility of further Q & A about 'suicide' rarely goes further than that.

But this was not what Ed Shneidman (1985/94) thought – or wrote about – in his classical text on what he called 'definition of suicide'. Suicide is known to be highly complex, both multidimensional and multifactorial, and can often be perceived by bereaved survivors and the general public as a 'grotesque, unprecedented, bizarre and unbelievable' event. In Ireland, an acronym – GUBU – that appropriated the four initial letters, was coined to describe sensational events, more immediately and specifically one that occurred in 1982 (Wikipedia, 2021a). For information regarding the 1982 event, see Annex 2 below.

Every suicide may share some, if not all of these descriptors. This might suggest a need for us, in seeking a deeper understanding of human self-destruction, to consider carefully the terminology we use in view of its importance for the communication of ideas, research and knowledge about this enigmatic human behaviour.

## The definition of suicide

Shneidman (1985/94) was a good starting point: his goal was 'to present as straightforwardly as possible, fresh notes on what suicide is'. As with most if not all published studies on suicide post-Durkheim, for Shneidman, suicide prevention per se seemed to be regarded as an essential, unavoidable companion. His concomitant goal therefore was 'to imply realistic and practical measures for preventing suicide' (Preface, v).

Shneidman (1985/94) was writing close to the centennial of Durkheim (1897/2002). He felt that it was timely to reconsider 'the nature of suicide, including of course the very definition of suicide itself' (p3). Shneidman, an academic and a professional, was addressing his colleagues: it is highly likely there was only a sparse readership of his erudition outside these hallowed circles.

Although he held that 'every adult knows instinctively what s/he means by it (i.e. suicide): it is the act of taking one's life' (p6), he noted that beyond this simple formula there was 'something more'. He cited several examples where 'something more' was necessary for a satisfactory definition:

'Are totally lethally intended acts which fail (e.g. shooting oneself in the head and surviving) suicide? Are non-lethal attempts on the life (e.g. ingesting a possibly lethal dose of barbiturates) suicidal? Are deleterious and inimical patterns of behaviour (e.g. continued smoking by a person with acute emphysema) suicidal? Are deaths which have been ordered by others or deaths under desperation (e.g. Cato's response to Caligula's requesting his death, or the deaths at Masada, or in Jonestown) suicide?' (Shneidman, 1985/94: 6).

The answers to these questions, and more, Shneidman held, 'constitute the indispensible periphery of the definition of suicide' (p6).

Although he concentrated on American suicidology, Shneidman might also have queried whether the deaths in Northern Ireland between May and August, 1981, of ten incarcerated men on hunger strike, were suicidal (Wikipedia, 2021d). Were he to rely upon Graber (1981), he would exclude such deaths on the basis of 'intentionality' – for suicide to be suicide, the deceased must intend that their action will in fact result in their death:

'Suicide is defined as something that results in one's death in the way that it was planned, either from the intention of ending one's life or the intention to bring about some other state of affairs (such as relief from pain) that one thinks it certain or highly probably can be achieved only by means of [one's] death' (Graber, 1981, cited by Shneidman, 1985/1994: 16).

Shneidman (1985/1994: 17) cited 'the fundamental dimensions of meanings that are required in the formal definition of suicide' as follows:

1. The initiation of an act that leads to the death of the initiator
2. The willing of an act that leads to the death of the willer
3. The willing of self-destruction
4. The loss of will
5. The motivation to be dead (or to die) which leads to the initiation of an act that leads to the death of the initiator
6. The knowledge of the actor that actions s/he initiates tend to produce the objective state of death (Douglas, 1967).

Moving forward from consideration of what we mean when we use the word 'suicide', we next explore the terminology of suicide and the importance of language in communications concerning our understanding of suicide.

## The language of suicide

A recent online survey of words used by adults aged over 18 years, affected by suicide in the UK, Australia and the US was promoted through the authors' research networks, as well as 'lived experience and charitable organisations', e.g. Samaritans, using email, organisation websites and social media (Padmanathan et al., 2019). [Ethical approval was granted by Bristol University (UK) Health Sciences Faculty Research Ethics Committee.] These authors did not feel any need to define 'suicide'. Their 33 question survey asked participants to 'rate descriptors pertaining to suicidal behaviour according to perceived acceptability' (p1). 2,719 responses were received, of which 1,679 (61.8%) were complete.

The survey explored language describing 'a situation where a person has performed an act of suicide or self-harm but has not died' in relation to how acceptable respondents felt certain phrases were, on a scale of 1 to 5 (1 – 'not acceptable' to 5 – 'acceptable'):

a) Cry for help; b) Suicidal gesture; c) Failed attempt at suicide; d) Attempted suicide; e) Unsuccessful suicide; f) Parasuicide; g) Near-miss; h) Non-fatal self harm; j) Suicide survivor.

'Attempted suicide' was rated most acceptable (845 respondents) while 'near-miss' was rated least acceptable. Most of the remaining phrases were deemed 'unacceptable'.

The survey also explored participants' feelings about language describing 'a situation where a person has performed an act of suicide or self-harm and has died' using a similar 'acceptability' rating scale, regarding how appropriate certain phrases were perceived to be:

k) Died by suicide; m) Suicide victim; n) Successful suicide; p) Topped themselves; q) Ended their life; r) Completed suicide; s) Took their [own] life; t) Committed suicide; u) Killed themselves; v) Fatal self-harm.

'Took their [own] life', 'Ended their life' and 'Died by suicide' were rated most acceptable while 'Topped themselves' and 'Successful suicide' were deemed least acceptable. The most controversial phrase, 'Committed suicide', divided opinion among participants that appeared to be related either to perceived criminal undertones, or to their varied experience of suicide whether 'through someone they knew' or 'solely through their own experiences' (p11). It seemed that the phrase 'committing suicide' will continue to be 'highly emotive for some participants' (p14).

These authors did not undervalue our need to be aware of, and to sympathise with bereaved survivors – including some participants – who held that 'talking about it' was a valid way to reduce the incidence of suicidal behaviour. However, they conceded that 'further research on the effect of English-language descriptors on attitudes and behaviour would be valuable [within] a broader conceptual framework, which explores the inclusion of reference to the intent and suicide itself' (Padmanathan et al., 2019: 13).

Unfortunately, they did not refer to earlier groundbreaking work that highlighted the potential blocking effect upon the integration of suicidology research, of indeterminate and confusing terminology. We now consider its relevance for suicide research today.

## A new nomenclature for suicidology

Over a quarter of a century ago, O'Carroll et al. (1996) published a proposal to think about and, perhaps, to begin to deal with the issue of suicidology's terminological inexactitude, in other words to seek to ensure that 'what you mean by a phrase or sentence is indeed what your listener/s understand by it':

'Suicidology finds itself confused and stagnated for lack of a standard nomenclature. This paper proposes a nomenclature for suicide-related behaviour in the hope of improving the clarity and precision of communications, advancing suicidological research and knowledge, and improving the efficacy of clinical interventions' (O'Carroll et al., 1996: 237).

A decade later, Silverman (2006) published an address he made a year before to fellow professional suicidologists that encapsulated his considered views on how this conundrum might be analysed and resolved:

'This 2005 Louis I. Dublin Award Address explores some of the basic difficulties and controversies inherent in the development and universal acceptance of a nomenclature for suicidology. Highlighted are some of the unresolved challenges with agreeing upon a mutually exclusive set of terms to describe suicidal thoughts, intentions, motivations, and self-destructive behaviours' (Silverman, 2006: 519).

The following year, the first section (Part 1) of a major article by the same author, in conjunction with colleagues, noted that most suicidologists 'agree that the use of inadequate and contradictory definitions of suicide and suicidal behaviour is often a limitation of suicide research and communication' (Silverman et al., 2007a).

But a decade before O'Carroll et al. (1996), in 1985, an alert was signalled by McIntosh (1985) regarding the paucity of precision regarding the suicide phenomenon. He asserted that no single term, definition or taxonomy existed that sufficiently represented the complex set of behaviours that were suicidal. He inferred that lack of standardising terms and definitions had the effect of impeding the advance of the science of suicidology by blocking both communication and understanding.

The second section (Part 2) of Silverman et al. (2007b) opened with an acknowledgement that although suicidology might not be able to construct 'universally unambiguous criteria' that would 'comprehensively characterise suicidal behaviours (and overall firmly establish the intention behind them), for scientific clarity it would be highly desirable that the set of definitions and the associated terminology be explicit and generalisable' (De Leo et al., 2006). It was suggested that 'rebuilding' the O'Carroll et al. (1996) 'tower of Babel' might increase the ability of all interested parties, inter alia clinicians, epidemiologists, policy makers and researchers to better communicate with each other.

'Babel', a Hebrew word, meant to mix or to confuse (McKenzie, 1995: 73). It seemed doubtful therefore whether 'rebuilding' that which was already mixed up and confused, was likely to remove the scales from suicidology's eyes. And so it has proved. Space did not permit a comprehensive analysis of the recommendations within the four above mentioned inter-related articles: hence we have chosen to examine a sample of four from the complex set of behaviours that were suicidal, to ascertain what level of precision, agreement and acceptance might be available therein in the real world of human self-destruction:

1. Suicide ideation; 2. Suicide plan; 3. Suicide attempt; 4. Death by suicide.

Two case study based dissertations (O'Keeffe, 2001; 2010) were examined to ascertain whether suicide-related language and terminology employed therein by the researcher and by their respondents were influential factors regarding the quality of inter-communications, in relation to identity development in bereaved survivors of family and client suicide.

## Family suicides

Six case studies, A to F (inclusive), were completed that employed Identity Structure Analysis (Weinreich and Saunderson, 2003) and Content Analysis (Weber, 1994) to assemble primary research evidence relating to the investigation of survivors' identity development, in the aftermath of a family suicide (O'Keeffe, 2001).

## Case A

Respondent 'A' was a 46 year-old woman living in Co Antrim with her husband. In October 1977, her 19 year-old sister was found hanged in her study bedroom at an educational establishment in Co Derry/Londonderry. At this time, the respondent was abroad and therefore unable to attend her late sister's funeral. At an inquest held later, photographs of the death scene and a 'suicide note' left by the deceased were shown to the respondent. Surviving members of the respondent's family of origin were her parents and two brothers, one older than her and the other younger than the deceased. Respondent 'A' contacted the investigator over 22 years after her intimate suicidal loss.

Only one of the sample of four behaviours – death by suicide – was evident in this case. None of the other three behaviours were referred to by the respondent. Long-standing, unresolved post-suicide grief was experienced by this vulnerable respondent, as evidenced in this interview extract:

'... to a certain extent I ... didn't really care ... I just I didn't actually care that much at the time ... sounds callous but I just didn't know what hit me ... I just thought 'Oh God' ... it was only afterwards ... subsequent to that ... I kept busy everybody said oh A's getting on great ... meanwhile I ... got my own life into a bit of a mess ... over the years this terrible thing – there's been this terrible thing ... I sort of ... hold it back you'll make up a story ... and that that's just pushing it away all the time ... and that just builds up and ... makes it worse ... you're just building up a bigger and bigger time-bomb for yourself' (O'Keeffe, 2001: 87).

## Case B

Respondent 'B' was a woman aged approximately 45 years, living and employed in Co Derry/Londonderry. In October 1996, her 23 year-old son was found dead in his bed at home by his younger brother. At this time, the respondent was staying overnight at her partner's home while her son socialised with some friends in her home. The coroner decided that in view of the circumstances of the death, an inquest hearing was unnecessary. Surviving members of the respondent's family were her mother – her father died when she was nine years old – two younger siblings, a brother and a sister, and her younger son. Respondent B contacted the investigator just under three and a half years after her suicidal loss.

As for respondent 'A', only one of the sample of four behaviours – 'death by suicide' – was evident for respondent 'B', although 'suicide ideation' may have been implicit in her use of the term 'suicidal tendencies' when, in this interview extract, she referred to:

'stages that people go through in depression and moving towards maybe suicidal tendencies. I could see every one of them in my son – after the fact' (O'Keeffe, 2001: 99).

There was no evidence of the remaining two sample behaviours – suicide attempt and suicide plan.

The respondent said she completed an in-depth study of the suicide phenomenon after she found counselling support to be ineffective. These interview extracts contained evidence of unresolved post-suicide trauma:

'I had a lot of people around me for about two weeks ... then people had to go back to their work ... and get on with their own life ... I had this terrible sense of isolation, loneliness, fear of death, fear of what it can do, how final it is ... it was a long struggle and I feel I had to do it on my own ... my family were all there for about the first two weeks ... after that I just don't feel I got much support ... I think they left me quite ... alone far too much ... I'm very angry at him for wasting his life ... you can only be angry at him for so long ... I only wish he'd talked to somebody ... me ... somebody ... I wouldn't say I loved him any more than ... my other son ... but feel a stronger relationship than ... my other boy ... I don't think I'll ever come to terms with his death ... I must have failed him as a mother that he didn't feel that he could come and speak to me as a mother whatever was bothering him ... suicide's a very brave thing ... goes against all your natural instincts to keep yourself alive ... something wrong with their mental processes ... my son certainly wasn't thinking straight ... I know that he's dead and that ... but I'll never understand it and I'll never get over it ... I've got over the stage where I'm expecting him to walk in the door ... bereavement by suicide carries its own special circumstances ... the fact that I've lost a child makes it all the more painful' (O'Keeffe, 2001: 95, 96, 102, 103).

## Case 'C'

Respondent 'C' was a man, aged about 42 years, living and employed in Belfast. He was temporarily living apart from his partner and their children for personal reasons. His father was found dead in a toxic gas-filled room in 1965. He was aged 29 years. At the time of his father's death, the respondent was seven years old and he and his younger brother were staying temporarily with an aunt – their remaining siblings were living with other relatives – while both of their parents were hospitalised. Surviving members of the respondent's family were his mother, his younger brother, four younger sisters, one older sister [viz. six siblings] and members of his parents' families. Respondent contacted the investigator 35 years after his suicidal loss.

In this case, it was evident that Respondent 'C' was familiar with all four sample behaviours: 'suicide ideation', 'suicide plan', 'suicide attempt' and 'death by suicide'. The interview extracts (below) contained evidence of long-standing unresolved post-suicide trauma.

At age 18, respondent started searching 'for the truth about his father's life and death':

'as I got older I wanted to know ... it wasn't until I was about eighteen ... always wondered why my father's brothers and sisters never bothered with my mother ... I seen other families and relations coming up ... but we never had anyone come ... especially my father's side ... I always claimed this must have something to do with the suicide like ... they must be blaming my mother ... when they don't visit her' (O'Keeffe, 2001: 107).

This respondent did not mention whether an inquest had been held. He said he recalled his aunt telling him and two of his siblings of his father's death:

'They took us into aunt A's living room ... she had kids herself ... older than me ... I knew they had been told before us because they were ... like an audience ... watching ... our response ... my aunt A just came straight out ... just turned round and dead cold "I have to tell you now your daddy's dead ... and he was buried yesterday" ... because we were so young there was no big response' (O'Keeffe, 2001: 108).

The respondent's unresolved grief was compounded by the 'magical disappearance of his father' without any 'final farewell' that attendance at the funeral might have offered:

'... that day ... robbed of it ... I used the word "robbed" although it doesn't sound like that. We didn't actually find out anything until he was actually buried ... then you didn't believe it ... because you never seen a funeral nor nothing' (O'Keeffe, 2001: 108).

The respondent described his own suicide attempt:

'Out of the seven of us, three have attempted it ... I'm beginning to think myself that when problems ... become too much for us, we turn to suicide for some reason because my dad did ... I attempted it ... none have been successful like ... it could be a cry for help. I'd split up with my family ... the whole family were away ... I remember saying to myself: "This is the way my father got out of it; this is the way I'm going" ... I set fire to the house. I lay down on the bed. The room was blazing ... choking with the smoke ... I was determined I would go through with it ... it would be painful but I didn't care. Maybe the drink helped me not to worry about it ... when I was lying on the bed ... I seen my son – just visually seen him in front of me ... and that stopped it ... what saved me personally was the thought of my father doing it leaving all the children behind. That stopped me from doing it' (O'Keeffe, 2001: 110).

There appeared in respondent's reflections, to have been strong elements in his mind of suicide ideation linked to a suicide plan to emulate his father's behaviour. Respondent did not have access to a firearm and he said this was crucial to his survival:

'You know one thing I'm glad and it's probably hard for you with me saying this but I hadn't got a gun with me because it only takes a second to do it when you've got a gun and I think I would've. If I had had a gun I would have shot myself and it would've been over' (O'Keeffe, 2001: 111).

## Case 'D'

Respondent 'D' was a woman aged early 40's, living and employed in Co Down. In September 1994, her older sister, then aged 39 years, was found hanged in the bathroom of a Co Down hospital where she was a patient. At this time the respondent was visiting relatives in Co Antrim and Co Derry/Londonderry. Surviving members of the respondent's family were her parents, a younger sister (domiciled in England), her husband, their three children and her deceased sister's husband and family. Respondent contacted the investigator five years after her sister's sad death.

In this case there was evidence that respondent was aware of at least three of the sample behaviours: suicide ideation, suicide plan/intention, and death by suicide.

There was evidence also for respondent's unresolved grief, compounded by a second serious loss, viz. miscarriage 12 weeks into a pregnancy that occurred 18 years into their marriage that had already produced three offspring. As recorded below in interview extracts, she said her sense of who she was, her identity, was altered by the suicide trauma:

'I just feel I'm just not ... the person I was just died when [my sister] died and I'm just ... totally different' (O'Keeffe, 2001: 124).

The investigator concluded that the respondent's identity development, related to her post-suicide trauma and her subsequent miscarriage, 'suggested a need to protect herself and to survive by reaching out to help people like herself' (O'Keeffe, 2001: 135).

Respondent said her sister had a difficult unplanned pregnancy about a year before her death: her work as a nurse, her diploma course, moving house and her husband's 'prospect of redundancy' all contributed to 'an anxious state'. Three months after a traumatic childbirth, respondent's sister was 'referred to a consultant psychiatrist and ... hospitalised after she voiced suicide ideation:

'Mammy would have constantly criticised [my sister] even to her dying day ... she'd come into the house and mammy would have been criticising what she was wearing or what the children were wearing or whatever she was doing ... [my sister] was convinced she wasn't a good mother ... the psychiatrist asked her ... did she ever think of killing herself ... my sister actually said she had and that alarmed her [the psychiatrist]. She was just going to give her Prozac and send her home ... and then she decided "She's voiced an intent to kill herself ... I'd better bring her in ..." ' (O'Keeffe, 2001: 130).

Some time before this, the respondent had mentioned suicide to her sister:

'... I remember [my sister] about a year before, somebody had killed themselves and I remember saying to ... her: "You would never think of doing that?" and she says "Oh no, no," she says, "God I know I'm bad ... but I'm not that bad" ... so I never gave it another thought' (O'Keeffe, 2001: 125).

In the event, respondent's sister sought contact on the night of her death with the nursing and religious personnel attached to the hospital but 'circumstances conspired to prevent all of the people she approached from reaching her before' she killed herself:

'... earlier in the evening, [my sister] had asked the ward sister could she speak to her ... the ward sister was called away to another ward ... she'd be back in twenty minutes ... she wasn't back ... only one other nurse ... and an auxiliary ... on the ward ... the nurse was assigned to a patient who was actively suicidal ... you can guarantee that the auxiliary ... wasn't looking near the other patients at all ... [my sister] also phoned the priest ... and asked if he could come and see her ... he would call up and see her after Mass. So nobody could speak to her when she wanted to speak to somebody ... they (hospital staff) didn't even notice she was missing ... And she never phoned me ... her husband came up ... at visiting time and he couldn't find her ... he saw two ... nurses absolutely running past him from another ward ... one of the nurses had gone in ... discovered her in the bathroom, didn't even attempt to take her down ...

administered oxygen ... [that] was certainly going to do [no] good to her ... she was dead' (O'Keeffe, 2001: 125, 131).

This apparently avoidable suicide generated complex grief reactions in family survivors. Respondent's parents were elderly and in poor health, and her mother's response was influenced by traditional Roman Catholic beliefs that, regrettably, 'reflected absence of pity or compassion for the victim ... focusing on the assumed culpability of the suicide, without any element of understanding or forgiveness':

' ... daddy's brother, [my uncle, who] is a priest ...and mammy's GP ... met me just round the corner ... the three of us went into the house together ... mammy and daddy were sitting in the living room ... you don't walk in with the GP and a priest ... and not knowing something was wrong uncle says "I'm sorry" he says "but bad news – [my sister] is dead' and daddy instantly said "Suicide". He just knew. And mammy's first words were "Will she go to hell?" and my uncle nearly died "Oh God ... no" he said, "don't be so silly" but that was the old school of thought ... you were damned for ever' (O'Keeffe, 2001: 126).

## Case 'E'

Respondent 'E' was a man, aged about 40 years, living and working in Belfast. On 11 June 1998, his younger brother, then aged 37 years, was found hanged in London. The respondent learned of the death two days later. At this time he was domiciled in Belfast having been reared in Co Tyrone. Surviving members of the respondent's family included his parents, several - number unknown - of his siblings, their families and his late brother's partner. The respondent contacted the investigator less than 18 months after his suicidal loss. In transcribed extracts from taped interviews, he described 'a suicide trajectory linked to alcoholism and related to mental disorder':

'... he'd gone back to drinking after a number of years ... he'd been taking drugs and stuff ... he had conflict about his sexuality ... lot of problems ... been in different treatment centres ... drinking heavily ... seemed to get involved in a cult thing ... his behaviour and messages he was sending home ... getting more and more bizarre ... he just went off the ropes ... he came home six months before he died ... he seemed ...

quite crazy in the way he was going on ... very, very angry ... ' (O'Keeffe, 2001: 139).

The effect upon the respondent and his family members included shock, anger, and traumatised impotence. He said his GP had zero involvement in the aftermath:

'Family was totally shattered so we weren't really in a position to support each other... I didn't get any help from my doctor. I didn't want any help from my doctor ... my doctor in Belfast doesn't really know me ... he wouldn't have known about this' (O'Keeffe, 2001: 139).

In this case, there was evidence that the respondent was aware of at least three of the sample behaviours: suicide plan/intention, suicide attempt and death by suicide.

Respondent described how the Cruse organisation offered him one-to-one counselling and access to a group for relatives of suicide victims. He said he also talked a lot to friends:

'I believe in talking to people ... twelve step fellowship support ... I met a woman going to meetings who lost her sister a couple of years ago and I used to talk a lot to her, I found it very helpful to find somebody that's in the same situation ... she understood what I was feeling ... it was OK to feel how I felt ... the woman I did counselling with was very good ... I felt I'd no right to grieve because he had committed suicide ... [she] pointed out to me that I didn't hang him ... that he did it himself' (O'Keeffe, 2001: 140, 141).

This respondent said 'he believed his mother's grief was exceptional, a mother's special grief on the loss of her son by suicide'. He inferred that he understood well many of the constituents of his brother's suicide trajectory that took him, weighed down by cross addictions (Dyer, 2020) to the suicide cul-de-sac:

' ... I feel I do know why he did it ... maybe ... arrogant point of view ... I've had problems with alcohol ... went through some very black times and could have done the same thing ... couple of years ago ... very black times ... phoned the Samaritans ... in a bad mess ... I feel that ... he went to that place and he went through with it ... I have had suicide attempts in my own life ... some pretty petty and cries for help ... but a number of years ago ... very black place ... thought I had no alternative but to take my own life ... it was a decision I had about putting up a rope ... I talked to someone ... he suggested "If you have a rope, get rid of it" and I did. I feel he [respondent's brother] must have gone to that same place ... he was in very active addiction ... drugs, alcohol and other things ... I think that's what happened to him' (O'Keeffe, 2001: 142).

The respondent suggested there was 'an iceberg effect' in relation to bereavement by suicide – only those traumatized individuals 'who find their way to Cruse – or into private counselling or other effective support – are likely to obtain life preserving and life enhancing help and support'. He said there was an issue of equity when appropriate therapeutic support was available to only a fraction of the estimated survivor community. He acknowledged the taboo/stigma aspect in suicide that may deepen the survivor's grief wound:

' ... there's a sensitivity needed around suicide ... I used to feel ashamed that my brother committed suicide ... at the church service the priest ... seemed to be very shaming ... of the family ... that we have been judged and ... condemned ... [but] my grief is as valid as anyone else's ... whether what he did was morally right or wrong ... he was a very sick boy ... my grief is valid ... [now] I can talk easily about it because I've been there ... I know what the story is ... one benefit of the whole experience ... if you can call it a benefit ... it is hard for people ... afraid to upset you or say the wrong thing ... so they say nothing ... assume we don't want to talk about it ... now I do know what it's like so I'm able to talk to people ... about my experience ... they're not going to turn round and say "What do you know about it?" I do know about it' (O'Keeffe, 2001: 143, 144).

**Case 'F'**

Respondent 'F' was a man, aged in his late fifties, living near Belfast and currently working in Belfast. On 13th October 1992, his only sibling, a single woman then aged 49 years, was found dead by police at her home in Belfast. She had died approximately two days earlier. At the time the respondent was domiciled in England and he learned about his sister's death following a telephone message from police to his residence. Other than the respondent, only an elderly aunt and a number of cousins survived the deceased. The investigator was contacted by the respondent seven years after the suicidal loss of his younger sister.

In this case, there was evidence that the respondent was aware of at least two of the sample behaviours: suicide plan/intention, and death by suicide.

This lady's death appeared to have been the outcome of a detailed suicide plan, without any element of cri-de-coeur: '... it could have no other endpoint than extinguishing her life', as outlined in the respondent's interview extract(s) :

'... on Sunday ... at some stage ... in the afternoon, she sat down and wrote a six page letter to me as to why and what it was all about ... pulled all the [electric power] plugs out in the flat ... and left a little note in the tea caddy ... opened the window so that... they wouldn't wreck any window frames ... filled two hot water bottles ... took an overdose with huge amounts of barbiturates ... later on the Sunday evening she would have died ... on the Tuesday... she was found dead in bed' (O'Keeffe, 2001: 156).

At work in England, the respondent received a message from his landlady to contact police in Belfast about the death of his sister. His initial shock-denial response was later compounded when police later confirmed 'no suspicious circumstances', viz. suspected suicide:

'... some chap from the company ... did all the phoning for me ... I was ashen ... and insecure ... the fact that it was suicide ... was just another thing on top of the fact she had died ... to say it was just one thing more is being very dismissive but it was just incredulity ... you just couldn't take anything on board ...' (O'Keeffe, 2001: 156).

Respondent said his work colleagues supported him, emotionally and physically, throughout the following days. He arranged the funeral 'at a distance', relied upon 'a lot of drinking and smoking', cried himself to sleep and thus was able to get the energy needed to organise everything:

'... I wouldn't have wanted anybody else to do it. She was my sister and the least I could do for her having not been around when I should have been, retrospectively ... I wanted to do it' (O'Keeffe, 2001: 157).

The respondent recognised a 'special survivor's grief' after his sister's death. Unlike normal family bereavements, his suicidal loss experience, he said, caused him to perceive it as fundamentally different in the sense that one 'cannot touch suicide':

' ... those of us who have been bereaved by suicide, you do have something left ... a feeling that nobody else has ... several deaths in the family ... you don't expect everybody to live forever ... people are bereaved and distracted and upset ... but you can touch that sort of a death. You can't touch suicide ... when somebody commits suicide you know nothing about it at all until you hear about it ... all sorts of things have led up to that suicide and nobody knows anything about them ... you can't touch it because you don't know what's going on in someone's mind ... the reasons why they do it' (O'Keeffe, 2001: 158).

The respondent was skeptical about the signs of suicide, including despair, a recently discussed tool in suicide prevention that may include four domains – cognitive, emotional, behavioural and biological:

'Although we now have the catchy term "deaths of despair," we have yet to study its central empirical claim: that conceptually defined and empirically assessed "despair" is indeed a common pathway to several causes of death [including suicide and drug-poisoning]. At the level of the person, despair consists of cognitive, emotional, behavioural, and biological domains. Despair can also permeate social relationships, networks, institutions, and communities' (Shanahan et al., 2019).

Respondent said he felt that 'the phenomenon of suicide signals, where a victim's agenda might enable a close observer to make a suicide prediction' was:

'... a hindsight thing ... how should you be tuned in to recognise those things – those signs and signals, because you're not looking for them' (O'Keeffe, 2001: 158).

Respondent added that he had noted in his diary the last time he visited his sister, two months before her demise, that he had not seen her looking so well:

'[They had] enjoyed each other's company for the first time in a long time ... again I didn't know she was being treated for depression ... someone told me that afterwards ... her doctor told me ... I didn't know that ... she hadn't told me ... all that could fall into place entirely' (O'Keeffe, 2001: 158).

The respondent raised the issue of his late sister's religious beliefs that would have considered suicide to be morally wrong. He did not understand how she could have acted against all the church's teachings:

'... but she had seemingly worked it out ... that if she confessed to Jesus long time since that she was a sinner, Jesus is there to save confessed sinners ... that's how she sorted it out ... how she could end her own life ... as opposed to waiting for the great call ... ' (O'Keeffe, 2001: 160).

Seven years after losing his sister, this respondent did not evidence symptoms of traumatic suicide-related grief. Rather he felt that survivors, temporarily burdened and focused upon their own loss, may not, with compassion, acknowledge that for victims, taking their own life had been construed by them, as a release from unbearable pain that no other suggested remedy offered:

'... the person having got to the stage where it was all too much for them, for whatever set of reasons ... what we feel sad about is all the things that led up to it but we shouldn't ... be sad for the person who actually did it because for them it was a way out ... it wasn't going to get any worse and hopefully it was going to get better' (O'Keeffe, 2001: 159).

## Client suicides

Twenty-three case studies formed the primary research evidence base in O'Keeffe (2010) that employed Identity Structure Analysis (ISA) (Weinreich and Saunderson, 2003) to investigate clinician survivors' identity development in the aftermath of the suicide of one or more of their clients. Eleven cases concerned clinician survivors of client suicide, six were comparison studies of clinician survivors by proxy, that is clinicians who were colleagues of clinician survivors, and six were control studies.

Space did not here permit a comprehensive analysis of language and terminology issues. However, as mentioned earlier, some progress followed, and was acknowledged in suicidology, when O'Carroll et al. (1996) questioned the validity of language usage in suicidology:

'A number of writers subsequently developed Shneidman's (1985/94) work arguing that 'suicidology finds itself confused and stagnated for want of a nomenclature' (O'Carroll et al., 1996: 237). They demonstrated how legitimate interpretations by clinicians of 'suicide attempt-related injuries' that varied with professional orientation, e.g. liaison psychiatrist, medical sociologist or epidemiologist, could lead to the term 'attempted suicide' meaning so many different things that 'it runs the risk of meaning nothing at all' (O'Carroll et al., 1996: 238). More recently Silverman (2006), Silverman et al. (2007a) and Silverman et al. (2007b), have attempted to take this work forward by proposing a revised nomenclature for the study of suicide and suicidal behaviour (O'Keeffe, 2010: 2, 3).

A glossary of terms used in the 2010 study featured in the doctoral dissertation (O'Keeffe, 2010: Appendix 9). This was included at Annex 1 to this chapter, for information.

In the following section, a sample of three case studies – three clinician survivors were summarised to illustrate the language and terminology used when identity development of clinicians was impacted by, and confronted with client suicide, directly. In these annotated cases, the 'gory death details' were largely excluded and ISA insights were rendered more comprehensible for the general reader. [At Annex 3 below, is a short extract from Black and Weinreich (2000) for readers seeking additional information about identity, identity development and Identity Structure Analysis.]

## Case A1 – Paula

Paula was a counselling director of a rehab unit for men with homelessness issues. Paula's client suicide experience over a year before interview was a very highly influential life event for her. This was evidenced by very high empathetic identifications [i.e. she saw in him many aspects of herself] with 'a client who died by suicide'. She saw within herself in the context of 'life's cruelties' and more so when 'working' with vulnerable clients, many of the characteristics that she perceived when reflecting upon her deceased client. The dual relationship that she participated in when working as a counsellor with the sibling of her deceased client was not without some negativity. It generated countertransference responses containing 'a lot of anger [and] very complicated emotions' connected back to Paula's family suicide experience with her cousin around 15 years before interview.

Her personal and professional life was permeated by problematic identifications with suicidal clients and with 'a suicide survivor' when 'working' and when 'relaxing'. Paula also recognised aspects of herself that were at odds with her values and beliefs. These were evident in her identical problematic identifications with 'a suicide survivor' and with a 'client who recovered after serious suicide attempt', before she became a counsellor: also later in practice before her client's suicide, and when 'enhanced by life's wonders' and when 'working'.

Paula's empathetic identifications, when working with vulnerable clients, with 'a suicide survivor' and with 'a client who died by suicide' pointed towards her distancing herself from her dual suicide survivor status while embracing, albeit subconsciously, key characteristics of her deceased client. This sub-conscious use by her of the psychological defence of denial clouded Paula's appreciation of her suicidal aspirations that were evidenced in how she acknowledged surprise and shock but also respect and admiration for those who acted on suicidal impulses.

Paula experienced areas of uncertainty including that suicide could not be predicted, feeling momentary bouts of psychological discomfort, wondering what life was all about, being totally changed by the suicide of her client, being highly sensitised to the issue of suicide and feeling that the person she was is dead. It was unclear whether Paula's system of values and beliefs was capable of addressing her areas of uncertainty with regard to suicide. She attempted to contend with these by pursuing her aspirational beliefs including her preference for alternative/complementary remedies, continuing to develop her personal values and beliefs, believing grief following suicide was uniquely painful, that each human being was of irreplaceable value and that most suicides are unavoidable and can occur 'out of the blue'.

Paula identified positively with her counselling supervisor in all counselling contexts and with regard to life's 'cruelties' and 'wonders', pointing to an anchor for her in her professional life. Such support was not replicated in non-counselling contexts in her personal life with family members, viz. partner/spouse, mother or father. All in all, Paula's ways of contending with the aftermath of client suicide were concerning not least because of her apparent, ongoing preoccupation with her deceased client, but also because of her own potential vulnerability in relation to suicidal behaviour (O'Keeffe, 2010: 155, 156).

<u>Comment</u>: There were no issues herein related to language or terminology in the context of client suicide and a suicide survivor.

## Case A2 – Basil

Basil was a part-time counsellor whose full time employment was in an educational institution. Basil's life experience until date of interview included several client suicides and he was designated a 'serial clinician survivor'. His most recent client suicide experience occurred up to five years before he upgraded his academic qualifications and commenced full-time employment in an educational setting and part-time activity as a counsellor.

In the current context, Basil's very low self-evaluation indicated failure to achieve his aspirational values and beliefs, in the irreplaceable value of each human when the 'cruelties' of armed conflict [in his past life] devalued his therapeutic pastoral contributions in support of self and vulnerable others. Basil contended successfully with his own propensity towards suicidality when he transitioned from focus upon life's 'cruelties' to its 'wonders', and reappraised himself much as having very high self-evaluation.

Basil's areas of uncertainty, included several aspects of suicide – whether it could be anticipated, whether it was brave or cowardly, whether grief after suicide was uniquely painful, whether depression and suicide were inextricably linked and in relation to the suicide survivor's predicament. He aspired to contend with stress around these problematic considerations by way of his perceived strengths including his above-mentioned belief in the irreplaceability of each human being, the safe expression of emotion, having warm feelings toward others, taking life for granted and being open to human relationships. Basil in his narrative said that he believed it was best for him to focus upon more positive, healthier options for change and progress than the terminal one of suicide.

When working, Basil did not construe himself as 'a suicide survivor' but rather recognised much more strongly the characteristics of his 'partner/spouse' in that identity state even than those of his counselling supervisor. His current academic activities were more dominant in his life than his counselling activities although his experiencing of 'wonders' and 'relaxing' were the predominant identity states by far.

The outcome of Basil's case was an insightful rejoinder to the notion that client suicide, or even serial client suicide, predisposed a counsellor to an indefinite hypervigilant future dominated by awareness of the possibility of client suicide. On the contrary even when he felt 'overwhelmed by life's cruelties' Basil was less 'a suicide survivor', as he perceived himself to be more like his 'mother', or 'a depressed client' or his 'father'.

Basil 'came through' identity determining past experiences that were permeated with 'suicide and the pain of suicide'. He succeeded in resolving difficult and potentially disabling identity conflicts in achieving his aspirations to 'seek and develop new relationships', to relegate 'thinking about people committing suicide' to a lower priority in his cognitive agenda and to deal with existential issues around life and death, first by remaining 'sure of who he is' and then by continuing 'to be the person he was into the foreseeable future'. Stimulating educational opportunities availed of in re-training for a new career met his aspirations to 'continue to develop personal values and beliefs' (O'Keeffe, 2010:156-158).

Comment: There were no obvious issues herein regarding language or terminology in this examination of a serial clinician survivor related to several historical client suicides.

## Case Study A5 – Michael

Michael worked full-time as a counsellor in private practice. He was 'shocked' by loss of his client 'out of the blue' in a unique 'first time in 20 years' of counselling practice client suicide event. In the context of 'life's cruelties', he was regarded as 'well adjusted' and well able to integrate the negative vagaries of client disclosures. This apparent stoicism was overlaid with anger at 'being conned' by his client's suicidal behaviour. The fact that his deceased client was a practitioner counsellor deepened Michael's negative response to being deceived.

Michael's uncertainties were dominated by suicide related issues, including being totally changed by his client's suicide, belief in an inextricable link between depression and suicide, being highly sensitised to the issue of suicide and feeling that grief after a suicide was uniquely painful. He contended with these problematic areas by aspiring to implement his personal strengths including belief in the irreplaceable value of each human being, continuing to develop personal values and beliefs, expressing his emotions safely, having warm feelings for others, believing people he was close to were entirely responsible for their own circumstances. He maintained an almost equally strong aspirational belief, despite his 'out of the blue' experience of client suicide, that suicide could be anticipated by perceptive observation.

Michael's view of self around his client suicide experience and the intensity of his engagement with it evidenced its impact upon his identity in the context of his working life. Although in the context of life's cruelties Michael construed himself as a clinician survivor, there was less in him of 'a suicide survivor' after his client's suicide or when working. The moderate level of his clinician survivor status indicated that while there was something of 'a clinician survivor' in him when he was with vulnerable clients, there was much more in him of a highly regarded person, a professional colleague and a family member.

Michael was predominantly defensive when contending with stress although he may not have been able to cope effectively. There were clues in his highly conflicted identifications with 'father', with suicidal thoughts and with death by suicide before he trained as a counsellor. His defensive stance about his own sense of identity blocked effective assimilation of and learning from his experience of the shock of suicide 'out of the blue' that was reinforced by his anger at being deceived.

Michael's psychological engagement comprised anger that was projected at the female client who took her own life, and also directed towards himself because he allowed himself to believe all was well while she was planning to kill herself. The impact of this suicide led him to review his counselling approach and to re-consider implementing a procedure for formal suicide assessment of all clients (O'Keeffe, 2010: 158,159).

Comment: There were no issues here regarding language use in this abbreviated summary.

## Discussion and Conclusions

The question remains: did I – personally – ever have any difficulty in communicating, recognising, understanding, engaging with or responding to 'suicide' – an intentional self-inflicted death – in my 39+ years from 1982 to date of personal, academic, and psychotherapeutic interest in and study/research into this age-old human behaviour? I do not recall anyone – relative, friend, colleague, client or student – asking me to clarify what I meant by 'suicide' in any of its multifarious manifestations.

However, it seemed that the four articles [O'Carroll et al., 1996; Silverman, 2006; Silverman et al., (2007a & b)] concentrated upon the need for standardisation of the nomenclature for preliminary behaviours – ideation, plan/intention, and attempt - that were understood in suicidology to precede death by suicide and how these might be better defined, confirmed, described, understood and communicated. These topics in my personal experience were unfortunately more often considered after a suicide death event, by grieving survivors and at formal inquests, than otherwise.

Northern Ireland's latest suicide prevention strategy, Protect Life 2(2019-24), made no reference to any of the four language/terminology related articles [O'Carroll et al., 1996; Silverman, 2006; Silverman et al., (2007a & b)]. Indeed it included few references to suicidology literature or research evidence. [See note below.] As such, it represented only the variously informed (or part-informed) opinions of local politicians, their civil servants and possibly some locally based counsellors/ psychotherapists. Clearly, no issue arose therein regarding language or terminology. If there were any, then its appendix 4: 'Glossary of Terms' (Protect Life, 2019: 75-77) addressed these descriptively in 17 titled statements, without any supporting source data, from 'Care Pathways' to 'Zero Suicide Approach'.

[Note: In September 2023, the Department of Health announced the extension of the Protect Life 2 Strategy (2019) for a further three years to the end of 2027, with the potential for an additional extension to 2029. As part of the Strategy extension, the Department agreed to undertake a Review of the Protect Life 2 Action Plan. This Review is to inform the future Action Plan and its implementation. The aims and objectives of the Protect Life 2 Strategy are not being reviewed and will not change at this point. The 61 page Report of the Review, published by the NI Department of Health in September 2024, included 8 recommendations, and an academic review of literature on suicide and suicidal behaviour in N Ireland. The latter review updated a paper, by O'Neill & O'Connor (2020) summarising the evidence published on suicide in populations in NI, since that earlier review was completed (March 2019- April 2024).]

Silverman (2006) concluded his persuasive case for standardisation of language and nomenclature by calling upon suicidologists, across the globe, 'to strive to reduce the subjectivity of labelling behaviours and to develop mutually exclusive operational definitions with clinical examples'. To this end he called for an international summit (Silverman, 2006: 530).

A year later, Silverman and colleagues specified four primary considerations in relation to agreeing universal language and nomenclature for the science of suicidology, as follows:

i) Intelligibility over precision
ii) Practicability over hard science
iii) Consistency over convenience
iv) Retention of commonly used parlance over the invention of new terminology (Silverman et al., 2007b: 275).

As I conclude this chapter, I have learned that an International Summit on Suicide Research was scheduled to be held virtually from October 24-27, 2021. A later event was scheduled to convene in Barcelona, Spain from October 15-18, 2023. Outcomes from these gatherings that might be relevant to this chapter's discussion were available on request from the joint organizers – International Academy of Suicide Research and American Foundation for Suicide Prevention.

## Annex 1 – Glossary, from Appendix 9, PhD Dissertation, (O'Keeffe, 2010)

### Glossary

1 Suicide: variously defined but essentially a person may be deemed to have died by suicide where it can be shown beyond a reasonable doubt and not [merely] on the balance of probabilities (Walsh, 2008) that the deceased acted alone and intended their lethal act against self to have a fatal outcome.

Note: The UK Supreme Court, in November 2020, held that the standard of proof ... required for the determination of the result of an inquest into a death where the question is whether the deceased committed suicide ... is the balance of probabilities. (UK Supreme Court, in the case of James Maughan, deceased, 2020).

1a Suicide ideation: an inner cognitive/affective process during which a person considers suicide as a possible coping strategy without any concrete intention to act out.

1c Suicide intention: may be considered as the next level in a person's cognitive/affective process, when psychache and lethality are predominant affects, and suicide emerges as a likely coping mechanism.

1d Serious suicide attempt: describes an outcome, excluding the death of the person who engages in normally lethal behaviour, where evidence exists that the person fully intended their own death by suicide.

2 Client: an individual who forms a voluntary, psychotherapeutic, counselling relationship with a clinician.

3 Counselling: an ethically structured, psychological process within which a clinician facilitates a client in addressing change issues raised by the client.

4 Clinician: a psychological counsellor, counselling psychologist, psychotherapist or other qualified counselling practitioner.

5 Client suicide: the death by suicide of an individual who was a clinician's current or former client.

6a Survivor syndrome: a pattern of reactions observed in those who remain alive after experiencing a traumatic event during which others lost their lives (Reber and Reber, 2001:728).

6b Survivor guilt: a deep sense of guilt or culpability [sometimes] experienced by those who remained alive following a catastrophic event which took the lives of many others. Observed in those who survived the Holocaust during WW2 or following subsequent wars, famines, earthquakes, fires or similar major disasters or calamities. Part of the sense of guilt or self-blame derived from a feeling that they did not do enough to save others who perished: another part derives from feelings of being unworthy relative to those who died (Reber and Reber, 2001: 728).

7 Suicide survivor: an individual who remains alive following the suicide death of someone with whom they had a significant relationship or emotional bond (AAS Clinician Survivor Task Force, 2008).

8a Clinician survivor: a clinician who has experienced one or more client suicides (AAS Clinician Survivor Task Force, 2008).

8b Clinician survivor (by proxy): Based upon Calhoun et al. (1982/84), current research designates the term 'clinician survivor (by proxy)' to acknowledge and identify the coincidental status of colleague clinician(s) who, although not clinician survivors per se, share a professional relationship with a clinician survivor.

9 Client suicide survivor: as for 8a above

10 Non-clinician: an individual who does not engage in formal psychotherapeutic relationships with clients or patients.

11 Non-client: an individual not currently or formerly a client, e.g. family member, personal friend or work colleague.

12 Family suicide survivor: a person, including a clinician, who experiences the loss by suicide of a family member, personal friend or work colleague.

**Annex 2** – The GUBU event of 1982

This called to mind former Taoiseach of the Irish Republic Charles Haughey's employment of the four metaphorical descriptors during his second term as Irish Taoiseach (Wikipedia, 2021b). At a press conference in 1982, Haughey was responding to the revelation of the infamous, albeit not illegal, circumstances surrounding the close relationship that his then Irish Attorney General Patrick Connelly, had with Malcolm McArthur, who following his two capital crimes, was a guest in Connelly's house. McArthur was later convicted of one murder but – for legal reasons – was not tried for a related second homicide. Haughey's remark was to become legend for notorious Irish public scandals:

"a bizarre happening, an unprecedented situation, a grotesque situation, an almost unbelievable mischance" (Dwyer, 1987, in Wikipedia, 2021a).

The above-mentioned double killer received a life sentence. McArthur was released on licence in 2012 after serving 30 years imprisonment (Wikipedia, 2021a)

**Annex 3** – Identity Structure Analysis – extract from Black, S. and Weinreich, P. (2000: 2-4)

## Identity Structure Analysis

Identity Structure Analysis (ISA) is a theoretical orientation used to analyse identity formation developed by Weinreich (1980, 1983, 1986, 1989). ISA explores the identity of individuals in relation to their social world. "Weinreich's perspective on identity views the person as a total entity, possessing a sense of self and identity situated in time and developing over time, through interaction and identification with others" (Phoenix, 1994, p.44). ISA is "an open-ended metatheoretical framework of concepts and postulates about content, structure and process relating to identity" (Weinreich, 1985a, 1986a). ISA draws upon concepts in the psychodynamic approach, social comparison theory, reference group theory, symbolic interactionism, personal construct theory and cognitive-affective consistency theory. Weinreich submits the following definition of identity based on those of Erikson (1963) and Laing (1961) that emphasises continuity and gives central place to the process of construal:

"One's identity is defined as the totality of one's self-construal, in which how one construes oneself in the present expresses the continuity between how one construes oneself as one was in the past and how one construes oneself as one aspires to be in the future" (Weinreich, 1969, 1980, 1989a).

ISA is operationalised for empirical work using customised identity instruments with the aid of IDEX for Windows (V3.0) (Weinreich and Ewart, 1999) (IDEX = identity exploration) which incorporates the above theoretical positions, and can either be presented as a pencil and paper instrument or be completed at a computer. ISA parameters are formulated algebraically with explicitly defined psychological concepts, for some of which the algorithms use Boolean algebra. "One of the strengths of this approach lies in the fact that the psychological concepts elucidating structure and process of identity are pre-defined and do not use crude post-hoc interpretations" (Weinreich, 1999).

Within ISA, the concept of identification is explicated in two modes of identification: empathetic identification and role model identification. "Empathetic identification with another refers to the degree of perceived similarity between the characteristics, whether good or bad, of that other and oneself" (Weinreich, 1989a, p.52). On the other hand, "one's role model identification refers to the degree to which one might wish to emulate another when the other is a positive role model (idealistic identification), or dissociate from the other when a negative role model (contra identification)" (Weinreich, 1989a, p.52). Weinreich further elaborates the distinction between the two modes: "...the role model identification mode refers to one's orientations in terms of aspirations and dissociations (the mode of wishing to emulate and wishing to dissociate to varying degrees), and the empathetic identification mode, situated from moment to moment in differing social contexts, refers to the de facto state of affinity with another of the current moment (the mode of being as the one or the other to varying degrees, at this moment now, or in this or that context, or doing this or that activity, and so on)" (Weinreich, 1989b, p.224).

Conflicted identifications occur when one simultaneously sees oneself as similar to another and recognises that other as having characteristics from which one wishes to dissociate. In relation to process postulates concerning attempted resolution of identification conflicts and the emergence of new identifications, ISA presents the following postulates (Weinreich, 1989a, p.53):

Postulate 1 – When one's identifications with others are conflicted, one attempts to resolve the conflicts, thereby inducing re-evaluations of self in relation to the others within the limitations of one's currently existing value system.

Postulate 2 – When one forms further identifications with newly encountered individuals, one broadens one's value system and establishes a new context for one's self-definition, thereby initiating a reappraisal of self and others which is dependent on fundamental changes in one's value system.

These process postulates are of direct importance in the context of this research where the resolution of past conflicts and the possible generation of new current conflicts are tracked as respondents appraise themselves in relation to the impact of a traumatic incident on the respondent's sense of identity.

In the ISA definition of identity above, a central place is given to the person's construal of self. Constructs, which are cognitive in form, are used to evaluate the characteristics of self and others. Affective associations are considered in the evaluative connotations of the cognitive constructs both in terms of the positive values (aspirations) and negative values (those from which one wishes to dissociate). Structural pressure is an ISA index that estimates the extent to which individuals consistently attribute favourable and unfavourable characteristics to particular entities. In relation to cognitive affective consistency and the structural pressure on constructs, ISA presents the following postulates (Weinreich 1989a, pp. 55-56):

Postulate 1 - When the net structural pressure on one of a person's constructs is high and positive, the evaluative connotations associated with it are stably bound.

Postulate 2 – When the net structural pressure on a construct is low, or negative as a result of strong negative pressures counteracting positive ones, the evaluative connotations associated with the constructs are conflicted: the construct in question is an arena of stress.

Postulate 3 – When the net structural pressure on a construct is low as a result of weak positive and negative pressures, the construct in question is without strong evaluative connotations.

In the context of this research, as ISA identifies the strength and intensity of one's core evaluative dimensions of identity, the professional orientation of respondents is examined in relation to both their core and conflicted evaluative dimensions of identity.

[FOOTNOTE - Coherent, consistent opposition to the universal 'suicide prevention' movement was articulated, albeit as a voice crying in the wilderness, in the extensive writings of the late psychiatrist Dr Thomas S. Szasz, whose existentialist philosophy held that each human being of sound mind, has a 'right to die', as regards when, where and how they wished to choose to exercise that right (Wikipedia, 2021c). Dr Edwin S. Shneidman did not accept in any way whatsoever Thomas Szasz's arguments – except to agree to differ wholeheartedly during a five hour debate, almost half a century ago, at the University of California (San Francisco) on 29 April 1972 between the two, in the presence Dr Jerome Motto, Ms Charlotte P Ross, Dr Robert Litman, Dr George Pickett and Dr Michael Scrivens (Ross, 1972/2021):

'The debate pitted Dr. Edwin S. Shneidman's views that one must always intervene in a suicidal crisis "on the side of life," even if that intervention includes "temporarily suspending one's civil rights" via involuntary hospitalization, against Dr. Thomas S. Szasz's views that "suspending one's civil rights is the job of totalitarian governments — not physicians and therapists." (Ross, 1972/2021)

More recently however, there were reports of descriptions of non-suicidal individuals who, being terminally ill and near death, appeared to 'chose when to die' in relation to events external to them, such as the arrival of a loved one:

'Hospice and palliative care clinicians routinely see cases in which people who are nearing life's end seem to will themselves to hold on until a certain point, after which time they let go. And while some people hold on long enough to see a loved one, others seem to do the opposite, clinging to life until they are left alone. Dr. Toby Campbell, an oncologist and palliative care specialist at the University of Wisconsin, Madison, said patients tend not to have a lot of control at the very end of their lives. But that doesn't mean they don't have any. "People in end-of-life care wouldn't bat an eye if you asked if they think people can, to a certain degree, control those final moments," Campbell said. "We'd all say, 'Well, yeah. Sure.' But it's inexplicable." If these well-timed deaths are anything but coincidental, medical scientists appear unlikely to be able to provide an explanation anytime soon. A body of scientific literature called "the will to live near death" explores questions at the fringe of this topic, but the research focuses more squarely on how one's will to live might affect life expectancy. When it comes to extending one's life by hours, seemingly through sheer will, Campbell believes the dying "probably have some kind of hormonal stimulus that's just a driver to keep them going. Then, when whatever event they were waiting for happens, the stimulus goes away, and there must be some kind of relaxing into it that then allows them to die.'" (Tedeschi, 2016).

Szasz's arguments, in relation inter alia to untreatable, unbearable pain and/or near-death terminal illness, were currently evidenced in the drive towards legalising euthanasia, in some or all of its various manifestations, in UK/Ireland (Szasz, 1999).]

**Myth:** (fictitious popular idea) If society developed high-level rational problem solving skills across their populations, much suicidal behaviour could be eliminated.

**Fallacy:** (misleading argument) Deaths by suicide globally will be reduced by reforming the language and terminology employed in addressing suicidal behaviour.

## References

AAS Clinician Survivor Task Force (2008) Formerly hosted by American Association of Suicidology; now known as Coalition of Clinician Survivors. Accessed on 18 March 2024 at https://www.cliniciansurvivor.org

Black, S. and Weinreich, P. (2000) An exploration of counselling identity in counsellors who deal with trauma. Traumatology. Vol 6 (1), p25-40. Accessed on 31 October 2021 at https://journals.sagepub.com/toc/tmta/6/1

Calhoun, L.G., Selby, J.W. and Selby, L.E. (1982) The psychological aftermath of suicide: An analysis of current evidence. Clinical Psychology Review

De Leo, D., Burgis, S., Bertolote, J. M., Kirkhof, A. J. F.M. and Bille-Brahe, U. (2006) Definitions of suicidal behaviour: Lessons learned from the WHO/EURO Multicentre Study. Crisis, 27, 4-15

DMR-Dark My Road (2008) Penacide or suicide: make the pain go away. A Lutheran view of depression. 4 December 2008. Accessed on 12 October 2021 at https://www.darkmyroad.org/2008/12/penacide-or-suicide-make-the-pain-go-away/

Douglas, J. D. (1967) The social meanings of suicide. Princeton, MA: Princeton University Press

Durkheim, E. (1897/2002) Suicide – a study in sociology. London: Routledge

Dwyer, T. R. (1987) Charlie, the political biography of Charles Haughey. Chapter 12. Irish Books and Media.

Dyer, T. (2020) Cross addiction. Accessed on 5 November 2021 at https://www.drugrehab.com/addiction/cross-addictions/

Graber, G. C. (1981) The rationality of suicide. In S. E. Wallace & A. Eser (eds.), Suicide and Euthanasia: the rights of personhood. Knoxville, TN: University of Tennessee Press

Hickey, G. and Kipping, C. (1996) A multi-stage approach to the coding of data from open-ended questions. Nurse Researcher Vol. 4 No. 1 (p81-91)

International Summit (2021) International Summit on Suicide Research – online – scheduled from October 24-27, 2021 [and later in Barcelona, Spain from October 15-18, 2023]. Accessed on 22 October 2021 at https://suicideresearchsummit.org/about-us/

Jordan, J.R. & McIntosh, J.L. (eds.) (2011) Grief After Suicide: Understanding the Consequences and Caring for the Survivors. New York, NJ: Routledge, Taylor & Francis Group.

McIntosh, J.L. (1985) Research on suicidology: a bibliography. Westport, CT: Greenwood Press.

Jordan, J.R. & McIntosh, J.L. (2011) Suicide Bereavement: Why Study Survivors of Suicide Loss. In J.R. Jordan & J.L. McIntosh, Grief after suicide: Understanding the Consequences and Caring for the Survivors (Chapter 1, page 7). New York, NY: Routledge, Taylor & Francis Group.

McKenzie, S.J., J. L. (1995) The dictionary of the Bible. New York, NY: Simon and Shuster

O'Carroll, P. W., Berman, A. L., Maris, R. W., Moscicki, E. K., Tanney, B. L. and Silverman, M. M. (1996) Beyond the tower of Babel: a nomenclature for suicidology. Suicide and Life-threatening Behaviour, Fall, 1996, 26, 3.

O'Keeffe, P. (2001) Suicidology, counselling and identity exploration: an investigation of postvention strategies for suicide survivors. Unpublished Master's Degree (MSc) dissertation. Jordanstown, Co Antrim, N. Ireland: Ulster University

O'Keeffe, P. (2010) Client suicide and clinician identity: an investigation of identity development in clinician survivors of client suicide. Unpublished doctoral (PhD) dissertation. Jordanstown, Co Antrim, N Ireland: Ulster University

O'Neill, S. and O'Connor, R. C. (2020) Suicide in Northern Ireland: epidemiology, risk factors and prevention. Lancet Psychiatry, 7(6), pp. 538-546

O'Neill, S. and Bond, N. (2024) Updated review of literature on suicide and suicidal behaviour in Northern Ireland. pp. 46-60. In Protect Life 2 – Review (2024) Action Plan: Report and Recommendations. September 2024. N Ireland Department of Health. Stormont, Belfast, N Ireland

Padmanathan, P., Biddle, L., Hall, K., Scowcroft, E., Nielsen, E. and Knipe, D. (2019) Language use and suicide: an online cross-sectional survey. Public Library of Science (PLoS), 14(6): e0217473. 13 June 2019. Accessed on 11 October 2021 at https://doi.org/10.1371/journal.pone.0217473

Protect Life 2 (2019) A strategy for preventing suicide and self-harm in Northern Ireland 2019-2024. 19 September 2019. Department of Health. An Roinne Slainte / Mannystie O Poustie. Stormont, Belfast, N Ireland

Protect Life 2 – Review (2024) Action Plan: Report and Recommendations. September 2024. N Ireland Department of Health. Stormont, Belfast, N Ireland

Reber, A. and Reber, E. (2001) Dictionary of Psychology. 3rd Edition, Penguin/Viking, London.

Ross, C. P. (1972/2021) A longstanding debate. Accessed on 10 October 2021 at https://charlotteswebsite.live/a-longstanding-debate/

Shanahan, L., Hill, S. N., Gaydosh, L. M., Steinhoff, A., Costello, E. J., Dodge, K. A., Mullan Harris, K. and Copeland, W. E. (2019) Does despair really kill? A roadmap for an evidence-based answer. June, 2019. AJPH, Vol 109, No 6

Shneidman, E. S. (1985/94) Definition of suicide. Northvale, NJ: Jason Aronson Inc

Silverman, M. M. (2006) The language of suicidology. Suicide and Life-threatening Behaviour, October, 2006, 36, 5.

Silverman, M. M., Berman, A. L., Sanddal, M. D., O'Carroll, P.W., and Joiner, Jr., T. E. (2007a) Rebuilding the tower of Babel: a revised nomenclature for the study of suicide and suicidal behaviours. Part 1: Background, Rationale and Methodology. Suicide and Life-threatening Behaviour, June 2007, 37, 3.

Silverman, M. M., Berman, A. L., Sanddal, M. D., O'Carroll, P.W., and Joiner, Jr., T. E. (2007b) Rebuilding the tower of Babel: a revised nomenclature for the study of suicide and suicidal behaviours. Part 2: Suicide-related ideations, communications and behaviours. Suicide and Life-threatening Behaviour, June 2007, 37, 3.

Szasz, T. E. (1999) Fatal freedom: the ethics and politics of suicide. Westport, CT: Praeger Publishers

Tedeschi, R. (2016) Can sheer willpower keep patients alive in their dying hours? 23 September 2016. Accessed on 11 October 2021 at https://www.statnews.com/2016/09/23/end-of-life-dying-willpower/

UK Supreme Court (2020) R (on application of Maughan) (Appellant) v Her Majesty's Senior Coroner for Oxfordshire (Respondent) [2020] UKSC 46. On appeal from [2019] EWCA Civ 809– Press Summary 13 November 2020. For full judgment: http://supremecourt.uk/decided-cases/index.html

Wallace, S. E. & Eser, A. (eds.) (1981) Suicide and Euthanasia: the rights of personhood. Knoxville, TN: University of Tennessee Press

Walsh, D. (2008) Suicide, attempted suicide and prevention in Ireland and elsewhere. Dublin: Health Research Board.

Weber, Max (1994) Content Analysis, cited in G.Hickey and C. Kipping (1996) A multi-stage approach to the coding of data from open-ended questions. Nurse Researcher Vol. 4 No. 1 (p81-91)

Weinreich, P. and Saunderson, W. (Eds.) (2003) Analysing Identity: Cross-cultural, Societal and Clinical Contexts. New York, NY: Routledge

Wikipedia (2021a) GUBU. 22 September 2021. Accessed on 2 October 2021 at https://en.wikipedia.org/wiki/GUBU

Wikipedia (2021b) Charles Haughey. 26 September 2021. Accessed on 2 October 2021 at https://en.wikipedia.org/wiki/Charles_Haughey

Wikipedia (2021c) Right to die. 7 October 2021. Accessed on 8 October 2021 at https://en.wikipedia.org/wiki/Right_to_die

Wikipedia (2021d) 1981 Irish Hunger Strike. Accessed on 11 October 2021 at https://en.wikipedia.org/wiki/1981_Irish_hunger_strike

* * *

# Chapter 16
# Suicide – Education for understanding: an approach to reduction and prevention

**Introduction**

'There are two ways to think about education: either as a means or as a lifestyle. Getting a qualification in plumbing or bricklaying is a respectable thing. But some people are uninspired by that kind of education. In contrast, education as a lifestyle means getting into the notion of learning and of transforming your thought patterns by reflecting on other people's experiences and reaching for the wealth available to us through books' (George 'The Poet' Mpanga, cited in Thorpe, 2021).

It seemed crystal clear to me, as Alvarez (1971/74: 14) suggested 50 odd years ago, that 'nearly everybody has his (sic) own ideas about suicide'. That may not be so surprising, since each of us, to a significant degree, is the sum of our life experiences, from womb to tomb. And so, when we first heard about it, as a human behaviour, it was most likely on the occasion of our earliest programming and conditioning in the family, in a place of worship, and/or at school.

For me, a good Catholic boy then 6 or 7 years of age (1948), at primary school I learned about Judas Iscariot, the betrayer of Jesus, who was condemned in these words: 'It would be better for him that he had never been born' (Matthew 26.23). And that later Judas was seized with remorse: 'I have sinned for I have betrayed innocent blood', returned the betrayal bounty of 'thirty pieces of silver' to the High Priests in the temple, and 'went away and hanged himself' (Matthew 27.3-5). I cannot recall, however, how either Miss McCartney (St Anthony's

Primary, Willowfield, Belfast) or Mr Cologhan (St Malachy's Christian Brothers Primary School, Oxford Street, Belfast) told that tragically sad story, but I retain a hazy, mental, pictorial representation, presumably imagined, of poor Judas's death scene that's lodged in my memory, its origin unknown.

Any further personal experiential 'education for understanding' suicide was delayed until over 50 years later when I examined a family suicide to complete a Research Methods module for a University diploma course (2000). During that interregnum, we experienced several family deaths, including two that were reported in local print media and were the subjects of public inquests. Little was learned from those catastrophic, traumatising losses (1982, 1989) as we endured the deep wound of a special scar (Wertheimer, 1991) twice over. Preoccupied as our society was then with lethal inter-communal strife, my personal efforts to engage with learning about suicide did not commence in an organised way until a fragile peace agreement emerged (GFA, 1998) that coincided with my formal university postgraduate counselling diploma studies.

## Education for understanding suicide – a way forward

Education for understanding suicide should at face-value benefit from what respected writers and researchers have said about their understanding of human self-destruction, at least since Durkheim. We know Shneidman's view that 'postvention is prevention' was key to the growth and development of the practice of caring for survivor-victims, or suicide survivors – that is: those bereaved by suicide who had a significant relationship or emotional bond with the deceased (Shneidman, 1973: 33-34). It was believed that suicide survivors were at higher risk of taking their own lives than persons not so bereaved: 'Exposure to the loss of a loved one to suicide increases the chances of suicidal thinking and behaviour in the person exposed' (Jordan, 2020: 2).

Perhaps at the outset it was best to define our terms. Education, as understood by O'Conner (1957/63: 5), was:

A set of techniques for imparting knowledge, skills and attitudes

A set of theories which purport to explain or justify the use of these techniques

A set of values or ideals [aims] embodied and expressed in the purposes for which knowledge, skills and attitudes are imparted and so directing the amounts and types of training that is given.

It was clear, in relation to education in O'Conner's terms, that techniques, theories and aims did not fit well in relation to the study of suicide, aka suicidology, not least because suicidology was rarely disassociated from therapeutic endeavours related to 'suicide prevention'.

In Western cultures, educational methods could include formal lectures, group discussions, class presentations, tutorials, essays, the study of longer written works, i.e. research dissertations and books, and more recently access to a plethora of internet-facilitated communications of varying relevance or credibility. Assessment for quality assurance of accredited courses of study was exercised in colleges and universities by way of awarding recognised certificates, diplomas and degrees.

In Northern Ireland, neither of the two universities, the Queen's University Belfast (QUB) nor Ulster University (UU), currently offered taught, third level courses in suicidology (Personal communication, 2021). This did not dissuade academics in both establishments from publishing valuable, occasionally radical, contributions on suicide-related issues in academic journals from multiple perspectives, including inter alia the NI civil conflict (aka 'The Troubles'), social sciences, sociology, psychology, nursing, mental health, public health, statistics, law and justice.

In most of these endeavours, it could be surmised that writers would necessarily deliberate on suicide within the limits of their professional disciplines, having chosen related terms of reference that met their university's ethical requirements. Their earlier education and training, if any, in the highly complex world of human suicide, prior to writing about suicide within their bounded, academic disciplines and locations, would remain to a large extent undisclosed and unknown. It might not be unreasonable, however, to suggest that their pre-academic interest in, or knowledge of suicide (with notable exceptions, viz. Dr Mike Tomlinson, and Dr Siobhan O'Neill) would not often reach beyond personal, often tragic family experience and/or run-of-the-mill media reports.

What seems clear is that, whatever the underlying rationale for Northern Ireland universities decisions to exclude suicidology from their third level course curricula, there was no obstacle to the pursuit of suicidological studies as long as these met their organisational objectives and ethical criteria. The question of a vacuum regarding third level studies remained unanswered, indeed unexplored, giving rise in this writer's mind, to the idea that a particular form of undeclared, perhaps unacknowledged taboo and/or stigma may remain unaddressed. On the other hand, it may more simply be explained by lack of interest from undergraduate students.

Next, the relationship that has developed between suicidology, suicide, suicide research, and suicide prevention was reviewed to highlight their connections and overlaps.

**Suicidology and Oncology**

Although far from analogous, the study of cancer, aka oncology offered insights into the study of suicide, aka suicidology. A reasonable assumption existed that understanding cancer may not be seen primarily as preventative: ultimately, of course, understanding should inform preventative activity. In a short article a UK cancer expert, Michael Stratton, stated that in the aftermath of new research findings: 'current understanding of [cancerous] tumour formation was inadequate ... we will have to rethink our ideas about the way in which some cancers develop' (McKie, 2021). It was beyond dispute that education for understanding cancer, viz. oncology, offered a medical student a way into engaging with a complex world containing a multiplicity of causes, effects and potential outcomes. A quality of uniqueness was rendered at the outset to each cancer diagnosis. Thus the need arose for an individualised, idiosyncratic prognosis and treatment for each patient, that may or may not prove to be successful, however that notion was defined. Clearly a high level of clinical understanding was essential for informed post-diagnosis treatment.

As partial comparators, it was clear that whereas 'suicidology' seemed enmeshed within 'suicide prevention', cancer and cancer prevention, i.e. to avoid a cancer diagnosis, were perceived as distinct if related entities: the former was a potentially lethal, multifactorial disease morass, while the latter appeared to be a conjunction, inter alia, of genetic inheritance, lifestyle choice and happenstance. [Note that cancer treatment, e.g. chemotherapy, was here considered distinct from cancer prevention.] Cancer research could be considered to be integral to oncology: in a similar way perhaps, suicide studies and suicide research might be designated more appropriately as suicidology, with suicide prevention, as such, identified as a related, but parallel activity or entity. Clearly treatment, e.g. by way of psychotherapy, of individuals who survived serious, but failed suicide attempts, could be considered distinct from suicide prevention. However, psychotherapists' insights that might emanate from treating suicide attempters could, in principle, perhaps as a byproduct, inform and even reform existing approaches to suicide prevention.

**Disease and Behaviour**

It was important to distinguish between a disease, such as cancer, that involved deleterious, potentially lethal physical changes to the human body, and a behaviour, such as suicide, that involved the outworking of a decision process within the mind/brain of a potential victim. This fundamental difference did not discourage the American Psychiatric Association (APA) from ambitiously and somewhat illogically, attempting to label 'suicidal behaviour' as a mental disorder for inclusion in their burgeoning DSM 5 manual of pathological symptoms.

All suicides could be considered and seen as suicide attempts, most of which did not result in death. A study by Owens and House (1994) estimated that about 25% of suicides were preceded by potentially lethal but non-fatal, self-harm, aka a failed suicide attempt, in the previous 12 months. It was believed that, although a suicide attempt by firearm, viz. a bullet to the brain, was almost certainly lethal, some other suicide attempt methods were neither fatal nor conclusive, e.g. self-poisoning by intentional overdose. In Northern Ireland, one third of suicide deceased 'had a previous recorded suicide attempt', indicating that failed suicide attempts were a major risk factor (O'Neill, S. et al., 2016). This pointed us towards consideration of whether repeated suicidal behaviour could be considered to be a pathological addiction.

## Pathological addictions

An addictive behaviour was commonly understood to be an action or activity engaged in repeatedly and compulsively by an addict to secure a perceived beneficial change. A broader definition followed:

'According to Science Direct, behavioural addictions are defined as, "an intense desire to repeat some action that is pleasurable or perceived to improve wellbeing or capable of alleviating some personal distress." What classifies some behaviours as addictive is the difficultly those affected have with stopping or reducing their participation in it. Some motivating factors for behavioural addictions include the perception of temporary decreased depression and anxiety making it a seemingly logical way to achieve calm or happiness. For example, gambling addiction lights up similar parts of the brain as some drugs, providing a dopamine rush to the user or player' (Murray, 2021).

What caused a behavioural addiction to become pathological was the likelihood, or risk, that it involved an action or activity that could lead to one or more adverse outcomes, including death. The question was whether repeated suicide attempts could be considered to be a pathologically addictive behaviour. A long-standing lacuna in the literature was recently filled by Blasco-Fontecilla et al. (2016) in their development of the work of Mynatt (2000), whose case-study based research examined the hypothesis that respondents' repeated 'suicide attempts were an addiction, similar to their addictions to alcohol and drugs'. The former writers' work consisted of an online literature review of suicidal behaviour, self-harming addiction, and 'major repeaters', defined as individuals with at least five lifetime suicide attempts. They concluded that their review 'suggests that both non-suicidal self-injury (NSSI) and suicidal behaviour (SB) can be conceptualised as addictions' (Blasco-Fontecilla et al., 2016).

# Education for understanding suicide – what the literature was saying

Thus, exploration of relevant knowledge, skills and attitudes, might reasonably point our discussion towards further consideration of what some modern writers have said about education for understanding suicide, following Durkheim (1897/2002). Our objective may therefore be to achieve a more informed position for examining education's potential for reducing the incidence of suicide, with its prevention as a more realistic longer term goal. Space restrictions meant that our brief discussion could consider only a fraction of the available and relevant voluminous literature. Time and space limitations also meant our consideration of these writers' opinions was sometimes restricted to their accessible online publications.

Ten selected writers were chosen from acknowledged expert suicidologists, including for example, Edwin S. Shneidman and Thomas S. Szasz, and then, randomly, from members of past/current editorial committees of four major academic journals: Suicide and Life-threatening Behaviour; Crisis – the journal of crisis intervention and suicide prevention; Suicidology-online and Archives of Suicide Research. The following individuals (underlines added) constitute the remaining sample of eight (8) out of a total 22 listed suicidology practitioners, who were recognised by their peers as global influencers in the development of suicidology, the scientific study of human self-destruction:

Suicide and Life-threatening Behaviour: Thomas Joiner; Morton Silverman; Ronald W. Maris; Craig Bryan; and Rory O'Connor.

Crisis – journal of crisis intervention and suicide prevention: Jane Pirkis; Maria A. Oquendo; Ella Arensman; Diego de Leo; and Keith Hawton.

Suicidology Online: Marco Sarchiapone; Erminia Colucci; Antoon Leenaars; David Lester and Paul Yip.

Archives of Suicide Research: Barbara Stanley; David Jobes; Maurizio Pompili; Kees van Heeringen and Thomas Niederkrotenthaler.

Also: Onja Grad and Heidi Hjelmeland. (Total 22)

## Edwin Shneidman

Robert Frost held that 'poetry is a way of taking life by the throat' (Frost, 1960). Shneidman spent his life in the study of suicidology, as an outsider while psychiatry grasped hold of suicide, ensuring that mental health (however defined) and self-destruction became cause and effect, excluding and/or minimising other potential explanations or paradigms. Shneidman pushed back against the psychiatric view that suicidal behaviour usually represented a symptom of serious mental illness for which treatment, including hospitalisation, medication and – perhaps – psychotherapy might be appropriate (Harding,2009). The problem for Shneidman was that he did not value the Diagnostic and Statistical Manual of Mental Disorders (DSM-5, 5th Edition, APA):

'Shneidman has a critical view of the established "facts" that almost all people who die by suicide suffer one or more mental disorder(s), and the causal link between the two. This he stated is a myth. Shneidman had a rather critical view of such reductionism. Shneidman has, in fact, always held a reasonable or unreasonable, supercilious view of the DSM. The DSM and its various revisions are seen as the end of wisdom' (Leenaars, 2010: 14).

This demonstrated, in my opinion, a major and deeply embedded block to establishing and carving out a realistic role for popular courses of education in suicidology, outwith the overwhelmingly suffocating dominance of psychiatry.

Shneidman's publications charted a 43 year period (1965-2008) that represented the beginnings and development of the scientific study of suicide, known as 'suicidology'. This field of knowledge was recognised primarily because it appeared to offer a social good: the reduction of the incidence of self-destruction by preventative processes rooted in understanding the phenomenon itself. In spite of his innovative, ground-breaking insights and their practical application in therapeutic engagement with persons at risk of suicide, Shneidman's suicidology was never accepted by academe as other than an adjunct to self-standing, bounded, knowledge-based disciplines including philosophy, psychology, psychiatry, sociology, anthropology, and theology.

A review of a short book, edited by Lester (2019), about future prospects for suicidology, surmised that 'some scholars have declared that we have reached our limits in understanding and predicting suicide'. Views were also cited 'that there is no empirical reason to believe that predictors of suicide exist, there is no theoretical foundation for believing that risk factors exist, and there is evidence that suicide may be predictably unpredictable!' (Lester, 2019).

So what was Shneidman's view regarding education for understanding suicide?

'As a researcher, theoretician, lecturer and author, he helped establish the study of suicide as an interdisciplinary field and devised many concepts now widely accepted' (Dicke, 2009).

A modest man, Shneidman, according to a professor of education, J. R. Rogers, proposed a humanitarian approach to suicide, rather than its medicalisation:

'A proponent of the psychological and sociological causes of suicide, Shneidman argued that suicide is not a drive towards death, but an escape from unbearable pain; for him, the therapist's goal was not to forbid suicide, but to work with the suicidal person to find other ways to ease their pain."Ed really worked to humanise the issue of suicide, to consider what's happening psychologically with folks who are suicidal, rather than neurochemically or otherwise", says James R Rogers, professor of education at the University of Akron in Ohio, USA, and the current President of the American Association of Suicidology, founded by Shneidman in 1968' (Harding, 2009).

## Thomas Szasz

Thomas Szasz was an archetypically lateral thinker whose views differed radically from almost all of his colleagues in psychiatry. 'He denounced any incursions on civil liberties in the name of psychiatry' distinguishing between compulsory and voluntary psychiatric treatment, asserting that the former was 'patronising and infantalising' while the latter must always acknowledge and respect the patient's right to give informed consent (Stadlen, 2012). Two of his 30+ books – 'The Myth of Mental Illness' (1961) and 'Suicide Prohibition: The Shame of Medicine' (2011) – represent fully and very fairly Szasz's existential and libertarian way of understanding suicide. In the former text, and for the next half-century:

'Szasz argued that "mental health" and "mental illness" are alienated, pseudo-scientific, pseudo-medical terms. He insisted that illness, in the modern, scientific sense, applies only to bodies, not to minds – except as a metaphor. A bodily organ, the heart, can be diseased, but to be heartsick or homesick, though real enough, is not to be medically, but only metaphorically, ill. Equally metaphorical, said Szasz, were such supposed mental illnesses as hysteria, obsessional neurosis, schizophrenia and depression' (Stadlen, 2012).

In keeping with that opinion, Szasz regarded suicide as a human right, and thus held that suicide prevention – by way of 'a vast bureaucratic legal-psychiatric enterprise' (Szasz, 2011: xii) – involving coercive psychiatric intervention, was a deprivation of that right:

'Laws that enable some people to lock up some other people whose behaviour they find upsetting have nothing to do with health, medicine or treatment. They are a system of extralegal social controls without the due-process safeguards of the criminal justice system. Calling the arrangement "suicide prevention" is deception and self-deception. The noncoercive prevention of death may, depending on circumstances, be a noble end. The coercive prohibition of it is, a priori, ignoble and unworthy of modern people in secular societies' (Szasz, 2011: xiii).

Szasz's family escaped in 1938 to the US when his homeland Hungary sided with the Nazis. He was a profoundly humane, compassionate man with a deeply held conviction about human freedom. He graduated in physics and medicine, trained in psychoanalysis, completed military service, and, as an educator, became a professor in psychiatry. He said he was 'viscerally upset' by 'the dehumanised language of psychiatry and psychoanalysis', but made sure that he never had to treat an involuntary patient (Stadlen, 2012):

'Szasz was an atheist, but he said his atheism was "religious". He called human beings ineffable, in the sense that they could not be ultimately described by a system or a science. Psychotherapy was likewise ineffable – a secular form of the "cure of souls". Psychotherapists were more like rabbis or priests than like medical doctors. This required absolute confidentiality, as in the confessional. It was no business of third parties or the state' (Stadlen, 2012).

I have not located many present-day writers who accepted Szasz's argument, but I remain open to readers' references.

## Thomas Joiner

Dr Thomas Joiner, described as 'an American academic psychologist and expert on suicide' (Wikipedia, 2021) was a survivor of his father's death by suicide. This sad loss was the pivotal event that pointed him towards a career in suicidology. His book 'Why people die by suicide' (2005) presented what to some, was an over-simplified conclusion to 100+ years of post-Durkheim suicide theory. This opinion posited that suicide desire is the inevitable consequence of a mental disorder, associated with a tripartite nexus of essential conditions within the victim's psyche: burdensomeness, isolation and lethal capability. This afterwards transitioned into the Interpersonal Theory of Suicide (Joiner et al., 2009). Dr Joiner edits the American Association of Suicidology's (AAS) house journal, Suicide and Life-threatening Behaviour. In this influentially decisive role, it has been alleged that he excluded idiographic/case study qualitative research articles about suicide, on the basis that such material was non-scientific, by comparison (presumably) with statistically driven quantitative research work (Joiner, 2011).

As an educator, Thomas worked as a professor of psychology at Florida State University, with the university's students on relevant courses. He has led many seminars on suicide around the world, has written, edited and/or published a significant number of suicide-related articles and contributed key chapters to important suicide-themed studies in addition to his third book 'Myths about Suicide' (2010).

## Rory O'Connor

Dr Rory O'Connor, an academic psychologist, was represented on his employer's website, University of Glasgow, as holding the Chair in Health Psychology (Psychology: Mental Health and Well-being), Director

(Suicidal Behaviour Laboratory), Associate (Institute of Neuroscience & Psychology), and Associate (School of Medicine, Dentistry & Nursing).

I cannot find a Wikipedia entry for Dr O'Connor.

Dr O'Connor was joint author with Dr Noel Sheehy (RIP) of 'Understanding Suicidal Behaviour' (2000). He recently published 'When it is darkest: why people die by suicide and what we can do to prevent it' (2021). Dr O'Connor was highly influential in academic publications devoted to the study of suicide, as follows: Associate Editor, Suicide and Life-threatening Behaviour [and Behaviour Therapy]; Editorial Board Member, Crisis – the journal of crisis intervention and suicide prevention; and Joint-Chief Editor, Archives of Suicide Research. It can reasonably be assumed therefore that anything and everything published in these journals was known to and approved by Dr O'Connor.

In his 'Darkest' book, Dr O'Connor noted, with deep regret, the tragic death by suicide of his former colleague and co-author in 2000, Dr Noel Sheehy (O'Connor, 2021: 2). It seemed to me it might be insightful for readers to consider what Dr O'Connor said about the death of his late friend Dr Noel Sheehy (RIP):

'I had been researching depression [at Queen's University Belfast] and … in 1994, just after my graduation, out of the blue, one of my professors Noel [Sheehy] … telephoned me [about] whether I'd be interested in doing a PhD on suicide. I jumped at the chance. Suicide is the most shocking outcome of depression [although] there had been little relevant research in Northern Ireland. That day, when I agreed, I couldn't envisage what a PhD in suicide would look like but I grabbed the opportunity with both hands and just ran with it. And there it began, suicide research was to become my life's passion. Little did I know … that many years later Noel [Sheehy] would lose his own mental health fight by his own hand. I often think of him reaching out to me, it was like my Sliding Doors moment … I doubt I would have become a suicide researcher without him … Perhaps I should have reached out to Noel [Sheehy] in his hour of need. I really wish I had. I'll always regret that I didn't do more for him. Guilt and regret are such common emotions after a suicide.' (O'Connor, 2021: 1, 2)

In neither of his books (2000 & 2021) were the words 'education' or 'training' indexed. However, the 'Darkest' book contains 48 pages of academic references/end-notes (p 289-337). As an educator, Dr Rory contributed to relevant course modules in his university and presented seminars across the UK, Ireland and further afield on suicide related matters, often focusing upon how he developed his IMV theory:

The Integrated Motivational-Volitional Model of Suicidal Behaviour (IMV) was first proposed in 2011 by Rory O'Connor (IMV; O'Connor, 2011) and it was refined in 2018 (O'Connor & Kirtley, 2018). Its aim was to synthesise, distil, and extend our knowledge and understanding of why people die by suicide, with a particular focus on the psychology of the suicidal mind. The model was developed from the recognition that suicide is characterised by a complex interplay of biology, psychology, environment, and culture (O'Connor, 2011), and that we need to move beyond psychiatric categories if we are to further understand the causes of suicidal malaise (Univ of Glasgow, 2021: Suicide Behaviour Research Laboratory).

It remains unclear if third level undergraduate courses in suicidology are offered currently, or planned for future terms in Dr O'Connor's University of Glasgow. Dr O'Connor confirmed that his continuing interest in understanding suicide by research was strongly influenced by the tragic suicides of close friends and colleagues:

'Although we can never bring back those we have lost, we can better support those left behind, and if we work together, we can save more lives. My ultimate hope is that as a society, if we are kinder and more compassionate, both to ourselves and to those around us, then we will go some distance in protecting all of us from the devastation of suicide' (O'Connor, 2021: 276 ).

## Diego de Leo

Dr. Diego de Leo is a professor at Griffith University, Brisbane, Queensland, Australia and a member of the editorial board of the Crisis Journal. Diego de Leo is Emeritus Professor of Psychiatry at Griffith University in Brisbane, where he is Director Emeritus of the World Health Organization (WHO) Collaborating Centre for Research and Training in Suicide Prevention. He was the creator and former convener of Graduate Certificate, and Postgraduate programmes including Master of Suicidology at the Australian Institute for Suicide Research and Prevention (AISRAP), at Griffith University. He is also co-founder of the journal Archives of Suicide Research. Prof De Leo has published extensively, with more than 500 peer-reviewed articles, 190 book chapters, 60 volumes and over 400 conference presentations. Winner of numerous national and international awards, in 2007 he was awarded the title of Doctor of Science by Griffith University for his research on suicide and psychogeriatrics. Prof De Leo is presently Director of the Psychology Department at Primorska University, Slovenia, and Director of the Slovene Center for Suicide Research.

It can be assumed that Professor De Leo knows more about suicide and suicidology than most of his contemporaries have ever been aware of, never mind understood. Significantly, he created and was actively involved in teaching third level, postgraduate and master's suicidology programmes. The question remains: why Professor De Leo was something of an outlier in his active participation in educational programmes in suicidology?

There was no chance that De Leo's massive literary legacy could be summarised – except by the author himself, perhaps. My best bet, therefore, was to check out as best I could – without the benefit of an internet-supported word search for 'education', 'suicide', and 'Diego De Leo' – this polymath's approach to 'education for prevention' of suicide. To advance this, I now briefly describe some of De Leo's recent work to ascertain what link existed between his academic research activities and its influence, if any, upon the issue of 'education for prevention'.

One recent study that De Leo participated in (Rimkeviciene et al., 2016) explored the utility of the construct 'acquired capability for suicide' (ACS) in the tripartite Interpersonal-Psychological Theory of Suicide (IPT) (Joiner, 2005; Van Orden et al., 2010) to 'predict proximal risk of death by suicide'. This construct was described as 'one of the most important breakthroughs in suicide research' (Bauer et al., 2018). These writers qualified this by referring to a study by Smith et al. (2016) that 'found that a large portion of an individual's ACS can be explained by genetic influences, [although] environmental influences still play a key role in a person's ACS, and how this remaining portion increases is largely unknown. Why some people are able to die by suicide and others are not is a significant question in the suicide literature' (Bauer et al., 2018).

Cutting to the chase, one of 20 factors – 'I could kill myself if I wanted to'- in the Acquired Capability for Suicide Scale (ACSS) was found to be among the strongest indicators of risk of suicidality (Rimkeviciene et al., 2016). However, Bauer et al. (2018) concluded that 'further research on this topic has the possibility to substantially inform foundational concepts of suicide theory, ultimately leading to clinical impact' (Bauer et al., 2018).

Three unanswered questions remained about any outcomes of this excellent study, and many more that Dr De Leo has carried out, jointly or with colleagues, over many years. First, did their insights ever reach further than a select but relatively small constituency of professional suicidologists? Second, what structure existed to channel new knowledge, and new learning towards Australia's population and further afield, so that it might transition towards, inform and influence clinical practice by way of public and/or professional educational programmes? And third, what read-across existed between any ongoing educational engagement at Griffith University (Brisbane) and its practical effect, if any, on moderating the incidence locally, nationally and globally of suicidal behaviour?

## Antoon Leenaars

Dr Antoon Leenaars, Ph.D., C. Psych (born 1951) is a Canadian clinical, mental health, public health, and forensic psychologist practicing in Windsor, Ontario. He is widely respected for his research on suicide. He has conducted influential research on death and suicide (including among indigenous people, police, and military), and was the founding Editor-in-Chief of the journal, Archives of Suicide Research. He is a recipient of numerous national and international awards and honours. Dr. Leenaars has provided forensic services in cases of wrongful death, suicide, homicide-suicide, homicide, and accidents involving inter alia ethical/legal issues. No specific references online, to formal 'education for prevention' roles or activities by Dr Leenaars were noted.

However his suicide-related literary output is considerable, including 230 published articles/chapters inter alia on violence, trauma, suicide, police suicide, military suicide, altruistic suicide, indigenous suicide, suicide notes, homicide, homicide-suicide, AIDS, genocide, terrorism, DNA analysis, forensic science, psychotherapy, and gun control. His 14 books have included 'Psychotherapy with Suicidal People' (John Wiley & Sons, UK), 'Suicide and Homicide-Suicide among Police' (Baywood Publ. Co., US/Taylor & Francis), 'Suicide among the Armed Forces' (Baywood Publ. Co. /Taylor & Francis), and 'The Psychological Autopsy' (Routledge, UK/US). Dr Leenaars has advised many national government agencies – including Norway, Netherlands, Sweden, Lithuania and India. (Career data via https://www.routledge.com/authors/i15248-antoon-a-leenaars# ).

It was difficult to summarise Dr Leenaars' philosophy on the place of education in suicidology – unlike for example Shneidman, Joiner, or O'Connor. Perhaps a brief, focused analysis of his approach to people at risk of suicide (Leenaars, 2004) could offer some partial if incomplete insights. In the preface to this comprehensive study (460 pages), Leenaars acknowledged a debt to his mentor, Edwin Shneidman, in his reference to the latter's guide and confidant, Henry (Harry) Murray: 'Never denigrate a fellow human being in less than 2,000 words' (p xi). Why? Because each of us, alive but suicidal or dead by suicide, is unique. He preferred the qualitative, idiographic approach to research that relied on intensive study of individuals: 'We must do justice to the individuality of each person ... humankind's complexity is as true for suicide as for any behaviour' (p 1).

Leenaars (2004: 9) reminded us that Shakespeare wrote a number of tragedies, that featured no fewer than 52 suicides in his plays, one of which – Hamlet, act 3, scene 1 – featured among the most famous passages ever written on the topic:

'To be, or not to be, that is the question:

Whether 'tis nobler in the mind to suffer

The slings and arrows of outrageous fortune,
Or to take arms against a sea of troubles
And by opposing end them. To die—to sleep,
No more; and by a sleep to say we end
The heart-ache and the thousand natural shocks
That flesh is heir to: 'tis a consummation
Devoutly to be wish'd. To die, to sleep;'

Leenaars referred to Shakespeare as 'a superb suicidologist' (p 9). Leenaars (2004) was addressing psychotherapists but he was well aware that most 'ordinary people', i. e. people who are not psychotherapists, may from time to time encounter a person/s at risk of suicide. Ideally, everyone at risk should be supported. But in the real world, in Northern Ireland, there were obstacles that blocked many at risk, who are in the grip of unendurable psychological pain, or psychache, from accessing professional life-saving help. We know this because a UK wide report from the Royal College of Psychiatrists (2020) confirmed that 'approximately 75% of persons who died by suicide have not been in contact with mental health services... and that people at risk of suicide were not being identified and/or offered the mental health treatment that could have prevented their death" (Black, 2021: 10, 11). Leenaars (2004: 311) devoted much of his text to descriptions of his psychotherapeutic endeavours with clients. He was clear that a deep understanding of suicide's multidimensional malaise was a prerequisite for helping people at risk of suicide. Such knowledge could be acquired and deployed but:

'Blocking suicide is best accomplished through prevention. Prevention is education. People – doctors, psychiatrists, psychologists, teachers, rabbis, ministers, [priests], crisis counsellors and so on must be educated. Such education is enormously complicated' (Leenaars, 2004: 311).

<u>Afternote</u>: Can society bridge the gulf between a) the level of expertise that Leenaars (2004) suggested was necessary for preventive engagement with those at risk of suicide and b) current, popular short-term campaigns in UK/Ireland to fund increased 'mental

health' activities, campaigns and publicity exercises? The latter economically affordable substitutes, were of questionable validity and/or effectiveness: can they realistically replace long-term investment in third level educational endeavours in psychotherapy and suicidology.

## David Jobes

Dr David Jobes was a board-certified clinical psychologist (American Board of Professional Psychology) and maintained a private, clinical and forensic practice at the Washington Psychological Center, PC. He was also a professor of psychology and associate director of clinical training at the Catholic University of America. His research and writing have led to numerous publications in suicidology, with a particular focus on clinical suicidology. A past president of the American Association of Suicidology (AAS), David served as a consultant the US Centers for Disease Control and Prevention (CDCP), the US National Institute for Mental Health (NIMH), US Department of Defence, and the US Department of Veteran Affairs.

Dr David Jobes began research in suicide prevention in the early 1980's as a graduate student at American University. His professional career began in 1987 in the Counselling Center of The Catholic University of America where he developed a valid and reliable suicide risk assessment tool and tracking method to ensure that the university's suicidal students didn't 'fall through the cracks'. This clinical research over several decades led to the development of the Suicide Status Form (SSF) and subsequent development of the Collaborative Assessment and Management of Suicidality (CAMS) methodology. For over 30 years, Dr David Jobes had trained thousands of mental health professionals in the assessment of suicide risk and the use of CAMS (Cams-care website, 2021).

Clearly, Dr Jobes supported an educated, informed, insightful, and compassionate approach to caring for people at risk of suicide. His CAMS model for clinical, therapeutic interaction with a client at risk emphasised the principle that the client's perspective, rather than that of the psychotherapist, was paramount. Seeing suicidal risk through the eyes of the patient was a central tenet of a person-centred CAMS approach, similar to Orbach's (2001) 'empathy with the suicidal wish' of the person. Indeed 'the primacy of the therapeutic alliance, between client and therapist, was essential ... for lifesaving clinical care' (Jobes, 2011).' The illustrations (below) represented the 'traditional' medical model approach to suicide and the 'collaborative' approach to suicide. The former conceptualised suicide as a symptom of psychiatric disorder while the latter illustrated the contrasting CAMS methodology, with clinician and client collaboratively working together, to come to terms with the how and why of suicide coping (Aeschi Model_T; Jobes, 2011).

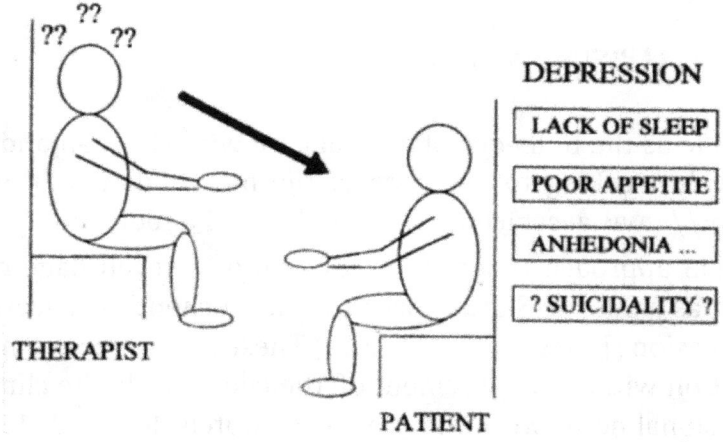

Fig 6: Critique of Current Approach to Suicide Risk The illustration above represents the 'traditional' medical model approach to suicide and the 'collaborative approach to suicide below. The former conceptualised suicide as a symptom of psychiatric disorder while the latter illustrated the contrasting CAMS methodology, with clinician and client collaboratively working together, to come to terms with the how and why of suicide coping (Aeschi Model_T; Jobes, 2011). http://www.aeschiconference.unibe.ch/T_Model.pdf

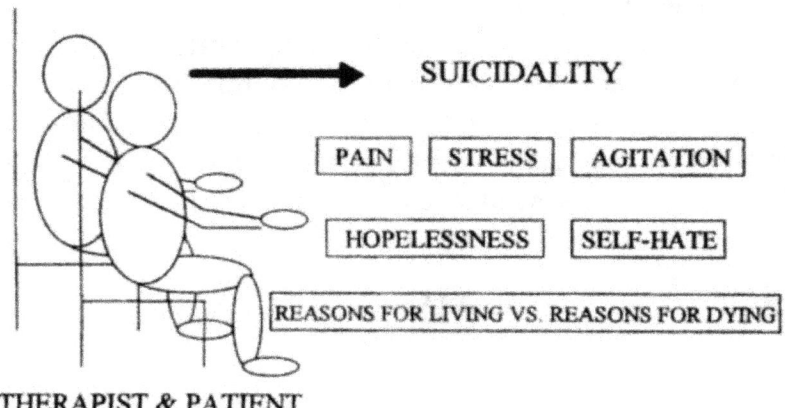

Fig 7: 'Suicide as the bulls-eye of clinical care with clinician and client collaboratively working to deconstruct the how and why of suicide coping' http://www.aeschiconference.unibe.ch/T_Model.pdf

The CAMS approach relied upon the use of a seven page clinical tool, known as a Suicide Status Form, to track a client's progress from session to session (Jobes, 2011, 221-227). These forms were completed in consultation with, and agreement of, the client while the clinician's own professional notes were completed separately. Jobes (2011: 228) described the SSF's distinct purposes:

i) The initial assessment and documentation of risk
ii) The initial development and documentation of a suicide-specific treatment plan
iii) The tracking and documentation of ongoing suicidal risk assessment and updates of the treatment plan
iv) The ultimate accounting and documentation of clinical outcomes.

Eligible clinicians were required prior to client work to have obtained certification following completion of training in CAMS practice.

The efficacy of four alternative interventions – medication, cognitive, cognitive-behavioural, and dialectical behaviour therapy –

was examined in a meta-analysis to ascertain the status of CAMS as a comparable intervention:

'In comparison to alternative interventions, CAMS resulted in significantly lower suicidal ideation and general distress, significantly higher treatment acceptability, and significantly higher hope/lower hopelessness. No significant differences for suicide attempts, self-harm, other suicide related correlates, or cost effectiveness were observed. The results of this meta-analysis support the efficacy of CAMS over alternative interventions for the treatment of suicidal ideation' (Swift et al., 2021)

Swift et al. (2021) were therefore content to extend CAMS proven efficacy with suicide ideation (SI) to 'suicide-related correlates' including self-harm and suicide attempts. It was clear that David Jobes' CAMS approach relied upon the priority that he placed upon SI as a high risk, dynamic state of mind, as he understood it. His Suicide Safety Form (SSF, 2017) described SI as a complex of thoughts and feelings about oneself and others that transitioned into 'feeling suicidal' inter alia because of psychological pain, stress, agitation, hopelessness and self-hate.

CAMS was undoubtedly an effective therapeutic approach. Its potency, of course, depended upon a potential client's direct acknowledgment, to a third party intermediary – friend, relative, family member, police, or ER medical staff – of their active suicidality and need for support. Communication and contracting between a sufferer and a potential healer was an evident prerequisite for CAMS or similar therapy. Unfortunately, as pointed out earlier, far too many suicidal people suffer and perish without accessing available potentially preventative support (Black, 2021: 10, 11).

## Heidi Hjelmeland

Dr Hjelmeland is a professor working at the Department of Mental Health, Norwegian University of Science and Technology, Trondheim, Norway. She specialised in researching suicidology and as a suicide researcher since 1992 and has participated in or led several multicenter studies in Europe and Africa. She has published on various aspects of suicidal behaviour, such as epidemiology, attitudes, intentionality, meaning, communication, gender and culture, as well as on theoretical and methodological issues. She was currently engaged in research projects in Norway, Ghana, and Uganda, and was especially focusing on cultural/contextual aspects of suicidality. She was also researching suicide research itself in the framework of critical suicidology. She established and led the Regional Resource Center for Suicide Research and Prevention in Central Norway from 1997 through 2003, and was there responsible for the implementation of the first Norwegian suicide prevention action plan in the region. She was Vice President of the International Association for Suicide Prevention (IASP) in the period 2007-2011. She was a member of the Editorial Board of Crisis – The Journal of Crisis Intervention and Suicide Prevention (since 2004 to date), and was Co-Editor of Suicidology Online (2010-2014), and a member of the Editorial Board of Suicide and Life-threatening Behaviour (2004-2015).

[Career data source on 29 Nov 2021:

https://www.mentalhealthacademy.com.au/team/lbp9z ]

For evidence of Dr Hjelmeland's views about education for understanding suicide, I refer to her career data, her published work over almost three decades, and also to an online interview in 2018 with the Network for Early Career Researchers in Suicide and Self-Harm (netECR, 2018). She also currently offered a one-hour online course described as 'specialised' entitled "To Prevent Suicide, We Need to Understand (the Meanings of) Suicidality" and available to members of the Mental Health Academy (https://www.mentalhealthacademy.com.au). Rather, Dr Hjelmeland endeavoured to show through numerous examples how qualitative research could help us prevent suicide by understanding the meaning of suicidality in context.

She strongly challenged 'one of the most well-established truths in suicidology ... that mental disorders play a significant role in almost all suicides' (p 1), and asserted that this view was 'permeated with ideology, politics, and power (for) positioning suicide as a predominantly medical/psychiatric issue' (Hjelmeland and Knizek, 2017: 8). She added:

'We do not claim that there is no relationship between mental disorders and suicide. But we do say that the evidence available does not support the claim that suicide almost always is a consequence of mental disorder' (Hjelmeland and Knizek, 2017: 8).

On the contrary, Hjelmeland said that we need to study suicide from a life history perspective involving qualitative research with people who have lived experience or have been bereaved by suicide (Hjelmeland, 2018). Hjelmeland was particularly scathing in relation to the dismissal of qualitative methodology as a valid approach to learning about suicide:

'by the editor-in-chief of the most comprehensive of the international suicide research journals, Suicide and Life-Threatening Behaviour (SLTB) (who) has stated in an editorial that he does not want to publish qualitative research (Joiner, 2011), that is, research with the greatest potential to study the complexity always involved in a suicide. This editor's stance has consequences far beyond SLTB not publishing qualitative research, because here he executes his editorial power to tell the world that qualitative research is not worth publishing. His arguments are ideological rather than scientific. One of the most basic tenets in philosophy of science is that you first choose the research question, and then the appropriate method by which to study it. This editor does it the other way around (chooses the method(s) first, that is, only quantitative) and thus prevents certain research questions from being studied (Hjelmeland, 2016)' (Hjelmeland and Knizek, 2017: 488).

Dr Hjelmeland said that she has experienced not only the alleged quasi-censorship referred to above but also an institutional resistance in the suicidology establishment from what she referred to as 'the people in power, toward some new insight or critical thinking' (Hjelmeland, 2018). Calling for more gender diversity in the study of suicide, she highlighted the absence of open debate in journals, at seminars and at conferences where 'those in power' shut down any sign of disagreement with the status-quo-ante regarding suicidology.

So much for the aspiration of many of us – including Dr Hjelmeland – towards a new paradigm for understanding the enigma of suicide in all of its complexity and brutality, that might reach beyond the deadwood of un-researchable brain chemistry, and mental health/

illness/disorders, towards exploration of the influence upon suicidal behaviour of individual differences, culture, global social systems (e.g. inter alia capitalism, socialism, democracy, and autocracy), context, lifestyle and life experience.

## Ella Arensman

Professor Ella Arensman, Research Professor, School of Public Health and Chief Scientist, National Suicide Research Foundation, at University College Cork, Ireland, is a leading influencer in Ireland and internationally, in the study of suicidology, the reduction / prevention of death by suicide, and academic research towards those objectives. For over three decades, Professor Arensman has conducted research into a wide range of topics relating to suicide, self-harm and public mental health.

Dr Arensman has fulfilled multiple leadership roles at national and international level, including President of the International Association for Suicide Prevention and Vice President of the European Alliance Against Depression. She was an Expert Advisor for the World Health Organization, Co-Director of the WHO Collaborating Centre for Surveillance and Research in Suicide Prevention and Visiting Professor with the Australian Institute for Suicide Research and Prevention, Griffith University, Brisbane.

The above data was obtained from the University College Cork website (www.ucc.ie). However, I could find no third level courses listed therein, whose titles included the word 'suicide' or the word 'suicidology' within the National Suicide Research Foundation's website. (https://www.nsrf.ie/). The Foundation's Chief Scientist, as mentioned above, was Professor Arensman and in that role, she led a multidisciplinary research team including staff members from public health, psychology, psychiatry, primary care and occupational health, who were responsible for 'more than 200 publications and numerous other outputs'.

Publications that mentioned Dr Arensman as a joint researcher date back to 1995 and are listed on the website. Unfortunately, to obtain more than an 'Abstract' for each study that briefly summarised research findings, a significant cash payment was invariably demanded which effectively meant that access was restricted to publicly funded academics and government employees and beyond the reach of interested, committed individuals in voluntary and community suicide-related organisations.

Dr Arensman was principally responsible for the creation of a National Self-Harm Registry, for both Ireland (2002) and later, Northern Ireland (2007):

'The National Self-Harm Registry Ireland has been operating in the Republic of Ireland since 2002, via the National Suicide Research Foundation. The registry collects data on persons presenting to hospital emergency departments as a result of an episode of self-harm, as defined by the Registry. The Registry had near complete coverage of the country's hospitals for the period 2002-2005 and, since 2006, all general hospital and paediatric hospital emergency departments in the Republic of Ireland have contributed data to the Registry.' (https://www.nsrf.ie/national-self-harm-registry-ireland/ )

'Under the Northern Ireland Suicide Strategy "Protect Life – A Shared Vision", the Registry was piloted in the Western Health & Social Care Trust area from 2007. Building upon the success of this pilot, the Registry was implemented across all five Health and social care trusts, with effect from 1$^{st}$ April 2012. The purpose of the registry is to improve understanding about self-harm and related behaviours in Northern Ireland. The information gathered will be used to monitor trends and patterns over time and, perhaps most importantly, will help shape the development of services and support to meet need' https://careappointments.com/features/reports-resources/130436/report-northern-ireland-registry-of-self-harm-annual-report-2017-2018/ )

The aims of the Registry are:
- To establish the extent and nature of hospital-treated deliberate self harm in Ireland/N Ireland
- To monitor trends over time and also by area
- To contribute to policy and development in the area of suicidal behaviour

- To help the progress of research and prevention.

Self-harm included all intentional drug overdoses, poisoning or self-injurious behaviour regardless of suicide intent (Arensman et al., 2014). Suicide risk was known to be high after self-harm but in Ireland 'no systematic linkage existed between the Self-Harm Registry and 'national data on completed suicide'. Five years later, Maguire et al. (2019) carried out a population-wide study of the link between self-harm and suicide, using the Northern Ireland Registry of Self-harm. They found that those who presented with self-harm were 24 times more likely to die by suicide compared to those who did not present with self-harm after adjustment for age and sex. They suggested that these results could inform suicide prevention strategies.

In summary, there was no doubt that the National Research Foundation, led by Dr Arensman, was one of the most important innovations in suicidology in Ireland. However, it was not possible to identify any NSRF- linked third level education courses in suicide and suicidology. This might be one limiting factor in an evidence-based assessment of the Foundation's educational contribution to enhanced understanding of suicide and hence its reduction and prevention.

**Craig Bryan – the last writer**

Dr Craig Bryan was a clinical psychologist and professor of psychiatry and behavioural health at Ohio State University Medical Center. He previously served in Iraq in the US military (2005-2009) as a psychologist during which time 'my commitment to researching and preventing suicide was cemented' (Bryan, 2022: 1). I do not know at this time whether Dr Bryan currently has an active role in suicidology education at third level and above at Ohio State.

Dr Bryan's book 'Rethinking Suicide' (2022) presented a rationale for moving beyond the widely accepted explanatory suicide/mental illness dyad. Dr Joiner, an advocate of the view that 'virtually everyone, approaching if not 100%, who dies by suicide had a mental disorder' (Joiner, 2010: 188), praised Dr Bryan's book's as 'lucid and thought-provoking' (Bryan, 2022: hardback cover) in its gentle questioning of Joiner's opinion (p 106, 107). Dr Bryan argued that understanding suicide was strongly influenced by the mental illness model because 'researchers who have conducted the bulk of suicide-focused studies in the past few decades have also come from mental health professionals and have tended to emphasise psychological processes' (p 106).

'Flawed and self-defeating' was the way a journalist recently described 'the very idea of a United Ireland' (O'Loughlin, 2021). In a similar way, and following Bryan's innovative study, pursuing a 'fix mental health to prevent suicide' strategy, seemed as over-optimistic as the century long Irish enigma. So what does Dr Bryan advocate as a way to escape from, or perhaps even to build upon and transform the contemporary approach to understanding suicide – its 'trauma, brutality and ruthlessness' (Bryan, 2022: 2, 4) – that was rooted in and dependent upon that mental disorder myth?

Bryan's skepticism about the concept of 'mental disorders' resonated with its categorical dismissal by Dr Thomas Szasz six decades earlier, although, curiously, I can find no index reference by Dr Bryan to Dr Szasz (1961) whose seminal work (as noted earlier):

'argued that mental health and mental illness are alienated, pseudo-scientific, pseudo-medical terms [insisting] that illness, in the modern scientific sense applies to bodies, not to minds – except as a metaphor' (Stadlen, 2012).

Perhaps this was explained by Bryan's (2021: 7) relegation of a problem-based approach to suicide prevention and his promotion of a process-based approach that majored on creating and building lives worth living that was less dependent upon opinions or assessments of mental health, and included these key features:

i) Becoming comfortable with what we don't know
ii) Embracing the inherent complexity of suicide
iii) Moving beyond a mental illness-based model of suicide
iv) Recognising the importance of context
v) Being willing to change what we do even when it's uncomfortable or inconvenient
vi) Attending to quality-of-life issues and social factors that influence the value of living.

Dr Bryan noted that reducing firearms availability could reduce US suicide rates, but would have little impact on those who did not own or have access to firearms, and would not necessarily reduce suicide by other methods (p 179). He cited a number of studies that identified how changes in some social and environmental factors, might in combination add up to significant reductions in overall deaths by suicide. These included:

i) Reducing economic uncertainty by increasing the minimum wage

ii) Making health insurance more accessible could have positive effects

iii) Reducing air-pollution levels, involving nitrogen dioxide, fine particulate matter and sulphur dioxide

iv) A range of city, state and national policy developments addressing debt, financial strain, underemployment, housing insecurity, discrimination [aka racism] and oppression, workplace harassment and bullying, and domestic abuse [aka partner violence] (Bryan, 2022: 179,180).

In summary, Bryan's revolutionary thesis offered an alternative suicide-reduction strategy involving a radical paradigm shift:

'Instead of classifying suicide as a mental health issue, careful analysis of research findings suggests it should instead be seen as a highly complex problem with many risk factors – from personal decision-making styles, to the availability of lethal means, to financial uncertainty ... we need process-based thinking that may, in some cases, defy or contradict many of our long held assumptions about suicide' (Bryan, 2022: hardback cover).

## Experience of recent suicidology teaching input

This writer presented four short educational programmes, ranging from 10 hours to 20 hours class contact, at the School of Education, QUB, from 2008 to 2014. These were entitled "Introduction to Suicidology", "Suicidology – further studies", "Insights into suicide" and "Researching suicide". These courses were included in an 'open learning programme' with no enrolment requirements. Many of the students who attended had previously completed introductory counselling courses, which may not have included suicide-related topics. One doctoral candidate shared some teaching input with the author. During the six years (2008-2014) these courses ran, zero interest was expressed by teaching staff in other QUB schools. It might not be too wide of the mark to conclude that there seemed to be an absence of any feeling of wanting to know more about the possibility or utility of studying suicidology: currently, eight years on that situation did not appear to have changed.

## Conclusions

The above synopses of 10 published suicidological authorities, albeit two deceased, include one Australian, five American, one Canadian, one Irish, one Norwegian and one UK. There was a clear dividing line between two windows on suicide – a predominant one that relied upon a psychiatric paradigm and a secondary one that emerged from a range of complex, cultural, contextual and individual, lifestyle situations and circumstances. What was missing – as far as I can determine – was any serious debate in academe or in the professional journals from either perspective that demonstrated recognition of the validity, or otherwise, of the other's viewpoint.

Educational courses across academe at third level and above invariably relied upon the presentation, analysis and development by research, of published material, in print or online. In assessing any educational content in the published writings of some of the above 10 suicidologists, I was struck by the energy that some of them continued to expend in attempting to explain suicidal behaviour within a comprehensive, all-enveloping theory or model or representation of suicide. It was as if it was still believed, by some academics, that there existed a way of conceptualising human self-destruction within an updated post-Durkheimian framework inside which all multifactorial and multidimensional aspects of human suicidal behaviour might find a perch.

This of course may in time be identified and described by scientific research, assisted perhaps by newly arrived IT-driven technologies like artificial intelligence (AI) and/or machine learning. At present perhaps it might even be agreed that such a possibility existed. But for the foreseeable future, such a recognised manifestation that might be entitled "A General Theory of Suicide", with practical life-saving and life-enhancing applications, was out of reach, perhaps even mission impossible.

The next chapter surveys the current state of research in suicidology, in particular what prospects exist, if any, of bridging the gulf between the psychiatric perspective and a less convenient, more complicated, idiosyncratic frame of reference. And what role, if any, could education for understanding suicide play.

**Myth:** (fictitious popular idea) Suicide is a mental health issue that's best left to be dealt with by medical doctors.

**Fallacy:** (misleading argument) The more science learns about how brain chemistry influences human behaviour, the better we'll be at preventing self-harm and suicide.

## References

Aeschi Model_T (2010) Aeschi Conference - CAMS v TAU diagram - Accessed on 27 August 2024 at http://www.aeschiconference.unibe.ch/T_Model.pdf

Alvarez, A. (1971/74) The savage god. London: Penguin Group

American Psychiatry Association, APA (2013) Diagnostic and Statistical Manual of Mental Disorders, 5th Edition. DSM5.Arlington, VA: American Psychiatric Publishing

Arensman, E., Larkin, C., Corcoran, C., Reulbach, U. and Perry, I. J. (2014) Factors associated with self-cutting as a method of self-harm. Findings from Irish National Registry of Self-harm. Eu. J. Public Health, 24(2), 292-297. April 2014

Bauer, B., Allan, N. P., Boska, R. L., Fink-Miller, E. L. and Capron, D. W. (2018) An investigation into the acquired capability for suicide. Suicide and Life-threatening behaviour. August 2018

Black, L-A (2021) Suicide in Northern Ireland. Northern Ireland Assembly - Research and Information Paper. Dr Lesley-Ann Black. 14 April 2021

Blasco-Fontecilla, H., Fernandez-Fernandez, R., Colino, L., Fajardo, L., Perteguer-Barrio, R. and de Leon, J. (2016) The addictive model of self-harming (non-suicidal and suicidal) behaviour. Frontiers in Psychiatry, February, 2016. Volume 7, Article 8

Bryan, C. J. (2022) Rethinking suicide: why prevention fails and how we can do better. New York, NY: Oxford University Press

CAMS-care website (2021) Accessed on 27 November2021 at https://cams-care.com/about-us/

Dicke, W. (2009) Edwin Shneidman, Authority on Suicide, dies at 91. William Dicke. New York Times, 21 May 2009

DSM-5, 5th Edition, APA (2013) Diagnostic and statistical manual of mental disorders, 5th edition. Washington, DC: American Psychiatric Association

Durkheim, E. (1997/2002) Suicide: a study in sociology. London: Routledge

Frost, R. (1960) The trial of existence. Citing E. S. Sergeant. Accessed on 10 November 2021 at https://quotepark.com/quotes/1350309-robert-frost-poetry-is-a-way-of-taking-life-by-the-throat/

GFA (1998) The Belfast Agreement / Good Friday Agreement. Accessed on 22 November 2021 at https://education.niassembly.gov.uk/post_16/snapshots_of_devolution/gfa

Harding, A. (2009) Edwin Shneidman: Obituary. The Lancet, Vol 374. 25 July 2009

Hjelmeland, H. (2018) Interview: career advice from Heidi Hjelmeland. 18 October 2018. Accessed on 29 November 2021 at https://netecr.org/

Hjelmeland, H. and Knizek, B. L. (2016) Time to change direction of research. In R. C. O'Connor and J. Pirkis (eds.) The International Handbook of Suicide Prevention, 2nd edition. Ch. 39, 696-709

Hjelmeland, H. and Knizek, B. L. (2017) Suicide and mental disorders: a discourse on politics, power and vested interests. Death Studies, 41(8), p 481-492

Jobes, D. A. (2011) Suicidal patients, the therapeutic alliance, and the collaborative assessment and management of suicidality. Chapter

12, p 205-229. In Konrad Michel and David A. Jobes, Eds. (2011) Building a therapeutic alliance with the suicidal patient. Washington, DC: American Psychological Association

Jobes, D. A. (2012) The Collaborative Assessment and Management of Suicidality (CAMS): an evolving evidence-based clinical approach to suicidal risk. Suicide and Life-threatening Behaviour, 42(6), p 640-653

Joiner, T. E. (2005) Why people die by suicide. Cambridge, MA: Harvard University Press

Joiner, T. E., Van Orden, K. A., Witte, T. K. and Rudd, M. D. (2009) The interpersonal theory of suicide: guidance for working with suicidal patients. Washington, DC: American Association of Psychology

Joiner, T. E. (2010) Myths about suicide. Cambridge, MA: Harvard University Press

Joiner, T. E. (2011). Editorial: Scientific rigor as the guiding heuristic for SLTB's editorial stance. Suicide and Life-threatening Behaviour, 41(5), 471–473

Jordan, J. R. (2020) Lessons learned: forty years of clinical work with suicide loss survivors. Front. Psychol. 29 April 2020. Accessed on 14 November 2021 at https://www.frontiersin.org/articles/10.3389/fpsyg.2020.00766/full

Leenaars, A. A. (2004) Psychotherapy with suicidal people. Chichester, West Sussex, England: John Wiley and Sons, Ltd

Leenaars, A. A. (2010) Edwin S. Shneidman on Suicide. Suicidology Online, 2010, 1: 5-18

Lester, D. (Ed.) (2019) The end of suicidology: can we ever understand suicide? [Stockton University, Galloway, NJ] New York, NY: Nova Science Publishers. Accessed on 11 November 2021 at https://novapublishers.com/shop/the-end-of-suicidology-can-we-ever-understand-suicide/

Maguire, A., Ross, E., Tseliou, F., O'Hagan, D. and O'Reilly, D. (2019) What happens after self-harm? An exploration of self-harm and suicide using the Northern Ireland Registry of Self-Harm. International Journal of Population Data Science, 4(3)

Matthew (2021a) Chapter 26, verse 23. Jesus' betrayal. Accessed on 21 November 2021 at https://www.biblegateway.com/passage/?search=Matthew%2026&version=NIV

Matthew (2021b) Chapter 27, verses 3, 4 & 5. Judas Ischariot, remorse & suicide. Accessed on 21 November 2021 at https://www.biblegateway.com/passage/?search=Matthew%2027&version=NIV

McKie, R. (2021) Mystery of the environmental triggers for cancer deepens. The Observer. Sunday 24 October 2021

Mental Health Academy (2022) Provider of online professional development (CPD) education for mental health professionals. Accessed on 12 October 2022 athttps://www.mentalhealthacademy.com.au/

Michel, K. and Jobes D.A. (eds.) "Building a Therapeutic Alliance with the suicidal patient" (2011) American Psychological Association

Murray, K. (2021) Behavioural addictions. 11 November 2021. Accessed on 13 November 2021 at https://www.addictioncenter.com/addiction/behavioral-addictions/

Mynatt, S. (2000) Repeated suicide attempts. J PsychosocNursMent Health Serv. Dec 2000, 38(12): 24-33. Memphis State University, Memphis, Tennessee

O'Connor, D. J. (1957/63) An introduction to the philosophy of education. London: Routledge and Kegan Paul

O'Connor, R. C. and Sheehy, N. P. (2000) Understanding suicidal behaviour. Leicester, England: BPS Books (The British Psychological Society)

O'Connor, R. C. (2011) Towards an integrated motivational-volitional model of suicidal behaviour. Crisis, 32, 295-298

O'Connor, R. C. and Pirkis, J. (eds.) (2016) The international handbook of suicide prevention. Second edition. West Sussex, UK: John Wiley and Sons

O'Connor, R. C. and Kirtley, O. J. (2018) The integrated motivational-volitional model of suicidal behaviour. Philosophical transactions of the Royal Society B., 373, 20170268

O'Connor, R. C. (2021) When it is darkest: why people die by suicide and what we can do to prevent it. London: Vermilion, an imprint of Ebury Publishing

O'Loughlin, M. (2021) We need to stop talking about a united Ireland. Michael O'Loughlin. The Irish Times. 22 November 2021

O'Neill, S., Corry, C., McFeeters, D., Murphy, S. and Bunting, B. (2016) Suicide in Northern Ireland: an analysis of gender differences in demographic, psychological and contextual factors. Crisis, Vol 37(1) January 2016

Orbach, I. (2001) Therapeutic empathy with the suicidal wish: principles of therapy with suicidal individuals. American Journal of Psychotherapy, 55(2) pp 166-184

Owens, D. and House, A. (1994) General hospital services for deliberate self-harm: haphazard clinical provision, little research, no central strategy. Journal of the Royal College of Physicians of London, V28(4) July/August 1994

Personal communication (2021) Responses by NI universities to enquiries about their third-level suicidology courses

Remkieviciene, J., Hawgood, J., O'Gorman, J. and De Leo, D. (2016) Capability for suicide scale: factor structure and discriminant validity. Journal of Psychopathology and Behavioural Assessment, 38(3) September 2016

Royal College of Psychiatrists (2020) Self-harm and suicide in adults. Final report of the Patient Safety Group. Accessed on 25 November 2021 at https://www.rcpsych.ac.uk/docs/default-source/improving-care/better-mh-policy/college-reports/college-report-cr229-self-harm--and-suicide.pdf?sfvrsn=b6fdf395_10

Shneidman, E. S. (1973) Deaths of man. New York, NY: Quadrangle/ The NY Times Book Co

Smith, P. N., Stanley, I. H., Joiner Jr, T. E., Sachs-Ericsson, N. J., & Van Orden, K. A. (2016). An aspect of the capability for suicide - fearlessness of the pain involved in dying - amplifies the association between suicide ideation and attempts. Archives of Suicide Research, 20(4), 650-662

SSF – Suicide Safety Plan (2017) CAMS Suicide Status form–4 (ssf-4) initial session. Accessed on 27 November 2021 at https://www.nevadacertboard.org/wp-content/uploads/2017/08/SSF-4.pdf

Stadlen, A. (2012) Thomas Szasz obituary. Andrew Stadlen. The Guardian, 4 October 2012

Suicidology Journals (2021) Editorial committees: Suicide and Life-threatening behaviour; Crisis – the journal of crisis intervention and suicide prevention; Suicidology Online; and Archives of Suicide Research. Accessed on 17 November 2021 at their respective websites

Swift, J. K., Trusty, W. T, and Penix, E. A. (2021) The effectiveness of the Collaborative Assessment and Management of Suicidality (CAMS) compared to alternative treatment conditions: a meta analysis. Suicide and Life-threatening Behaviour, 2021, 00: 1-15

Szasz, T. S. (1961/1974) The myth of mental illness: foundations of a theory of personal conduct. New York, NY: Harper and Row

Szasz, T. S. (2011) Suicide prohibition: the shame of medicine. Syracuse, NY: Syracuse University Press

Thorpe, V. (2021) George the Poet: 'It's easier to change the lives of offenders in prison than on the outside'. Vanessa Thorpe. The Observer, 7 November 2021

University of Glasgow (2021) The Integrated Motivational-Volitional Model of Suicidal Behaviour. Accessed on 18 November 2021 at https://suicideresearch.info/the-imv/

Van Orden, K. A., Witte, T. K., Cukrowicz, K. C., Braithwaite, S. R., Selby, E. A., & Joiner, T. E., Jr. (2010). The interpersonal theory of suicide. Psychological Review, 117(2), 575–600

Wertheimer, A. (1991) A special scar. Oxford, UK: Routledge

Wikipedia (2021) Thomas Joiner. 3 January 2021. Accessed on 18 November 2021 at https://en.wikipedia.org/wiki/Thomas_Joiner

\* \* \*

## Chapter 17
# Suicide research: impediments, lateral thinking and critical suicidology

## Introduction

'Peter Shilton (1949- ) is regarded as one of soccer's greatest ever goalkeepers. As a metaphor for autonomic suicide prevention, the goalkeeper is a soccer team's last line of defence ... In sum, the expectation is that the adaptive problem of suicide would have been addressed by the evolution, through the co-option and adaptation of pre-existing biological systems, of special-purpose mechanisms specifically designed to prevent suicide, mobilising in response to environmental cues of suicide risk. These defences [are] described, and defined as last-line, reactive, anti-suicide, evolved psychological mechanisms, henceforth, as a working name, shiltons' (Soper, 2017: 146).

Readers will recall in the following discussion, as stated in Chapter 16 above, that I distinguish between suicidology, designated as suicide studies and suicide research, and suicide prevention, identified as a related but parallel activity or entity.

The purpose of research, in scientific terms, is the discovery of new knowledge, to locate and describe an important entity, or vital aspect(s) of that entity, that was unknown, or at least previously unrecognised, and that adds in a significant and non-trivial way to the sum of human knowledge/wisdom.

Soper's (2017: 3) doctoral dissertation presented a 'novel and defensible' theoretical framework, viz. 'new knowledge', to account for the emergence of suicide in the human species. He asserted that:

'suicidality most likely evolved as an unfortunate side-effect of two important primary adaptations in the human species, 'pain and brain': the aversive emotional experience of pain, which is biologically designed to aid self-preservation by motivating adaptive escape action combined with a cognitive sophistication that offers most mature humans the means to escape pain maladaptively by self-killing' (p5).

Soper (2017) accepted 'natural selection's "survive and reproduce rule of thumb" in his attempt to investigate suicide's "evolutionary puzzle"' (p5). He coined the term 'shilton' to describe the human species' 'last line of defence', otherwise psychological mechanism(s) against suicide (p146). [This Northern Irish writer might have substituted the name of our own 'Northern Irish greatest ever goalkeeper' – Patrick Anthony Jennings – aka 'jennings' for Soper's English equivalent, Peter Leslie Shilton – aka 'shilton'!]. There were echoes of Baumeister's Escape Theory (1990, 1991) in Soper's presentation.

In my academic and research approach to understanding suicide, I have tended to focus upon each individual suicide rather than attempting to investigate the whys and wherefores of the roughly estimated global total of deaths annually by suicide that range from 700,000 to over a million (WHO, 2021). This has located my work within a qualitative, case study-based, idiographic methodology, augmented by Identity Structure Analysis (Weinreich and Saunderson, 2003): other methodologies, including the quantitative approach, underpinned by statistical analysis, and mixed methods, were available.

## Impediments to advancing suicide research

What represented a substantial, if understandable but immovable, block to research in suicidology was the permanent absence of the possibility of direct or indirect access to the mind, aka the decision-taking process, of the suicide deceased. Some have argued that 'psychological autopsy' offered indirect access to the deceased through retrospective observations of others (See Chapter 8 above). This meant that 'new knowledge' regarding any suicide event relied almost totally on identifying important clues – that were almost invariably 'hidden in plain sight' (Free Dictionary, 2021) – and that might potentially illuminate the pathway to that individual death by suicide and perhaps, how that life might have been saved. Shneidman (2004) speculated that 'suicide notes' represented the 'royal road to understanding suicide' by appearing to permit post-mortem access to the deceased:

"We believed (with excessive optimism) that, like Freud's notion about dreams being the royal road to the unconscious, suicide notes might prove to be the royal road to the understanding of suicidal phenomena", Shneidman wrote in Autopsy of a Suicidal Mind (2004). That royal road turned out to be a dead end' (Harding, 2009).

Shneidman (2004: 7, 8) did concede that 'words and phrases in the [suicide] note can take on special meanings' in the context of the known details of the note writer's life. A more recent attempt to create a 21$^{st}$ century royal road was represented by the 'survivors of attempted / failed suicide' movement, that purported to offer insights into the state of mind of persons whose effort/s to kill themselves were unsuccessful. I remain unsure if any advocates of this latter approach have as yet emulated the refutation by Shneidman and Farberow (1957) of their regal route hypothesis via suicide notes that involved investigating real and made-up suicide notes.

Rivlin et al. (2013: 336) expressed some skepticism regarding any direct read-across from suicide attempters to suicide completers:

'(I)nterviewing suicide attempters can be problematic because there is little evidence to suggest that it is possible to generalise about those that complete suicide from those generally making attempts. Research has consistently found significant differences in terms of populations and causal factors between those attempting and dying by suicide (Beautrais, 2001), for instance, in terms of age (those who attempt suicide are younger than those who die by suicide) (Pallis, Barraclough, Levey, Jenkins, & Sainsbury, 1982), sex (females more likely to attempt, but males more likely to die by suicide) (Dorpat & Boswell, 1963; Dorpat & Ripley, 1967; Linehan, 1986; Michel, 1987; Stengel & Cook, 1958), psychiatric diagnosis (higher rates in suicides) (Pallis, D.J. et al., 1982), and intent to die (weaker in attempted suicides than suicides) (Pallis, D.J. and Sainsbury, P. 1976)' (Rivlin et al., 2013).

Meyer et al. (2017: 26) pointed to a fundamental systemic weakness in any serious research process aimed at understanding suicide:

'Coroners obtain information for investigative purposes not for research purposes (Rivlin et al., 2013)'.

This situation almost seemed to be deliberately (or otherwise) designed to obfuscate the emergence of comprehensive information about suicide deaths. As mentioned earlier in this book, the coroner's limited remit excluded consideration of the 'why' of any suicide death, being restricted to ascertaining 'who/when/where/how' data only. Hence, the pathway to self-destruction was of no legal or statutory interest to coroners (or anyone else) unless it informed that strictly limited agenda.

The importance of a postmortem investigation of each suicide event had not yet been officially/legislatively acknowledged in Ireland/UK. Occasional coroner's public inquests, at the discretion of each coroner, were organised where the public interest demanded it. My personal experience of public inquests in Northern Ireland into two family deaths (1982 & 1989) confirmed the restricted nature of these affairs: they added little if anything in terms of 'new knowledge' regarding either how each death might have been prevented or what lessons, if any, might have been learned from either catastrophic loss. It was important to confirm that this situation, embedded in centuries of law and legal practice, was unlikely to change any time soon. This meant that targeted research represented the only avenue towards improved understanding of a suicide event, and highlighting any insights from that understanding regarding how that awful event might have been anticipated, foreseen, avoided, or prevented. However, a coroner's discretion was total regarding access by researchers to their case files, representing yet another potential block to suicide research.

## Lateral thinking – Professor Dr Heidi Hjelmeland, Department of Mental Health, Norwegian University of Science and Technology

In a published interview, Dr Hjelmeland (2018) said that, early in her career, she found that quantitative suicide research was limited 'in terms of finding anything useful':

'I realised I had to change completely from quantitative to qualitative because quantitative research can only scratch the surface. Many researchers tend to find the same risk factors over and over again and therefore the field seems to be sort of stuck in this repetitive risk factor research that is not getting us anywhere' (Hjelmeland, 2018).

She believed that the context and complexity of suicidal behaviour could not otherwise be investigated:

'We should stop pretending that we are going to be able to find all of the relevant risk factors for suicide and put them together into a predictive model to predict suicide. I don't believe that is possible. I believe that we need to study suicide in a life history perspective, which means we need to have qualitative research. We need to conduct qualitative research with people who have lived experience, or have been bereaved by suicide, to tell the story of the suicide' (Hjelmeland, 2018).

Professor Hjelmeland was skeptical about reliance upon psychological autopsy as an accurate window into the deceased suicide's mindset, since opinions of family members, clinicians, friends and colleagues regarding the deceased may not necessarily be in agreement, because of their different, perhaps conflicted perspectives:

'For the family members it might be important to keep up a façade, whereas a friend might have no problems revealing a family secret of sexual abuse, for example. This showed that it is important to have several voices, covering different types of relationships when conducting psychological autopsies. However, it is also important to conduct research with people who have first-hand experience, by exploring the life stories of people who have experienced serious suicidal thoughts or made suicide attempts too. This will allow us to understand more about their lives and the context surrounding the suicidal acts so that we can understand what suicidality is all about for those who are suicidal and then I think we will be better equipped to prevent suicide' (Hjelmeland, 2018).

Heidi Hjelmeland was critical of the pressure placed upon some academic researchers to publish a set or contracted number of journal articles per annum in order to retain their academic employment status. [The mirror image of this unfair predicament was my personal experience of being unable to find a publisher because of my non-university, independent status – hence the current publication.]

'This publish or perish thing leads to so much rubbish research because researchers are pressured to publish a high number of articles, rather than producing quality work which will really move the field forward. Instead of repeating for the hundredth time that depression is a risk factor for suicide, developing some new knowledge is much more important' (Hjelmeland, 2018).

Dr Hjelmeland also highlighted the absence of open discussion and debate between researchers whose endeavours have located them quite legitimately in positions, with arguments and opinions that might not fully coincide with those of other researchers. [Galileo's ancient predicament comes to mind (Finocchiaro, 2009)]:

'As academics we should be having open debates to hear the viewpoints of people who disagree with one another, both at conferences or in journals. But those in power do not want that, they shut it down and in my view that is not just unscientific but also unethical. But I think we need to hear more of these discussions, both in journals and at conferences. Because I am sorry to say, but at conferences it tends to be the same old men, saying the same old things. I have been arguing about that for years. When I was Vice-President of IASP [International Association for Suicide Prevention] I was involved in the planning of two conferences and I argued that we should have more women. I mean there are so many clever, brilliant women working in this area, we should be aiming at 50:50. But this was seen as impossible; because others felt people would expect to hear from the same old men. I said no. I don't. I want to see more courage from conference organisers to invite not just more women to present, but also newer faces. Perhaps people maybe from outside this field who can offer a viewpoint from a different perspective. Not just the same old, same old. And I am not talking about one particular conference, but this seems to be the pattern across most conferences with few exceptions' (Hjelmeland, 2018).

The obvious danger here, cited by Hjelmeland, was the quasi-censorship involved in diluting the enrichment of the field by excluding the presentation of alternatives to established dogma. [Loincloths and trousers come to mind.] If research activity was to be worthwhile, and much more than going through the motions, it was inevitable that 'new knowledge' would emerge that must be taken on board, by integration with the accepted canon rather than by quasi-censorship that valued peace and quiet above deepening our understanding of the complex enigma of suicide:

'(T)he key thing I would advise everyone to do, is to question well-established truths. Even though that may sound obvious, as that should be part of our duty as researchers, there are powerful forces working to prevent that in order to keep the status quo and retain their power' (Hjelmeland, 2018).

Professor Hjelmeland's words resonate with my own experience in suicide studies. Because of stigma and taboo, challenging the supposed cause/effect relationship between 'mental health disorders' and suicidal behaviour, advocated in particular by US psychology, psychiatry, and pharmacology, risked ridicule by otherwise sincere colleagues, who were reluctant to think beyond this 'simple answer to a complex problem'. She said that what helped her to continue her research was the support of like-minded academics and students:

' ... because of all the pressure and resistance at all levels ... to have some support is just essential. If it hadn't been for the critical suicidology network we have formed, with members across the globe working together to change the direction of suicide research and prevention, I probably wouldn't still be a suicide researcher. I am so fed up with all the resistance towards new thinking and all of the different strategies that are used to keep you out. So to have a forum or group that you will get support from no matter what you say or do, that is so essential' (Hjelmeland, 2018).

The critical suicidology network (CSN) was established in 2016 with the objective of moving beyond the established canon when that was no longer successful in advancing the understanding of suicide:

'Critical suicide studies (Chandler et al., 2022) present(s) an approach to understanding, theorising and intervening in suicide from alternative perspectives that seeks new ways to thinking about suicide from a critical perspective to help address suicide where traditional approaches have failed ... Many within suicide research have become frustrated by the limitations of dominant pathologising and medicalised approaches to suicide research and prevention practices. Believing that suicidology is in need of a critical re-thinking of its subject matter and a broadening of its disciplinary basis, they look at cultural practices of making sense of suicide, taking into account how suicide is shaped by history, politics, gender, identity, culture, media and power (Critical Suicidology Network, 2021).

The Network already listed books and published journal articles and essays dating from 1992 to the present. The CSN's direction involved sixteen working group members, including Professor Hjelmeland, who were based in the Czech Republic, UK (7), Australia (3), Norway, US (2), Canada and Ghana. Only time and published outcomes will reveal what further progressive developments emerge from the CSN's endeavours.

In the next section, current, planned and prospective research work, with particular reference to Northern Ireland was summarised in relation to its potential, if any, to enhance the understanding of suicide.

## Current, planned and prospective research in Northern Ireland

In Northern Ireland, the Protect Life 2 (2019) strategy document, under the sub-heading 'Areas for enhancement in post-vention services' (pp 50-54), proposed 'research and data-collection/analysis (achieving a better understanding of suicide)' with the following objectives:

'Data gathering on suicide and self-harm is through the mechanisms of the Self-Harm Registry, the Sudden Death Notification Process, National Confidential Inquiry, the Serious Adverse Incident Process, and the General Register Office – these data systems are not linked at present.

'On a wider basis, a range of organisations hold intelligence that is relevant to understanding the context and patterns of suicide. They include general practice, mental health services, ambulance services, social services, police services, housing, education, probation, and many others.

'Research has commenced by Queen's University to link some of these data sources and this should provide very useful information to guide suicide prevention initiatives in the coming years. It is hoped that it may be possible to identify particular subgroups that are at higher risk and inform preventative services, e.g. identifying which people who self-harm are more likely to die by suicide' (Protect Life 2, 2019: 50-54).

Linking data systems and data sources within a unified suicide information management system (SIMS) would appear to be a straightforward, if complex, IT supported undertaking dependent inter alia upon access to appropriate financing and cooperation across relevant government organisations and agencies within the NI bureaucracy mentioned above. At the time of writing (December 2021) I have requested, but not yet received, a progress report on the development of an emergent SIMS, from the Queen's University and the NI Department of Health, that might facilitate 'a better understanding of suicide' in Northern Ireland.

Within the UK there was no shortage of existing models – in Scotland and England – and preliminary work in Belfast, upon which to develop, and benefit hugely from a Northern Ireland SIMS:

'The Scottish Suicide Information Database (ScotSID) and the Northern Ireland Suicide Database (established temporarily to inform research commissioned under Protect Life) provide potential models for improved data collection and linking of data sources encompassing information on medical records, contact with addiction services, emergency department attendances, contact with justice services, as well as demographic data. The Public Health England Suicide Prevention Profile provides another potential model' (Protect Life 2, 2019: 50-54).

In its action plan, the NI Protect Life 2 strategy, referred to research options to be led by the NI Department of Health and its Public Health Agency:

'10.1 Identify priorities for local research into suicide, self-harm & their prevention including data linkage; promote, encourage and commission local research' (Protect Life 2, 2019: 61).

Suggested areas for investigation included suicide attempters, bereaved families, the characteristics of those [suicide attempters and deceased] not known to core services (mental health and primary care), links between self-harm presentation at hospital and later suicide, and research into, and evaluation of the efficacy of existing suicide-related programmes (Protect Life 2, 2019: 50-54).

The recent report of a review of the NI Protect Life 2 Strategy (2024) included a summary of recent NI-related suicide studies and offered a further insight into one important potential research topic. O'Neill and Bond (2024) suggested that 'more research is needed on the controllability of suicide ideation (viz. serious thoughts of suicide) and ways of detecting and measuring ideation and treatments to reduce the frequency, intensity or duration of suicide ideation':

'there is evidence that clinical providers may avoid patients who are suicidal (out of fear and perceived concerns about malpractice liability) and that too many rely on interventions (i.e. inpatient hospitalisation and medications) that have little to no evidence for decreasing suicidal ideation and behaviour (and may even increase risk)... there is an emerging and robust evidence-based clinical literature, supported by replicated randomized controlled trials, on suicide-related assessment, acute clinical stabilisation, and the actual treatment of suicide risk through psychological interventions' (Jobes and Barnett, 2024).

An earlier study by O'Neill and O'Connor (2020) sought to 'inform suicide prevention policies and practice' linked to the NI Protect Life 2 Strategy (2019), by making a number of research proposals within a 'suicide prevention' rubric. They recommended that suicide prevention research should prioritise 'actions ... delivered across the lifespan, embracing the early years and the school context, championing resilience and emotional literacy ... [in the context of] the Troubles' legacy ... and emerging evidence of the biological transgenerational transmission of trauma ... [and] ongoing risk'. Other areas where 'huge gaps in knowledge existed included minority groups, including [Irish] Travellers and minority ethnic groups, those in contact with the criminal justice system ... ex-prisoners and their families ... and drug and alcohol services'.

In the next section, research prospects in relation to enhancement of understanding suicide were discussed in relation to the lived experience of human populations.

## Suicidology research and lived experience of human populations

A further significant limitation that blocked research aimed at understanding suicidal behaviour was its focus upon prevention of suicide at the local or community level. This resulted in an emphasis upon risk/protective factors without sufficient regard to deeply embedded political and social systems that determined the cultural context for the lived experience of human populations. Button (2016) offered a radical perspective that located suicidality in a social justice context:

'While individual cases of suicide can frequently generate widespread feelings of loss and grief, a collective sense of political responsibility for the enduring and differential conditions of suicidality remains missing today. [My] aim ... is to develop the broad outlines of a political approach to suicide as a matter of social justice. In contrast to the dominant psychological and psychiatric approaches to the study and prevention of suicide [I discuss] the thesis that suicide is a solitary "answer" to a set of collective and institutional questions about the conditions of a dignified human existence that we (i.e. most political societies) have not confronted in a meaningful or sustained way. I argue that a political account of suicide should ultimately point in the direction of a new right to life movement, the aim of which is to secure the conditions of human dignity for all persons' (Button, 2016: 270).

Button (2016) was careful to add that he wished to 'supplement, not fully dislodge, the dominant psychological and psychiatric approaches to the study of suicide, with greater attention to the sociocultural dynamics that are part of the enduring conditions of the possibility of suicide today' (p 270). There was little new in the thesis that suicide was a political issue – Durkheim's (1897/2002) treatise located suicide within the individual's response to their political – in his term 'sociological' – realities.

## Austerity suicide

Fisher (2012) had refuted the simplistic notion that UK government cuts in welfare benefits, ostensibly aimed at 'encouraging' unfit claimants to return to work, were unrelated to suicides among older men:

'The NHS like the education system and other public services, has been forced to try to deal with the social and psychic damage caused by the deliberate destruction of solidarity and security ... once workers would have turned to their trade unions when they were put under increasing stress, now they are encouraged to go to their GP or, if they are lucky enough to be able to get one on the NHS, a therapist. It would be facile to argue that each single case of depression can be attributed to economic or political causes; but it is equally facile to maintain – as the dominant approaches to depression do – that the roots of all depression must always lie either in individual brain chemistry or in early childhood experiences' (Fisher, 2012).

Mills (2018) developed Fisher's (2012) thesis by identifying a causal link between post financial crisis austerity in the UK and an increase in the numbers of suicides, especially by people who may have experienced the lethal cutting edge of welfare reform. He developed an analytic framework of psychopolitical autopsy to explore media coverage of 'austerity suicide' and to take seriously the psychic life of austerity (self-blame, shame, anxiety), embedding it in a context of social disease. Mills concluded that understanding austerity suicide meant recognising the stigma associated with being a welfare recipient that intensified the toxic anxiety around welfare entitlement being perceived by self and others as an economic burden. The significance of this approach was its ability to relocate suicide from an individual and psychocentric locus, to illuminate potential culpability of government reforms while still retaining the complexity of suicide, and provide a stimulus for relevant policy insights about welfare reform.

## Narrative therapy with community work: suicide risk and quality of life

White and Morris (2019) introduced a novel approach to engagement with those at risk of suicide that differed radically from their 'normal' way of working, by employing narrative therapy allied with community work. This relied upon the idea that problems are manufactured in social, cultural and political contexts:

'This is a way of working that challenges familiar psychological understandings of persons and problems, which often start from the assumption that problems like suicide reside inside persons. Narrative therapy is based on the simple principle that problems are separate from people and thus the therapeutic (or community or pedagogical) task is to elicit, link, and circulate new stories, discourses, and cultural practices that are in keeping with the individual's or group's preferred future' (p2).

Both of these authors were community practitioners with decades of experience working with indigenous Coast Salish peoples on the west coast of Canada: White, a suicide prevention counsellor, educator, policy consultant, and researcher and Morris, starting out as a youth volunteer on a national crisis line service at 16 years-old, and working as a youth suicide prevention educator, community developer, researcher, policy-maker, and non-profit leader.

White and Morris (2019) were careful to acknowledge that suicide involved the death of an individual and the potential for great distress for bereaved survivors. But they argued that when society's response was couched in exclusively individualistic and scientific terms motivated by an imperative to prevent it at any cost – including involuntary hospitalisation – then the opportunity was missed to be more creative and compassionate in our responses. They supported provision of high quality, individual care and treatment to individuals who are suicidal, but stressed that we need to do more than that if we want to respond to suicide in all its complexity and multiplicity.

Their conclusion was worth citing at some length for its humanistic, life-enhancing, life-preserving emphasis, that suggested a newly invigorated way ahead for suicidology, in the development of the critical suicidology network (CSN), locating concern for each 'at risk' human life with equal acknowledgement of their lived experience in family, community and society:

'To conclude, we would like to suggest that together, narrative therapy and critical suicide studies (Chandler et al., 2022) can become a creative site of world making. When we move away from a narrow focus on death prevention, towards co-creating a world worth living in, we may be better able to see suicide prevention work as a collective responsibility that is thoroughly ethical in its vision for a more caring, just, relationally engaged, and interdependent future. We hope that this [vision] can remind us of what is possible when we go beyond the accepted wisdom—which renders suicide as an individual private trouble—and begin to see its multiplicity, historical contingency, and the implications that a narratively informed approach might have for a re-invigorated public conversation about suicide. We see this way of working as hopeful and life-giving for suicidal persons and those who offer care and support, as well as for communities seeking to create the conditions for increased connection, belonging, and ultimately, liveability' (White and Morris, 2019).

We have sketched out an alternative vision for the development of suicidology beyond its seeming incarceration in a closed, cold, impersonal world, bounded by combinations of a) inscrutable, statistical, quantitative methodology; b) the identification of additional risk factors and protective factors; c) further attempts to predict individual suicide, including transition from ideation to attempt; together with d) psychiatric diagnoses and pharmacological treatments.

In the following concluding sections, we considered suicide research's mission, its aims and objectives, its potential contribution to our understanding of suicide, and what stubbornly remained unknown and un-investigated. This facilitated an assessment of suicide research's potential influence upon society's attitude to citizens at risk of suicide, and the bereaved survivors of persons deceased by suicide.

## Suicide research 1: strategy, outcomes and influence upon society's attitude to suicide

There was nothing good about suicide. This seemed an obvious, even facile observation: except that for those who died by suicide, an assumption existed – at least among those left alive – that for the deceased, their unbearable psychological pain, or existential psychache, had now ceased. Sadly and paradoxically, this apparently consoling aspect of suicidal loss might intensify a survivor's grief with unrealistic guilt about their perceived pre-mortem inability to ease the deceased's mental pain.

Orbach (2003) offered four models of what he termed 'mental pain' related to risk of suicide:

'a) the literary model, that is based on a content analysis of Styron's book 'Darkness Visible: A memoir of madness'(1990), describes mental pain as an inner turmoil of hostile forces; (b) the narrative model based on a qualitative analysis of pain narratives by patients, defines pain as a sense of brokenness (Bolger, 1999); (c) the phenomenological-psychache model focuses on psychache as a frustration of the most important needs (Shneidman, 1993); (d) .... .and (e) the empirical model views mental pain as a perception of negative changes in the self and its function (Baumeister, 1990)', adding that 'the common aspects in all models include intense negative emotions, loss of self, surfeit of the negative' (Orbach, 2003: 191).

Orbach's models represented mental pain as occurring within a sufferer's mind, out of sight and awareness of others. What was absent here was acknowledgement that human lives were experienced in association with others, in family, community, and society. The critical suicidology network (CSN), through the medium of critical suicide studies (Chandler et al., 2022) – as mentioned above – addressed this in its approach to understanding, theorising and intervening in suicide from alternative perspectives that sought new ways for thinking about suicide from a critical perspective to help address suicide where traditional approaches have failed:

'Many within suicide research have become frustrated by the limitations of dominant pathologising and medicalised approaches to suicide research and prevention practices. Believing that suicidology is in need of a critical re-thinking of its subject matter and a broadening of it disciplinary basis, they look at cultural practices of making sense of suicide, taking into account how suicide is shaped by history, politics, gender, identity, culture, media and power' (CSN, 2021).

Critical suicidology argued, for instance, that the psychological perception of an individual's death by suicide needed to be located beyond the mantra of a coroner's inquested conclusions detailing who/when/where/how. In addition to the personal, circumstantial characteristics of the deceased and their family, their lived reality was essential. White et al. (2016) have persuasively argued that suicide's 'multidimensional malaise' (Leenaars, 1996) cried out for a more comprehensive representation, in the only available public forum, the coroner's inquest. Instead of becoming:

'too narrowly focused on questions of individual pathology and deficit, [critical suicidology] takes as its starting point the idea that suicide is characterised by multiplicity, instability, social context, complexity, and historical contingency' (White et al., 2016, p. 4).

## Suicide research 2: reaching beyond the limitations of traditional approaches

Changing the direction of suicidology – suicide studies and research – and its cousin suicide prevention, from questions of individual pathology and deficit may take some time. Meanwhile the dominant, entrenched triumvirate of mental illness and disorders, psychopharmacology and suicide rates, might continue to reign supreme as the Western world's way of misunderstanding human self-destruction, while failing to address its enormous cost in human misery and financial misinvestment. However, a change process was available.

Ranasinghe et al. (2019) reflected upon bringing about change in health care systems in order to 'identify deficient practices and make appropriate corrections by implementing new and improved techniques and treatments' (p507). They cautioned that this could involve 'a long arduous process consisting of several small and successive deviations from the norm, analogous to "turning the oil tanker"' (p507). They also identified a 'three-pronged' approach that had allowed successful innovators to overcome resistance to change:

i) A determined opinion leader with a network of like-minded opinion leaders

ii) The presentation of hard evidence with adequate praise for current practice and the generation of clearly worded, specific guidelines

iii) The use of simple reminders and continuous analysis of outcomes (p 507).

'Mainstream' suicidology as currently extant in the Western world, according to Marsh (2015), was moribund at present:

'The authoritative voices in the field – the editors of the main suicide journals, the keynote speakers at conferences, the heads of professional associations, and the recipients of the large research grants – are almost always drawn from academic psychiatry or psychology departments, and so suicide tends to be conceptualised in ways congruent with the epistemological and ontological assumptions and commitments of those disciplines' (Marsh, 2015: 5).

This located suicide as perceived by these dominant 'authoritative voices' to the bounded domains of mental health, mental illness, and/or mental disorder and that, consequently, an individual's suicidal behaviour was essentially a consequence or outworking of feelings, thoughts and actions within their disordered mind and/or distorted decision-making process. Involved as I have been in trying to understand suicide for almost four decades, I cannot yet identify that 'determined opinion leader' otherwise than, perhaps, within the critical suicidology network (CSN). The shrill tone of the above mentioned extant 'authoritative voices' had inadvertently restricted debate and discussion to a wider, less censorious tranche of published journals and essays including, inter alia, 'Death Studies', 'Social Epistemology', 'Social Epistemology Review and Reply Collective', 'Suicidology Online' and 'International Journal of Environmental Research and Public Health'. Thus advocates of 'mainstream suicidology' were firmly entrenched in their positivistic scientism (Kral, 2015). In other words: 'Positivists believe society shapes the individual and use quantitative methods while anti-positivists or interpretivists believe individuals shape society and use qualitative methods' (Thompson, 2015).

| Positivism | Interpretivism |
|---|---|
| *Relationship between society and the individual* | |
| Society shapes the individual - 'Society consists of '*social facts*' which exercise coercive control over individuals' | Individuals have consciousness and are not just puppets who react to external social forces as Positivists believe. |
| People's actions can generally be explained by the social norms they have been exposed to through their socialisation. | Individuals are intricate and complex and different people experience and understand the same 'objective reality' in different ways |
| *General focus of social research* | |
| The point of research is to uncover the laws that govern human behaviour, just as scientists have discovered the laws that govern the physical world. | The point of research is to gain in-depth insight into the lives of respondents, to gain an empathetic understanding of why they act in the way that they do. |
| Prefer quantitative methods which allow for the researcher to remain detached from the respondents. | Prefer qualitative methods which allow for close interaction with respondents. |
| *Preferred research methods* | |
| Quantitative | Qualitative |
| Require research to be valid, reliable and representativeness | Prepared to sacrifice reliability and representativeness for greater validity |

[Table 6: accessed from Thompson (2015), contrasts 'positivism' and 'interpretivism' in social research.]

As illustrated in the diagram above, it was clear that critical suicidology favoured an interpretivist approach to suicide research, while the predominant mainstream perspective was strongly positivist. But unless the Goliath guarding the current mainstream paradigm was courageous and confident enough to engage genuinely, and discuss and debate openly with the David of the critical suicidology network (CSN) and critical suicide studies (Chandler et al., 2022), then suicide rates, as a measure of success, or otherwise, in understanding suicide and related suicide prevention strategies, will continue to misrepresent the actualité of global human self-destruction. And no one knew for sure, whether 'suicide rates', however differentiated regarding gender, ethnicity, nationality, age, marital status, occupation, method employed, et al., as variously recorded and reported in multiple locations anywhere and everywhere, were accurate or reliable.

## Conclusions 1 – Latest textbooks on suicide

It would be unfortunate and well beyond my intentions in this penultimate chapter to end on a downbeat note. So what I propose to do is to comment upon some of the optimistic conclusions reached by the authors of two recently published books on suicide, and suicide prevention by O'Connor (2021) and Bryan (2022). Both of these influential suicidologists were members of the editorial board of the 'Suicide and Life-threatening Behaviour' journal that was considered to be the flagship of mainstream suicidological research. It was safe to assume therefore that, unlike me, both would be au fait with the latest published research findings.

Both texts focused upon suicide prevention: O'Connor on 'what we can do to prevent it' and Bryan on 'why prevention fails and how we can do better'.

Both writers were supportive of Joiner's (2005) Interpersonal Theory though O'Connor (2018) had advanced his own ideas in his theory, the Integrated Motivational-Volitional model of Suicidal Behaviour (p 101/2) that incorporated Joiner's key ideas. Neither wholly accepted Joiner's (2010: 188) later assertion that almost every

– 'approaching if not 100%' – suicide deceased had a mental disorder at death, whether diagnosed or not. O'Connor (2021: 81-84) was clear that 'suicide is not explained by mental illness'. And Bryan (2022: 32) challenged the arguments of originators of this widely-held and widely promulgated view, Cavanaugh et al. (2003), in a 'maybe or maybe not' paragraph that allowed for the possibility that mental ill-health – however that was defined or understood – had not yet been totally erased as – possibly – explicating suicidal behaviour:

'Instead of assuming that most or all individuals who die by suicide have a mental illness, a more balanced and accurate perspective would be that some individuals who die by suicide have a mental illness and some individuals who die by suicide do not. Likewise, assuming that suicide is caused by or results from mental illness, a more balanced and accurate perspective would be that suicide sometimes occurs within the context of a mental illness and sometimes does not. Finally, although mental illness probably influences the emergence of suicidal behaviour, this does not mean that it is necessarily causing suicidal behaviour' (Bryan, 2022: 48).

Both authors were content to allude to case studies to illustrate aspects of their thinking about what they have learned about suicidal behaviour that might be deployed more widely. O'Connor made nine references to the suicide in 2008 of his friend Clare (RIP), almost all of which considered the aftermath for him of her death that involved shock, grief, regret, and guilt. He also mentioned with deep sadness the suicide of his former colleague the late Dr Noel Sheehy (RIP), who died by suicide in 2011. Bryan made eleven references involving two suicides, a near-lethal suicide attempt and an at-risk patient in relation to four topics: i) psychological autopsy; ii) challenging the widely-believed 90% statistic linking suicide with mental illness; iii) cases where mental illness was absent; and iv) recovery following PTSD and relevance of context and quality of life. However, neither author attempted to develop an idiographic (case-study based) approach to understanding these personal encounters with lethal and near-lethal suicidal behaviour. This might be viewed by some as an opportunity missed, since understanding suicide must be considered to be a major element for the bereaved in the work of integrating their loss experience.

Perhaps it was fairest to both writers to cite their concluding remarks about reducing the incidence of human self-destruction:

'If we are surrounded by things that improve our quality of life, we can reduce the probability of suicidal behaviour and facilitate the creation of post-suicidal lives by strengthening the value of living. This is to me the true heart and soul of the oft cited mantra suicide prevention is everyone's business. Suicide prevention does not mean that everyone needs to be conducting suicide risk screenings and repeatedly imploring people to pursue mental health treatment. Rather it means that we should be working together on a daily basis to create lives worth living' (Bryan, 2022: 198).

'I have tried ... to dispel many of the myths that surround suicide, to illustrate the complex pathways from suicidal thoughts to suicidal acts and what works to prevent suicidal behaviour. In so doing I have tried to provide hope. Hope for those who have been suicidal and hope for those who have been bereaved. Although we can never bring back those whom we have lost, we can better support those left behind, and if we work together we can save more lives. My ultimate hope is that, if we as a society are kinder and more compassionate, to ourselves and to those around us, then we will go some distance in protecting all of us from the devastation of suicide' (O'Connor, 2021: 276).

## Conclusions 2 – Social justice and human rights

It was somewhat disappointing that neither author addressed comprehensively the relevance, or otherwise, of human rights or social justice, to suicide.

From the perspective of critical suicidology, as discussed above, to make sense of suicide it was necessary to 'look at cultural practices, taking into account how suicide is shaped by history, politics, gender, identity, culture, media and power' (CSN,2021). A developing literature was investigating the significance of both social justice and human rights in understanding suicide.

For example, Button (2016) argued, as mentioned above, that:

'While individual cases of suicide can frequently generate widespread feelings of loss and grief, a collective sense of political responsibility for the enduring and differential conditions of suicidality remains missing today' (Button, 2016).

Platt (2016) considered arguments that advocated changes in government policy related to social justice that went beyond simply reducing inequalities, and that he felt could positively challenge suicide's attrition across society:

'The approach to tackling inequalities in suicidal behaviour depends on the overarching philosophy of health inequality reduction that is adopted by the government. A concentration on reducing the overall level of suicide in society or on reducing suicide risk only among the most disadvantaged may result in little change in relative risk between the most and least privileged, and it may even result in an increased relative risk by widening inequalities. On the other hand, the development and delivery of effective public policy interventions that reduce poverty, boost educational performance, improve housing conditions, and reduce unemployment would address the fundamental sources of disadvantage faced by many population groups, leading to a reduction in their risk of suicidal behaviour' (Platt, 2016).

Three years later, the UN Special Rapporteur on the Right to Health followed Button's (2016) lead when they pulled no punches in challenging what they perceived were current ineffective approaches:

'We cannot effectively prevent suicide by increasing the use of prescription medicines. Instead, we need to acknowledge that emotional pain frequently comes from social problems, including being a victim of violence, discrimination, or exclusion ... mental distress is frequently poorly managed. Targeting the brain chemistry of individuals often exacerbates stigma and social exclusion, aggravates loneliness and helplessness and fails to reduce the risk of suicide.

'Treating individual responses to adversity as if they are medical conditions disempowers individuals and perpetuates social exclusion and stigma. Interpersonal and gender-based violence, and child abuse and neglect, all contribute to the high incidence and the economic burden of mental health conditions.

'If we are serious about preventing suicide, we must pursue new approaches that fortify healthy, respectful and trusting relationships which also include connecting people with communities. Suicide prevention must address the structural factors that make lives unliveable and examine how distress arises within power imbalances and within harmful relationships.

'A targeted, individual response to each person's situation is vital in suicide prevention, and each response should be careful to avoid excessive use of medication, coercion, and isolation.

'To help people to want to stay alive and thrive, it is necessary to have ongoing community-based care within robust support systems that can adequately reach people where they live, work, learn and play. States should adopt rights-based strategies to suicide prevention that avoid excessive medicalisation and [that] address societal determinants, promoting autonomy and resilience through social connection, tolerance, justice, and healthy relationships' (Puras, 2019).

Unfortunately, translating some or all of the admirable sentiments in these three writers' (viz. Button, Platt and Puras) potential ways ahead, would involve progressive change away from, or perhaps initially alongside, the dominant individualistic, psychological/psychiatric diagnosis and treatment of each 'pathological suicidal patient' towards an as yet not fully defined alternative. This transition could represent a community-based, right-to-life approach, politically empowered and resourced to address suicide as a matter of social justice involving every member of society.

**Myth:** (fictitious popular idea) Understanding suicide is well beyond the capacity of most people. It's best to leave the whole thing to the experts.

**Fallacy:** (misleading argument) Only by treating each suicidal patient with the latest medications can we help them to move away from harming themselves.

# References

Baumeister, R. F. (1990) Suicide as escape from self. Psychological Review, January, 1990, 97(1), 90-113

Baumeister, R. F. (1991) Escaping the self: alcoholism, spirituality, masochism, and other flights from the burden of selfhood. New York, NY: Basic Books

Beautrais, A. L. (2001) Suicides and serious suicide attempts: Two populations or one? Psychological Medicine, 31, 837– 845

Bolger, E. A. (1999) Grounded theory analysis of emotional pain. Psychother Res 1999; 9: 342–362

Bryan, C. J. (2022) Re-thinking suicide: why prevention fails and how we can do better. Oxford: Oxford University Press

Button, M. E. (2016) Suicide and social justice: towards a political approach to suicide. Political Research Quarterly, 69(2), June 2016, pp 270-280

Cavanaugh, J. T., Carson, A. J., Sharpe, M. and Lawrie, S. M. (2003) Psychological autopsy studies of suicide: a systematic review. Psychological Medicine, 33, 395-405

Chandler, A.D., Cover, R. and Fitzpatrick, S. J. (2022) Critical suicide studies, between methodology and ethics: Introduction. Health 26(1), 3-9

CSN-Critical Suicidology Network (2021) Accessed on 22 December 2021 at https://criticalsuicidology.net/

Dorpat, T. L. and Boswell, J. W. (1963). An evaluation of suicide intent in suicide attempts. Comprehensive Psychiatry, 4, 117–125

Dorpat, T. L. and Ripley, H. (1967). The relationship between attempted suicide and committed suicide. Comprehensive Psychiatry, 8, 74–79

Durkheim, E. (1897/2002) Suicide – a study in sociology. London: Routledge

Finocchiaro, M. (2009) The Galileo Affair. In Physics World Magazine. Accessed on 23 June 2022 at https://physicsworld.com/a/the-galileo-affair/

Fisher, M. (2012) Why mental health is a political issue. Mark Fisher. The Guardian. 16 July 2016

Free Dictionary (2021) Meaning of 'hidden in plain sight': Accessed on 16 December 2021 at https://idioms.thefreedictionary.com/hide+in+plain+sight

Harding, A. (2009) Obituary: Edwin Shneidman. Pioneer in the study and prevention of suicide. Born on May 13, 1918, in York, PA, USA, he died on May 18, 2009, of natural causes, in Los Angeles, CA, USA, aged 91 years. Lancet, Vol 374, page 286, 25 July 2009

Hjelmeland, H. (2018) Interview: career advice from Heidi Hjelmeland. 18 October 2018. Accessed on 21 December 2021 at https://netecr.org/2018/10/10/interview-career-advice-from-heidi-hjelmeland/

Jobes, D. A. & Barnett, J. E. (2024) Evidence-based care for suicidality as an ethical and professional imperative: how to decrease suicidal suffering and save lives. American Psychologist. Advance online publication. http://psycnet.apa.org/record/2024-78987-001

Joiner, T. E. (2005) Why people die by suicide. Cambridge, MA: Harvard University Press

Joiner, T. E. (2010) Myths about suicide. Cambridge, MA: Harvard University Press

Kral, M. J. (2015) Critical suicidology as an alternative to mainstream revolving-door suicidology. Michael J Kral, Wayne State University. Social Epistemology Review and Reply Collective, Vol 4(6), 10-11

Leenaars, A. A. (1996) Suicide: a multidimensional malaise. Suicide and Life-Threatening Behaviour, Vol. 26(3), Fall 1996

Linehan, M. (1986). Suicidal people. One population or two? In J. J. Mann & M. Stanley (eds.), Psychobiology of suicidal behaviour (pp. 16–33). New York, NY: Annals of the New York Academy of Sciences

Mann, J. J. & M. Stanley, M. (eds.) (1986) Psychobiology of suicidal behaviour. New York, NY: Annals of the New York Academy of Sciences

Marsh, I. (2015) 'Critical Suicidology': Toward an Inclusive, Inventive and Collaborative (Post) Suicidology. Social Epistemology Review and Reply Collective, 2015 Vol. 4, No. 6, 5-9. [Ian Marsh, Canterbury Christ Church University]

Meyer, C. L., Irani, T. H., Hermes, K. A. and Yung, B. (2017) Explaining suicide: patterns, motivations, and what notes reveal. London: Academic Press (Elsevier)

Michel, K. (1987). Suicide risk factors: A comparison of suicide attempters with suicide completers. British Journal of Psychiatry, 150, 78–82

Mills, C. (2018) 'Dead people don't claim': A psychopolitical autopsy of UK austerity suicides Crit. Soc. Policy 2018, 38, 302–322

O'Connor, R. C. (2018) The integrated motivational-volitional model of suicidal behaviour. Philosophical Transactions of the Royal Society B., 373, 20170268

O'Connor, R. C. (2021) When it is darkest: why people die by suicide and what we can do to prevent it. London: Vermilion, an imprint of Ebury Publishing

O'Neill, S. and Bond, N. (2024) Updated review of literature on suicide and suicidal behaviour in Northern Ireland. In Protect Life 2 – Review (2024) Action Plan: Report and Recommendations. Annex 2. pp 46-60. September 2024. N Ireland Department of Health. Stormont, Belfast, N Ireland

O'Neill, S. and O'Connor, R. C. (2020) Suicide in Northern Ireland: epidemiology, risk factors, and prevention. Lancet Psychiatry, 7(6), pp 538-546

Orbach, I. (2003) Mental pain and suicide. Israel Journal of Psychiatry and Related Sciences, 40(3) 191-201

Pallis, D. J. and Sainsbury, P. (1976). The value of assessing intent in attempted suicides. Psychological Medicine, 6, 487–492

Pallis, D. J., Barraclough, B. M., Levey, A. B., Jenkins, J. S. and Sainsbury, P. (1982). Estimating suicide risk among attempted suicides: The development of new clinical scales. British Journal of Psychiatry, 141, 37–44.

Platt, S. (2016) Suicide prevention: it's a social justice issue. Stephen Platt. 13 May 2016. Social Justice, a journal of crime, conflict and world order

Protect Life 2 (2019) Protect Life 2 – a strategy for preventing suicide and self-harm in Northern Ireland 2019-2024. 19 September 2019. NI Department of Health, Stormont, Belfast

Protect Life 2 – Review (2024) Action Plan: Report and Recommendations. September 2024. N Ireland Department of Health. Stormont, Belfast, N Ireland

Puras, D. (2019) Human Rights Approaches to Suicide Prevention Make Life "More Liveable". Dainius Puras, UN Special Rapporteur on the right to health. Health & Human Rights Journal, 9 Oct 2019

Ranasinghe, L., Dor, F. J. M. F. and Herbert, P. (2019) Turning the oil tanker: a novel approach to shifting perspectives in medical practice. Advances in Medical Education and Practice, 2019:10, pp 507-511

Rivlin, A., Ferris, R., Marzano, L., Seena, F. and Hawton, K. (2013) A typology of male prisoners making near-lethal suicide attempts. Crisis: Journal of Crisis Intervention and Suicide Prevention, 34(5), 335-347

Shneidman, E. S. (1993) Suicide as psychache: a clinical approach to self-destructive behaviour. London: Jason Aronson Inc

Shneidman, E. S. (2004) Autopsy of a suicidal mind. Oxford, England: Oxford University Press

Shneidman, E. S. and Farberow, N. L. (eds.) (1957) Clues to suicide. New York, NY: McGraw-Hill Book Company Inc

Soper, C. A. (2017) Towards solving the evolutionary puzzle of suicide. A thesis submitted to the University of Gloucestershire for the degree of doctor of philosophy (PhD) in the School of Natural and Social Sciences

Stengel, E. N., and Cook, R. (1958). Attempted suicide. London, UK: Chapman and Hall

Styron, W. (1990) Darkness visible: a memoir of madness. London: Random House

Thompson, K. (2015) Positivism and interpretivism in social research. Accessed on 5 January 2022 at https://revisesociology.com/2015/05/18/positivism-interpretivism-sociology/

Weinreich, P. and Saunderson, W. (eds.) (2003) Analysing Identity: Cross-Cultural, Societal and Clinical Contexts. London: Routledge

White, J., Kral, M., Marsh, I. and Morris, J. (eds.) (2016) Introduction: Re-thinking suicide. In J. White, M. Kral, I. Marsh, & J. Morris (eds.) Critical Suicidology: Transforming Suicide Research and Prevention for the 21st Century. (pp. 1–11). Vancouver, Canada: University of British Columbia Press

White, J., M. Kral, M., Marsh, I. & J. Morris (eds.) Critical Suicidology: Transforming Suicide Research and Prevention for the 21st Century. (pp. 1–11). Vancouver, Canada: University of British Columbia Press

White, J. and Morris, J. (2019) Re-thinking Ethics and Politics in Suicide Prevention: Bringing Narrative Ideas into Dialogue with Critical Suicide Studies. Int. J. Environ. Res. Public Health 2019, 16, 3236

WHO (2021) World Health Organisation (WHO). Suicide. Accessed on 19 December2021 at https://www.who.int/news-room/fact-sheets/detail/suicide

\* \* \*

## Chapter 18
# Suicide – Afterthoughts and recommendations

**Raison d'être**

The book's contents page was initially drafted in early 2015, two years after I set up the Belfast Centre for Study of Suicide (www.philipokeeffe.com), a registered company, as an accessible repository for some of my thoughts and with the objective of engaging interested students in suicide studies and research. While the manuscript for this book eventually reached a conclusion, the Belfast Centre continues to remain dormant.

This book's origins rest in the suggestion of my doctoral supervisor, the much missed Emeritus Professor Dr Peter Weinreich (RIP), that it might be an appropriate substitute for peer-reviewed journal articles that I was unable to publish regardless of quality, due perhaps inter alia, to my independent, self-funded status outside any university. Some of the contents herein represent my perspective on suicide as a bereaved survivor of family death(s) by suspected suicide up to four decades ago.

My research studies at Ulster University at master's degree and doctorate levels, investigated the aftermath of suicide for families and clinicians, respectively. They were related indirectly to my personal experience. Both dissertations are accessible at the Belfast Centre's (2024) website and also at the Identity Exploration (2022) website.

I did succeed in publishing several 'opinion' articles in a 'Mind Matters' column of a local Belfast newspaper, The Irish News, in the Irish Association of Suicidology newsletter and more recently in a Belfast quarterly social affairs magazine 'The View'. I also published some papers on the Researchgate website.

I worked as a lecturer (2001-2014) in N Ireland further education colleges and at the School of Education, Queen's University Belfast. My subject areas included diploma/advanced diploma courses in counselling / psychotherapy and short, introductory courses in suicidology. I also worked with clients, as a counsellor in private practice from November 1998 until September 2021, when I retired having earned the status in 2013, as a registered, accredited British Association of Counselling and Psychotherapy (BACP) psychotherapist.

## Afterthoughts

Readers of the book's 17+ chapters will no doubt gather that I remain somewhat skeptical of society's – and government's – current attitude, approach and policy in relation to human suicidal behaviour in Ireland/UK. In particular, I reject the medicalisation of suicide (Szasz, 2010), just as much as I reject the perpetration of state, individual or group violence, power-lusting terrorism and authoritarian forms of government, in Ireland, UK and elsewhere. I need not rehearse again what underpins my conviction. Instead, I shall briefly set down – call them recommendations – my priorities for a different way ahead in our understanding and response, as a society, to the catastrophe of any and all suicidal behaviour by our citizens.

## Priorities and/or Recommendations

1. Reformation of the administration of the Irish/UK Coroners' service to facilitate reasonable access by qualified, competent researchers to the complete Coroners' service records of deaths by suspected or actual suicide. Currently at 'the discretion of the Coroner "properly interested persons" may see notes of evidence or any document put in evidence at an inquest and may also obtain copies of these on payment of a fee' (Coroners Service, 2022). The recommended reasonable access should be extended to include the Coroners' findings, conclusions and recommendations. It should when appropriate be made clear by the Coroners' Service that any coroner's inquest findings and conclusions in relation to deaths by suspected suicide are

required to be based upon 'the balance of probabilities' aka the civil standard of proof (UK Supreme Court, 2020).

2. Introduction of any necessary changes in the educational syllabi and professional practice inter alia of police officers, emergency service personnel, medical practitioners, social workers, and counselling practitioners including mandatory continuous professional development (CPD): this is essential to match the needs, including knowledge and skills, of public employees tasked with 'first responder' and 'ongoing care' responsibilities when they encounter during their employment any individual's suspected or evident, suicidal behaviour, including lethal and non-lethal self harm.

3. Progressive removal, in relation to suicidal behaviour, of the use of stigmatizing language, including umbrella terms 'mental health', or 'mental illness' or 'mental disorder' in the context of any individual's problems in living reasonably and contentedly in the context of their personal, or family, or work-place, or neighbourhood, or community circumstances.

4. In relation to interaction with individuals engaging in suspected suicidal behaviour, the early phasing out – leading to ultimate removal – of coercive, medical, psychiatric 'treatment', including so-called electric shock treatment, and prescription of pharmaceutical medications, associated with compulsory detention in hospital ('sectioning'). This practice calls out for its replacement with and by caring, compassionate attention, advice and support as deemed necessary and effective by qualified, competent practitioners and as agreed to and with the explicit, voluntary consent of any affected individual, experiencing problems in living reasonably and contentedly in society.

5. Introduction at third level educational institutions, including further education colleges and universities, of comprehensive suites of accredited certificate, diploma/advanced diploma, and first degree courses in suicidology including access to relevant modules by enrolled students inter alia of police, emergency

service, medical, social worker, and counselling practitioner courses (Muehlenkamp, J.J. and Thoen, S.K., 2019).

6  Amendment as necessary of syllabi at 'O', 'A' and 'S' levels for second level courses in psychology, religious studies and sociology so as to include age / stage / maturity appropriate content on suicidology.

7.1 My informal survey of relevant NI public services found that psychological autopsy post-suicide was not normally practised at present. Coroners are restricted by statute, custom and practice, in their investigative enquiry or inquest to ascertain answers to factual 'who / when / where/ how' questions in relation to the suicide deceased. My view is that in conjunction with #1 above, the 'why' question – ever present in suicide's aftermath – might be explored indirectly. Currently, the deceased's pathway to a brutal, secret death remains largely untouched, overgrown, ignored, hidden and excluded from most inquests.

7.2 An amended form of psychological autopsy – normally limited to a hopeless quest for speculative insights into the suicide deceased's 'state of mind' at death – might be extended to consideration by any and all interested parties regarding how might this death have been avoided, prevented, delayed, postponed, and ultimately cancelled by the deceased when alive. This situation contrasted starkly with mandatory outcomes of UK public enquiries [e.g Moore-Bick (Grenfell, ongoing), Dame Janet Smyth (Shipman Enquiry), Redfern (Alder Hey Organs Scandal), Pitchford (Undercover policing), Levy/Khan (Pindown Child Abuse), and many others (Wikipedia, 2022)] that invariably address three crucial questions:

i   How was this catastrophic situation permitted to occur?
ii  How might it have been prevented?
iii What lessons, if any, have been learned such that it may never happen again?

Coroners' inquests into suspected suicide rarely engage comprehensively with the enormous potential within these pertinent questions.

8. Linking depression with suicide as a cause/effect phenomenon is as useless as supposing that there is a causative relationship between stress and cancer. Correlation perhaps in some limited circumstances, but causation? No, being stressed doesn't directly increase the risk of cancer. The best quality studies have followed up many people for several years. They have found no evidence that those who are more stressed are more likely to get cancer (Cancer Research UK, 2021). New data on depression that has followed people over long periods of time suggests that about 2 percent of those people ever treated for depression in an outpatient setting will die by suicide (US HHS Gov, 2022).

9. Every death by suspected suicide should be the subject of an investigation as rigorous as if that death was by other than natural causes. My informal survey of students' opinions in regarding this proposal related to the subject of responsibility – what, and more specifically, who caused the death? In suicide deaths, the 'who' by definition is the deceased while the 'what' aspect, including any identifiable responsibility beyond the deceased is largely ignored as an irrelevant unknown by our existing hamstrung, inquisitorial bureaucracy.

10. The discussion in Chapter 17's conclusions (above) referred to a raft of issues beyond the influence or control or responsibility of an individual suicide deceased, but where some situational and/or circumstantial responsibility, albeit indirectly, may more than likely have rested. These included:

i. Quality of life that strengthens the value of living
ii. Better support for survivors of suicide bereavement
iii. A collective sense of political responsibility for the enduring and differential conditions of suicidality
iv. Development and delivery of effective public policy interventions that reduce poverty, boost educational performance, improve housing conditions, and reduce unemployment [that] would address the fundamental sources of disadvantage faced by many population groups

v.   Emotional pain frequently comes from social problems, including being a victim of violence, discrimination, oppression or exclusion ... mental distress is frequently poorly managed

vi.  Treating individual responses to adversity as if they are medical conditions disempowers individuals and perpetuates social exclusion and stigma. Interpersonal and gender violence, and child abuse and neglect, all contribute to the high incidence and the economic burden of adverse, psychological health conditions

vii. Pursuit of new approaches that fortify healthy, respectful and trusting relationships, which also include connecting people with communities, [and] address the structural factors that make lives unliveable. [Also] examine how distress arises within power imbalances and within harmful relationships

viii. A targeted, individual response to each person's situation is vital in suicide prevention ... and each response should be careful to avoid excessive use of medication, coercion, and isolation

ix.  To encourage people to identify 'reasons to stay alive' (Haig, 2016). This may mean that it is necessary to establish, fund and locate ongoing, accessible community-based care facilities, within robust support systems, that can adequately engage with those individuals and families who could benefit from them where they live, work, learn and play

x.   States should adopt rights-based strategies to [address suicidal behaviour] that avoid[s] excessive medicalisation and address[es] societal determinants, promoting autonomy and resilience through social connection, tolerance, justice, and healthy relationships.

**Endnote**

Few if any of the issues listed at #10 above are expected to appear to my knowledge in current or prospective Irish/UK political party manifestos. I conclude that little is likely to change in the near term in relation to our societal approaches to suicide. Continuation of existing policies and strategies will unfortunately ensure that the incidence of suicidal behaviour, including deliberate self-harm, will remain probably at current and perhaps enhanced levels into the foreseeable future.

Suicide is without question a political issue that has for decades been mislabelled a 'mental health' matter, and hived off to our overburdened, under resourced Irish/UK publicly funded, independent and 'private for profit' health sectors. It is therefore not wholly surprising that the catastrophic phenomenon of suicide that devastates individuals, families and communities, and traumatizes many bereaved survivors, shows little or no sign of going away any time soon.

## References

Belfast Centre for Study of Suicide (2024) Accessible at https://www.philipokeeffe.com

Cancer Research UK (2021) Together we will beat cancer. Accessed on 6 March 2022 at https://www.cancerresearchuk.org/about-cancer/causes-of-cancer/cancer-myths/can-stress-causecancer# #

Coroners Service for Northern Ireland (2022) Information about the work of the Coroners Service, the inquest process and ... the coroners system. Accessed on 6 March 2022 at https://www.justice-ni.gov.uk/articles/coroners-service-northern-ireland

Haig, M. (2016) Reasons to stay alive. Edinburgh: Canongate Books Ltd

Muehlenkamp, J.J. and Thoen, S.K. (2019) Short- and Long Term Impact of an Undergraduate Suicidology Course. Suicide and Life-threatening Behaviour, 49(6), 1573-1586. December 2019

Szasz, T. (2010) The medicalisation of suicide. The Freeman, October 2010. Accessed on 5 March 2022 at http://www.szasz.com/3medicalizationofsuicide.pdf

UK Supreme Court (2020) R (on the application of Maughan) (Appellant) v Her Majesty's Senior Coroner for Oxfordshire (Respondent) (2020) UKSC 46. On appeal from [2019] EWCA Civ 809. Press summary, 13 November 2020

US HHS Gov (2022) US Dept of Health and Human Services. Answers: mental health and substance abuse. Accessed on 6 March 2022 at https://www.hhs.gov/answers/mental-health-and-substance-abuse/does-depression-increase-risk-of-suicide/index.html#

Wikipedia (2022) UK public enquiries. Accessed on 26 June 2022 at https://en.wikipedia.org/wiki/Public_inquiry

\* \* \*

# Index

For technical reasons, this index mostly cites proper names with the surname only and without forename initials. In the few cases where two or more people have the same surname, the initial is given in separate references. However, full references with initials are given for all names within the book's body and in bibliographies at the end of each chapter.

**A**

Abrutyn 170, 189, 192
Abrutyn et al 170
abuse 74, 75, 78, 79, 80, 81, 82, 86, 114, 157, 210, 213, 436, 448, 464, 476, 477, 478
abusive behaviour 206
academically gifted student 210, 219
accidental death 9, 117, 160, 217, 300, 305
accidental suicide 200, 306
acquired capability for suicide 422, 423, 438
Acquired Capability for Suicide Scale (ACCS) 423
Acute management of a person at risk of self-harm 37
addiction 45, 52, 282, 283, 285, 299, 347, 386, 387, 407, 414, 441, 452
Addiction Northern Ireland Team 282
adolescent 20, 70, 85, 221, 289, 293
Advocacy After Fatal Domestic Abuse 78
affect 31, 45, 102, 121, 125, 130, 131, 170, 179, 202, 331, 404
aftermath 9, 12, 24, 40, 59, 91, 103, 104, 105, 106, 107, 114, 115, 121, 122, 123, 124, 130, 133, 134, 150, 154, 155, 158, 161, 183, 187, 220, 269, 272, 288, 291, 304, 336, 349, 366, 379, 386, 390, 393, 405, 412, 462, 471, 474
age 15, 35, 42, 59, 66, 77, 93, 102, 105, 179, 184, 185, 211, 231, 262, 277, 278, 280, 288, 305, 310, 337, 381, 396, 409, 434, 446, 461, 474
alcohol 20, 80
alcoholism 58, 186, 233, 385, 465
Alexander 60, 109, 144
Alexander et al., 109
Alliance Party 178, 193
Allport 231, 244, 253, 260, 262, 264

Altruistic suicide 40, 424
Alvarez 7, 8, 11, 18, 226, 244, 255, 256, 257, 258, 265, 409, 438
American Association of Suicidology 36, 92, 104, 107, 109, 144, 198, 199, 242, 293, 330, 404, 417, 419, 426
American Foundation for Suicide Prevention 146, 398
American Psychiatric Association 31, 35, 36, 190, 230, 232, 244, 338, 413, 439
Andreissen 92, 93, 144
anguish 30, 31, 84, 94, 122, 278, 317
anomic suicide 41
anorexia nervosa 226
anticipation 122
antidepressant 29
anti-social criminality 65
anti-social personality 226
anxiety 27, 28, 35, 180, 210, 226, 230, 272, 414, 455
apparent 6, 12, 23, 25, 26, 70, 77, 78, 115, 121, 155, 164, 279, 334, 393, 395
apparent suicide 6, 25, 70, 77, 78
Applied Suicide Intervention Skills Training 17-19
Archives of Suicide Research 219, 340, 415, 420, 422, 423, 442, 443
Arensman 71, 415, 432, 433, 434, 438
Arrested flight model 235
Asberg, M., Nordstrom, P. and Traskman-Bendz, L. 244
Applied Suicide Intervention Skills Training (ASIST) 16-19
aspirational systems of values and beliefs 112
assessment 17, 26, 27, 71, 99, 113, 117, 127, 128, 129, 131, 133, 134, 146, 147, 149, 151, 152, 167, 171, 208, 222, 238, 249, 294, 335, 362, 396, 426, 428, 434, 439, 453, 457
assessment and management 146, 147, 152, 167, 439
assessment and prevention 171
Assessment and Qualifications Alliance 39
assisted dying 155, 344, 357, 360, 361, 362, 363, 364, 365, 367, 368, 372
Assisted Dying Survey Report 362
assisted suicide 9, 11, 19, 224, 336, 343, 344, 345, 346, 347, 357, 360, 362, 364, 368, 370, 372
Associative Network Model 235
Atkinson 53, 84, 165, 218, 307, 315
Auerbach 44
Australia 17, 159, 174, 177, 204, 308, 309, 341, 375, 421, 423, 451

## B

Baker  349, 350, 351, 368
balance of probabilities  5, 23, 59, 60, 86, 155, 224, 306, 398, 473
Barnes  3, 80, 84
Barry  45, 167
Baton Rouge Crisis Intervention Centre  304
Battin  11, 18, 232, 244
Bauer  145, 146, 422, 423, 438
Baumeister  51, 53, 235, 241, 244, 445, 458, 465
Baumeister's EscapeTheory  445
Beasley-Murray  60
Beautrais  446, 466
Beck  51, 53, 211, 218, 227, 235, 241, 250
Belfast Centre for Study of Suicide  471, 477
Belfast Domestic Violence Partnership  80, 84
Belfast Health and Social Care Trust  289, 293
Benning  333, 334, 338
Bereaved by Suicide Support Group  304
bereavement  15, 19, 22, 24, 47, 72, 73, 91, 94, 97, 98, 102, 147, 159, 183, 189, 197, 198, 199, 205, 221, 242, 269, 271, 278, 305, 307, 326, 340, 381, 387, 475
Berman  20, 35, 38, 92, 93, 106, 145, 192, 222, 233, 249, 406, 407
Bertolete  332, 338
Beskow, J. et al.  330
beyond a reasonable doubt  5, 23, 59, 306, 398
Biedenweig and Gross-Camp  154
biopsychosocial assessment  71
Bipolar  27, 100
Black and McKay  181, 182, 280, 313, 323
Black Dog Institute  309, 315
Black, L.A.  265  Blakely et al.  48
Blasco-Fontecilla et al. 414
Boland  71, 90
Boldt  170, 189
borderline personality disorder  54, 226
Boston University School of Public Health  45
Braithwaite  56, 207, 218, 443
Brennock  301, 316

Brexit 178 Bridge et al 62
Britain 5, 7, 24, 174, 269, 317, 344, 349, 365
British Association for Counselling 109, 145
British Medical Association 360, 368
Brown 41, 53, 85, 122, 145, 167, 245, 316
Brown, H. N. 145
Brown, M.M. 85,145
Brown, S.T. 167
Bryan, C. 439, 466
Bryan, D. 36, 189
Bryan, W. J. 339
Buie, D.H. 166
bulimia 226
Bunney and Fawcett 234
Bunting et al. 175, 179, 232

## C

Cain 94, 109, 128, 133, 145, 152, 183, 190, 293, 297
Cameron 164, 165
CAMHS cf. Child and Adolescent Heath Service (Irish Government)
CAMS cf. Collaboration and Management of Suicidality 253, 266, 426, 427, 428, 429, 438, 439, 440, 443
Camus, A. 9, 253-269
Capacity Building & Support 312
Capital punishment 321, 342
caregiver's reaction 147
Carroll, R. 316
Carswell 69, 90, 272, 293
Carty 68, 89
case history 211
case study 42, 43, 51, 98, 111, 112, 125, 126, 152, 160, 182, 196, 211, 242, 243, 271, 378, 419, 445
Causes 189
Cavanaugh 214, 218, 462, 466
Census 178
Cerel 59, 60, 85, 92, 145, 304, 316
Chandler 313, 316, 450, 456, 458, 461, 466
character disorder 31

Chemtob et al. 109
Chesney et al. 332
child abuse 464, 476
Child and Adolescent Health Service (CAMHS) 70, 71
child contact 80
Choron 232, 245
Chu 170, 171, 190, 246
client 93, 99, 103, 104, 105, 106, 107, 108, 109, 111, 112, 114, 115, 116, 117, 118, 119, 121, 122, 123, 124, 125, 126, 127, 128, 129, 130, 131, 132, 133, 134, 135, 136, 138, 140, 146, 147, 148, 149, 150, 151, 162, 171, 183, 192, 227, 237, 238, 248, 262, 297, 334, 335, 379, 390, 391, 392, 393, 394, 395, 396, 398, 399, 406, 426, 427, 428, 429
client at risk 124, 126, 131, 262, 426
client suicide 104, 105, 106, 107, 108, 111, 114, 116, 121, 122, 123, 124, 125, 129, 130, 131, 132, 133, 146, 147, 148, 150, 192, 248, 297, 379, 390, 391, 393, 394, 395, 406
clinical 11, 21, 26, 34, 37, 55, 64, 68, 98, 110, 122, 145, 146, 148, 149, 151, 153, 163, 164, 167, 171, 185, 194, 195, 215, 229, 233, 235, 238, 246, 247, 249, 266, 285, 322, 331, 335, 351, 362, 371, 377, 397, 405, 408, 412, 423, 426, 427, 428, 434, 440, 442, 453, 468, 469
clinician 124, 125, 126, 129, 134, 158, 162
clinician survivor 104-118, 121, 123, 130, 131, 132, 133, 391, 393, 394, 395, 399, 406
clinician survivor by proxy 104, 112, 116, 117, 118, 133
Clinician Survivors Task Force 107
Clusters 61
coercive actions 163
coercive behaviour 79
Cognitive-Affective Consistency Theory 99, 400
Cognitive Behaviour Model 237
Cognitive-Behavioural Therapy 253
Collaborating Centre for Research and Training in Suicide Prevention 421
Collaborative Assessment and Management of Suicidality 253, 266, 426, 427, 428, 429, 438, 439, 440, 443
Colucci 169, 170, 171, 190, 191, 415
community 5, 13, 26, 29, 41, 42, 68, 99, 102, 118, 155, 156, 159, 162, 178, 180, 181, 189, 198, 270, 286, 287, 311, 312, 313, 322, 325, 339, 348, 350, 387, 433, 454, 455, 456, 458, 465, 473, 476
compulsory treatment order 58

Comte, A. 39

confirmatory bias 331

conflict 24, 25, 29, 33, 42, 43, 55, 81, 113, 126, 159, 160, 170, 173, 174, 175, 180, 181, 183, 190, 232, 272, 275, 276, 277, 278, 292, 294, 297, 300, 302, 327, 347, 361, 363, 385, 393, 411, 468

conflicted 112, 114, 117, 119, 125, 126, 130, 157, 184, 363, 395, 402, 403, 448

connectedness 47, 106, 121, 225, 332

Connelly 257, 400

consciousness 12, 22, 32, 44, 50, 228, 252, 257, 286

consent 16, 27, 64, 94, 97, 109, 111, 202, 224, 345, 417, 473

contagion 82, 83

Corrigall-Brown, C.J. 41, 53

coroner 5, 12, 15, 23, 24, 25, 58, 59, 60, 64, 66, 67, 71, 74, 82, 84, 88, 116, 186, 198, 199, 200, 201, 206, 208, 216, 219, 223, 224, 245, 268, 269, 272, 274, 280, 281, 282, 287, 288, 289, 290, 308, 310, 315, 380, 447, 458, 472

cost of crime in Northern Ireland 316

costs of suicide 311

Cotton et al. 122

counselling 28, 67, 69, 72, 93, 97, 98, 99, 102, 103, 104, 109, 114, 115, 116, 117, 118, 137, 145, 149, 150, 158, 159, 162, 165, 186, 187, 192, 264, 296, 380, 386, 387, 391, 392, 394, 396, 398, 404, 406, 410, 437, 472, 473, 474

counsellor 95, 99, 103, 104, 109, 114, 115, 116, 135, 149, 151, 284, 298, 336, 391, 392, 393, 394, 395, 398, 456, 472

countertransference 107, 116, 121, 127, 129, 157, 158, 392

Coveney, C.M. et al. 17

Covid-19 30, 41, 52, 162, 172, 187, 353, 354, 355, 356

criminal charges 63, 73

criminal gangs 49

Criminal Injuries Compensation Authority 303

Crisis 16, 19, 20, 30, 37, 38, 55, 113, 144, 147, 153, 166, 167, 189, 191, 218, 219, 246, 249, 266, 293, 295, 304, 317, 338, 405, 415, 420, 421, 430, 441, 442, 443, 469

crisis care 309

Cruse 151, 185, 186, 187, 386, 387

Cryan, E.M.J., Kelly, P. and McCaffrey146 CSTF 107

CTH 127, 128, 129

Cubic Theory 228, 231, 234

cultural contexts 172, 191, 354, 454

cultural drivers 207, 363

cultural theory of suicide 170
culture 5, 41, 43, 47, 65, 168, 169, 170, 171, 172, 173, 191, 193, 215, 218, 360, 367, 368, 421, 430, 432, 451, 458, 463
Curtice and Sandford 322
cutting 33, 438, 455
Cvinar 330, 339

# D

Dana 168, 190
D'Andrade 170, 190
Daubert Standard 212, 213
Davidson 210, 219
Davidson and Linnoila 210
Dawes 260, 265, 267
death certificate 22, 230, 345
death certification practices 349
death penalty 322
de Beauvoir 257
decriminalisation 269
decriminalised 182, 303
Deeney 281, 293
defamation 62
definition of suicide 11, 21, 59, 83, 88, 153, 193, 217, 249, 298, 373, 374, 375, 407 407
De Leo 202, 204, 212, 218, 220, 221, 270, 293, 338, 378, 405, 422, 423, 442
Demographics 213
Denmark 308
Department of Health 30, 69, 166, 199, 221, 246, 266, 289, 310, 311, 316, 318, 322, 323, 327, 337, 338, 341, 355, 370, 397, 406, 407, 452, 468, 469
Department of Health, Social Services and Public Safety (DHSSPS) 289
depression 22, 27, 28, 29, 31, 63, 65, 67, 74, 94, 101, 105, 114, 136, 141, 144, 158, 170, 180, 185, 187, 210, 211, 226, 229, 230, 232, 238, 254, 261, 266, 286, 297, 312, 380, 389, 393, 395, 405, 414, 418, 420, 449, 455, 475, 478
depression and suicide 136, 141, 144, 230, 393, 395
depressive disorder 22, 214
deprivation 42, 179, 180, 181, 192, 195, 418
Descartes, R. 254
determinants 28, 34, 45, 121, 465, 476

development 4, 39, 50, 98, 102, 103, 105, 111, 120, 123, 128, 130, 132, 133, 134, 150, 170, 171, 178, 192, 209, 224, 225, 235, 237, 238, 248, 264, 297, 304, 307, 308, 310, 314, 316, 320, 332, 357, 366, 377, 379, 383, 390, 391, 406, 410, 414, 415, 416, 426, 428, 433, 437, 441, 452, 456, 457, 464, 468, 473

Diagnostic and Statistical Manual (DSM) 22, 31, 35, 36, 37, 38, 174, 190, 226, 244, 245, 338, 339, 413, 416, 438, 439

diathesis 235, 238

Diathesis–stress–hopelessness Model 235

Dicke 417, 439

Differential Activation Theory 235

Dignity in Dying 365

disability 18, 22, 29, 33, 180, 327, 337

distress 17, 27, 48, 64, 67, 68, 69, 70, 73, 74, 82, 106, 115, 122, 148, 155, 167, 170, 205, 252, 285, 303, 365, 414, 429, 456, 464, 465, 476

Doctrine of Double Effect 366

Doerr 329, 339

Doherty and Mageean 25

domestic abuse 78, 79, 80, 82, 86, 436

domestic violence 52, 63, 80, 81, 82, 88, 90

Doran, G.T. 339

Doran, C.M. and Kinchin 308-312

Dorpat 207, 219, 446, 466

Dorpat and Ripley 207

double suicide 25, 84

Douglas 232, 245, 369, 375, 405

Drazin 257, 258, 265

Dressler et al. 129

drivers to suicide 32, 33, 44, 207, 237, 238, 363

drowning 60, 80, 119, 164, 281

drug 28, 40, 45, 58, 60, 70, 84, 108, 160, 210, 216, 217, 306, 348, 389, 434, 453

Drug-Abuse Deaths 221, 318

drug dependency 28

drug use 58

DSM 22, 31, 35, 36, 37, 38, 174, 190, 226, 245, 249, 334, 335, 338, 339, 413, 416, 439

Duffy and McClements 275

Durkheim 9, 15, 19, 26, 36, 39, 40, 41, 42, 43, 48, 49, 50, 51, 53, 56, 169, 179, 190, 207, 209, 219, 232, 241, 245, 253, 254, 268, 294, 330, 338, 339, 342, 374, 405, 410, 415, 419, 439, 454, 466

Dwyer  400, 405
Dyer  386, 405
Dyregrov  19, 148, 176, 191, 193, 204, 206, 219, 220, 340

## E
Easton  48, 53
ECHR  321, 322, 325, 338, 339
economics  300
Economics of Youth Suicide  308
education for prevention  313, 422, 424
education for understanding  18, 410, 412, 415, 417, 430, 438
Edwards and Young  292, 294
ego-involvement  101, 112, 114, 127, 128
elderly  24, 187, 214, 261, 348, 354, 357, 365, 385, 387
emergency admissions  180
emergency departments  433
emotion  31, 120, 185, 228, 393
emotional health and wellbeing  312
enigma of suicide  253, 269, 278, 431, 450
entrapment  66, 82, 235, 238
epistemology  7, 244
Epstein, J.  73, 273, 274, 294, 298, 318
equivocal death  213
erectile dysfunction  35
Erikson, E. E.  263
escalation  46, 71
ethics  7, 8, 22, 145, 330, 331, 338, 368, 372, 407, 466
ethnicity  206, 461
European Alliance Against Depression  432
European Convention of Human Rights  321, 339
euthanasia  11, 155, 224, 344, 345, 346, 347, 356, 358, 359, 360, 361, 363, 365, 366, 367, 369, 370, 372, 404
euthanasia, voluntary  346
Ewart  111, 153, 401
ex-paramilitaries  63

**F**

fake psychiatrist 352
fallacy 5, 56
family conflict 170
family discord 326
family disfunction 101
family history 154, 335
family liaison officers 312
Family Liaison Service 304, 305
Farberow 98, 105, 106, 128, 146, 149, 199, 201, 219, 220, 221, 231, 246, 249, 271, 446, 469
Fazel 64, 339
Fehling and Selby 35, 334, 335
femicide 78
Ferry 174, 182, 190, 191, 192, 297
financial loss 33
Finnis 348, 368
firearms 45, 77, 81, 436
Firestone 279, 294
first responders 207
Fisher 454, 455, 466
Fitzmaurice 282, 294
Fitzpatrick, S. J., Hooker, C. and Kerridge, I. 146, 265
Flack 60, 85
Flint 60, 82, 88
Flint, Keith 60, 82, 88
Flourish 313
Foley and Kelly 105, 107
Foot, M. 369
Foster 60, 106, 147, 195, 196, 203, 204, 219, 243, 292, 294
foster care 58
Foster Wallace, David 60, 243
Fowles 232, 245
Frankl 211, 219, 255, 259, 260, 261, 262, 263, 264, 265, 266, 267
Frankl, Victor 259, 260, 264, 265, 267
Freud 224, 226, 227, 233, 234, 242, 245, 246, 247, 253, 263, 446
friends 15, 59, 64, 72, 73, 75, 76, 89, 93, 119, 120, 186, 187, 195, 201, 270, 271, 276,

280, 282, 284, 285, 287, 305, 311, 319, 380, 386, 421, 448
Frost 416, 439
frustrated psychological needs 32, 228, 254
Fulton 77, 90

## G
Gaffney 105, 106, 147
gatekeeper 16, 17
Gender 54
gender diversity 431
General Medical Council 348, 352
general practice 309, 350, 351, 357, 362, 368, 451
general practitioner 26, 28, 36, 101, 272, 325
General Theory of Suicide 91, 438
genetic 42, 210, 234, 247, 413, 423
Germany 61, 204, 308, 358, 359
Gerson 363, 364, 369
Giles 77, 90
Giles, Billy 77, 90
Girard, R. 209, 219
Gitlin 106, 131, 133, 147
Goethe 61
Goldsmith, R. 42, 53, 54
Good Friday Agreement 42, 43, 53, 76, 77, 80, 160, 165, 173, 189, 439
Gorkin 106, 147
Gould et al. 17
Gould, M. S. 62, 85
government investment 327
Registrar General Northern Ireland 43
General Practitioner (GP) 26, 28, 66, 67, 70, 71, 94, 95, 101, 185, 261, 272, 305, 325, 347, 348, 385, 386, 455
Graber 375, 405
Grad and Michel 107
Grad, O. T. 105, 106, 107, 131, 132, 146, 147, 415
Graunt 230, 231, 245
Great Britain 5, 7, 24, 344

grief 9, 23, 24, 91, 93, 98, 100, 101, 105, 106, 115, 121, 122, 134, 135, 139, 142, 146, 185, 187, 197, 198, 208, 221, 254, 291, 304, 311, 326, 341, 379, 382, 383, 385, 386, 387, 389, 390, 392, 393, 395, 454, 457, 462, 463
Guidance and Counselling Programme 96
guilt 94, 105, 106, 121, 158, 229, 258, 278, 399, 457, 462
Gulfi 105, 122, 147

# H
Haig 476, 477
Hamill 65, 85
Hamilton 54, 227, 246, 360, 366, 367, 369
hanging 60, 63, 67, 73, 77, 78, 85, 157, 200, 290, 291, 321
Harding 227, 246, 416, 417, 439, 446, 467
Harré 111, 148
Harris and Barraclough 332
Harte 283, 295
Hawe 67, 68, 69, 89, 90
Hawe, Clodagh 69, 89
Hawton et al. 330
Hawton, K. 340, 469
health and social Care 39, 274, 289, 293, 304, 312
health deprivation 180
health, right to 464
Health Trust 64
Helmore 331, 340
Henderson 25, 36
Hendin 106, 131, 148, 163, 164, 166, 232, 246, 367, 369
Hendricks 257, 258, 259, 265
hermeneutic interpretive 197
Hjelmeland 15, 19, 96, 148, 169, 171, 176, 191, 214, 215, 219, 220, 225, 240, 241, 246, 329, 331, 340, 415, 429, 430, 431, 439, 447, 448, 449, 450, 451, 467
Hoffman 24, 36, 60
Hoffman, Philip Seymour 60
Hogan and Grumet 44
Hollinger and Offer 231
Holmes 211, 220
Holt 148, 149, 244, 303, 317
homelessness 391

homicide data 307
hopelessness 42, 82, 170, 197, 211, 225, 228, 229, 235, 243, 250, 346, 429
Horn 106, 148
human development 307, 308, 310, 316
humanitarian impulse 336
Human Rights Act 1998 321, 339
Hume 254
Hume, David 254
hunger strike 268, 272, 293, 371, 375

# I

IASP 52, 54, 166, 430, 449
identity 74, 97, 98, 99, 100, 101, 102, 103, 105, 110, 111, 112, 114, 115, 117, 119, 120, 122, 123, 124, 125, 128, 129, 130, 132, 133, 145, 149, 150, 178, 179, 183, 188, 192, 210, 248, 263, 280, 284, 296, 297, 314, 379, 383, 390, 391, 394, 395, 400, 401, 402, 403, 404, 406, 451, 458, 463
identity diffusion 101, 112, 114, 117, 120
Identity Structure Analysis (ISA) 97, 98, 99, 100, 102, 104, 110, 111, 112, 113, 115, 116, 118, 123, 125, 132, 150, 153, 184,185, 188, 379, 390, 391, 400, 401, 402, 403, 445
ideographic case study 51
idiographic approach 424
Iga 232, 246
IJpelaar et al. 180
Illich 32, 33, 34, 35, 36, 37
imitation 61, 82
Imprisonment 33, 43
IMVM cf. Integrated Motivational Model
Independent Counselling Service for Schools 73
Independent Press Standards Organisation 60, 82, 83, 86
individual pathology 458, 459
Inquest 59, 86, 293
insurance companies 34
Integrated motivational-volitional model 51
Integrated Motivational-Volitional Model (IMVM) 51, 150, 236, 237, 238, 239, 248, 421, 443, 468
Integration 9, 154, 161
intellect 31

intensified treatment 344
intergenerational transmission 277
International Academy of Suicide Research 398
International Association for Suicide Prevention (IASP) 52, 54, 430, 432, 449
International Handbook of Suicide Prevention 54, 248, 439
International Journal of Environmental Research and Public Health 460
Interpersonal-Psychological Model 234
Interpersonal Psychological Theory of Suicide 225, 226, 236, 238, 239, 240, 241, 242, 243, 244 225, 238, 239, 332, 419
Interpersonal Suicide-Trajectory Model 211
Intervention 17, 19, 20, 55, 304, 430, 469
intervention project 312
intimidation 24, 65, 66, 86
IPSO cf. Independent Press Standards Organisation
IPTS cf. Interpersonal Psychological Theory of Suicide
Irish Association of Suicidology 97, 145, 147, 148, 150, 471
Irish nationalist 178
Irish National Suicide Research Foundation 71
ISA cf. Identity Structural Analysis
Isaac et al. 16
ISA IDEX software 111, 112

# J

Jacob and Klein-Benheim 330
jealous behaviour 80
JED Foundation 162, 166
Jobes 107, 116, 127, 148, 415, 426, 427, 428, 429, 439, 440, 441, 453, 467
Johns Hopkins Bloomberg School of Public Health 46
Johnson 235, 246
Joiner T.E. 51, 54, 55, 56, 68, 86, 91, 148, 170, 175, 191, 196, 224, 225, 226, 227, 229, 234, 236, 238, 239, 240, 241, 242, 243, 244, 246, 247, 249, 251, 252, 253, 265, 266, 269, 295, 329, 332, 340, 407, 415, 419, 422, 424, 431, 434, 440, 442, 443, 461, 467
Jordan, J.R. 19, 155, 166, 405, 406
Jordan, J.R. & McIntosh, J.L. 405, 406
journalism 23, 59, 82
Journal of Crisis Intervention and Suicide Prevention 19, 55, 430, 469

# K

Kahn 107, 148
Kahne 105, 148
Kapoor 107, 149
Kato 232, 247 Kelly, B. D., 340
Kelly, G. A. 246
Kelly, Paul 73
Kendell, R. E. 340
Kennaway, J 77, 78, 87
Kety, S. 234, 247
Kivisto 49, 54
Klapp 99, 149
Kleespies et al. 122
Klonsky and Dixon-Luinenburg 243
Klonsky and May 225
Kraepelin 232, 247, 254
Kral 170, 191, 460, 467, 469, 470

# L

Lall, Conor 69, 89
Lally 69, 89
Lange 125
language of suicide 268, 375
law 24, 25, 27, 35, 57, 62, 79, 80, 81, 108, 122, 168, 177, 184, 186, 214, 227, 314, 319, 320, 321, 325, 327, 336, 343, 354, 358, 360, 361, 362, 365, 371, 411, 447
Law Commission 58
Leavey et al. 28
Leckey 6, 8, 23, 36
Lester D. 191
lethality 31, 32, 124, 129, 229, 398
level of suicidality 124, 126, 131, 165
Lichter, D. H. 330, 340
life expectancy 45, 55, 102, 180, 404
life history 215, 230, 270, 284, 431, 448
Lifeline 16, 17, 19, 70, 76, 159, 312
Life-threatening Behaviour 19, 20, 21, 85, 149, 151, 220, 242, 247, 249, 267, 318, 338, 340, 341, 406, 407, 415, 419, 420, 430, 440, 443, 461, 477
Lifton 232, 247

Lindemann 94
Linder 359, 360, 369
Linehan 51, 54, 241, 446, 467
Litman, R.E. 20, 105, 149, 199, 201, 220, 221, 233, 234, 242, 243, 247, 271, 317, 403
Litman, R.E., et al 317 Lizardo 170, 192
logotherapy 219, 260, 263, 266

# M

MacKinnon 149
Magill, Martin 65
Maguire 147, 434, 440
Maguire, A. et al. 440
Maishman 354, 355, 369
Mallon 36, 65, 66, 86
Maltsberger 107, 116, 127, 148, 149, 157, 164, 166, 271, 295
Manchester University's Centre for Suicide Prevention 303
manslaughter 74, 307, 310, 344
Maris 10, 11, 12, 13, 14, 16, 20, 175, 192, 232, 247, 271, 406, 415
marital status 231, 305, 337, 461
Marlowe 256, 266
marriage 47, 68, 89, 95, 185, 383
Marsh 459, 460, 467, 469, 470
Maughan 5, 8, 59, 86, 88, 250, 398, 408, 477
Maxwell 73
Maze Prison 77, 272
McConville 89, 286, 288, 289, 295, 298, 301, 302, 317, 318
McCready and Waring 331
McGlade et al. 345, 346, 347, 360
McGonagle 55, 281, 287, 295, 296
McGowan et al. 43
McIntosh, J.L. 405, 406
McKay 181, 182, 189, 251, 265, 275, 280, 293, 296, 313, 316, 323, 339
McKee 275, 277, 278, 296
McKee, Lyra 275, 278
McKenzie 378, 406
McKeown 25, 36
McKie 412, 441

McKinney 285, 296
McKinnon and Farberow 128
McKitterick 43, 275, 296
McLeod 108, 149
McQueen 60
McQueen, Alexander 60
Meade 106, 107, 149
meaning and interpretation 171
meaning-making 204, 221
meaning of suicide 171, 189, 245
medicalisation 30, 34, 207, 243, 303, 334, 417, 465, 472, 476, 477
medical records 66, 67, 202, 452
medicine 22, 26, 32, 33, 34, 41, 110, 175, 255, 320, 333, 336, 342, 351, 352, 357, 358, 362, 366, 367, 368, 418, 443
Meirion 348, 351, 352, 353, 357, 369
Mencken 225, 247, 329, 340, 341
Menninger 147, 233, 247, 253
mental disability 22
mental disease 5, 22, 230, 254
mental disorder 5, 22, 28, 37, 164, 165, 175, 176, 195, 196, 204, 207, 220, 225, 226, 233, 236, 326, 327, 334, 385, 413, 416, 419, 431, 434, 435, 460, 462, 473
mental health 5, 8, 15, 27, 28, 29, 30, 32, 37, 43, 54, 55, 58, 70, 72, 79, 81, 85, 90, 98, 147, 161, 163, 168, 180, 195, 203, 208, 216, 275, 276, 280, 284, 286, 289, 293, 295, 299, 304, 305, 312, 324, 325, 326, 327, 328, 329, 332, 339, 341, 342, 352, 411, 416, 418, 419, 420, 423, 425, 426, 429, 430, 431, 432, 435, 436, 438, 441, 447, 450, 451, 452, 460, 463, 464, 466, 473, 477
mental health establishment 203
Mental Health Northern Ireland Order (1986) 326
mental health promotion 312
mental health services 29, 275, 280, 304, 305, 325, 328, 341, 425, 451
mental illness 5, 29, 33, 48, 67, 68, 168, 172, 176, 200, 206, 218, 227, 243, 276, 313, 324, 325, 326, 327, 329, 330, 331, 332, 333, 335, 338, 340, 341, 342, 365, 416, 418, 434, 435, 443, 459, 460, 462, 473
mercy killing 344, 360
metaphysics 7
metatheoretical framework 99, 400
method 14, 20, 21, 60, 61, 67, 82, 100, 196, 202, 207, 208, 209, 305, 314, 350, 426, 431, 438, 461

methodology  5, 15, 64, 104, 171, 182, 197, 204, 207, 215, 218, 252, 329, 330, 426, 427, 431, 445, 457, 466
Meyer  446, 467
Michel  107, 147, 440, 441, 446, 468
Michel, K.  107, 147, 440, 441, 446, 468
military suicide  424
Miller, B.  44, 53, 54, 231, 248, 438
Miller, J. G.  248
Mills  455, 468
Milner 207, 220
minister of religion  185
minority  106, 107, 170, 352, 453
Mishara  17, 20, 145
Monaghan  173, 288, 296
mood disorders 226
Moriarty  303, 317
Morris  290, 291, 296, 455, 456, 457, 469, 470
Morris, A.  89
Morrissey  25, 37
Muehlenkamp, J.J. and Thoen, S.K.  474, 477
Mueller  169, 170, 189, 192
multifactorial  5, 171, 215, 225, 242, 244, 373, 413, 437
Munro and Aiken  82
murder  9, 25, 35, 67, 68, 69, 77, 78, 82, 86, 89, 90, 95, 173, 233, 257, 268, 269, 270, 278, 290, 296, 300, 301, 302, 303, 306, 307, 308, 310, 316, 317, 322, 343, 344, 350, 351, 400
Murder disguised as suicide  25
murder-suicide  67, 68, 69, 89
Murray  37, 60, 231, 234, 248, 253, 285, 296, 414, 424, 441
My identity  99
Mynatt  414, 441
myth  265, 267, 333, 335, 340, 342, 416, 435, 443
Myth of Sisyphus  253, 256, 258, 265
Myths about Suicide  175, 419

# N

narrative  96, 99, 100, 101, 270, 292, 293, 294, 295, 367, 393, 455, 456, 457
NASH  11, 12, 200, 220, 306, 307
National Confidential Inquiry  313, 451
National Health Service  182, 304, 361
National Institute for Health Clinical Excellence (NICE)  26, 27, 28, 3726
National Institute for Mental Health  426
nationalist  81, 168, 178
National Self-Harm Registry  433
National Suicide Prevention Alliance  318
National Suicide Prevention Line  159
National Suicide Research Foundation  69, 71, 432, 433
National Violent Deaths Reporting System  332
Nazi  256, 259, 358, 359, 365
negligence  199, 298, 306, 314, 317, 318, 322
Nelson  77
Netherlands  308, 365, 424
neurosis  31, 418
newsworthiness  57, 62
New Zealand  57, 58, 74, 85, 88, 174, 204, 344
NHS  26, 182, 304, 352, 354, 357, 361, 362, 369, 454, 455
NIACRO cf. Northern Ireland Association for the Care and Resettlement of Offenders
NICE cf. National Institute for Health Excellence)
NI Coroner's Office  6, 216
NI Department of Health  199, 318, 355, 397, 452, 468
Niederkrotenthaler, T.  85, 87
Niederkrotenthaler T. et al.  61
NI-HSE Health & Care Board  355, 370
NIMDM cf. Northern Ireland Multi-Deprivation Measure  180, 192
NISRA (cf. Northern Ireland Statistics and Research Agency)  84, 160, 161, 166, 178, 192, 216, 217, 218, 220, 223, 248, 306, 307, 317, 355, 362, 370
NI Suicide Prevention Strategy  311
non-fatal bodily injury  33
non-publication order  58
Northern Ireland  5, 6, 7, 8, 16, 17, 24, 25, 28, 29, 30, 32, 33, 35, 36, 37, 40, 41, 42, 43, 49, 52, 54, 55, 56, 64, 65, 66, 69, 70, 72, 76, 80, 81, 83, 84, 86, 87, 90, 159, 160, 161, 162, 164, 166, 167, 168, 172, 173, 174, 175, 178, 179, 180, 181, 182, 188, 189, 190, 191, 192, 193, 198, 204, 207, 216, 218, 219, 220, 223, 224, 232, 245, 251, 256, 265,

266, 268, 269, 272, 274, 275, 276, 277, 278, 279, 280, 281, 282, 283, 284, 287, 290, 292, 293, 294, 295, 296, 297, 299, 300, 301, 302, 303, 304, 305, 306, 307, 308, 309, 310, 311, 313, 314, 315, 316, 317, 318, 320, 322, 323, 325, 326, 327, 328, 329, 337, 339, 341, 343, 344, 345, 347, 349, 355, 357, 362, 369, 370, 374, 396, 406, 411, 412, 413, 420, 425, 433, 434, 438, 440, 442, 447, 451, 452, 468, 477

Northern Ireland Act 1998 337

Northern Ireland Ambulance Service 198

Northern Ireland Assembly 35, 86, 265, 274, 293, 299, 313, 316, 438

Northern Ireland Association for the Care and Resettlement of Offenders 64

Northern Ireland Coroners' Office 307

Northern Ireland Coroners' Service 84, 198

Northern Ireland Department of Health 370

Northern Ireland Education Authority Critical Incident Response Team 72

Northern Ireland multiple deprivation measure 192

Northern Ireland Multiple Deprivation Measure 180

Northern Ireland Prison Service 64

Northern Ireland Programme for Government 311, 317

Northern Ireland Registry of Self-harm 434

Northern Ireland Statistics and Research Agency 83, 160, 166, 178, 216, 306, 317, 355

Northern Ireland Suicide Prevention Strategy 311, 329

Norway 17, 169, 193, 308, 424, 429, 430, 451

no-suicide contract 163

nutrition 34

# O

Obegi 35, 37

O'Brien 15, 20, 85, 90, 144

O'Carroll 377, 378, 390, 391, 396, 406, 407

O'Connor, R.C. 8, 37, 54, 150, 248

O'Connor, R.C., and Kirtley, O.J. 248

O'Connor, R.C., Sheehy, N.P. and O'Connor, D.B. 8, 37

O'Donnell White, J. 279

O'Keeffe, Adrian Francis 4, 23

O'Keeffe, Gerard, Henry, Aidan 4, 23

O'Keeffe, P. 95, 97, 98, 111, 151, 152, 185, 194, 229, 250, 299, 382-398, 400, 402, 410

O'Keeffe T. 296

O'Loughlin, M. 442

O'Mahony  33, 34, 37
O'Neill, S.  6, 8, 23, 24, 37, 87, 175, 190, 191, 192, 245, 251, 266, 277, 297, 309, 317, 406, 414, 442, 468
opinion leader  459, 460
Oquendo  35, 37, 415
Oranga Tamariki  58
Orbach  18, 20, 131, 150, 262, 263, 266, 426, 442, 457, 458, 468
Oregon  363
O'Reilly and Rosato  178, 179
O'Riordan  60
Osman  269, 297
Owens, D. and House, A.  442

**P**
Padmanathan  375, 377, 406
pain, emotional  464, 466, 476
pain, psychological  91, 135, 137, 138, 141, 142, 143, 171, 227, 228, 229, 234, 249, 252, 254, 269, 286, 425, 429, 457
pain, unendurahle  31, 32
palliative care  345, 361, 362, 363, 364, 367, 368, 369, 371, 403, 404
Pallis, D.J. and Sainsbury, P.  446, 468
Pallis, D.J. et al.  446, 468
Palmer, S.  109, 149, 151
Paniagua  241, 242, 248
Papageno effect  76, 82, 83
paracetamol  309
paramilitaries  63, 65, 77
paramilitary  49, 63, 65, 76, 77, 81, 86, 89, 275, 278, 302, 303
paramilitary organizations  49
pathologising  450, 458
pathways to suicide  16, 170
patient suicide  103, 105, 122, 132, 146, 147, 151, 227
Patterson, A.  79
Patterson, O.  79, 169, 193
Pepper  232, 248
Personal Construct Theory  99, 400
Pfeffer  232, 249

pharmaceutical industry 34, 45, 334
pharmacotherapy treatments 309
phenomenological lens 210
Phillips 88, 106, 151, 207, 221
philosophy 7, 10, 13, 64, 150, 253, 255, 258, 259, 260, 341, 403, 416, 424, 431, 441, 464, 469
Physician Assisted 362
PIRA (cf. Provisional Irish Republican Army)
Pirkis 85, 415, 439, 441
Plath Nicholas 60
Plath, Sylvia 60, 243
poisoning 40, 45, 389, 413, 434
Pokorny 128, 151, 230
police 23, 25, 32, 41, 48, 58, 63, 74, 75, 78, 81, 88, 94, 95, 177, 185, 187, 199, 200, 201, 207, 214, 275, 281, 290, 291, 302, 303, 305, 307, 310, 312, 314, 317, 348, 358, 387, 388, 423, 424, 429, 451, 473
Police Service of Northern Ireland (PSNI)180, 87, 198, 300, 302, 303, 304, 305, 312, 314
political system 48, 53
politics 48, 156, 175, 176, 182, 191, 302, 317, 354, 358, 407, 430, 439, 451, 458, 463
Pompili 415
Pope John Paul II 301, 318
Pope, K.S. and Tabachnik, B.G. 151 Positivism and interpretivism 469
post-mortem 5, 16, 22, 36, 198, 199, 207, 291, 301, 446
postsuicidal 152
post-traumatic stress disorder (PTSD) 28, 29, 181, 190, 277
postvention 94, 97, 98, 102, 106, 107, 119, 122, 130, 131, 150, 192, 269, 278, 291, 292, 296, 406, 410
Pouliot and De Leo 202, 204, 212
poverty 33
power 24, 34, 48, 49, 57, 175, 191, 206, 226, 257, 263, 334, 354, 388, 430, 431, 439, 449, 450, 451, 458, 463, 465, 472, 476
PPAS cf Psycological Pain Assessment Scale CF
Prediction 146, 151
predictors of suicide 36, 170, 417
pregnancy 80
prescription drugs 43, 45
presuicidal 152

prevention Blues 310
Prevention of Future Deaths 74
prevention strategy 161, 314, 321, 322, 325, 396
prevention training 16
priest 65, 384, 385, 387
prison 23, 58, 59, 63, 64, 73, 77, 79, 199, 268, 272, 273, 274, 298, 303, 318, 322, 352, 353, 443
prisoner 63, 64, 78, 260, 273
Probert-Lindström et al. 226
problematic identifications 114, 117, 392
professional autobiography 111
protection 321, 325, 327, 355, 360, 361
protective factors 44, 47, 146, 276, 454, 457
Protect Life 2 (2019) 166, 266, 311, 318, 341, 345, 370, 406, 451, 468
Protect Life 2 - Suicide Prevention Strategy 161
Protestant 41, 48, 176, 179
Provisional Irish Republican Army (PIRA or PROVOS) 301, 302, 343
PSNI cf. Police Service of Northern Ireland
PSNI Legacy Investigation Branch 303
psychache 21, 32, 33, 37, 55, 124, 129, 152, 229, 234, 249, 252, 254, 269, 270, 286, 398, 425, 457, 458, 469
psychiatric autopsy 340
psychiatric disorder 201, 203, 226, 235, 334, 427
psychiatric epidemiology 175
Psychiatric history 213
psychiatric paradigm 437
psychiatrist 27, 67, 71, 95, 137, 140, 143, 147, 157, 176, 204, 220, 221, 233, 254, 255, 260, 264, 271, 272, 279, 331, 332, 333, 340, 352, 358, 371, 384, 391, 403
psychiatry 5, 9, 10, 13, 22, 26, 30, 35, 68, 105, 149, 170, 171, 172, 175, 189, 192, 215, 227, 247, 255, 327, 330, 331, 332, 333, 334, 335, 342, 416, 417, 418, 432, 434, 450, 459
psychological autopsy 9, 148, 194, 198, 208, 218, 222, 340, 341, 466
psychological burnout 285
psychological disorders 28
psychological needs 32, 228, 234, 254
Psychological Pain Assessment Scale (PPAS) 229
psychologist 30, 68, 70, 93, 104, 116, 122, 176, 208, 251, 398, 419, 423, 426, 434
psychology 5, 10, 13, 15, 26, 52, 87, 104, 105, 110, 202, 203, 209, 220, 221, 263,

331, 411, 416, 419, 421, 426, 432, 450, 459, 474
psychometric scale 110
psychopharmacology 215, 459
psychopolitical 455, 468
psychosis 27, 31, 180
psychosocial factors 195
psychotherapy 20, 148, 149, 150, 221, 265, 266, 418, 424, 440, 442, 472
Public Health 21, 45, 46, 55, 88, 178, 245, 304, 305, 311, 318, 355, 356, 370, 432, 438, 452, 460, 470
Public Health Scotland 355
Public Information Campaigns 312
public investment 102, 314
Public Prosecution Service Northern Ireland 345, 370
punishment attacks 65
Puras 465, 469

## Q

QPR 16, 18
Question Persuade and Respond 16 Quinton 5, 7, 8

## R

Ranasinghe 459, 469
rape 47
Rasmussen 176, 191, 193, 219
reducing ruicide 44, 46, 47, 48, 49, 53, 54
reducing youth suicide 310
Reece 79, 288, 289, 296
Rees 179, 193
reference group theory 99, 400
Regional Resource Center for Suicide Research and Prevention 430
Registrar General Northern Ireland 43, 55, 160, 166
Reizler 99, 151
religion 41, 48, 156, 168, 178, 179, 185, 258, 259, 276, 301
religiosity 48, 179
religious activities 48
religious attitudes 81
religious beliefs 48, 188, 263, 390

religious denomination  176, 177, 178, 179, 182
religious practice  41
Republic of Ireland  308, 433
reputation  23, 33, 102, 104, 331, 333, 353
Research Ethics Committee  97, 108, 375
Resnik  122, 151
responsibility  2, 15, 25, 26, 27, 34, 107, 115, 120, 121, 134, 136, 139, 142, 162, 201, 260, 289, 314, 330, 333, 335, 350, 358, 361, 366, 454, 456, 464, 475
retraumatisation  197
Richman  232, 249
Rimkeviciene  422, 423
risk factor  226, 332, 414, 448, 449
risk factors  37, 51, 62, 69, 80, 151, 164, 170, 194, 199, 210, 214, 215, 226, 249, 406, 417, 436, 447, 448, 457, 468
risk management  16, 163
risk of suicide  47, 48, 51, 98, 124, 126, 127, 129, 131, 134, 156, 158, 162, 167, 176, 179, 186, 193, 226, 234, 236, 238, 240, 242, 262, 278, 279, 291, 321, 322, 332, 334, 338, 416, 424, 425, 426, 455, 457, 464
Rivlin  446, 447, 469
Roberts  78, 79, 82, 88
Rockett  40, 55
Rogers, J.R.  151, 341
Rogers, J.R. and Lester, D.  341
Rogers, J.R. et al.  126
Roman Catholic  41, 385
Roush  163, 167
Roy  234, 244, 247, 249, 329, 341
Royal College of General Practitioners  350
Runyon  231, 249
Rural Needs Act NI  338
Rural Needs Impact Assessment Template  338

## S

Safer Custody  312
safeTALK  16
Salvatore  3, 329, 330, 331, 332, 341
Samaritans  16, 69, 70, 72, 156, 158, 159, 162, 167, 284, 337, 375, 386
Sands, D.  196, 197, 198, 203, 204, 221, 326, 341

sanitation 34
Sarchiapone, S 415
Sargent 211, 221
SBD cf. Suicide Behaviour Disorder
Schaler 336, 340, 341, 342
Schematic appraisal model 235
schizophrenia 27, 233, 246, 418
schools 52, 72, 177, 437
Schotte and Clum 237, 249
Scotland 17, 23, 24, 174, 269, 274, 296, 343, 354, 355, 362, 452
Scottish Law 23
Scourfield 206, 209, 221
secularization 41
self care 34, 124
self-destruction 5, 30, 44, 49, 50, 91, 155, 159, 165, 181, 196, 200, 223, 225, 228, 252, 255, 278, 279, 286, 374, 375, 378, 410, 415, 416, 437, 447, 459, 461, 463
self esteem 181, 193, 211, 343
self-evaluation 101, 112, 113, 115, 119, 124, 129, 393
self-harm 26, 29, 33, 37, 63, 64, 71, 74, 78, 108, 161, 166, 194, 211, 248, 266, 310, 311, 312, 316, 318, 323, 328, 329, 332, 341, 370, 376, 406, 413, 429, 432, 433, 434, 438, 440, 442, 451, 452, 468, 477
Self-Harm Registry 312, 433, 434, 451
separation 47, 93
separation (child contact) 80
Serious Adverse Incident Process 451
sexual abuse 74, 448
Sexual assault 80
sexuality 163, 186, 385
sexual orientation 206, 337
Shahtahmasebi 176, 193
Shakespeare, 297
Shanahan 389, 407
Shannon 99, 151
Sheehy 8, 37, 43, 54, 194, 195, 215, 221, 226, 248, 420, 441, 462
Shelley 270, 297
Shilton 444, 445
Shipman Effect 349, 351

Shipman Enquiry  348, 349, 370, 474
Shipman, Harold  347, 368, 371
Shneidman, E.S.  10, 11, 14, 15, 20, 21, 30, 31, 32, 37, 51, 55, 59, 88, 91, 92, 93, 94, 97, 98, 121, 124, 129, 151, 152, 171, 172, 193, 199, 201, 211, 215, 220, 221, 227, 228, 229, 230, 231, 234, 241, 243, 244, 246, 247, 249, 252, 253, 254, 255, 266, 268, 269, 271, 278, 291, 293, 297, 298, 306, 318, 340, 373, 374, 375, 391, 403, 407, 410, 415, 416, 417, 424, 439, 440, 442, 446, 458, 467, 469
shyness 35
Silverman  20, 35, 38, 192, 233, 249, 271, 377, 378, 391, 396, 397, 406, 407, 415
Singapore 308
Sisyphus syndrome 34
Skills Training On Risk Management 16 SLTB  242, 318, 431, 440
Snider  204, 207, 212, 213, 222
Social Care Trusts 312
social class 206
social comparison theory  99, 400
social conditions 33
social context  99, 459
social deviance  330
social discord 170
Social Epistemology  146, 265, 460, 467
Social Epistemology Review and Reply Collective  460, 467
social exclusion  464, 476
social integration  40, 43, 46
Social isolation 33
social justice  454, 463, 464, 465, 466, 468
socially acceptable option 170
social networks 189
social policy 195
social regulation  40, 41, 43, 50
social relationships  169, 389
social roots 192
social services  185, 451
social suicide  49, 75
social suicide rate 49
social supports 213
social work  118, 119
social world  100, 110, 111, 124, 129, 130, 184, 192, 400

society and culture 43
sociocultural context 17, 172
socioeconomic disadvantage 48
socioeconomic status 48
sociological autopsy 206, 221, 275
Soderland 105, 107, 152
Soper 444, 445, 469
spiritual adviser 184
spiritual resources 186, 261
Stack, S. 21, 55, 85, 222
Stadlen 417, 418, 419, 435, 443
stalking 79
standardisation 204, 396, 397
Stanley 50, 51, 55, 415, 442, 467
statistics 12, 13, 18, 30, 42, 44, 80, 81, 83, 84, 160, 161, 166, 181, 189, 192, 194, 205, 209, 216, 218, 220, 231, 265, 276, 293, 307, 316, 317, 339, 355, 370, 411
Stefan 344, 371
stigma 45, 83, 95, 102, 109, 201, 304, 305, 326, 339, 387, 412, 450, 455, 464, 476
Stillion and McDowell 94, 98
strangulation 66, 291
stress 27, 28, 29, 31, 118, 149, 170, 181, 190, 229, 235, 277, 278, 287, 393, 395, 403, 429, 455, 475, 477
structural pressures 112, 113, 115
student suicide 183, 210, 219, 282, 426
sub-poena 108
substance abuse 213
Sudden Death Notification Process 451
suffering 31, 32, 34, 68, 74, 158, 195, 198, 254, 261, 262, 264, 270, 311, 334, 335, 336, 347, 362, 365, 366, 367, 467
suicidal ideation 53, 62, 95, 170, 175, 218, 225, 235, 237, 238, 250, 253, 429, 453
suicidality disorder 35
suicidality level 31
suicidal syndrome 35
suicidal thoughts 65, 81, 143, 171, 226, 236, 377, 395, 448, 463
suicide and life-threatening behaviour 19, 20, 21, 85, 149, 151, 220, 242, 247, 249, 267, 318, 338, 340, 341, 406, 407, 415, 419, 420, 430, 440, 443, 461, 477
Suicide as escape from self 53, 235, 244, 465

suicide attempt 15, 17, 33, 114, 115, 124, 126, 127, 136, 140, 226, 273, 276, 380, 381, 382, 386, 391, 392, 398, 413, 414, 462
suicide behaviour disorder (SBD)334, 335
suicide model 198
suicide note 15, 67, 68, 194, 271, 283, 379
suicide prevention 5, 10, 11, 13, 14, 16, 17, 18, 32, 35, 40, 50, 52, 56, 71, 73, 83, 87, 88, 102, 118, 119, 120, 155, 160, 161, 162, 164, 165, 169, 172, 175, 180, 192, 193, 195, 206, 209, 215, 232, 233, 238, 251, 252, 293, 309, 311, 312, 313, 314, 315, 320, 321, 322, 323, 325, 364, 374, 389, 396, 403, 411, 412, 413, 415, 418, 420, 426, 430, 434, 435, 441, 443, 444, 451, 453, 456, 459, 461, 463, 465, 476
Suicide Prevention Day 52, 56, 176
Suicide Prevention Profile 452
Suicide Prevention Resource Centre 88
Suicide Status Form 426, 428
Suicide Trajectory Model 211, 385, 385,386
suicide, unsuccessful 376
suicidologist 15, 30, 98, 164, 166, 213, 241, 377, 397, 415, 423, 425, 437, 461
Suicidology 7, 9, 10, 20, 21, 36, 92, 97, 104, 105, 107, 109, 144, 145, 146, 147, 148, 150, 164, 192, 198, 199, 227, 231, 242, 255, 264, 265, 293, 296, 330, 377, 404, 406, 412, 415, 417, 419, 422, 426, 430, 436, 440, 443, 451, 453, 460, 466, 467, 469, 470, 471, 477
Survivor syndrome 399
suspected suicide 5, 6, 58, 73, 187, 218, 273, 280, 289, 312, 388, 471, 472, 474, 475
Sussmilch, J. 231, 250
Swift 253, 266, 429, 443
Swift, J.K. et al. 253, 429
Switzerland 308, 342, 344
symbolic interactionism 99, 400
systems-based approach 309
Szasz 27, 38, 320, 332, 333, 334, 335, 336, 338, 340, 341, 342, 403, 404, 407, 415, 417, 418, 419, 435, 443, 472, 477

# T

teachers 110, 155, 210, 211, 425
Tedeschi 404, 407
telephone crisis services 17
tendencies 16, 170, 176, 380
testosterone-deficiency syndrome 35
The Journal of Crisis Intervention and Suicide Prevention 19, 430

The National Action Alliance for Suicide theology 416
theory 7, 28, 49, 50, 51, 56, 68, 99, 104, 153, 170, 190, 223, 225, 228, 234, 235, 236, 238, 239, 240, 242, 243, 244, 245, 246, 248, 250, 266, 295, 330, 342, 400, 419, 421, 423, 437, 440, 443, 461, 466
therapeutic alliance 107, 121, 427, 439, 440
therapeutic empathy 18, 262
therapeutic relationship 129, 131
the Troubles 37, 56, 275, 292, 294, 299, 300, 344, 453
Thompson 460, 461, 469
Thorpe 409, 443
threats to kill 80
thwarted needs 32
Tillman 131, 152
Tomlinson 40, 42, 43, 44, 50, 55, 56, 57, 160, 166, 167, 174, 193, 268, 275, 276, 277, 299, 412
Tonge 178, 193
Torney 3, 42, 56, 299
trafficking 108, 273
training packages 16
training programme 17
transformation programme 312
transgenerational 33, 453
Tripartite Model of Suicide Grief 221
Troubles Permanent Disablement Payment Scheme 344
Tuckey, L. and Slowther, A. 371
Tyler 231, 250

## U

Ubido and Scott-Daniel 16
UK Department for Digital, Culture, Media and Sport 75
UK Supreme Court 5, 59, 224, 250, 398, 408, 473, 477
Ulster Unionists 168
Ulster University 3, 80, 81, 90, 93, 96, 97, 103, 150, 152, 153, 191, 245, 296, 297, 406, 411, 471
unaddressed countertransference hate 107, 127, 129, 157, 158
unbearable pain 227, 390, 404, 417
Unemployment 33, 48, 53
Unionist 178

United Ireland  178, 343, 442
United Nations Development Programme  308, 318
United States  17, 51, 53, 74, 222, 308
unlawful killing  79, 86, 270
US Centers for Disease Control and Prevention  44, 332, 426
US Institute of Medicine  44

## V

Vaisey  170, 193
Valente  107, 152
Validity  202
van Heeringen  415
Van Poppel and Day  43
Vasudevan  208, 222
Viktor Frankl Institute of Logotherapy in Israel  260, 267
Violence  21, 24, 33, 78, 80, 84, 90
voluntary organisations  155, 159

## W

Walby  81, 90
Wales  24, 290, 320, 341, 343, 362
Wallace  60, 243, 405, 408
Walsh  398, 408
Walter and Pridmore  207
ward of state  58
Wasserman  209, 222, 338
Watts and Morgan  107, 116, 127
Weber, Max  100, 379, 408
Web, T.  177
Weinreich, P.  145, 152, 153, 167, 400, 404, 408, 469
Weinreich, P. and Saunderson, W.  153, 167, 408, 469
Weisman, A.D.  271
welfare  50, 56, 161, 305, 352, 356, 360, 361, 454, 455
Wenzel, A. and Beck, A.T.  227, 235
Wertheimer  410, 443
Werther Effect  61, 82, 83
Western Health and Social Care Trust  304

White and Morris 455, 456, 457
White-Bowden, S. 279, 299
White et al. 458, 459
White, J. 469, 470
White, J. and Morris, J. 470
why suicide? 251
Wilkins 116, 131, 153, 244, 247, 249
Williams, J. M. G. 90, 250
Williams, Robin 60
Women's Aid Federation 80
Woodruff, R. 372
World Health Organisation 12, 40, 56, 62, 268, 277, 299, 309, 318, 324, 342, 362, 371, 470
World Health Survey 175
World Suicide Prevention Day 52, 56, 176
Wray 42, 50, 56
Wurst 105, 122, 123, 153

## Y

Yalom 257, 258, 263, 264, 267
Yip 85, 415
young 42, 61, 65, 72, 76, 94, 95, 160, 166, 174, 184, 193, 201, 214, 250, 262, 277, 278, 282, 285, 286, 287, 310, 319, 326, 328, 382
young adult 160, 166, 174, 201
youth 42, 47, 149, 170, 189, 211, 219, 246, 259, 307, 308, 309, 310, 314, 316, 318, 319, 354, 456
youth suicide 42, 189, 219, 307, 308, 309, 310, 314, 316, 318, 456
Yuill 365, 372
Yur'yev 49, 50, 56

## Z

Zavasnik 107, 147
Zhang 208, 222
Zilboorg, G. 233, 250, 253